D1590467

On the Margin of the Visible

Contemporary Religious Movements:
A Wiley-Interscience Series

Edited by IRVING I. ZARETSKY

On the Margin of the Visible

SOCIOLOGY, THE ESOTERIC, AND THE OCCULT

Edited by

EDWARD A. TIRYAKIAN

A WILEY-INTERSCIENCE PUBLICATION

JOHN WILEY & SONS, New York • London • Sydney • Toronto

Library of Congress Cataloging in Publication Data

Tiryakian, Edward A.   comp.
  On the margin of the visible.

  (Contemporary religious movements: a Wiley-Inter-
science series)
  "A Wiley-Interscience publication."
  Bibliography: p.
  1. Occult sciences.   2. Religion and sociology.
I. Title.

BF1411.T57   301.2′2   73-21981
ISBN 0-471-87435-3

Printed in the United States of America

10 9 8 7 6 5 4 3 2 1

To my wonderful Aquarian wife Josefina

Series Editor's Foreword

Not a few social scientists consider the untraditional and unconventional aspects of human social life, not being a neutral area of study, to be ill-suited for serious scholarly endeavor. Hence the unorthodox religious views and social doctrines held by some individuals and groups dedicated to the pursuit of the esoteric and occult have suffered scholarly neglect. This book challenges that position and aims to demonstrate that the occult is a legitimate and important area of investigation in its own right and as an avenue leading to greater understanding of the society of which it is a part.

Until a few years ago occult and esoteric pursuits were thought to be unpopular within the mainstream of American life. Religious groups organized around esoteric doctrines were regarded as numerically marginal and pariah. Social scientists therefore argued that serious research is better expended on more significant social domains.

Popular interest in the esoteric and the occult, however, has a long history in Western civilization. Every society in every historical period has had social groups, frequently organized as religious institutions, devoted to the accumulation of "hidden" knowledge and the search for power to apply that knowledge in daily life. In retrospect we often view such past efforts primarily in terms of the philosophical and literary traditions to which they have contributed.

Contemporary religious movements associated with the occult cannot be studied merely for their philosophical interest or traditional textual exegeses. We must examine their living component—the efforts of many people to build religious institutions and form movements devoted to the understanding of esoteric doctrines and their daily application.

This book is divided into three parts, each of which deals with a significant component in the study of the occult and its institutional forms. One component is esoteric doctrines; formulated by charismatic leaders and handed down through generations, they are central to the social organization of the groups interested in the occult. Learning, explicating, practicing, and transmitting such doctrines are the activities around which individuals group themselves. They link contemporary groups with those no longer extant. Part Two is a case study of one genre of the occult—witchcraft. We examine the nature of witchcraft activity, how it is defined by practitioners, how it is institutionalized in a society, and the resulting social relationships. The third component deals with contemporary efforts to introduce dispassionate and rational inquiry into this field. We are interested in getting away from the stereotype of the scientist who studies the esoteric for spurious, personal, and unscholarly reasons and from the efforts of some to become spokesmen for the material they have investigated and to present declarations of faith framed within scientific results of research.

Among contemporary movements concerned with esoteric doctrines and their application are Theosophy, Spiritualism, Scientology, the Society for Krishna Consciousness, Satanic churches, and a variety of groups organized around Hindu-based and other Eastern traditions.[1] These movements fall interstitially between our categories of secular and religious groups. Some define themselves as secular groups devoted to learning about the "laws of nature and life" and to applying them so that the individual lives according to the "rhythm and harmony of the universe." Other groups define themselves as religious bodies performing the tasks of orthodox religious groups as orientation systems for the parishioner. How a group defines itself is of great interest, since it reveals the nature of society's relationship to particular interest groups. Such relationship further serves as an index for the content and process of social change.

This book acquaints the reader with a range of esoteric doctrines well known in the West and with a series of problems that emerged when followers

---

[1] Irving I. Zaretsky and Mark P. Leone, *Religious Movements in Contemporary America* (Princeton: Princeton University Press, 1974).

of such doctrines were confronted by their societies. Such confrontations have been instrumental in creating new strategies for the formation of small social groups, and, conversely, they have further defined the level of tolerance of the larger society for the free exercise of individuals' beliefs. The renaissance of religious activity in the United States and Europe—especially of esoteric and occult pursuits—enables us today to conduct field research among newly forming groups. This gives us a unique opportunity to observe groups *ab ovo* and to address areas that still need further explication. For example, we need to know how doctrines are formulated by leaders; what the relationship is between a group's organization for maximum flexibility and responsiveness to its members and the impinging social pressures; and how belief systems evolve to reflect and promote a particularly advantageous form of organization.

Our task is to understand these groups as social institutions searching for a pattern of organization to achieve their institutional goals, and for a *modus vivendi* with the society so that they may remain readily available to those who seek them and a visible part of the social landscape.

IRVING I. ZARETSKY

New Haven, Connecticut
December 1973

Acknowledgments

I am indebted to several sources of support, encouragement, and assistance in the preparation of this book. The Duke Research Council has provided me with modest but useful grants. The Department of Sociology at Duke University has enabled me to draw on secretarial assistance in the preparation of various manuscripts. My thanks also extend to the undergraduate participants of a seminar I gave on the Sociology of Esotericism at Duke University some years ago; their receptivity, enthusiasm, and activities in the course of the semester encouraged me to collect the various materials we had discussed into a single volume.

My appreciation for intellectual support of the line of sociological inquiry into the nature of sociocultural change that I have been carrying out goes to two overseas colleagues and friends, Professor Georges Balandier of the Sorbonne and Professor S. N. Eisenstadt of Hebrew University. The execution of this book owes much to the timely suggestions and efforts of Dr. Irving I. Zaretsky and Mr. Eric Valentine, and lastly to the great variety of invaluable research assistance that Jeffrey Johnson has given me.

EDWARD A. TIRYAKIAN

Duke University
Durham, North Carolina
December 1973

Contents

PART III   SOCIOLOGICAL PERSPECTIVES AND RESEARCH ON THE ESOTERIC AND THE OCCULT

On the Margin of the Visible

Edward A. Tiryakian

Preliminary Considerations

This volume deals with complex sociocultural phenomena which occupy a marginal position in the development of Western civilization. They are the belief systems and symbolism characterized as "esoteric" teachings; their propagation in initiatory, secret or publicly invisible voluntary associations; and their derivative applications in magical arts and/or occult practices. These phenomena seem out of place in the context of Western development; they seem atavistic, vestiges of "premodern" society and premodern thought. Religious and scientific authorities alike have treated the esoteric and the occult as delusions and superstitions. The belief systems, the practices related to them, and the social groups associated with their propagation have been treated not only as innocuous frailties of the human mind, but also as "heresies"—religious, scientific, and political—which must be stamped out lest they bring irreparable harm to humanity. Although publicly condemned and repressed by various social means at the disposal of religious, scientific, and political "establishments," the esoteric and the occult have survived as social phenomena throughout the development of Western civilization. They have remained on the margin of the socially visible, a covert if not underground aspect of the Western cultural system. Some of its artifacts, symbols, and major figures have entered the mainstream of popular culture; others have retained their cloak of invisibility.

A comprehensive investigation of the esoteric tradition, that seemingly archaic side of Western culture, can, we believe, shed much light on major sources of ideational change in the structure of Western society, changes at the core of collective representations of physical and social reality. Our present aim is not a full documentation of this rather bold contention which goes counter to most standard interpretations, but to introduce the reader, whether sociologist or not, to the unfamiliar field of the esoteric and the occult in its Western manifestations. We take this field as representing a crucial missing link between the cultural systems of "modern" and "traditional" Western society; the esoteric consciousness, at heart, is both ultramodern and ultratraditional. The study of this field is particularly appropriate in a period such as ours, one representing the most advanced state of "modernity," in which we are confronted with the paradox of an unexpected renaissance of public interest in the esoteric and the occult, ranging from the personal identity symbols of Zodiac signs and computerized horoscopes, Eastern imports of Yoga, Transcendental Meditation, the widely read works of Roszak and Castaneda,[1] to the demonological side of the occult, reflected in the popularity of the movie "Rosemary's Baby," the establishment of covens and Satanic "churches" in metropolitan centers, and even warnings from church and evangelistic leaders about the reality of Satan whose followers are seen as spreading.[2]

What is the sociological significance of these surface manifestations of the esoteric and the occult? From the standpoint of our customary way of interpreting central trends of modern society, they can be interpreted as odd deviations or as "breakdowns of modernization,"[3] as flights into the irrational, as escapes from the strains imposed by the complexity of the technological social order, as aberrations from the major lines of progress. In itself, this perspective provides room enough for sociological research and theorizing. To posit that a flourish of the occult represents a "breakdown of modernization" is not an explanation of why it should occur at this time, nor an explanation of its meaning and social forms to various social strata. Further, an adequate sociological explanation should be extended to other time periods in Western civilization when other renewal of interest and participation in the esoteric and the occult took place, notably during the Renaissance and Reformation and during the closing stages of the Roman Empire.

If the surfacing of the esoteric and the occult into public awareness occurs only at certain periods of Western civilization, is the correlation a fortuitous one or is there a significant linkage between the cultural system of the larger (or exoteric) society and the esoteric and the occult? This should be seen as a major sociological question. If we think of "normal" social life as "routinely" unfolding along the lines of a basic cultural paradigm underlying social institutions, then the analysis of changes in the structure of cultural paradigms gives us greater sensitivity to periods of transition, that is, to periods of normative crises (or "anomie," to borrow from Emile Durkheim), cultural revolutions, and renovations. It is in these crucial periods that esoteric doctrines, and occult groups and practices, surface from their covert level in society and attain public visibility. The flourishing of the esoteric and the occult has, therefore, a definite sociological significance. It might, conceivably, be an indicator of a very advanced state of cultural decadence; it is also conceivable that it may be a harbinger of a new cultural paradigm.

The latter possibility arises if we avoid the common-place judgment that the esoteric element of Western civilization is an atavistic trait, a throwback to "primitive" mentality. Why not approach the esoteric tradition as a source of new cultural paradigms, new models of reality? This, essentially, is what we have done. To state our thesis as boldly as possible, it is that a key component of the dynamism of Western civilization, the "theurgic restlessness" at the heart of the Western historical process, is in part a function of the marginal status of esoteric subculture as an active "counterculture" which has been a seedbed of innovations and inspirations in religion, science, politics, and other domains (such as art and literature). Stated differently, we propose that the esoteric tradition, the covert side of Western civilization, has been a catalyst in the modernization process (spanning many centuries), both in its "breakdowns" and in its "build-ups."[4] We have in an earlier essay[5] treated some of these themes, particularly that of the relation of the esoteric to the modernization process. We would now like to add some new considerations.

We shall limit ourselves here to seeking the core of consciousness in esoteric doctrines, and occult practices and groups, so as to lay the groundwork for treating their sociocultural manifestations in a sociological manner. The following remarks approach this from considerations of a sociology of knowledge influenced by phenomenology.

A social order is organized around the knowledge of reality which is shared and accepted by the majority of its members. The knowledge of reality has

conventional definitions, conventional techniques of acquisition and transmission, and conventional categorizations. This is knowledge which makes
sense to those who participate in the institutional framework surrounding
everyday social life. Is is the "common sense" knowledge with which we interpret the world about us, our relations to the social and physical environ-
ments, and so forth.

Our knowledge of the world and our place in it is to a large part given to us
by our direct experiences, mediated by our sensory apparatus and feelings,[6]
along with the "common sense" we acquire in the socialization process. There
is also the knowledge we "learn about," from courses we take, from the mass
media, and so forth. We may never experience a quantum jump, but we accept
its reality as it is established by physicists. Likewise, we may never experience
direct contact with, say, the Kwakiutl Indians or exotic tribes in distant lands,
yet we take for granted their existence based on anthropological knowledge.
Both components of the stock of knowledge which is publicly shared and publicly accessible may be termed "exoteric knowledge."

One form of consciousness of reality is that only the tangible, physical,
visible world there-before-us, given by the physical senses and/or capable of
objective measurements, is real—a view manifest in the philosophical positions
of "materialism" and "radical empiricism." In contrast, there is an apprehension of reality that what exists before us is an "appearance," that what
is visible is only part of the total picture of the world. One radical form of this
consciousness is that the visible, tangible, factual is illusory; this perception is
manifest in the philosophical position of "absolute idealism." The first stance
has an affinity for an extreme form of objectivism. Its polar extreme emphasizes subjectivism, which can lead to solipsism. Although philosophically
intriguing, neither of these ontological perspectives can provide the basis for
the organization of human society.

More typical, in both Western and non-Western societies, modern and premodern alike, is a general perspective that the world of appearance is an outward manifestation of a background reality, that the relationships and interrelationships among observed phenomena derive from their linkage to covert
factors or forces "behind" the world of appearance. What is the social importance of this view? If the familiar, everyday world is contingent on the
operations of a knowable but hidden reality, one not accessible to the senses,
then those who gain knowledge of the hidden reality are superior to those who
do not. *Such knowledge of hidden truths is therefore a source of power.* It is a
source of power because knowledge of the workings of forces that govern the

manifest world implies the ability to use these forces to bring about changes in the appearance of things, to transform the world of appearances. And, since the transformation of the world of appearances affects people's lives, it is a source of social power.

The visible world there-before-us is an ensemble of physical things, of bodies which we can touch, localize, measure. The invisible world is hidden from our view. We cannot situate ourselves in relation to aspects of it the way we can take our distance from objects in the visible world. It is both very much "inside" us and very much "outside" us; the spatio-temporal continuum does not seem to apply to it. The two worlds, however, are not in a state of radical discontinuity vis-à-vis one another. There is a "medium" which relates the two, the medium of *symbols*. A "symbol" is an empirical referent, it is capable of being grasped by the senses. It is an image, a gesture, a phrase, a physical object, etc.—anything which can act as an interchange between the two worlds, a point of contact between the manifest and the hidden reality. The ability to utilize these symbols, which when properly activated can harness the energy or forces of the invisible, ultimate reality to bring about changes in the conditions of the world of appearances is, at heart, a *magical* ability. It is an ability, obviously, not given to everyone.

"Magic" is intimately connected to the occult, but it has broader social import. It is worthwhile to give some attention to it now, prior to treating the esoteric tradition, which rests upon the careful acquisition and transmission of knowledge of ultimate reality.

A very important ingress to the sociological significance of magic is to be found in a neglected monograph of Henri Hubert and Marcel Mauss, two collaborators of Emile Durkheim, the founder of modern sociology. The monograph in question, *A General Theory of Magic*, was first published in 1904, and has just recently become available in an English edition.[7]

The authors drew upon a great variety of comparative materials pertaining to magic, including ancient Veda texts, ethnographic materials on Australia, Melanesia, and North America, and also materials from Western civilization. They point out the social character of magic at several levels, for example, the collective nature of beliefs, actions, rituals, and roles which constitute the magical world. Beyond arguing that magic is grounded in the existence of the collectivity and that magic depends upon its social validations[8] —major points in themselves—Hubert and Mauss also relate magic to science and religion, a consideration which greatly adds to the significance of magic.[9] A reflection on some of the points raised by this seminal monograph is in order.

The relationships of those who participate in activities recognized as
"magic" to the larger societal setting in which they occur are, to an important
extent, those of a marginal group. Hubert and Mauss were quick to note that
the magical virtues attributed to persons were as much, if not more, a function
of social categories occupied by these persons than of their physical characteristics. There are social strata, even occupational and ethnic groups, whose social
situation predisposes them to be regarded by the larger social communities as
practicing magic: women, young children, professions such as barbers and
physicians, strangers, and others. In brief, a disproportionate number of
magical practitioners (or their auxiliaries) come from the ranks of those oc-
cupying a marginal social status.[10]

Social marginality—or liminality[11]—is a state or condition on the
boundaries of society's institutional framework, not subject to its regulations
yet not altogether disjoint from it. The groups who occupy a liminal position
in the social structure are both in a position of inferiority and power; the
norms and regulations of everyday life do not apply to them. Magic exists in a
marginal or liminal social world. It is present in the larger society (and
provides services to the latter), yet is not institutionally recognized. However
widely practiced, magic does not have the legitimation given to it which other
institutional practices receive; everyday "social" religion is very circumspect in
dealing with magic and looks askance upon it, even though religious rites have
magical elements.[12]

Magic is, in effect, a subculture of society, a deviant social world. Its very
existence, however, is a socially defined one since it is contingent upon the
popular imagination (in the words of Hubert and Mauss), which bestows on
the magician (or the sorcerer, the witch, etc.) the powers and virtues that the
practitioners of magic possess. One is not born a magician; one learns to become a magician in a socialization process wherein one internalizes the public
definitions concerning the cluster of role characteristics associated with being a
magician. Once one has become a magician, he cannot doubt the efficacy of his
techniques. If a magical rite or charm does not produce the desired effect, it is
the fault of the client of magic, or practitioner's own error, or a more powerful
"countermeasure" used by a third person.

The foundation of magic is broader than the social delimitation of magic itself, at least in terms of the customary image of magic and its specialists. The
magician uses procedures to transform empirical reality by bringing into play
forces of the invisible world that act on visible things. Beliefs in magic are part
of a broader collective belief that some human agents are or can become

endowed with the capability of invoking the fundamental forces of the universe.

The ultimate force which can operate on the quiddity of entities has received many names. Hubert and Mauss adopted the term "mana," originating in Melanesia, which has been extended to other cultural contexts to represent the referent of magic, the virtue of a special force capable of affecting things (making them move, changing their shape and form, operating on other things, etc.). We might add in passing that the notion of "mana," taken from the context of non-Western culture, has an important linkage in Western society with the notion of "charisma."[13] The latter has a more individualistic connotation: it designates an extraordinary spiritual force (a state of divine grace) which attaches itself to some human agents, giving them an authority that transcends other authority structures which frame daily, routine and institutionalized society.

From the standpoint of institutionalized society, the direct tapping by a human agent of the ultimate forces of the world is a short-cutting of established, traditional and legitimate authority structures. Hence, the possession of "mana" or "charisma" is always a potential threat to civil authority, for it necessarily implies that the possessor of mana can command a social following and can upset the established social order. He who has the power to transform reality, can upset the balance of things, and can, consequently upset the social equilibrium in the process. Therefore, he who has access to the ultimate forces of reality, or to the knowledge of these forces, has to be an important social figure (not necessarily an approved social figure), a figure of power whose source does not derive from institutional activities.

The attainment of the knowledge of the ultimate forces behind the visible world is itself always a dangerous thing. It is equally dangerous to the individuals who seek such knowledge and to the larger collectivity in which such a person lives. The knowledge of the ultimate workings of the cosmos is "divine knowledge,"—*theosophy* in a generic sense. That such knowledge is not meant for everyone is also conveyed by its designation as "forbidden knowledge," which can lead to the downfall of he who seeks it. This knowledge which is not meant for ordinary man is esoteric knowledge par excellence. And in various streams of the esoteric tradition there is a conception of a "safe"and an "unsafe" path to the attainment of this ultimate knowledge of reality, a "Right Way" and a "Left Way," the one benefic and the other malefic in its consequences for those who seek "divine knowledge."[14]

Hazardous as the quest for ultimate knowledge may be, that is, dangerous as the quest for knowledge of the ultimate workings of the world may be, it is one which always has had Promethean appeal—to the most sophisticated minds as much if not more than to the ordinary man. There is a fascination to danger, for *danger* (as the etymology of "danger" indicates) is closely linked to *power*,[15] and therefore to domination: knowledge of how to utilize forces of the world is not only to place oneself in a position of domination over these forces but also over the lives of others.

The magician is not the only human agent whose social activity and meaning derives from his knowledge and active participation in the forces which underlie the visible world. There are other social figures who share this quality with the magician: the priest, the scientist, the prophet, and the charismatic political leader (the latter two being often fused in the same historical person, for example, the Anabaptist "King" John Beukels of Münster, or in a more recent period, Simon Kimbangu of the Congo).

The priest in traditional society and the scientist in modern society have a degree of social acceptance within the institutional framework of the on-going society, whereas the prophet/charismatic leader has a more marginal status. Yet all three are potential threats to the authority structure of society, and on various occasions in the history of Western civilization, the conflict has been an open one. This is so because, like the magician, each of these figures (and the collectivities which rally around them) can lay claim to a special authority to direct or intervene in human affairs by virtue of participatory knowledge of the ultimate forces of the world. The magician, the priest, the scientist, and the prophet/charismatic leader (even if the latter appears in his modern secular guise) can perform "miracles" whose common denominantor is the transformation of the world of appearances. They share in common an extraordinary consciousness of reality, a vision of a dimension of reality other than that experienced by the ordinary sense; each is a sort of visionary who does not operate under the constraints of the "natural attitude." Typically, the norms of ascetism and disinterestedness operate on their conduct, certainly to a degree not expected of ordinary men. The vows of poverty of the priesthood may be an explicit formulation of norms which tacitly structure the conduct of the magician, the scientist, and the charismatic revolutionary leader (as well as its antecedent figure, the prophet). It is as if the energy of each, his ability to relate to the ultimate truths and forces of the world—his ability to do great wonders—is contingent on and reflected in forgoing material enhancement and affluence. In fact, if one succumbs to the temptations of improving his material situation by his gifts, if he seeks material gains, he may well lose his "mana" or "charisma" and suffer a "fall from grace."

I have stated that a distinguishing feature of these social figures is a consciousness of reality which transcends the frames of the "natural attitude"; each has an apprehension of a hidden reality. Such a consciousness is conducive to viewing the factual world as a *possibility*, one among many possible orderings, and not as the sole actuality now-and-forever or one whose relationships among its parts are immutable. Each of these figures perceives the relationships between the visible and the invisible in terms of what might be called a *grammar of symbols*. The rules of the grammar differ from one to the other, and from the grammar of the layman and his social institutions.[16] The grammar of the magician of the priest, of the scientist, and of the prophetic charismatic leader operates within a different logic from that of everyday common sense," from the logic of everyday practical activity.

A discussion of the grammar of symbols from each standpoint is beyond the scope of this essay. But we might suggest a typification of the respective forms of consciousness involved. The priest will tend to see the invisible reality in terms of personalized forces (e.g., good and evil deities) towards which he relates by means of prescribed rituals. The scientist will tend to see this reality in terms of impersonal forces (e.g., gravitation, rays, atomic energy) towards which he relates by means of impersonal (objective, experimental) procedures. The charismatic leader will see it in terms of impersonal collective forces (e.g., nationalism, class struggle as an historical process) with which he is in direct contact. The magician, as such, will see the invisible reality in terms of both personal and impersonal forces which he relates to by means of prescribed rituals, a mirror image of those of the priest.

Although the symbolic conceptions and the grammar of each differ from one another, they have points in common. They tend to have the consciousness that the interplay between the forces and basic structures of hidden reality is characterized by dualistic tension and conflict: conflict between the spiritual forces of good and evil in the religious vision; between impersonal physical forces in the scientific vision (e.g., matter and antimatter, positive and negative charges of matter, etc.); between sociopolitical groups (e.g., the bourgeoisie and the proletariat) in the consciousness of the revolutionary leader. A second common element is the belief that the conflicting tensions between the forces of the cosmos underlie the changes which punctuate the world before us. Finally, each symbolic conception also encompasses the view that the conflicting forces form necessary parts of a whole, or constitute a unity, a cosmic harmony. The knowledge of this ultimate "fitting-together" (the harmony of conflict) is the ultimate knowledge of the meaning of the world, and consequently the ultimate source of power. If the world of appearances, the visible world, is a possible arrangement of parts that derives from the invisible reality, then knowledge of the invisible can make possible the rearrangement of the visible. Knowledge of the invisible is power to transform the visible. It is awesome, fascinating, dangerous knowledge. It is the knowledge of the Magus, whether he be socially designated as a magician, a priest, a scientist, or a charismatic leader.

We now wish to give a brief consideration to the esoteric tradition in Western civilization. Knowledge of the reality behind the world of appearances, we have said, is tantamount to "divine knowledge." It is knowledge of hidden truths, of the inner workings of the structures of the visible. Access to such knowledge is not immediate; the recipient of this knowledge must undergo long preparation, a process of initiation which will demonstrate whether he is worthy of knowing the secrets of the world. The procedures involved in the training of the priesthood before ordination and the prolonged scientific training necessary to receive the doctorate—both taking place under careful supervision by "elders"— have structural linkages with the socialization process operative in the esoteric tradition. Each involves a dissociation from the "natural attitude" perspective of laymen and also involves the acquisition of specialized skills in dealing with the reality not given by the ordinary senses (including "common sense").

The esoteric tradition in Western civilization is closely tied to the development of both religion and science. At the religious level it has been a covert part of Judaism, Hellenism, and Christianity, and it has straddled theology and philosophy. In this context, it has been designated or has had manifestations under various labels: Pythagoreanism, Neo-Platonism, Gnosticism, kabbalism, or even mysticism. To be sure, each branch has had various "schools" of adepts, and different forms of social organization and symbolic consciousness, some of which are "familiar" or publicly recognized. Each social branch (for example, that of Freemasonry, of Rose Croix, etc.) has its own history and rites. Behind the diversity of symbols and figures, however, the esoteric tradition professes a unity and a continuity which transcends specific religio-philosophical currents.[17]

The religious aspect of the esoteric does not discredit major religious figures of Western civilization, such as Moses or Christ; on the contrary, it claims them as important participants—not as saviors or exalted leaders but as teachers who imparted "divine knowledge" to a small group of followers, an oral knowledge to be handed down in successive generations by a small, highly qualified group, whose membership must remain anonymous in terms of the larger society, and therefore who constitute an "invisible college" of sages.

The esoteric tradition has many linkages to the development of Western science and scientific thought, if not to its very social organization. Modern science rests on a "dynamic" conception of the cosmos and of nature (physis), one in sharp contrast to the static Weltanschauung of the Middle Ages.[18] The very notions of the earth moving in the celestial sphere, of the circulation of the blood, of the propagation of light, of the gravitational attraction of heavenly bodies are manifestations of this conception—just as modern social science was galvanized by Saint-Simon's and Marx's dynamic conception of social reality and Freud's dynamic conception of personality. The affinity of these cardinal ideational "innovations" with the esoteric perspective on reality leads us to speculate, as a topic of subsequent investigation, on the nexus between scientific innovative figures—such as Copernicus, Newton, Descartes, and more recent ones—and the esoteric tradition.[19] Certainly, to err on the conservative side, one can affirm that the experimentations, theorizings, and symbolizations of the esoteric sciences, notably alchemy and astrology, provided the necessary chrysalis, the Jacob's ladder, of modern science.[20]

Esoteric and scientific thought are profoundly interrelated, just as esoteric and religious thought are profoundly interrelated. The esoteric world-view asserts the primacy of the existential nexus between the knowing self and the workings of the world, between the subject and the object. Esoteric knowledge and praxis form an indissoluble unity. In the esoteric assertion "As it is above, so it is below," the Microcosm is not the world of appearance external to man. Man—the Anthropos—is revealed in Nature and Nature is revealed in Man. This view relates esoteric thought to the world-view of traditional thought, whereas the development process of modern science in its institutionalization carried it beyond "the edge of objectivity."[21]

Science and technology have been driving forces in the formation of modern society, at least in the past two hundred years. The esoteric context in which they developed may be thought of as the "booster" from which they "took-off" into distant space ventures. But stripped of its subjectivity, of its apprehension of a symbolic reality which interrelates man and society with the cosmos, the space capsule of modernity shows signs of floundering in search of the ontological "sense" of being. The one-sided emphasis on objectivity has led to increasing reactions of protests at the political and cultural level, reactions as varied as Nazism, Surrealism, and the drug culture.

Perhaps now is the period when we shall witness a new cultural paradigm replacing the one that may have spent its creative energy. And perhaps it is the esoteric tradition that will again come to the fore of the visible and act as a new booster. If the "right path" of the esoteric tradition is followed, it may be possible for the new cultural paradigm to realize a synthesis of science and religion, since the esoteric tradition has channels to both. Without it, the "Weberian dilemma" will become even more accentuated, the dilemma of the "iron cage" of modern, depersonalized society: mechanized petrification or blind following of false prophets.[22]

To strike a viable balance between subjectivity and objectivity, that is a central problem of the modern period, a problem at the very core of the direction of modern society, and therefore a crucial sociological problem. It is in this context that an awareness of the esoteric and the occult takes on an added sociological meaning, for sociology must participate in the formulation of the cultural paradigm adequate for modern society. To prepare this, sociology must familiarize itself with these sociocultural phenomena which have been a major although latent aspect of Western civilization. Sociology must become conscious of the cultural unconscious of Western society, and like the earlier explorations of Freud and Jung, it must learn to decipher the codes, the workings, and the meanings to actors of the cultural unconscious, so much of which can be unraveled by the study of the esoteric and the occult as sociocultural phenomena.

The rationale for this volume, then, has many aspects. I hope that I have indicated enough to justify the reader's interest in discovering, if not recovering, what lies on the margin of the visible.

NOTES

1. Theodore Roszak, *The Making of a Counter Culture*, (Garden City, N.Y.: Doubleday Anchor, 1969; Carlos Castaneda, *The Teachings of Don Juan: A Yaqui Way of Knowledge*, Berkeley: University of California Press, 1968; C. Castaneda, *A Separate Reality: Further Conversations with Don Juan*, New York: Simon and Schuster, 1971: C. Castaneda, *Journey to Ixtlan: The Lessons of Don Juan*, New York: Simon and Schuster, 1972.

2. Pope Paul VI delivered for the first time a public warning about Satan and Satanic cults on November 15, 1972. The evangelist Billy Graham has issued similar statements recently.

3. The sociological treatment of "breakdowns in modernization" has received considerable attention in the writings of S. N. Eisenstadt; see in particular his essay "Breakdown of Modernization," in S. N. Eisenstadt, ed., *Readings in Social Evolution and Development*, New York: Pergamon Press, 1970, pp. 421–452. For an economist's perspective, see Joseph J. Spengler, "Breakdowns in Modernization," in Myron Weiner, ed., *Modernization*, New York: Basic Books, 1966, pp. 321–333.

4. In this sense, the "latency" functions of the esoteric subcultural system vis-à-vis institutionalized society are analogous to those of the "unconscious" for the organization and development of the personality system.

5. "Toward the Sociology of Esoteric Culture, "*American Journal of Sociology*, **78** (November, 1972), 491–512. Reprinted elsewhere in this volume.

6. See Erwin Straus, *The Primary World of Senses*, New York: Free Press, 1963.

7. Henri Hubert and Marcel Mauss, "Esquisse d'une Théorie Générale de la Magie," *L'Année Sociologique*, **VII** (1902–1903), pp. 1–146. The English edition is *A General Theory of Magic*, Robert Brain, trans., London: Routledge and Kegan Paul, 1972. Citations in this essay are taken from the original. The concluding chapter of their monograph is to be found elsewhere in this volume, but the entire work deserves reading for the richness of its insights.

8. Hubert and Mauss, *op. cit.*, p. 140. They even proposed that there is an inexhaustible ground of diffuse magic in society itself, and that society generates new magicians and experiments with new magical rituals in every age. Such rituals, we might add, would be modern secular adaptations of both "white" and "black" magic.

9. The relation of magic to science and religion is treated in the well-known essay of Malinowski, "Magic, Science, and Religion" (1925), reproduced in Bronislaw Malinowski, *Magic, Science and Religion and Other Essays*, Boston: Beacon, 1948. Although critical of the Durkheimian approach to religion, this is an important complementary perspective.

10. Hubert and Mauss, *op. cit.*, pp. 22–28.

11. For a pertinent discussion of liminality and social structure, see Victor W. Turner, *The Ritual Process, Structure and Anti-Structure*, Chicago: Aldine, 1969, pp. 94–130.

12. Emile Durkheim noted a fundamental antagonism between magic and religion: "Magic takes a sort of professional pleasure in profaning holy things; in its rites, it performs the contrary of religious ceremony. On its side, religion, when it has not condemned and prohibited magic rites, has always looked upon them with disfavor." (*The Elementary Forms of the Religious Life,* Joseph Ward Swain, trans., New York: Collier, 1961, p. 58.) It is significant that the priest and the magician *invert* their normal procedures when they step into the domain of each other. As an extension, magic may be thought of as the prototype of a "counterculture" in the depth of the structure of the established social order.

13. The classical sociological treatment of charisma is, of course, that of Max Weber; see his "The Sociology of Charismatic Authority" in Hans Gerth and C. Wright Mills, eds., *From Max Weber: Essays in Sociology*, New York: Oxford University Press, 1958, pp. 245–252. I have not found in Weber reference to "mana"; Hubert and Mauss (and Durkheim, for that matter) do not refer to "charisma."

14. This apprehension is found, for example, in the Tantric Yoga magical tradition of Hinduism, but is also expressed in other traditions, such as that of Jewish mysticism. The legend of the *golem* is an instance of the following: "Spiritual activism, when all realistic and practical outlets are closed, easily turns into magical activism, and Jewish legend knows of

Kabbalist masters who decided to force the messianic advent by means of extreme mortifications, special meditations, and Kabbalist incantations. These legends . . . usually end with the kabbalist adept falling a prey to the daemonic powers which he had meant to vanquish." (R. J. Zwi Werblowsky, "Messianism in Jewish History," in H. H. Ben-Sasson and S. Ettinger, eds., *Jewish Society Through the Ages*, New York: Schocken, 1971, p. 40.)

15. See the insightful study of Mary Douglas, *Purity and Danger*, London: Routledge and Kegan Paul, 1966. She gives a particular emphasis to the interplay between power and organized social life in terms of notions of taboo and pollution.

16. Alfred Schutz, one of the influential figures of phenomenological sociology, has given major impetus to an understanding of the grammar of the everyday world. See his *Collected Papers*, 3 vol., The Hague (Holland): Martinus Nijhoff, 1962–1966; and his *The Phenomenology of the Social World*, Evanston, Ill.: Northwestern University Press, 1967.

17. The following statement by the noted art historian Gombrich in his recent study of the Renaissance is apposite:"We are familiar with the doctrine of an esoteric tradition which reaches back to the mysterious origins of time and which is both revealed and concealed in the Wisdom of the East. The writings of the Florentine Neo-Platonists belong to this current of thought. . . . We are constantly referred to the mythical sages of the East, to the Egyptian Priests, to Hermes Trimegistos, to Zoroaster, and, among the Greeks, to those who were believed to have been in possession of this secret lore, to Orpheus, to Pythagoras and last but not least to Plato, whose use of myths and whose reverence for Egypt fitted in well with this picture of an unbroken chain of esoteric tradition." (E. H. Gombrich, *Symbolic Images, Studies in the Art of the Renaissance*, New York: Phaidon, 1972, p. 149.)

18. Concerning the latter, see William J. Brandt, *The Shape of Medieval History*, New York: Schocken, 1973.

19. The nexus between esoteric thought and innovations in scientific thought is a challenging but difficult avenue of research. For partial indications, see, on the influence of Neo-Platonism in astronomy, Thomas S. Kuhn, *The Copernican Revolution*, New York: Random House, 1959, *Passim;* on esoteric thought and Newton, see D. Geoghegan, "Some Indications of Newton's Attitude Towards Alchemy, *Ambix*, **6** (1957–1958), 102–06, and F. Sherwood Taylor, "An Alchemical Work of Sir Isaac Newton," *Ambix*, **5** (October, 1953), 59–84; on Rose Croix, see the intriguing note of Leontine Goldschmidt, "The Symbolic Meaning of Fahrenheit's Temperature Scale," *Ambix*, **6** (August 1957). 107–108; for a critical discussion of Rose Croix and Descartes, see Paul Arnold, *La Rose Croix et ses Rapports avec la Franc-Maçonnerie*, Paris: Maisonneuve and Larose, 1970; on the influence of esoteric Judaism on Freud, see David Bakan, *Sigmund Freud and the Jewish Mystical Tradition*, Princeton: Van Nostrand, 1958.

20. The penultimate aphorism of Wittgenstein's *Tractatus Logico Philosophicus* (one of the most significant works of modern philosophy) is (unwittingly) as good a statement describing the relationship between modern scientific thought and its esoteric background as can be found:

"My propositions are elucidatory in this way: he who understands me finally recognizes them as senseless, when he has climbed out through them, on them, over them. (He must so to speak throw away the ladder after he has climbed up on it).

"He must surmount these propositions; then he sees the world rightly." (Ludwig Wittgenstein, *Tractatus Logico-Philosophicus,* New York: Harcourt, Brace, 1933, aphorism 6.54).

The ultimate aphorism of Wittgenstein is not so much a riddle of logical positivism, perhaps, as it is a statement strikingly esoteric in character, that of the esoteric sage-teacher who has spoken to the initiated as much as possible, having disclosed in words all that language can disclose:

"Whereof one cannot speak, thereof one must be silent" (*Tractatus*, aphorism 7).

In passing, it is tempting to think that the *Tractatus* itself may have an esoteric meaning. If we think of each aphorism as a seal that Wittgenstein opened, a seal of the truth of the world (and that his investigations are logical investigations about the world are indicated in the first set of aphorisms), one is led to the intriguing speculation of a nexus between the seven sets of aphorisms that constitute the *Tractatus* and the Seven Seals of *Revelation* (one of the most pronounced esoteric aspects of the New Testament). I am not in the position to affirm that Wittgenstein had familiarity with esoteric culture but am suggesting it as a possibility, in keeping with the working hypothesis that radical innovations in the categorization of the world may have a likely inspirational source in esoteric thought.

21. Charles C. Gillespie, *The Edge of Objectivity,* Princeton, N.J.: Princeton University Press, 1960. For a very perceptive comparison of traditional and scientific thought, see Robin Horton, "African Traditional Thought and Western Science," *Africa,* 37, Nos. 1 and 2 (January and April, 1967).

22. Max Weber, *The Protestant Ethic and the Spirit of Capitalism,* Talcott Parsons, trans., New York: Scribner, 1958, p. 182.

Part One

Representative Esoteric Doctrines and Their Social Forms of Expression

The selections in this part provide an initial exposure to esoteric culture and its social context in Western civilization. The reader will become aware of the differences between esoteric belief systems and commonplace assumptions about the nature of the world, of the interrelationships between various strands of esotericism, and of the linkages between esoteric cosmological notions and empirical techniques and practices, such as alchemy and divination by the Tarot. The selections also indicate areas of convergence and divergence between esoteric consciousness and more familiar forms of Western social consciousness, including religious and scientific consciousness.

One major strand of esoteric culture is Gnosticism; the selections by Bouisson and Voegelin indicate how interwoven with the development of Western civilization this heterodox esoteric religion has been, in its guises and disguises.

The relationship of esoteric thought to science is brought out in several selections. Alchemy provides an important nexus between esotericism and science. The selection of Jung introduces some basic concepts of alchemy, and prepares the reader for the excerpt from Paracelsus (1493–1541), a major figure who bridges esoteric culture and the dawn of modern empirical science. The piece by Pauwels and Bergier discusses alchemy in our own day. Although Francis Bacon (1561–1626), who played a key role in the early formulation of the scientific method, had harsh things to say about "degenerate natural magic, alchemy, astrology and the like" (*Of the Proficience and Advancement of Learning,* Book II), the selection from his *New Atlantis* depicts a scientific fraternal community which acts as an "invisible college" of benefac-

17

tors to mankind. As such, one may intimate its filiation with the esoteric tradition, particularly with the early Brotherhood of Rosicrucians, which was flourishing in Europe in Bacon's later years (and which attracted other eminent scientists and mathematicians, such as Descartes and Leibnitz).

Part One also includes selections from more recent historical figures who renovated Western esotericism: P. D. Ouspensky, a trained mathematician and physicist, who became acquainted with the enigmatic Gurdjieff in 1915 and subsequently became the best-known interpreter of Gurdjieff's teachings; Papus (Gérard Encausse) who brought out the complex and profound symbolisms of the Tarot (perhaps *the* synthesis of esoteric culture); H. P. Blavatsky, who after extensive travels in India launched the modern Theosophical movement in America and England; Rudolf Steiner, the founder of Anthroposophy and undoubtedly one of the most profound and influential esoteric writers of this century, who was also a Goethe scholar, an architect, and an educator; finally in this context, Max Heindel, who was instrumental in activating the Rosicrucian Order in the United States.

Esoteric consciousness is imparted by those who obtain knowledge of it in a complex process of socialization. Sometimes this takes place in a single teacher-pupil relationship. More often the secret knowledge is imparted in rituals of initiation into a group. The selection by the sociologist Georg Simmel remains the most penetrating analytical study of secrecy and secret social organizations. The selection on the Carbonari (an Italian patriotic secret society of the nineteenth century which played an important role in the development of Italian nationalism, and from which the Mafia may have evolved) illustrates one of the forms of initiation rituals of fraternal orders which require secrecy; Dewar's and Cohen's selections provide complementary materials on that most complex of brotherhoods, Freemasonry.

The selection by the well-known literary figure William Butler Yeats has a whimsical side. Yeats' interest in both folk and esoteric culture was related to his interest in Irish nationalism. The connections between archaic elements of culture and modern political movements, especially Nazism, are suggested in the other selection by Pauwels and Bergier.

P. D. Ouspensky (1878–1947)

Esotericism and Modern Thought

The idea of a knowledge which surpasses all ordinary human knowledge, and is inaccessible to ordinary people, but which exists somewhere and belongs to somebody, permeates the whole history of the thought of mankind from the most remote periods. And according to certain memorials of the past a knowledge quite different from ours formed the essence and content of human thought at those times when, according to other opinions, man differed very little, or did not differ at all, from animals.

"Hidden knowledge" is therefore sometimes called "ancient knowledge." But of course this does not explain anything. It must, however, be noted that all religions, all myths, all beliefs, all popular heroic legends of all peoples and all countries are based on the recognition of the existence sometime and somewhere of a knowledge far superior to the knowledge which we possess or can possess. And to a considerable degree the content of all religions and myths consists of symbolic forms which represent attempts to transmit the idea of this hidden knowledge.

From P. D. Ouspensky, *A New Model of the Universe,* New York: Alfred A. Knopf, 1931, pp. 11–17. Reprinted by the permission of the publisher and the Estate of P. D. Ouspensky.

On the other hand, nothing demonstrates so clearly the weakness of human thought or human imagination as existing ideas as to the content of hidden knowledge. The word, the concept, the idea, the expectation, exist, but there are no definite concrete forms of percept connected with this idea. And the idea itself has very often to be dug out with great difficulty from beneath mountains of lies, both intentional and unintentional, from deception and self-deception and from naïve attempts to present in intelligible forms adopted from ordinary life that which in its very nature can have no resemblance to them.

The work of finding traces of ancient or hidden knowledge, or even hints of its existence, resembles the work of archaeologists looking for traces of some ancient forgotten civilisation and finding them buried beneath several strata of cemeteries left by peoples who have since lived in that place, separated possibly by thousands of years and unaware of one another's existence.

But on every occasion that an investigator comes upon the attempts to express in one way or another the content of hidden knowledge he invariably sees the same thing, namely, the striking poverty of human imagination in the face of this idea.

Humanity in the face of the idea of hidden knowledge reminds one of the people in fairy-tales who are promised by some goddess, fairy or magician that they will be given whatever they want on condition that they say *exactly* what they want. And usually in fairy-tales people do not know what to ask for. In some cases the fairy or magician offers to grant as many as three wishes, but even this is of no use. In all fairy-tales of all periods and peoples, men get hopelessly lost when confronted with the question of what they want, and what they would like to have. They are quite unable to determine and formulate their wish. Either at that minute they remember only some small unimportant desire, or they express several contradictory wishes, which cancel one another; or else, as in the fairy-tale of "The Fisherman and the Fish,"[1] they are not able to keep within the bounds of possible things and, always wishing for more and more, they end by attempting to subjugate higher forces, not being conscious of the poverty of their own powers and capacities. And so again they fall, again they lose all that they have acquired, because they themselves do not clearly know what they want.

In a jocular form this idea of the difficulty of formulating desires and of men's rare success in it is set forth in an Indian tale:

A beggar, who was born blind, led a single life, and lived upon the charity of his neighbours, was long and incessantly assailing a particular deity with his prayers. The latter was at last moved by this continual devotion, but fearing that his votary might not be easily satisfied, took care to bind him by an oath to ask for no more than a single blessing.

It puzzled the beggar for a long while, but his professional ingenuity at last came to his aid.

"I hasten to obey the behest, generous Lord!" quoth he, "and this solitary boon is all I ask at thy hands, namely, that I should live to see the grand-child of my grand-child playing in a seven-storied palace and helped by a train of attendants to his meal of milk and rice, out of a golden cup." And he concluded by expressing his hope that he had not exceeded the limit of a single wish vouchsafed to him.

The deity saw that he had been fairly done, for though single in form, the boon asked for comprised the manifold blessings of health, wealth, long life, restoration of sight, marriage and progeny. For very admiration of his devotee's astuteness and consummate tact, if not in fulfilment of his plighted word, the deity felt bound to grant him all he asked for.[2]

In the legend of Solomon (I Kings, 3, 5–15) we find an explanation of these tales, an explanation of what it is that men can receive if they only know what to wish for.

In Gibeon the Lord appeared to Solomon in a dream by night; and God said, Ask what I shall give thee.

And Solomon said . . . I am but a little child: I know not how to go out or how to come in . . .

And thy servant is in the midst of thy people . . .

Give therefore thy servant an understanding heart to judge thy people, that I may discern between good and bad . . .

And the speech pleased the Lord that Solomon had asked this thing.

And God said unto him, Because thou hast asked this thing and hast not asked for thyself long life; neither hast asked riches for thyself, nor hast asked the life of thine enemies; but hast asked for thyself understanding . . .

Behold, I have done according to thy words; lo, I have given thee a wise and understanding heart; so that there was none like thee before thee, neither after thee shall any arise like unto thee.

And I have also given thee that which thou hast not asked, both riches and honour . . . and I will lengthen thy days.

The idea of hidden knowledge and the possibility of finding it after a long and arduous search is the content of the legend of the Holy Grail.

The Holy Grail, the cup from which Christ drank (or the platter from which Christ ate) at the Last Supper and in which Joseph of Arimathea collected Christ's blood, was according to a medieval legend brought to England. To those who saw it the Grail gave immortality and eternal youth. But it had to be guarded only by people perfectly pure in heart. If anyone approached it who was not pure enough, the Grail disappeared. On this followed the legend of the quest of the Holy Grail by chaste knights. Only the three knights of King Arthur succeeded in seeing the Grail.

Many tales and myths, those of the Golden Fleece, the Fire-Bird (of Russian folklore), Aladdin's lamp, and those about secret riches and treasures guarded by dragons or other monsters, serve to express the relation of man to hidden knowledge.

The "philosopher's stone" of alchemists also symbolised hidden knowledge.

All views on life are divided into two categories on this point. There are conceptions of the world which are entirely based on the idea that we live in a house in which there is some secret, some buried treasure, some hidden store of precious things, which somebody at some time may find and which occasionally has in fact been found. And then from this point of view, the whole aim and the whole meaning of life consist in the search for this treasure, because without it all the rest has no value. And there are other theories and systems in which there is no idea of "treasure-trove," for which all alike is visible and clear, or all alike invisible and obscure.

If in our time theories of the latter kind, that is, those which deny the possibility of hidden knowledge, have become predominant, we must not forget that they have become so only very recently and only among a small, although a very noisy, part of humanity. The very great majority of people still believe in "fairy-tales" and believe that there are moments when fairy-tales become reality.

But it is man's misfortune that at those moments at which something new and unknown becomes possible he does not know what he wants, and the opportunity which suddenly appeared as suddenly disappears.

Man is conscious of being surrounded by the wall of the Unknown, and at the same time he believes that he can get through the wall and that others have got through it; but he cannot imagine, or imagines very vaguely, what there may be behind this wall. He does not know what he would like to find there or what it means to possess *knowledge*. It does not even occur to him that a man can be in different relations to the Unknown.

The Unknown is not known. But *the Unknown* may be of different kinds, just as it is in ordinary life. A man may not have *precise* knowledge of a particular thing, but he may think and make judgements and suppositions about it, he may conjecture and foresee it to such a degree of correctness and accuracy that his actions and expectations in relation to what is unknown in the particular case may be almost right. In exactly the same way, in regard to the Great Unknown, a man may be in different relations to it; he may make more correct or less correct suppositions about it, or he may make no suppositions at all, or he may even altogether forget about the very existence of the Unknown. In the latter cases, when he makes no suppositions or forgets about the existence of the Unknown, then even what was possible in other cases, that is, the accidental coincidence of conjectures or speculations with the unknown reality, becomes impossible.

In this incapacity of man to imagine what exists beyond the wall of the known and the possible lies his chief tragedy, and in this, as has already been said, lies the reason why so much remains hidden from him and why there are so many questions to which he can never find the answer.

In the history of human thought there are many attempts to define the limits of possible knowledge. But there are no interesting attempts to conceive what the extension of these limits would mean and where it would necessarily lead.

Such an assertion may seem an intentional paradox. People clamour so loudly and so often about the unlimited possibilities of knowledge, about the immense horizons opening before science, and so forth, but in actual fact all these "unlimited possibilities" are limited by the five senses—sight, hearing, smell, touch and taste—plus the capacity of reasoning and comparing—beyond which a man can never go.

We do not take sufficient account of this circumstance or forget about it, and this explains why we are at a loss when we want to define "ordinary knowledge," "possible knowledge" and "hidden knowledge," or the differences between them.

In all myths and fairy-tales of all times we find the idea of "magic," "witchcraft" and "sorcery," which, as we come nearer to our own period, take the form of "spiritualism," "occultism" and the like. But even people who believe in these words understand very imperfectly what they really mean and in what respect the knowledge of a "magician" or an "occultist" differs from the knowledge of an ordinary man; and therefore all attempts to create a theory of magical knowledge end in failure. The result is always something indefinite and, though impossible, not fantastic, because the "magician" usually appears as an ordinary man endowed with some exaggerated faculties in one direction. And the exaggeration of anything on already long-known lines cannot create anything fantastic.

Even if "miraculous" knowledge is an approach to knowledge of the Unknown, people do not know how to approach the miraculous. In this they are greatly hindered by the interference of "pseudo-occult" literature, which often strives to abolish the divisions mentioned above and prove the unity of scientific and "occult" knowledge. Thus in such literature one often finds assertions that "magic" or "magical" knowledge is nothing but knowledge which is in advance of its time. For instance, it is said that some medieval monks may have had some knowledge of electricity. For their times this was "magic." For us it has ceased to be magic. And what may appear magic for us would cease to be magic for future generations.

Such an assertion is quite arbitrary, and, in destroying the necessary divisions, it prevents us finding and establishing a right attitude towards facts. Magical or occult knowledge is knowledge based upon senses which surpass our five senses and upon a capacity for thinking which surpasses ordinary thinking, *but it is knowledge translated into ordinary logical language, if that is possible or in so far as it is possible.*

In speaking of ordinary knowledge, it is necessary to repeat once more that, though the content of knowledge is not constant, that is, though it changes and grows, it always grows along definite and strictly fixed lines. All scientific methods, all apparatus, all instruments and appliances, are nothing but an improvement upon and a broadening of the "five senses," whereas mathematics and all possible calculations are nothing but the broadening of the ordinary capacity of comparison, judgement and the drawing of conclusions. But at the same time some mathematical constructions go as far beyond the realm of ordinary knowledge as to lose any connection with it. Mathematics finds such relations of magnitudes or relations of relations as have no equivalents in the physical world we observe. But we are unable to make use of these mathematical attainments, because in all our observations and reasonings we are bound by the "five senses" and the laws of logic.

In every historical period human knowledge, that is to say, "ordinary knowledge" or the "known," the "accepted" knowledge, embraced a definite cycle of observations and the deductions made from them. As time went on this cycle grew larger but, if it may be so expressed, it always remained on the same plane. It *never* rose above it.

Believing in the possibility and existence of "hidden knowledge," people always ascribed new properties to it, always regarded it as rising above the plane of ordinary knowledge and stretching beyond the limits of the "five senses." This is the true meaning of "hidden knowledge," of magic, of miraculous knowledge and so on. If we take away from hidden knowledge the idea that it goes beyond the five senses, it will lose all meaning and importance . . . .

NOTES

1. A fairy-tale in verse by Pushkin, very popular in Russia and based upon an old fairy story.
2. 184 *Indian Tales,* published by G. A. Natesan and Co. (Madras, 1920), p. 134.

Maurice Bouisson

Gnosticism and Its Survivals in Christianity

Long before the compilation of the *Sepher Yetsira* there appeared another esoteric doctrine that was impregnated with magic and especially with the magic of incantation. This was Gnosticism, which developed in the Near East, principally at Alexandria, during the first three centuries of our era, side by side with Christianity. Gnosticism both influenced and deeply perturbed the Fathers of the Church.

Gnosis is the Greek for 'knowledge,' and the Epistle of Barnabas (*Codex sinaiticus*, between A.D. 79 and 100) calls *gnōsis teleia*, or 'perfect knowledge,' the understanding of the allegorical mysteries of the Old Testament.

It is, according to a Gnostic fragment, 'the knowledge of that which we are and of that which we have become, of whence we came and to where we have fallen, of the goal towards which we hasten, and of the conditions of our redemption, of our birth and of our rebirth. Its ways are illumination by ecstasis and by asceticism which free the spirit from matter.'

Reprinted from Maurice Bouisson, *Magic, Its Rites and History*. London: Rider and Company, 1960, pp. 116–122. Reprinted by permission of Hutchinson Publishing Group, Ltd. Footnotes have been renumbered consecutively.

Gnosticism may, therefore, be defined as initiatory knowledge drawn from the interpretation of the sacred texts, in the light of a revelation reserved to the predestined alone and which consists of a familiarity with the formulae and rites of magic. Gnosticism is entirely dominated by the problem of the origin of evil, linked with that of the creation and redemption.

Gnosticism was the product of a great intermingling of peoples and was made up of elements borrowed from Judaism, polytheism and Christianity.

It was, however, from Judaism that Gnosticism derived its foundation. 'If we regard it from the purely mystical point of view, Judaism stands out, above all, as the most important source of Gnosticism, that which implies, in a peculiar manner, a metaphysical tendency, that is to say a *revealed* knowledge of the world, of life and of all that relates to happiness. This tendency, characterized by direct communication with the real nature of things, is very marked among the Prophets of Israel.'[1]

'The Gnostic crisis had begun in Judaism long before the preaching of the Gospel and it was co-ordinated with a religious syncretism, with an outburst of salvation *gnōsēs* which, in the world of the East, resulted from the Hellenic conquest which followed the domination of Persia.'[2]

The Book of Enoch and the Book of Daniel bear marks of such influences. The Sect of the Essenes certainly had their own brand of Gnosticism.[3]

The Gnostics[4] have left but very few writings and their ideas are known to us, for the most part, from the works of the Fathers of the Church, St. Hippolytus, St. Epiphanius, St. Irenaeus, St. Justin, Clement of Alexandria, and the ecclesiastical historian Eusebius, Bishop of Caesaraea—that is to say, from adversaries of the Gnostics. However, the doctrines of Mani and the history of his life were first revealed by the Arabic chronicles of An-Nadim and AlBirūni. In more recent times, Manichaean MSS. have been found (1893) in Chinese Turkestan and Upper Egypt (1933).

The *Pistis-Sophia* and 'The Great Treatise according to the Mystery' of the *Bruce Codex* were until recently the only Gnostic works which had come intact down to us. In the January 29th, 1954, number of the German-Swiss review *Atlantis* there appeared an account of the discovery in Egypt of a Gnostic MS—the *G. Jung Codex*—containing the 'Gospel of Truth' attributed to Valentinus. Nine years earlier (in 1945) some peasants in Upper Egypt had come across a jar which had been buried for fifteen hundred years. It contained fifty treatises in Coptic. These writings have been the subject of an erudite study by Jean Doresse entitled *Les Livres secrets des Gnostiques d'Egypte* (1958).

'What these Gnostic documents reveal,' says Doresse, 'is the spiritual attitude of those who were most tragically sensitive to the problems of Man's fate. Their anonymous authors attributed them to Adam, Seth, Jesus, Zoroaster, and even Hermes Trismegistus. But these Gnostic documents may be compared with the Dead Sea Scrolls, inasmuch as the former contributes as much as the latter to our understanding of the religious unrest in which early Christianity developed.'

In the creation, according to the Gnostics, many intermediaries come between the infinite, perfect Creator and the World that is cramped, condemned to suffering and death. These intermediaries are the powers, the aeons and the logoi. The demiurge is a maleficent spirit that rules matter, Yahveh, the Demon, Satan.

Evidence from Celsus and Origen enables us to reconstruct the plan of the world according to the Naassene sect, the diagram is in the form of concentric circles. From top to bottom these are: the Heaven of the Father, the circle of light (yellow), that of the shades (blue), the heaven of fixed stars with the Garden of Eden and the signs of the zodiac, then the serpent that bites its tail, dominating the planetary circles. Below the circle of Behemoth (the hippopotamus, spirit of chaos), the air, and, finally, the earth and, in its depths, Tartarus.

The soul must free itself from the material element proceeding from the evil demiurge and rise up, through the circles, towards the light, a spark of which the soul preserves within it.

In its journey towards the upper regions the soul cannot pass through the successive circles if it does not know the name of the aeons (in this following a tradition of the Egyptian *Book of the Dead*) and it must hold in its hand the seals with magic power on which are engraved the signs and *numbers* of the aeons.

The *Book of the Saviour* describes (after the revelation of Jesus to the Apostles during his sojourn among them in the months which followed the Resurrection) the magical acts by which he exorcises the maleficent aeons. Over the heads of the Apostles he pronounces the 'Great Name.'

In the 'Hymn of the Soul' (from the 'Acts of Thomas'), which also belongs to Gnostic writings in Coptic, human destiny is symbolized by a mystical journey of the soul in the land of Egypt. Though shorn of its mantle of light, the soul will regain it, if it can possess itself of the peerless stone hidden in the folds of the serpent. Then, when the soul is in danger of succumbing to the traps laid by the demons, the Father sends it a 'letter' in the form of a vulture 'which becomes the magic word.' By the power of the *name* of its father and mother, the soul triumphs over the serpent, regains its mantle of light, and passes once more through the circles of light and the gate of the princes, and takes its place 'among the great ones.'

Gnostic papyri and amulets contain many lists of magical names and formulae:

The names of the aeons, angels and archangels; Kilhabriel, Gabriel, Michael, Raphael, those of the three kings or Magi and those of the three Jews cast into the fiery furnace (as related in the Book of Daniel) and those of the seven sleepers of Ephesus.

Conjurations and imprecations, *Sabaeiao (Iao Sabaoth), Sphragis theou* . . . 'The Seal of God'.

There may be seen often a curious mixture of Hebrew and Greek ingredients—sometimes disfigured by faulty transcription—such as Mithraz for Mithra, Or Rou for O Eros, Uphlaze, 'cured.'

Abraxas, or Abrasax, which we have already mentioned, may come from the Hebrew, BRK, *barak*, 'to bless.'

From various Hebrew roots has also been derived the magic 'Abracadabra' written in triangular form.

The original Hebrew formula, transliterated into Latin characters, contains eleven letters:

```
A B R A C A D A B R A
A B R A C A D A B R
A B R A C A D A B
A B R A C A D A
A B R A C A D
A B R A C A
A B R A C
A B R A
A B R
A B
A
```

It is also found in abridged forms, such as:

```
A B R A C A D A B R A
B R A C A D A B R
R A C A D A B
A C A D A
C A D
A
```

In his *Precepts of Medicine* the Gnostic physician Serenicus Sammonicus (second century) recommends that it should be written upon a sheet of paper folded in four so that none of the lines is visible. The paper was suspended by a white thread to the neck of the patient, who must wear it in this way for nine days. Then he must rise from his bed, go out, very early in the morning, to the banks of a river flowing eastwards, take off the amulet and, while taking care not to open it, throw it over his shoulder into the water.

Another formula, of similar sort, is the ABLANATHANALBA. It is read from left to right, like the Christian formula SATOR, which we shall deal with in the chapter on talismanic magic. Several Hebrew words have been recognized in this formula, among them AB, that is 'father.'

```
A B L A N A Th A N A L B A
A B L A N A Th A N A L B
A B L A N A Th A N A L
A B L A N A Th A N A
A B L A N A Th A N
A B L A N A Th A
A B L A N A Th
A B L A N A
A B L A N
A B L A
A B L
A B
A
```

In their system of the world the Gnostics imagined a connexion between the seven Greek vowels and the seven planets, as well as with the seven strings of the lyre. The Qabalah proceeded further in this direction by establishing more complex correlations between the divine names, the Sephiroth, the various parts of the human body,[5] colours, and precious stones, an obscure presentiment, as one might say, of the theories of modern physics.[6]

Among the Gnostic incantations we may cite the following mystical formula from the *Leyden Papyrus,* written in Greek, but of Egyptian origin, and which derives its efficacy from the sonority and rhythm of the words, from the power of the vowels and from ritual gestures:

'Facing East, both hands extended to the left, thou shalt say "A"; towards the North, the right fist extended, thou shalt say "E"; extending thy two hands thou shalt say, turning towards the South, "Ē"; then, towards the

South, with the hands pointing to thy stomach, thou shalt say "I"; spitting upon the ground and touching the tips of thy feet, thou shalt say "O"; looking upwards into the air, and with thy hand upon they heart, thou shalt say "U"; looking up at the sky, and with thy two hands on thy head, thou shalt say "Ō".' (Translation by H. Leclercq in *Dict. Arch. chrét.*)

Survivals in Christianity. Since Christianity developed side by side with Gnosticism, and since the Fathers of the Church, even those who were the most ardent opponents of the *Gnosis,* were profoundly influenced by it, we should not be astonished to find, for instance, in the Fourth Gospel, the 'Creative Word,' the *Logos,* nor should we be surprised to come across many traces of Gnostic magic in Christian traditions. Sometimes the sign of the cross, after each invocation of the divine name, was substituted for the ritual gestures mentioned in the *Leyden Papyrus.*

A formula of exorcism taken from the Grimoire of Armadel (*Bibliothèque de l'Arsenal,* No. 88, p. 3)[7] thus uses divine names in order to subjugate a demon:

'I adjure thee, by virtue of the Great Names of God, immediately and without delay, to appear to me in an agreeable shape and without noise or hurt to my person, to reply to all that I shall order thee, and I adjure thee by the Great Name of the Living God, and by these Holy Names, El, Elohim, Eloho, Elohim, Sabaoth, Elion, Eiech, Adies, Eiech, Adonay, Jah, Saday, Tetragrammaton, Saday, Agios o Theos, Ischiros, Athanatos, Agla, Amen.'

The divine names mentioned here are, as so often, in Gnostic incantations, a mixture of Hebrew (El, Elion, Shadai) and Greek, Ischuros, 'strong,' Athanatos, 'immortal.' Some words are misspelt, e.g. 'Eiech' for 'Eieh,' 'Adies,' perhaps, for 'Hades.' We find here again the magic word, Agla, which we have already mentioned, composed, according to cabalistic custom, of the *notaricon,* the first letters of *Aieth gadol leolam Adonia,* that is, 'The Lord will be great for ever.'

We may compare with the foregoing these two exorcisms from the *Rituale Romanum*: the first is to cure possession by demons and the second is the 'exorcism of salt' for the blessing of holy water.[8]

'I adjure thee, thou ancient Serpent, by the Judge of the living and the dead, by thy Creator, by the Creator of the World, by Him who hath the power to cast thee into hell, remove thyself, without delay from this servant of God who hath had recourse to the Church.'

'I exorcise thee, creature called salt, by the living God' (sign of the cross), 'by the true God' (sign of the cross), 'by God the Most Holy, through the intervention of the Prophet Elisha who had thee cast into water to purify it. Be salt exorcised for the salvation of believers, be a cause of salvation for the soul and the body of those who shall take thee. In every place where thou shalt be spread, may the phantoms and the ills produced by the wiles of the Devil, disappear, may there disappear also all unclean spirits, by the order of Him who shall come to judge the quick and the dead and the world by fire.'

NOTES

1. Henri Sérouya, *La Kabbale*, p. 33.
2. A. Loisy, *La Naissance du Christianisme*, p. 396.
3. To whom some authorities attribute part of the MSS., especially *The Manual of Discipline*—belonging to the Dead Sea Scrolls discovered from 1947 onwards near Qumran.
4. Among the greatest of whom were Simon Magus of Gittoi in Samaria, Basilides, Valentinus, and Mani, and founder of Manichaeism, a doctrine strongly marked by Iranian Mazdaism and which made its appearance again among the Albigensians.
5. In the Qabalah, the ten Sephiroth are written upon the body of *Adam Kadmon*, 'Adam the Ancient.'
6. One may compare this belief with the famous sonnet of Arthur Rimbaud, written so many centuries later:

    'A, black, E, white, I, red, U, green, O, blue, vowels . . . '

    and with this interpretation by certain Tibetan Buddhist sects of the Hinduistic formula of incantation:

    Aum mani padme hum (mani padme, the jewel in the lotus) whose repeated recitation assures a blessed rebirth in the Western Paradise of Great Beatitude:

    > Aum *is white and relates to the gods.*
    > Ma *is blue and relates to non-gods.*
    > Ni *is yellow and relates to men.*
    > Pad *is green and relates to animals.*
    > Me *is black and relates to non-men.*
    > Hum *is black and relates to dwellers in the purgatories.*

    'Non-gods' are a sort of Titan, the Hindu *Asuras,* who struggle with the gods and 'non-men' are monsters or genii, benevolent or harmful. *Vide* Alexandra David-Neel, *Initiations and Initiates in Tibet.* (Rider, London, second edition, 1958.)

    'Black is the colour of chaos. Nothing better than dark and swirling water conveys an idea of what chaos may be. Black is the mother of all colours, because black contains, potentially, all colours. But when chaos became differentiated yellow separated from black. Black is "the Lady Thai Xing" who gave birth to the "thaikiet fluid." The black, the heavier, sank down to the lower regions while the yellow, less coarse, floated. "Black and yellow are the two fundamental colours of the universe." But fire became differentiated through its temperature and its rarefied state, and manifested itself as red. There remained the blue and the white.

Blue, lighter than all other hues, followed the aerial fluid which formed the firmament, while white stayed inseparable from the metal.' *Vide* L. Chochod, *Occultisme et magie en Extrême-Orient,* p. 330. On pp. 309 and 310 of that work will be found tables, used in Chinese magic, setting out the correlations relating to the eight trigrams: (1) Orientation; position, colour, element, season, stars; (2) Physical metaphysical and augural correlations. Concerning the trigrams, *vide* 'Talismanic Magic,' p. 126.

7.   Cited by Jacob in *Curiosités des Sciences occultes,* p. 336.

8.   Salt, which arrests putrefaction, is held in horror by devils—on the golden table-cloth of the witches' Sabbath only dishes without salt are served.

Eric Voegelin

Ersatz Religion

The term "gnostic mass movement" is not in common use. Therefore, when one encounters it one expects it first to be defined. This, however, is not possible, since for methodological reasons definitions come at the end of the analytical process and not at the beginning. And if the analysis has been carefully carried out, definitions are no longer of any great importance, for they can provide no more than a summary of the results of the analysis. We shall follow the Aristotelian method and speak first illustratively of the subject to be examined, and then, when it is secured at the common-sense level of our experience, proceed with the analysis.

I

By gnostic movements we mean such movements as progressivism, positivism, Marxism, psychoanalysis, communism, fascism, and national socialism. We

Reprinted from Eric Voegelin, *Science, Politics & Gnosticism*. Chicago: Henry Regnery Company, 1968, pp. 83–92. Copyright © 1968 Henry Regnery Company. Reprinted by permission of the publisher.

are not dealing, therefore, in all of these cases with political mass movements. Some of them would more accurately be characterized as intellectual movements—for example, positivism, neo-positivism, and the variants of psychoanalysis. This draws attention to the fact that mass movements do not represent an autonomous phenomenon and that the difference between masses and intellectual elites is perhaps not so great as is conventionally assumed, if indeed it exists at all. At any rate, in social reality the two types merge. None of the movements cited began as a mass movement; all derived from intellectuals and small groups. Some of them, according to the intentions of their founders, should have grown into political mass movements, but did not. Others, such as neo-positivism or psychoanalysis, were meant to be intellectual movements; but they have had, if not the form, at least the success of political mass movements, in that their theories and jargons have shaped the thinking of millions of people in the Western world, very often without their being aware of it.

A brief outline of Comteian positivism may serve as a representative example of how mass and intellectual movements are connected. Positivism was an intellectual movement that began with Saint-Simon, with Comte and his friends, and was intended by its founders to become a mass movement of worldwide extent. All mankind was expected to compose the fellowship of the positivist congregation under the spiritual leadership of the "fondateur de la religion de l'humanité." Comte tried to enter into diplomatic correspondence with Nicholas I, with the Jesuit General, and with the Grand Vizier, in order to incorporate into positivism Russian Orthodoxy, the Catholic Church, and Islam. Even though these grandiose plans fell through, something significant was achieved. There have been strong positivist movements, especially in South America; and to this day the Republic of Brazil has on its flag the Comteian motto "Order and Progress." Comteian positivism engaged the best minds of the time in Europe. It decidedly influenced John Stuart Mill; and the echo of the Comteian view of history can still be heard in the philosophy of Max Weber, Ernest Cassirer, and Edmund Husserl. Finally, the entire Western world can thank Comte for the word "altruism"—the secular-immanent substitute for "love," which is associated with Christianity: altruism is the basis of the conception of a brotherhood of man without a father. In the case of positivism one can see perhaps most clearly how problems concerning intellectual and mass movements converge.

II

We have located the subject of our inquiry at the level of common sense, and must now proceed to clarify further the degree to which the movements cited can be characterized as gnostic.

Again, we cannot give definitions, only allusions to the historical instances. Gnosticism was a religious movement of antiquity. It can be confirmed as having been approximately contemporary with Christianity—so contemporary, in fact, that it was assumed for a long time that gnosis involved no more than a Christian heresy. This notion can no longer be held today. Although there are no gnostic sources that can be dated with certainty before the birth of Christ, gnostic influences and terminology are indeed so clearly recognizable in St. Paul that they must stem from a powerful movement in existence before his time. On the historical continuity of gnosticism from antiquity to modern times, let it be said here only that the connections in the development of gnostic sects from those of the eastern Mediterranean in antiquity through the movements of the high Middle Ages up to those of the Western Renaissance and Reformation have been sufficiently clarified to permit us to speak of a continuity.

More important for our purposes than definitions and questions of genesis are the features by which we can recognize gnostic movements as such. Let us list, therefore, the six characteristics that, taken together, reveal the nature of the gnostic attitude.

1. It must first be pointed out that the gnostic is dissatisfied with his situation. This, in itself, is not especially surprising. We all have cause to be not completely satisfied with one aspect or another of the situation in which we find ourselves.

2. Not quite so understandable is the second aspect of the gnostic attitude: the belief that the drawbacks of the situation can be attributed to the fact that the world is intrinsically poorly organized. For it is likewise possible to assume that the order of being as it is given to us men (wherever its origin is to be sought) is good and that it is we human beings who are inadequate. But gnostics are not inclined to discover that human beings in general and they themselves in particular are inadequate. If in a given situation something is not as it should be, then the fault is to be found in the wickedness of the world.

3. The third characteristic is the belief that salvation from the evil of the world is possible.

4. From this follows the belief that the order of being will have to be changed in an historical process. From a wretched world a good one must evolve historically. This assumption is not altogether self-evident, because the Christian solution might also be considered—namely, that the world throughout history will remain as it is and that man's salvational fulfillment is brought about through grace in death.

5. With this fifth point we come to the gnostic trait in the narrower sense— the belief that a change in the order of being lies in the realm of human action, that this salvational act is possible through man's own effort.

6. If it is possible, however, so to work a structural change in the given order of being that we can be satisfied with it as a perfect one, then it becomes the task of the gnostic to seek out the prescription for such a change. Knowledge—gnosis—of the method of altering being is the central concern of the gnostic. As the sixth feature of the gnostic attitude, therefore, we recognize the construction of a formula for self and world salvation, as well as the gnostic's readiness to come forward as a prophet who will proclaim his knowledge about the salvation of mankind.

These six characteristics, then, describe the essence of the gnostic attitude. In one variation or another they are to be found in each of the movements cited.

III

For its appropriate expression, the gnostic attitude has produced a rich and multiform symbolism in the modern mass movements. It is so extensive that it cannot be completely described in this essay. We shall deal with only a few of the most important complexes of symbols. Let us begin with that complex of symbols which can be recognized as modifications of the Christian idea of perfection.

This idea represents the insight that human nature does not find its fulfillment in this world, but only in the *visio beautifica,* in supernatural perfection through grace in death. Since, therefore, there is no fulfillment in this world, Christian life on earth takes its special form from the life to come in the next. It is shaped by *sanctificatio,* by the sanctification of life. Two components can be distinguished in the Christian idea of perfection. The first component is that of the movement toward the goal of perfection, which is described by the expression "sanctification of life"—in English Puritanism, by the notion of the *pilgrim's progress*. As movement toward a goal, it is referred to as the *teleological* component. Further, the goal, the *telos*, toward which the movement is directed, is understood as ultimate perfection; and since the goal is a state of highest value, this second component is called the *axiological*. The two components, the teleological and the axiological, were identified by Ernst Troeltsch.

The gnostic mass movements derive their ideas of perfection from the Christian. In accordance with the components just described, there are on principle three possibilities of derivation. In gnostic perfection, which is supposed to come to pass within the historical world, the teleological and axiological components can be immanentized either separately or together. There follow a few examples of the three types of immanentization.

To the first type of derivation, the teleological, belongs progressivism in all variants. When the teleological component is immanentized, the chief emphasis of the gnostic-political idea lies on the foreward movement, on the movement toward a goal of perfection in this world. The goal itself need not be understood very precisely; it may consist of no more than the idealization of this or that aspect of the situation, considered valuable by the thinker in question. Eighteenth-century ideas of progress—for example, Kant's or Condorcet's—belong to this teleological variant of gnosis. According to the Kantian idea of progress, humanity is moving in an unending approach toward the goal of a perfect, rational existence in a cosmopolitan society—although, to Kant's credit, it must be said that he was able to find in the unending progress of mankind no salvation for the individual man, and the relevance of progress for the fulfillment of the person therefore seemed doubtful to him. Condorcet was somewhat less patient than Kant. He chose not to leave the perfection of man to the unending progress of history, but to accelerate it through a directorate of intellectuals. However, his progressivist idea thereby approaches the third type, the activist effort toward perfection; for the three types of derivation are rarely found in pure form in the individual gnostic thinkers, but usually in multifarious combinations.

In the second type of derivation, the axiological, the emphasis of the idea falls on the state of perfection in the world. Conditions for a perfect social order are described and worked out in detail and assume the form of an ideal image. Such an image was first sketched by Thomas More in his *Utopia*. But the design for perfection need not always be as carefully worked out as it is in More. Much more common are those depictions of a desirable final state that are designed as negatives of some specific evil in the world. The list of these evils has been familiar since antiquity; it was drawn up by Hesiod. Chiefly, it includes poverty, sickness, death, the necessity for work, and sexual problems. These are the principal categories of the burden of existence, to which correspond the models of society offering specific deliverance from one ill or another. Incomplete notions of perfections of this sort may be called *ideals,* in order to distinguish them from the complete models of the utopian kind. Under ideals, therefore, should be included fragments of utopias, such as the notion of a society without private property or of one free from the burdens of labor, sickness, or anxiety. It is characteristic of the whole class of these axiological derivatives that they draw up a comparatively lucid picture of the desirable condition, but are concerned only vaguely with the means of bringing it about.

In the third type of derivation the two components are immanentized together, and there is present both a conception of the end goal and knowledge of the methods by which it is to be brought about. We shall speak of cases of this third type as *activist mysticism.* Under activist mysticism belong primarily movements that descend from Auguste Comte and Karl Marx. In both cases one finds a relatively clear formulation of the state of perfection: in Comte, a final state of industrial society under the temporal rule of the managers and the spiritual rule of positivist intellectuals; in Marx, a final state of a classless realm of freedom. And in both cases, there is clarity about the way to perfection: for Comte, through the transformation of man into his highest form, positivist man; for Marx, through the revolution of the proletariat and the transformation of man into the communist superman.

Carl G. Jung (1875–1961)

Basic Concepts of Alchemy

Introduction. Slowly, in the course of the eighteenth century, alchemy perished in its own obscurity. Its method of explanation—"obscurum per ob-scurius, ignotum per ignotius" (the obscure by the more obscure, the unknown by the more unknown)—was incompatible with the spirt of enlightenment and particularly with the dawning science of chemistry towards the end of the century. But these two new intellectual forces only gave the *coup de grâce* to alchemy. Its inner decay had begun at least a century earlier, at the time of Jakob Böhme, when many alchemists deserted their alembics and melting-pots and devoted themselves entirely to (Hermetic) philosophy. It was then that the chemist and the Hermetic philosopher parted company. Chemistry became natural science, whereas Hermetic philosophy lost the empirical ground from under its feet and aspired to bombastic allegories and inane speculations which were kept alive only by memories of a better time.[1] This was a time when the mind of the alchemist was still grappling with the problems of matter, when the exploring consciousness was confronted by the dark void of the unknown, in which figures and laws were dimly perceived and attributed to matter al-

From THE COLLECTED WORKS OF C. G. JUNG, ed. by G. Adler, M. Fordham, and H. Read, trans. by R. F. C. Hull, Bollingen Series XX, vol. 12, *Psychology and Alchemy* (copyright 1953 and (c) 1968 by Bollingen Foundation), pp. 227–241, reprinted by permission of Princeton University Press. Figures and some footnotes in the original have been left out in this selection.

41

though they really belonged to the psyche. Everything unknown and empty is filled with psychological projection; it is as if the investigator's own psychic background were mirrored in the darkness. What he sees in matter, or thinks he can see, is chiefly the data of his own unconscious which he is projecting into it. In other words, he encounters in matter, as apparently belonging to it, certain qualities and potential meanings of whose psychic nature he is entirely unconscious. This is particularly true of classical alchemy, when empirical science and mystical philosophy were more or less undifferentiated. The process of fission which separated the φυσικά from the μυστικά set in at the end of the sixteenth century and produced a quite fantastic species of literature whose authors were, at least to some extent, conscious of the psychic nature of their "alchemystical" transmutations. On this aspect of alchemy, especially as regards its psychological significance, Herbert Silberer's book *Problems of Mysticism and Its Symbolism* gives us abundant information. The fantastic symbolism bound up with it is graphically described in a paper by R. Bernoulli,[2] and a detailed account of Hermetic philosophy is to be found in a study by J. Evola.[3] But a comprehensive study of the ideas contained in the texts, and of their history, is still lacking, although we are indebted to Reitzenstein for important preparatory work in this field.

The Alchemical Process and Its Stages.   Alchemy, as is well known, describes a process of chemical transformation and gives numberless directions for its accomplishment. Although hardly two authors are of the same opinion regarding the exact course of the process and the sequence of its stages, the majority are agreed on the principal points at issue, and have been so from the earliest times, i.e., since the beginning of the Christian era. Four stages are distinguished, characterized by the original colours mentioned in Heraclitus: *melanosis* (blackening), *leukosis* (whitening), *xanthosis* (yellowing), and *iosis* (reddening).[4] This division of the process into four was called the τετραμερεῖν τήν φιλοσοφῖαν, the quartering of the philosophy. Later, about the fifteenth or sixteenth century, the colours were reduced to three, and the *xanthosis*, otherwise called the *citrinitas,* gradually fell into disuse or was but seldom mentioned. Instead, the *viriditas* sometimes appears after the *melanosis* or *nigredo* in exceptional cases, though it was never generally recognized. Whereas the original tetrameria corresponded exactly to the quaternity of elements, it was now frequently stressed that although there were four elements (earth, water, fire, and air) and four qualities (hot, cold, dry, and moist), there were only three colours: black, white, and red. Since the process never led to the desired goal and since the individual parts of it were never carried out in any standardized manner, the change in the classification of its stages cannot be due to extraneous reasons but has more to do with the symbolical significance of the quaternity and the trinity; in other words, it is due to inner psychological reasons.[5]

The *nigredo* or blackness is the initial state, either present from the beginning as a quality of the *prima materia*, the chaos or *massa confusa*, or else produced by the separation (*solutio, separatio, divisio, putrefactio*) of the elements. If the separated condition is assumed at the start, as sometimes happens, then a union of opposites is performed under the likeness of a union of male and female (called the *coniugium, matrimonium, coniunctio, coitus*), followed by the death of the product of the union (*mortificatio, calcinatio, putrefactio*) and a corresponding *nigredo*. From this the washing (*ablutio, baptisma*) either leads direct to the whitening (*albedo*), or else the soul (*anima*) released at the "death" is reunited with the dead body and brings about its resurrection, or again the "many colours" (*omnes colores*), or "peacock's tail" (*cauda pavonis*), lead to the one white colour that contains all colours. At this point the first main goal of the process is reached, namely the *albedo, tinctura alba, terra alba foliata, lapis albus*, etc., highly prized by many alchemists as if it were the ultimate goal. It is the silver or moon condition, which still has to be raised to the sun condition. The *albedo* is, so to speak, the daybreak, but not till the *rubedo* is it sunrise. The transition to the *rubedo* is formed by the *citrinitas*, though this, as we have said, was omitted later. The *rubedo* then follows direct from the *albedo* as the result of raising the heat of the fire to its highest intensity. The red and the white are King and Queen, who may also celebrate their "chymical wedding" at this stage.

Conceptions and Symbols of the Goal. The arrangement of the stages in individual authors depends primarily on their conception of the goal: sometimes this is the white or red tincture (*aqua permanens*); sometimes the philosophers' stone, which, as hermaphrodite, contains both; or again it is the panacea (*aurum potabile, elixir vitae*), philosophical gold, golden glass (*vitrum aureum*), malleable glass (*vitrum malleabile*). The conceptions of the goal are as vague and various as the individual processes. The *lapis philosophorum*, for instance, is often the *prima materia*, or the means of producing the gold; or again it is an altogether mystical being that is sometimes called *Deus terrestris, Salvator*, or *filius macrocosmi*, a figure we can only compare with the Gnostic Anthropos, the divine original man.[6]

Besides the idea of the *prima materia*, that of water (*aqua permanens*) and that of fire (*ignis noster*) play an important part. Although these two elements are antagonistic and even constitute a typical pair of opposites, they are yet one and the same according to the testimony of the authors. Like the *prima materia* the water has a thousand names; it is even said to be the original material of the stone. In spite of this we are on the other hand assured that the water is extracted from the stone or *prima materia* as its life-giving soul (*anima*). This perplexity comes out very clearly in the following passage from the "VIII Exercitatio in Turbam":

> Many dispute in long controversies whether the stone, under different names, consists of several substances, or of two, or only of one. But this philosopher [Scites] and Bonellus say that the whole work and the substance of the whole work are nothing but the water; and that the treatment [*regimen*] of the same also takes place in nothing but the water. And there is in fact one substance in which everything is contained and that is the *sulphur philosophorum*, [which] is water and soul, oil, Mercurius and Sol, the fire of nature, the eagle, the *lachryma*, the first *hyle* of the wise, the *materia prima* of the perfect body. And by whatever names the philosophers have called their stone they always mean and refer to this one substance, i.e., to the water from which everything [originates] and in which everything [is contained], which rules everything, in which errors are made and in which the error is itself corrected. I call it "philosophical" water, not ordinary [*vulgi*] water but *aqua mercurialis*, whether it be simple or composite. For both are the philosophical water, although the vulgar mercury is different from the philosophical. That [water] is simple [and] unmixed, this [water] is composed of two substances: namely of our mineral and of simple water. These composite waters form the philosophical Mercurius, from which it must be assumed that the substance, or the *prima materia* itself, consists of composite water. Some [alchemists] put three together, others, only two. For myself two species are sufficient: male and female or brother and sister. But they also call the simple water poison, quicksilver [*argentum vivum*], cambar, *aqua permanens*, gum, vinegar, urine, sea-water, dragon, and serpent.

This account makes one thing very evident: the philosophical water is the stone or the *prima materia* itself; but at the same time, it is also its solvent, as is proved by the prescription immediately following:

Grind the stone to a very fine powder and put it into the sharpest celestial [*coelestino*] vinegar, and it will at once be dissolved into the philosophical water.

It can also be shown that fire played the same role as water. Another, no less important, idea is that of the Hermetic vessel (*vas Hermetis*), typified by the retorts or melting-furnaces that contained the substances to be transformed. Although an instrument, it nevertheless has peculiar connections with the

prima materia as well as with the *lapis*, so it is no mere piece of apparatus.
For the alchemists the vessel is something truly marvellous: a *vas mirabile*.
Maria Prophetissa says that the whole secret lies in knowing about the
Hermetic vessel. "Unum est vas" (the vessel is one) is emphasized again and
again. It must be completely round, in imitation of the spherical cosmos, so
that the influence of the stars may contribute to the success of the operation. It
is a kind of matrix or uterus from which the *filius philosophorum*, the miraculous stone, is to be born. Hence it is required that the vessel be not only round
but egg-shaped. One naturally thinks of this vessel as a sort of retort or flask;
but one soon learns that this is an inadequate conception since the vessel is
more a mystical idea, a true symbol like all the central ideas of alchemy. Thus
we hear that the *vas* is the water or *aqua permamens*, which is none other
than the Mercurius of the philosophers. But not only is it the water, it is also
its opposite: fire.

I will not enter further into all the innumerable synonyms for the vessel.
The few I have mentioned will suffice to demonstrate its undoubted symbolical
significance.

As to the course of the process as a whole, the authors are vague and
contradictory. Many content themselves with a few summary hints, others
make an elaborate list of the various operations. Thus in 1576, Josephus
Quercetanus, alchemist, physician, and diplomat, who in France and French
Switzerland played a somewhat similar role to that of Paracelsus, established a
sequence of twelve operations as follows:

1. *Calcinatio*
2. *Solutio*
3. *Elementorum separatio*
4. *Coniunctio*
5. *Putrefactio*
6. *Coagulatio*
7. *Cibatio*
8. *Sublimatio*
9. *Fermentatio*
10. *Exaltatio*
11. *Augmentatio*
12. *Proiectio*

Every single one of these terms has more than one meaning; we need only look
up the explanations in Ruland's *Lexicon* to get a more than adequate idea of

this. It is therefore pointless to go further into the variations of the alchemical procedure in the present context.

Such is, superficially and in the roughest outline, the framework of alchemy as known to us all. From the point of view of our modern knowledge of chemistry it tells us little or nothing, and if we turn to the texts and the hundreds and hundreds of procedures and recipes left behind by the Middle Ages and antiquity, we shall find relatively few among them with any recognizable meaning for the chemist. He would probably find most of them nonsensical, and furthermore it is certain beyond all doubt that no real tincture or artificial gold was ever produced during the many centuries of earnest endeavor. What then, we may fairly ask, induced the old alchemists to go on labouring—or as, they said, "operating"—so steadfastly and to write all those treatises on the "divine" art if their whole understanding was so portentously futile? To do them justice we must add that all knowledge of the nature of chemistry and its limitations was still completely closed to them, so that they were as much entitled to hope as those who dreamed of flying and whose successors made the dream come true after all. Nor should we underestimate the sense of satisfaction born of the enterprise, the excitement of the adventure, of the *quaerere* (seeking) and the *invenire* (finding). This always lasts as long as the methods employed seem sensible. There was nothing at that time to convince the alchemist of the senselessness of his chemical operations; what is more, he could look back on a long tradition which contained not a few testimonies of such as had achieved the marvellous result.[7] Finally the matter was not entirely without promise, since a number of useful discoveries did occasionally emerge as byproducts of his labours in the laboratory. As the forerunner of chemistry alchemy had a sufficient *raison d'être*. Hence, even if alchemy had consisted in—if you like—an unending series of futile and barren chemical experiments, it would be no more astonishing than the venturesome endeavours of medieval medicine and pharmacology.

NOTES

1. An alarming example of this kind of "alchemy" is to be found in the illustrated work *Geheime Figuren der Rosenkreuzer*, belonging to the 16th and 17th centuries. The so-called Sachse Codex, belonging to the first half of the 18th century, also gives an excellent idea of this amazing literature. (Cf. Hall, *Codex Rosae Crucis*).

2. "Spiritual Development as Reflected in Alchemy and Related Disciplines."

3. *La tradizione ermetica.*

4. This word comes from *iós* (poison). But since it has about the same meaning as the red tincture of later alchemy I have translated *iosis* as "reddening."

5. This is particularly evident in the writings of Dorn, who violently attacked the quaternity from the trinitarian standpoint, calling it the "quadricornutus serpens" (four-horned serpent). See Jung, "Psychology and Religion," pars. 103f.

6. Cf. Jung, "Paracelsus as a Spiritual Phenomenon," pars. 165ff., 203ff.

7. Even Meyrink (in the 20th century) still believed in the possibility of the alchemical procedure. We find a remarkable report of his own experiments in his introduction to *Aquinas: Abhandlung über den Stein*, pp. xxixff.

Paracelsus (1493–1541)

On Magic and Alchemy

Magic is the most secret of the arts and the highest wisdom concerning the supernatural on earth. . .

Magic has power to experience and fathom things which are inaccessible to human reason. For magic is a great secret wisdom, just as reason is a great public folly. Therefore it would be desirable and good for the doctors of theology to know something about it and to understand what it actually is, and cease unjustly and unfoundedly to call it witchcraft.

After all, God has permitted magic, and this is a sign that we may use it; it is also a sign of what we are; but we must not interpret this sign as a summons to practice magic. For if a man practices false magic, he tempts God . . . . And if he tempts God, woe to his soul!

All skills and arts come from God, and nothing comes from any other source . . . and therefore no one may vilify astronomy, alchemy, or medicine,

Reprinted from *Paracelsus: Selected Writings*, ed. by Jolande Jacobi, trans. by Norbert Guterman, New York: Pantheon Books, for Bollingen Foundation, Bollingen Series XXVIII, pp. 211–223. Copyright 1951 and © 1958 by Bollingen Foundation. Reprinted by permission of Princeton University Press.

or philosophy, or theology, acting, poetry, music, geomancy . . . or any other high art. Why not? What then does man invent of himself? Not even the slightest rag with which to patch his breeches. What new thing can the devil invent? Nothing on earth, nothing pure and simple; not even so much as is needed to catch and kill a louse on your head. But as soon as something is kindled in us by the light of nature, the devil pretends to be our guide and makes bold to falsify all things that God has given us, to slander them, and to make them deceptive, and thus does he spoil everything. . . . The devil makes bold to brand God's works as lies, in order to abuse Him; he seduces those who are weak in their faith and leads them astray in order to make them desert God and cultivate false arts and grievously affront Him. They spend their time in lies, and although they too brood, and inquire and explore, they nevertheless must die without finding the truth.

A test and a proof are always required to distinguish the sacred from the profane, and to discover from what virtues the various miracles derive. A careful examination is required before one can establish whether it is the spirit of nature or the spirit of God which appears to us in such a miracle. Learn to recognize this distinction well! It is most indispensable to know what comes from *divinatio* and what from *divinitas*. These terms are alike, they derive from the same root, but not so the miracles—these spring from different sources.

The Holy Scriptures call sorcerers—without distinction—all those who were versed in supernatural things and were not at the same time holy. But this matter must be given some consideration. God wills us to live simply, like the apostles, and not to brood over things and explore hidden things which occur in a supernatural manner, because it is not His will that we misuse such knowledge to the injury of our fellow men, and thus damn our bodies and souls. For this reason we must not regard as sorcerers all those who are so called in the Holy Scriptures. If we did we should have to look upon the three Wise Men of the East as arch-sorcerers, for they were more versed in the arts and things supernatural than anyone before them or anyone living in their time. But Holy Writ speaks of them not as sorcerers but as magi; and how should we interpret this? Only to mean that they did not misuse their art and their great occult wisdom. For magic is an art which reveals its highest power and strength through faith. It is true, however, that if it is misused, it can give rise to sorcery.

As God awakens the dead to new life, so the "natural saints," who are called magi, are given power over the energies and faculties of nature. For there are holy men in God who serve the beatific life; they are called saints. But there are also holy men in God who serve the forces of nature, and they are called magi. God shows His miracles through His holy men, both through those of the beatific life and through those of nature; what others are incapable of doing they can do, because it has been conferred upon them as a special gift.

———————

Who can be an enemy of alchemy, since it bears no guilt? Guilty is he who does not know it properly and who does not apply it properly.

Let it be for you a great and high mystery in the light of nature that a thing can completely lose and forfeit its form and shape, only to arise subsequently out of nothing and become something whose potency and virtue is far nobler than what it was in the beginning.

Nothing has been created as *ultima materia*—in its final state. Everything is at first created in its *prima materia*, its original stuff; whereupon Vulcan comes, and by the art of alchemy develops it into its final substance. . . . For alchemy means: to carry to its end something that has not yet been completed. To obtain the lead from the ore and to transform it into what it is made for. . . .Accordingly, you should understand that alchemy is nothing but the art which makes the impure into the pure through fire. . . . It can separate the useful from the useless, and transmute it into its final substance and its ultimate essence.

The transmutation of metals is a great mystery of nature. However laborious and difficult this task may be, whatever impediments and obstacles may lie in the way of its accomplishment, this transmutation does not go counter to nature, nor is it incompatible with the order of God, as is falsely asserted by many persons. But the base, impure five metals—that is, copper, tin, lead, iron, and quicksilver—cannot be transmuted into the nobler, pure, and perfect metals—namely, into gold and silver—without a *tinctura*, or without the philosophers' stone.

Since ancient times philosophy has striven to separate the good from the evil, and the pure from the impure; this is the same as saying that all things

die and that only the soul lives eternal. The soul endures while the body
decays, and you may recall that correspondingly a seed must rot away if it is to
bear fruit. But what does it mean, to rot? It means only this—that the body
decays while its essence, the good, the soul, subsists. This should be known
about decaying. And once we have understood this, we possess the pearl which
contains all the virtues.

Decay is the beginning of all birth. . . . It transforms shape and essence, the
forces and virtues of nature. Just as the decay of all foods in the stomach
transforms them and makes them into a pulp, so it happens outside the
stomach. . . . Decay is the midwife of very great things! It causes many things
to rot, that a noble fruit may be born; for it is the reversal, the death and
destruction of the original essence of all natural things. It brings about the
birth and rebirth of forms a thousand times improved. . . . And this is the
highest and greatest *mysterium* of God, the deepest mystery and miracle that
He has revealed to mortal man.

The great virtues that lie hidden in nature would never have been revealed
if alchemy had not uncovered them and made them visible. Take a tree, for
example; a man sees it in the winter, but he does not know what it is, he does
not know what it conceals within itself, until summer comes and discloses the
buds, the flowers, the fruit. . . . Similarly the virtues in things remain
concealed to man, unless the alchemists disclose them, as the summer reveals
the nature of the tree. And if the alchemist brings to light that which lies hidden in nature, one must know that those hidden powers are different in each
thing—they are different in locusts, different in leaves, different in flowers, and
different in ripe and unripe fruits. For all this is so marvellous that in form
and qualities the last fruit of a tree is completely unlike the first one. . . . And
each thing has not only one virtue but many, just as a flower has more than
one colour, and each colour has in itself the most diverse hues; and yet they
constitute a unity, one thing.

Alchemy is a necessary, indispensable art. . . . It is an art, and Vulcan is its
artist. He who is a Vulcan has mastered this art; he who is not a Vulcan can
make no headway in it. But to understand this art, one must above all know
that God has created all things; and that He has created something out of
nothing. This something is a seed, in which the purpose of its use and function
is inherent from the beginning. And since all things have been created in an

unfinished state, nothing is finished, but Vulcan must bring all things to their completion. Things are created and given into our hands, but not in the ultimate form that is proper to them. For example, wood grows of itself, but does not transform itself into boards or charcoal. Similarly, clay does not of itself become a pot. This is true of everything that grows in nature.

———————

The *quinta essentia* is that which is extracted from a substance—from all plants and from everything which has life—then freed of all impurities and all perishable parts, refined into highest purity and separated from all elements. . . . The inherency of a thing, its nature, power, virtue, and curative efficacy, without any . . . foreign admixture . . . that is the *quinta essentia*. It is a spirit like the life spirit, but with this difference that the *spiritus vitae*, the life spirit, is imperishable, while the spirit of man is perishable. . . . The *quinta essentia* being the life spirit of things, it can be extracted only from the perceptible, that is to say material, parts, but not from the imperceptible, animated parts of things . . . . It is endowed with extraordinary powers and perfections, and in it is found a great purity, through which it effects an alteration or cleansing in the body, which is an incomparable marvel. . . . Thus the *quinta essentia* can cleanse a man's life. . . . Therefore each disease requires its own *quinta essentia*, although some forms of the *quinta essentia* are said to be useful in all disease.

Only what is incorporeal and immortal, what is endowed with eternal life, what stands above all natural things and remains unfathomable to man, can rightly be called an arcanum. . . . Like the divine curative powers, it has power to change us, to renew us, and to restore us. . . . And although the arcana are not external and although they do not constitute a symphony to the divine essence, they must be considered heavenly as compared with us mortals, for they can preserve our bodies, and by their influences achieve marvels in us that reason cannot fathom. . . . The arcanum is the entire virtue of a thing, multiplied a thousandfold. . . . Up until the present epoch, which is still young, only four arcana have come to our knowledge. . . . The first arcanum is the *prima materia*, the second the *lapis philosophorum*, the third the *mercurius vitae*, and the last the *tinctura*. . . . The *prima materia* can consume a man's old age and confer a new youth upon him—thus a young herb from a new seed grows in a new summer and a new year. . . . The second arcanum, the *lapis philosophorum*, purifies the whole body and cleanses it of all its filth by developing fresh young energies. . . . *Mercurius vitae*, the third arcanum, has a purifying action; like a halcyon, which puts on new feathers after moulting it can remove the impurities from man—down to the nails and the skin—make him grow anew. Thus it renovates the old body. . . . *Tinctura*, the last arcanum, is like the *rebis*—the bisexual creature—which transmutes silver and other metals into gold; it "tinges," i.e., it transforms the body, removing its harmful parts, its crudity, its incompleteness, and transforms everything into a pure, noble, and indestructible being.

Here on earth the celestial fire is a cold, rigid, and frozen fire. And this fire is the body of gold. Therefore all we can do with it by means of our own fire is to dissolve it and make it fluid, just as the sun thaws snow and ice and makes them liquid. In other words, fire has not the power to burn fire, for gold itself is nothing but fire. In heaven it is dissolved, but on earth it is solid-ified. . . .God and nature do nothing in vain, or without a purpose. The place of all things indestructible is not subject to time, it has no beginning or end, it is everywhere. Those things are efficacious when all hope has been given up, and they may accomplish miraculously what is considered impossible, what looks hopeless, absurd, or even desperate.

———————

But to write more about this mystery is forbidden and further revelation is the prerogative of the divine power. For this art is truly a gift of God. Wherefore not everyone can understand it. For this reason God bestows it upon whom He pleases, and it cannot be wrested from Him by force; for it is His will that He alone shall be honoured in it and that through it His name be praised for ever and ever.

Louis Pauwels and Jacques Bergier

A Modern Alchemist

It was in March 1953 that I met an alchemist for the first time. It was at the Café Procope in Paris which was then coming into fashion again. A famous poet, while I was writing my book on Gurdjieff, had arranged the meeting, and I was often to see this singular man again, though I never succeeded in penetrating his secrets.

My ideas about alchemy and alchemists were rudimentary and derived from popular literature on the subject, and I had no idea that alchemists still existed. The man seated opposite me at Voltaire's table was young and elegant. After a thorough classical education he had studied chemistry. He was then earning his living in business and knew a lot of artists as well as some society people. I do not keep a regular diary, but sometimes, on important occasions, I jot down my impressions and make comments. That night, when I got home, I wrote as follows:

"How old can he be? He says thirty-five. That seems surprising. He has white, curly hair, trimmed so as to look like a wig. Lots of deep wrinkles in a pink skin and full features. Few gestures, but slow, calculated and effective

From Louis Pauwels and Jacques Bergier, *The Morning of the Magicians*. New York: Avon, 1968, pp. 103–107. Copyright © 1964 by Stein and Day in the United States. Reprinted with permission of Stein and Day/Publishers.

when he does make them. A calm, keen smile; eyes that laugh, but in a detached sort of way. Everything about him suggests another age. In conversation, highly articulate and completely self-possessed. Something of the sphinx behind that affable, timeless countenance. Incomprehensible. And this is not merely my personal impression. A.B. who sees him nearly every day, tells me he has never, for a second, found him lacking in a 'superior degree of objectivity.' . . .

"I asked him some questions about alchemy which he must have thought completely foolish. Without showing it, he replied:

"'Matter is everything; contact with matter, working with matter, working with the hands.' He made a great point of this:

" 'Are you fond of gardening? That's a good start; alchemy is like gardening. Do you like fishing? Alchemy has something in common with fishing. Woman's work and children's games.

" 'Alchemy cannot be taught. All the great works of literature which have come down to us through the centuries contain elements of this teaching. They are the product of truly adult minds which have spoken to children, while respecting the laws of adult knowledge. A great work is never wrong as regards basic principles. But the knowledge of those principles and the road that led to this knowledge must remain secret. Nevertheless, there is an obligation on first-degree searchers to help one another.'

"Around midnight I asked him about Fulcanelli (author of *Le Mystère des Cathédrales* and *Les Demeures philosophales*) and he gave me to understand that Fulcanelli is not dead: 'It is possible to live infinitely longer than an unawakened man could believe. And one's appearance can change completely. I know that there is such a thing as the philosopher's stone. But this is matter on a different level, and not as we know it. But here, as elsewhere, it is still possible to take measurements. The methods of working and measuring are simple, and do not require any complicated apparatus: women's work and children's games. . . .'

"He added: 'Patience, hope, work. And whatever the work may be, one can never work hard enough. As to hope: in alchemy hope is based on the certainty that there is a goal to attain. I would never have begun had I not been convinced that this goal exists and can be attained in this life.' "

Such was my first contact with alchemy. If I had begun to study it in the books of "magic," I do not think I should have got very far for lack of time, and because I have little taste for literary erudition. No sense of vocation either—such as an alchemist (though he does not know yet that he is one) feels when for the first time he turns the pages of some old treatise. My vocation is not for doing, but for understanding; I am a spectator rather than an actor. . . .

I am a man in a hurry, like most of my contemporaries. I had the most recent contact imaginable with alchemy: a conversation in a *bistro* at Saint-Germain-des-Près. Later, when I was trying to grasp the real meaning of what that "young" man had told me, I met Jacques Bergier, who doesn't work in a dusty old garret full of old books, but in places where the life of our century is concentrated—a laboratory and an information bureau. Bergier, too, was seeking something along the line of alchemy, but not with the idea of making a pilgrimage into the past. This extraordinary little man, completely preoccupied with the secrets of atomic energy, had taken this path as a short cut. I dashed at supersonic speed, hard on his heels, through ancient texts compiled by wise men in love with leisureliness, intoxicated with patience. Bergier enjoyed the confidence of some of those men who still engage in alchemy. He was also in touch with modern scientists.

I soon became convinced, from what he told me, that there is a close connection between traditional alchemy and *avant-garde* science. I saw how intelligence was building a bridge between two worlds. I ventured on to this bridge, and found that it held. This made me very happy and relieved me of my anxieties. Having for a long time taken refuge in anti-progressist thought, along Hindu lines and influence by Gurdjieff, seeing the world of today as a prelude to the Apocalypse, full of despair at the prospect of a disastrous end to everything and not very sure of myself in my proud isolation, suddenly I saw the old past and future shaking hands. The alchemists' metaphysics, thousands of years old, had concealed a technique which at last, in the twentieth century, had become almost comprehensible. The terrifying modern techniques opened up metaphysical horizons very like those of ancient times. My retreat from reality was nothing but false romanticism. On either side of the bridge, men's immortal souls had kindled the same fires.

In the end I came to believe that in the far distant past men had discovered the secrets of energy and matter. Not only in thought, but by manipulation; not only spiritually but technically.

Now the modern mind, by a different approach and by the methods, which I had long found distasteful, of pure reason and irreligion and by methods which displeased me, was in its turn preparing to discover the same secrets, with a mixture of curiosity, enthusiasm and apprehension. It was face to face with essentials in the spirit of the best tradition.

I then perceived that the opposition between age-old "wisdom" and contemporary "madness" was the invention of feeble and backward minds, a compensatory product for intellectuals incapable of keeping up with the times.

There are several ways of gaining access to essential knowledge. Our age has its own methods; older civilizations had theirs. And I am not speaking only of theoretical knowledge.

Finally I realized that, with modern techniques being apparently more efficient than those of yesterday, this essential knowledge that the alchemists (and other wise men before them) no doubt possessed, would reach us with still greater force and weight and would be more dangerous and more demanding. We are getting to the same point as the Ancients, but on a different level. Rather than condemn the modern spirit in the name of the initiatory wisdom of the Ancients, or repudiate this wisdom on the grounds that real knowledge only began with our civilization, we should do better to admire and even venerate the power of the mind which, under different aspects, traverses the same point of light, mounting upwards in a spiral ascent. Instead of condemning, repudiating and choosing, we ought to love. Love is everything: both rest and movement at the same time.

Papus (1865–1916)

Introduction to the Tarot

We are on the eve of a complete transformation of our scientific methods. Materialism has given us all that we can expect from it, and inquirers, though disappointed as a rule, hope for great things from the future, and are unwilling to spend more time in pursuing the path adopted in modern days. Analysis has been carried, in every branch of knowledge, as far as possible, and has only deepened those moats which divide the sciences.

Synthesis becomes necessary; but how can we realize it?

If we would condescend to waive for one moment our belief in the indefinite progress and necessary superiority of later generations over the ancients, we should at once perceive that the colossal civilizations of antiquity possessed Science, Universities and Schools.

India and Egypt are even now strewn with valuable remains, which reveal to archaeologists the existence of this ancient science.

We are in a position to affirm that the dominant character of its teaching was synthesis, which condenses in a few very simple laws the whole of acquired knowledge.

Selections from Papus (Gérard Encausse), *The Tarot of the Bohemians*, rev. ed., A.P. Morton, trans. New York: Samuel Weiser, 1958, pp. 3–13,305–310. By permission of Samuel Weiser. The original French edition appeared in 1889 (Paris: G. Carré) and the revised English edition was first published in 1910.

But the use of synthesis has been almost entirely lost, through several causes, which it is important to enumerate.

Amongst the ancients, knowledge was only transmitted to men whose worth had been proved by a series of tests. This transmission took place in the temples, under the name of Mysteries, and the adept assumed the title of Priest or Initiate.[1] This science was therefore secret or occult, and thus originated the name of Occult Science, given by our contemporaries to the ancient synthesis.

Another reason for the limited diffusion of the higher branches of knowledge, was the length and difficulty of the journeys involved before the most important centres of initiation could be reached.

However, as the Initiates found that a time was approaching when their doctrines might be lost to humanity, they made strenuous efforts to save the law of synthesis from oblivion. Three great methods were used for this purpose—

1. Secret societies, as a direct continuation of the Mysteries;

2. The cultus, as a symbolic translation of the higher doctrines, for the use of the people;

3. Lastly, the people itself became the unconscious depository of the doctrine.

Let us now see what use each of these groups made of the treasure confided thereto.

The Secret Societies.   The school of Alexandria was the principal source from which the secret societies of the West arose.

The majority of the Initiates had taken refuge in the East, and recently (in 1884) the West discovered the existence in India, and above all in Thibet, of an occult fraternity, which possessed, practically, the ancient synthesis in its integrity. The Theosophical Society was founded with the object of uniting Western initiation with Oriental initiation.

But we are less interested in the existence of this doctrine in the East than in the history of the development of initiatory societies in the West.

The Gnostic sects, the Arabs, Alchemists, Templars, Rosicrucians, and lastly the Freemasons, form the Western chain in the transmission of occult science.

A rapid glance over the doctrines of these associations is sufficient to prove that the present form of Freemasonry has almost entirely lost the meanings of those traditional symbols which constitute the trust that it ought to have transmitted through the ages.

The elaborate ceremonials of the ritual appear ridiculous to the vulgarian good sense of a lawyer or grocer—those actual modern representatives of the profound doctrines of antiquity.

We must, however, make some exceptions in favour of great thinkers, like Ragon and a few others.

In short, Freemasonry has lost the doctrine confided to it, and cannot by itself provide us with the synthetic law for which we are seeking.

The Cultus. The secret societies were designed to transmit in their symbolism the scientific side of primitive initiation, and the religious sects were to develop the philosophical and metaphysical aspects of the doctrine.

Every priest of an ancient creed was one of the Initiates; that is to say, he knew perfectly well that only one religion existed and that the cultus merely served to translate this religion to the different nations according to their particular temperaments. This fact led to an important result, that a priest, no matter which of the gods he served, was received with honour in the temples of all other deities, and was allowed to offer sacrifice to them. Yet this circumstance must not be supposed to imply any idea of polytheism. The Jewish High Priest in Jerusalem received one of the Initiates, Alexander the Great, into the Temple, and led him into the Holy of Holies, to offer sacrifice.

Our religious disputes for the supremacy of one creed over another would have caused much amusement to any of the ancient initiate-priests; they were unable to suppose that intelligent men could ignore the unity of all creeds in one fundamental religion.

Sectarianism, chiefly sustained by two creeds, equally blinded by their errors, the Christian and the Mussulman, was the cause of the total loss of the secret doctrine, which gave the key to Synthetic Unity.

Still greater labour is required to re-discover Synthesis in our Western religions than to find it in Freemasonry.

The Jews alone possessed no longer the spirit but the letter of their oral or Kabalistic traditions. The Bible, written in Hebrew, is marvellous from this point of view, for it contains all the occult traditions, although its true sense has never yet been revealed. Fabre d'Olivet commenced this prodigious work, but the ignorant descendants of the Inquisition at Rome have placed such studies on the list of things prohibited.[2] Posterity will judge them.

Yet every cultus has its tradition, its book, its Bible, which teach those who know how to read them the unity of all creeds, in spite of the difference existing in the ritual of various countries.

The *Sepher Bereshith* of Moses is the Jewish Bible; the *Apocalypse* and the

Esoteric Gospels form the Christian Bible; the *Legend of Hiram* is the Bible of Freemasonry; the *Odyssey* is the Bible of the so-called polytheism of Greece; the *Eneid* that of Rome; and lastly the *Hindu Vedas* and the *Mussulman Koran* are well known to all students of ancient theology.

To any one possessing the key, all these Bibles reveal the same doctrine; but this key, which can open Esotericism, is lost by the sectarians of our Western creeds. It is therefore useless to seek for it any longer amongst them.

The People.   The Sages were under no illusions respecting the possible future of the tradition which they confided to the intelligence and virtue of future generations.

Moses had chosen a people to transmit through succeeding ages the book which contained all the science of Egypt; but before Moses, the Hindu Initiates had selected a nation to hand down to the generations of the future the primitive doctrines of the great civilizations of the Atlantides.

The people have never disappointed the expectations of those who trusted them. Understanding none of the truths which they possessed, they carefully abstained from altering them in any way, and treated the least attack made upon them as sacrilege.

Thus the Jews have transmitted intact to us the letters which form the *Sepher* of Moses. But Moses had not solved the problem so authoritatively as the Thibetans.

It was a great thing to give the people a book which it could adore respectfully, and always guard intact; but to give it a book which would enable it to live, was yet better.

The people intrusted with the transmission of occult doctrines from the earliest ages were the Bohemian or Gypsy race.

The Gypsies.   The Gypsies possess a Bible which has proved their means of gaining a livelihood, for it enables them to tell fortunes; at the same time it has been a perpetual source of amusement, for it enables them to gamble.

Yes; the game of cards called the Tarot, which the Gypsies possess, is the Bible of Bibles. It is the book of Thoth Hermes Trismegistus, the book of Adam, the book of the primitive Revelation of ancient civilizations.

Thus whilst the Freemason, an intelligent and virtuous man, has lost the tradition; whilst the priest, also intelligent and virtuous, has lost his esotericism; the Gypsy, although both ignorant and vicious, has given us the key which enables us to explain all the symbolism of the ages.

We must admire the wisdom of the Initiates, who utilized vice and made it produce more beneficial results than virtue.

The Gypsy pack of cards is a wonderful book according to Court de Gébelin[3] and Vaillant.[4] This pack, under the name of TAROT,[5] THORA,[6] ROTA,[7] has formed the basis of the synthetic teachings of all the ancient nations successively.[8]

In it, where a man of the people only sees a means of amusement, the thinker will find the key to an obscure tradition. Raymond Lully based his *Ars Magna* upon the Tarot; Jerome Cardan wrote a treatise upon subtility from the keys of the Tarot;[9] William Postel found therein the key to the ancient mysteries; whilst Louis-Claude de Saint-Martin, the Unknown Philosopher, discovered within it the mysterious links which unite God, the Universe and Man!

Through the Tarot we are now able to discern and develop the synthetic law, concealed in all these symbolisms.

The hour is approaching when the missing word will be restored. Masters, Rosicrucians and Kadosh, you who form the sacred triangle of Masonic initiation, do you remember!

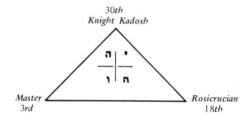

Remember, MASTER, that illustrious man, killed through the most cowardly of conspiracies; remember Hiram, whose resurrection, promised by the Branch of Acacia, thou art looking for in faith!

Remember, ROSICRUCIAN, the mysterious Word which thou hast sought so long, of which the meaning still escapes thee!

Remember, KADOSH, the magnificent symbol, which radiated from the centre of the luminous triangle, when the real meaning of the letter G was revealed to thee!

HIRAM—INRI—YOD-HE-VAU-HE—indicate the same mystery under different aspects.

He who understands one of these words possesses the key which opens the tomb of Hiram, the symbol of the synthetic science of the Ancients; he can open the tomb and fearlessly touch the heart of the revered Master, the symbol of esoteric teaching.

The whole Tarot is based upon the word ROTA, arranged as a wheel.

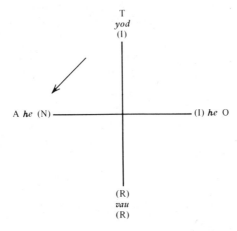

INRI is the word which indicates the Unity of your origin, Freemasons and Catholics! *Igne Natura Renovatur Integra; Iesus Nazareus Rex Iudeorum*; are the opposite poles, scientific and religious, physical and metaphysical, of the same doctrine.

YOD-HE-VAU-HE (יהוה) is the word which indicates to you both, Freemasons and Kabalists, the unity of your origin. TAROT, THORA, ROTA are the words which point out to you all, Easterns and Westerns, the unity of your requirements and of your aspirations in the eternal Adam-Eve, the source of all our knowledge and of all our creeds.

All honour, therefore, to the Gypsy Nomad, to whom we are indebted for the preservation of this marvellous instrument, the synthetic summary of the whole teaching of antiquity.

Our Work.   We will commence by a preliminary study of the elements of the Kabalah and of numbers.

Supplied with these data, we will explain the construction of the Tarot in all its details, studying separately each of the pieces which compose our machine, then studying the action of these pieces upon each other. Upon this point we shall be as explicit as possible. We will next touch upon some applications of the machine, but upon a few only, leaving to the genuine inquirer the work of discovering others. We must confine our personal work to the gift of a key, based upon a synthetic formula; we can only supply the implement of labour, in order that those who wish for knowledge may use it as they like; and we feel assured that they will understand the utility of our efforts and of their own.

Lastly, we will do out best to explain the elements of divination by the Tarot as practised by the Gypsies.

But those who think that occult science should not be revealed must not be too angry with us. Experience has taught us that everything may be fearlessly said; those only who should understand can understand; the others will accuse our work of being obscure and incomprehensible.

We have warned them by placing at the head of this volume—*For the exclusive use of Initiates.*

It is one characteristic of the study of true occult science that it may be freely explained to all men. Like the parables, so dear to the ancients, it appears to many as only the expression of the flight of a bold imagination: we need, therefore, never be afraid of speaking too openly; the Word will only reach those who should be touched thereby.

To you all, philosophers of Unity, enemies of scientific, social and religious sectarianism, I now address myself, to you I dedicate this result of several years' study. May I thus aid in the erection of the temple which you are about to raise to the honour of the Unknown God, from whom all the others emanate throughout Eternity!

First Lesson: Simplification of the Rules of Fortune-Telling by the Tarot. The great difficulty encountered by a beginner in the study of divination by the Tarot, is the number of meanings to be remembered in reading the cards.

Open any treatise upon this subject, and you will see that you must first master the different significations of the 78 cards. You must then learn the variations in their meaning when reversed, and this does not include the pairings and other complications, which bring up the sum total to about 200 different meanings. All these must be retained in the memory before anyone can become a good fortune-teller by cards. Habit only will enable the student to remember such details, and in this case intuition becomes an important aid to the memory.

Now complication of this kind always points to an imperfect system. Nature is synthetic in its manifestations, and simplicity is found at the bottom of the most outwardly involved phenomena. Whilst admitting that our work upon the Tarot may have its errors, no one can deny the absolute simplicity of the constituent principles. We will therefore apply the same method to the divining Tarot, and endeavour to establish a system which will enable us to dispense with memory almost entirely, or at least to reduce its work considerably. We shall thus allow a certain scope for scientific data, although we are unwilling to create any prejudice by this influence, considering the subject that we are dealing with.

The first point to retain from the commencement of this study is the necessity for clear, simple rules, by which the divining Tarot may be read. We will explain them in the following lessons.

Second Lesson: Minor Arcana: Signification from the Divining Point of View. The Tarot pack is composed of 78 cards or plates; 22 of them bear symbolical names (the Juggler, Sun, Moon, Hanged Man, etc.), and they should be separated from the 56 others, which are divided into four great series: Sceptres, Cups, Swords, and Pentacles.

These four suits each contain 14 cards (King, Queen, Knight, Knave, Ace, 2, 3, 4, 5, 6, 7, 8, 9 and 10), corresponding with the four suits of common playing cards (clubs, hearts, spades, diamonds), but called Sceptres, Cups, Swords, Pentacles. These are the Minor Arcana.

The 22 symbolical cards on the Major Arcana or Great Arcana.

1. Minor Arcana, formed of four sequences of 14 cards each, or 56 cards in all.

2. Major Arcana, formed of 22 cards.

These are the two great divisions which must first be remembered.

We have already said that the minor arcana are divided into four sequences: Sceptres, Cups, Swords, Pentacles. Each of these suits represents one of the four great principles, as follows—

The Sceptres	represent	*Enterprise and Glory.*
The Cups	represent	*Love and Happiness.*
The Swords	represent	*Hatred and Misfortune.*
The Pentacles	represent	*Money and Interest.*

Enterprise, Love, Hatred, Fortune are the four great principles which must be remembered.

If you now take one of these packets of 14 cards, you will see that it is formed of four pictures, and of 10 other cards, which bear numbers formed by the symbols.

We will first look at the 4 picture cards—

The King	represents	*Man.*
The Queen	represents	*Woman.*
The Knight	represents	*A Young Man.*
The Knave	represents	*A Child.*

The Man represents the creator, the one who undertakes the enterprises; the woman characterizes love; the young man, conflict, struggle, rivalry, hatred; the child symbolizes the absolute neuter, the second *He,* which varies according to circumstances, money, which addresses itself to all, and applies itself to all, univeral transition. Man, Woman, Young Man, Child are therefore the same symbols applied to the family as the four great principles applied to humanity, and to know them in one case is to know them in the other.

To sum up all this, we may say that the first element represents the positive, the second the negative, the third the opposition between the two; finally, the last the absolute neuter; and these elements are symbolized by the four picture-cards of each of the minor arcana.

But even as the cards are divided into two colours, red and black, so humanity is divided into *dark* and *fair.*

The eight picture-cards of Sceptres and Swords therefore represent dark people, and the eight of Cups and Pentacles, fair people.

The picture-cards of Sceptres and Cups are *good*; those of Swords and Pentacles, *bad.*

We shall presently repeat this in connection with each suit, and will now recapitulate the meanings of the four pictures of Sceptres.

King of Sceptres	:	Dark man; good; a friend.
Queen ,,	:	Dark woman; good.
Knight ,,	:	Dark young man; good.
Knave ,,	:	Dark child or messenger; good.

Besides our four pictures we have to consider the 10 cards bearing numbers. How can we discover the meaning of these 10 cards, and above all how can we memorize it?

We have nothing new to learn, but need only apply all that we already know. We divide our 10 cards into four packets: three packets of 3 cards each, and one packet formed of a single card, the 10th. When this is done we say—

The first packet of 3 cards, formed of the ace, 2, and 3, will have the meaning as the Man, enterprise, commencement, the creation of some undertaking (enterprise, love, hatred, or money).

The second packet, composed of the 4, 5 and 6, represents Woman, and all the ideas of negation, of reflection, associated with her; that is to say, the contrary of man, antagonism, opposition in any matter.

The third packet signifies the equilibrium which results from the action of the two opposites upon each other, represented by the Young Man.

Lastly, the Child, the absolute neuter, will be represented by the 10th card.

Each of the 3 cards in these packets have the same meaning.

The first card of these 3 packets will indicate the commencement; the second, opposition, antagonism; the third, equilibrium, which gives us the following general sequence in our 10 cards.

KEY TO THE DIVINING TAROT

1. Commencement
2. Opposition   } *of Commencement.*
3. Equilibrium

4. Commencement
5. Opposition   } *of Opposition.*
6. Equilibrium

7. Commencement
8. Opposition   } *of Equilibrium.*
9. Equilibrium

10. Undetermined: The card which follows will explain it.

Thus the three words, Commencement, Opposition, Equilibrium, the synonyms of Thesis, Antithesis, Synthesis, or of *Brahma, Siva, Vishnu,* etc., suffice for the explanation of all the minor arcana of the Tarot. We need only add the words love, hatred, enterprise or fortune to each of the series, and we can define the meaning of every card without wearying the memory. This we will now do. . . .

NOTES

1. See Jamblichus, Porphyry and Apuleius.
2. See Fabre d'Olivet, *La Langue Hébraïque Restituée*.
3. Court de Gébelin.—*Le Monde Primitif.*
4. Vaillant.—*Les Romes, Histoire des Bohémiens.*
5. Eliphas Lévi.—*Rituel de la Haute Magie.*
6. Vaillant.—*Op. cit.*
7. William Postel.—*Clavis.*
8. Vaillant.—*Op. cit.*
9. Eliphas Lévi—*Op. cit.*

H. P. Blavatsky (1831–1891)

Occultism Versus the Occult Arts

"I oft have hear, but ne'er believed till now, There are, who can by potent magic spells Bend to their crooked purpose Nature's laws."
—Milton

In this month's Correspondence several letters testify to the strong impression produced on some minds by our last month's article "Practical Occultism." Such letters go far to prove and strengthen two logical conclusions: —

(a) There are more well-educated and thoughtful men who believe in the existence of Occultism and Magic (the two differing vastly) than the modern materialist dreams of: and —

(b) That most of the believers (comprising many theosophists) have no definite idea of the nature of Occultism and confuse it with the Occult sciences in general, the "Black art" included.

From Helene Petrovna Blavatsky, *Studies in Occultism,* Pasadena, Cal.: Theosophical University Press, n.d., pp. 11–20. Reprinted by permission of Theosophical University Press.

Their representations of the powers it confers upon man, and of the means
to be used to acquire them are as varied as they are fanciful. Some imagine
that a master in the art, to show the way, is all that is needed to become a
Zanoni. Others, that one has but to cross the Canal of Suez and go to India to
bloom forth as a Roger Bacon or even a Count St. Germain. Many take for
their ideal Margrave with his ever-renewing youth, and care little for the soul
as the price paid for it. Not a few, mistaking "Witch-of-Endorism" pure and
simple, for Occultism—"through the yawning Earth from Stygian gloom, call
up the meager ghost to walks of light," and want, on the strength of this feat,
to be regarded as full blown Adepts. "Ceremonial Magic" according to the
rules mockingly laid down by Éliphas Lévi, is another imagined *alter ego* of
the philosophy of the Arhats of old. In short, the prisms through which Occultism appears, to those innocent of the philosophy, are as multicolored and
varied as human fancy can make them.

Will these candidates to Wisdom and Power feel very indignant if told the
plain truth? It is not only useful, but it has now become *necessary* to disabuse
most of them and before it is too late. This truth may be said in a few words:
There are not in the West half-a-dozen among the fervent hundreds who call
themselves "Occultists," who have even an approximately correct idea of the
nature of the Science they seek to master. With a few exceptions, they are all
on the highway to Sorcery. Let them restore some order in the chaos that
reigns in their minds, before they protest against this statement. Let them first
learn the true relation in which the Occult Sciences stand to Occultism, and
the difference between the two, and then feel wrathful if they still think
themselves right. Meanwhile, let them learn that Occultism differs from Magic
and other secret Sciences as the glorious Sun does from a rush-light, as the immutable and immortal Spirit of Man—the reflection of the absolute, causeless,
and unknowable *all*—differs from the mortal clay—the human body.

In our highly civilized West, where modern languages have been formed,
and words coined, in the wake of ideas and thoughts—as happened with every
tongue—the more the latter became materialized in the cold atmosphere of
Western selfishness and its incessant chase after the goods of this world, the
less was there any felt for the production of new terms to express that which
was tacitly regarded as obsolete and exploded "superstition." Such words
could answer only to ideas which a cultured man was scarcely supposed to
harbor in his mind. "Magic," a synonym for jugglery; "Sorcery," an
equivalent for crass ignorance; and "Occultism," the sorry relic of crack-
brained, medieval Fire-philosophers, of the Jacob Boehmes and the St.
Martins, are expressions believed more than amply sufficient to cover the

whole field of "thimble-rigging." They are terms of contempt, and used generally only in reference to the dross and residues of the Dark Ages and its preceding aeons of paganism. Therefore have we no terms in the English tongue to define and shade the difference between such abnormal powers, or the sciences that lead to the acquisition of them, with the nicety possible in the Eastern languages—pre-eminently the Sanskrit. What do the words "miracle" and "enchantment" (words identical in meaning after all, as both express the idea of producing wonderful things by *breaking the laws of nature* [!!] as explained by the accepted authorities) convey to the minds of those who hear, or who pronounce them? A Christian—*breaking* "of the laws of nature," notwithstanding—while believing firmly in the *miracles,* because said to have been produced by God through Moses, will either scout the enchantments performed by Pharaoh's magicians, or attribute them to the devil. It is the latter whom our pious enemies connect with Occultism, while their impious foes, the infidels, laugh at Moses, Magicians, and Occultists, and would blush to give one serious thought to such "superstitions." This, because there is no term in existence to show the difference; no words to express the lights and shadows and draw the line of demarcation between the sublime and the true, the absurd and the ridiculous. The latter are the theological interpretations which teach the "breaking of the laws of Nature" by man, God, or devil; the former—the *scientific* "miracles" and enchantments of Moses and the Magicians *in accordance with natural laws,* both having been learned in all the Wisdom of the Sanctuaries, which were the "Royal Societies" of those days— and in true OCCULTISM. This last word is certainly misleading, translated as it stands from the compound word *Gupta-Vidyâ*, "Secret Knowledge." But the knowledge of what? Some of the Sanskrit terms may help us.

There are four (out of the many other) names of the various kinds of Esoteric Knowledge or Sciences given, even in the exoteric Puranas. There is (1) *Yajña-Vidyâ*,[1] knowledge of the occult powers awakened in Nature by the performance of certain religious ceremonies and rites. (2) *Mahâ-Vidyâ*, the "great knowledge," the magic of the Kabalists and of the *Tântrika* worship, often Sorcery of the worst description. (3) *Guhya-Vidyâ*, knowledge of the mystic powers residing in Sound (Ether), hence in the *Mantras* (chanted prayers or incantations) and depending on the rhythm and melody used; in other words a magical performance based on Knowledge of the Forces of Nature and their correlation; and (4) *Âtma-Vidyâ*, a term which is translated simply "Knowledge of the Soul," *true Wisdom* by the Orientalists, but which means far more.

This last is the only kind of Occultism that any Theosophist who admires

Light on the Path, and who would be wise and unselfish, ought to strive after. All the rest is some branch of the "Occult Sciences," i.e., arts based on the knowledge of the ultimate essence of all things in the Kingdom of Nature— such as minerals, plants, and animals—hence of things pertaining to the realm of *material* Nature, however invisible that essence may be, and howsoever much it has hitherto eluded the grasp of Science. Alchemy, Astrology, Occult Physiology, Chiromancy exist in Nature, and the *exact* Sciences—perhaps so called because they are found in this age of paradoxical philosophies the reverse—have already discovered not a few of the secrets of the above *arts.* But clairvoyance, symbolized in India as the "Eye of Śiva," called in Japan, "Infinite Vision," is *not* Hypnotism, the illegitimate son of Mesmerism, and is not to be acquired by such arts. All the others may be mastered and results obtained, whether good, bad or indifferent; but *Âtma-Vidyâ* sets small value on them. It includes them all, and may even use them occasionally, but it does so after purifying them of their dross, for beneficient purposes, and taking care to deprive them of every element of selfish motive. Let us explain: Any man or woman can set himself or herself to study one or all the above specified "Occult Arts" without any great previous preparation, and even without adopting any too restraining mode of life. One could even dispense with any lofty standard of morality. In the last case, of course, ten to one the student would blossom into a very decent kind of sorcerer, and tumble down headlong into black magic. But what can this matter? The *Voodoos* and the *Dugpas* eat, drink and are merry over hecatombs of victims of their infernal arts. And so do the amiable gentlemen vivisectionists and the *diplomaed* "Hypnotizers" of the Faculties of Medicine; the only difference between the two classes being that the Voodoos and the Dugpas are *conscious,* and the Charcot-Richet crew *unconscious* Sorcerers. Thus, since both have to reap the fruits of their labors and achievements in the black art, the Western practitioners should not have the punishment and reputation without the profits and enjoyments they may get therefrom. For we say it again, *hypnotism* and *vivisection* as practised in such schools, are *Sorcery* pure and simple, *minus* a knowledge that the Voodoos and Dugpas enjoy, and which no Charcot-Richet can procure for himself in fifty years of hard study and experimental observation. Let then those who will dabble in magic, whether they understand its nature or not, but who find the rules imposed upon students too hard, and who, therefore, lay Âtma-Vidyâ or Occultism aside—go without it. Let them become magicians by all means, even though they do become *Voodoos* and *Dugpas* for the next ten incarnations.

But the interest of our readers will probably center on those who are invincibly attracted towards the "Occult," yet who neither realize the true nature of what they aspire towards, nor have they become passion-proof, far less truly unselfish.

How about these unfortunates, we shall be asked, who are thus rent in twain by conflicting forces? For it has been said too often to need repetition, and the fact itself is patent to any observer, that when once the desire for Occultism has really awakened in a man's heart, there remains for him no hope of peace, no place of rest and comfort in all the world. He is driven out into the wild and desolate spaces of life by an ever-gnawing unrest he cannot quell. His heart is too full of passion and selfish desire to permit him to pass the Golden Gate; he cannot find rest or peace in ordinary life. Must he then inevitably fall into sorcery and black magic, and through many incarnations heap up for himself a terrible Karma? Is there no other road for him?

Indeed there is, we answer. Let him aspire to no higher than he feels able to accomplish. Let him not take a burden upon himself too heavy for him to carry. Without ever becoming a "Mahâtma," a Buddha, or a Great Saint, let him study the philosophy and the "Science of Soul," and he can become one of the modest benefactors of humanity, without any "superhuman" powers. *Siddhis* (or the Arhat powers) are only for those who are able to "lead the life," to comply with the terrible sacrifices required for such a training, and to comply with them *to the very letter*. Let them know at once and remember always, that *true Occultism* or *Theosophy* is the "Great Renunciation of *self*," unconditionally and absolutely, in thought as in action. It is *altrusim,* and it throws him who practises it out of calculation of the ranks of the living altogether. "Not for himself, but for the world, he lives," as soon as he has pledged himself to the work. Much is forgiven during the first years of probation. But, no sooner is he "accepted" than his personality must disappear, and he has to become *a mere beneficent force in Nature*. There are two poles for him after that, two paths, and no midward place of rest. He has either to ascend laboriously, step by step, often through numerous incarnations and *no Devachanic break,* the golden ladder leading to Mahâtmaship (the *Arhat or Bodhisattva* condition), or—he will let himself slide down the ladder at the first false step, and roll down into *Dugpaship*. . . .

All this is either unknown or left out of sight altogether. Indeed, one who is able to follow the silent evolution of the preliminary aspirations of the candidates, often finds strange ideas quietly taking possession of their minds. There are those whose reasoning powers have been so distorted by foreign influences that they imagine that animal passions can be so sublimated and elevated that their fury, force, and fire can, so to speak, be turned inwards; that they can be stored and shut up in one's breast, until their energy is, not expanded, but turned toward higher and more holy purposes; namely, *until their collective and unexpanded strength enables their possessor to enter the true Sanctuary of the Soul* and stand therein in the presence of the *Master*—the *Higher Self!* For this purpose they will not struggle with their passions nor slay them. They will simply, by a strong effort of will put down the fierce flames and keep them at bay within their natures, allowing the fire to smolder under a thin layer of ashes. They submit joyfully to the torture of the Spartan boy who allowed the fox to devour his entrail rather than part with it. Oh, poor, blind visionaries!

As well hope that a band of drunken chimney-sweeps, hot and greasy from their work, may be shut up in a Sanctuary hung with pure white linen, and that instead of soiling and turning it by their presence into a heap of dirty shreds, they will become masters in and of the sacred recess, and finally emerge from it as immaculate as that recess. Why not imagine that a dozen of skunks imprisoned in the pure atmosphere of a Dgon-pa (a monastery) can issue out of it impregnated with all the perfumes of the incenses used? . . . Strange aberration of the human mind. Can it be so? Let us argue.

The "Master" in the Sanctuary of our souls is "the Higher Self"—the divine spirit whose consciousness is based upon and derived solely (at any rate during the mortal life of the man in whom it is captive) from the Mind, which we have agreed to call the *Human Soul* (the "Spiritual Soul" being the vehicle of the Spirit). In its turn the former (the *personal* or human soul) is a compound in its highest form, of spiritual aspirations, volitions and divine love; and in its lower aspect, of animal desires and terrestrial passions imparted to it by its associations with its vehicle, the seat of all these. It thus stands as a link and a medium between the animal nature of man which its higher reason seeks to subdue, and his divine spiritual nature to which it gravitates, whenever it has the upper hand in its struggle with the *inner animal*. The latter is the instinctual "animal Soul" and is the hotbed of those passions, which, as just shown, are lulled instead of being killed, and locked up in their breast by some imprudent enthusiasts. Do they still hope to turn thereby the muddy stream of the animal sewer into the crystalline waters of life? And where, on what neutral ground can they be imprisoned so as not to affect man? The fierce passions of love and lust are still alive and they are allowed to still remain in the place of their birth—*that same animal soul*; for both the higher and the lower positions of the "Human Soul" or Mind reject such inmates, though they cannot avoid being tainted with them as neighbors. The "Higher Self" or Spirit is as unable to assimilate such feelings as water to get mixed with oil or unclean liquid tallow. It is thus the mind alone—the sole link and medium between the man of earth and the Higher Self—that is the only sufferer, and which is in the incessant danger of being dragged down by those passions that may be reawakened at any moment, and perish in the abyss of matter. And how can it ever attune itself to the divine harmony of the highest Principle, when that harmony is destroyed by the mere presence, within the Sanctuary in preparation, of such animal passions? How can harmony prevail and conquer, when the soul is stained and distracted with the turmoil of passions and the terrestrial desires of the bodily senses, or even of the "Astral man"?

For this "Astral"—the shadowy "double" (in the animal as in man)—is not the companion of the *divine Ego* but of the *earthly body*. It is the link between the personal *Self*, the lower consciousness of *Manas* and the Body, and is the vehicle of *transitory, not of immortal life*. Like the shadow projected by man, it follows his movements and impulses slavishly and mechanically, and leans therefore to matter without ever ascending to Spirit. It is only when the power of the passions is dead altogether, and when they have been crushed and annihilated in the retort of an unflinching will; when not only all the lusts and longings of the flesh are dead, but also the recognition of the personal Self is killed out and the "astral" has been reduced in consequence to a cipher, that the Union with the "Higher Self" can take place. Then when the "astral" reflects only the conquered man, the still living, but no more the longing, selfish personality, then the brilliant *Augoeides*, the divine *Self*, can vibrate in conscious harmony with both the poles of the human Entity—the man of matter purified, and the ever pure Spiritual Soul—and stand in the presence of the *Master Self*, the Christos of the mystic Gnostics, blended, merged into, and one with IT for ever.[2]

NOTES

1. "The *Yajña*," say the Brâhmans, "exists from eternity, for it proceeded forth from the Supreme One . . . in whom it lay dormant from 'no beginning.' It is the key to the *Traividya*, the thrice sacred science contained in the Rig verses, which teaches the Yajus or sacrificial mysteries. 'The Yajña' exists as an invisible thing at all times; it is like the latent power of electricity in an electrifying machine, requiring only the operation of a suitable apparatus in order to be elicited. It is supposed to extend from the *Ahavaniya* or sacrificial fire to the heavens, forming a bridge or ladder by means of which the sacrificer can communicate with the world of gods and spirits, and even ascend when alive to their abodes."—Martin Haug's *Aitareya Brâhmana*.

"This *Yajña* is again one of the forms of the *Âkuśa*; and the mystic word calling it into existence and pronounced mentally by the initiated Priest is the *Lost Word* receiving impulse through *will power.*"—*Isis Unveiled,* Vol. I. Introduction. See *Aitareya Brâhmana,* Haug.

2. Those who would feel inclined to see three *Egos* in one man will show themselves unable to perceive the metaphysical meaning. Man is a trinity composed of Body, Soul and Spirit; but *man* is nevertheless *one* and is surely not his body. It is the latter which is the property, the transitory clothing of the man. The three "Egos" are *man* in his three aspects on the astral, intellectual or psychic and the Spirtual planes, or states.

Georg Simmel (1858–1918)

The Sociology of Secrecy and of Secret Societies

. . . While secrecy, therefore, is a sociological ordination which characterizes the reciprocal relation of group elements, or rather in connection with other forms of reaction constitutes this total relation, it may further, with the formation of "secret societies," extend itself over the group as a whole. So long as the being, doing, and having of an individual persist as a secret, his general sociological significance is isolation, antithesis, egoistic individualization. In this case the sociological meaning of secrecy is external; as relationship of him who has the secret to him who does not have it. So soon, however, as a group as such seizes upon secrecy as its form of existence, the sociological meaning of the secrecy becomes internal. It now determines the reciprocal relations of those who possess the secret in common. Since, however, that relation of exclusion toward the uninitiated exists here also with its special gradations, the

Translated by Albion W. Small.
Abridged from *The American Journal of Sociology,* XI (January, 1906): 441–498. Kurt H. Wolff has also translated this essay in his volume, *The Sociology of Georg Simmel,* New York: Free Press, 1950.

sociology of secret societies presents the complicated problem of ascertaining the immanent forms of a group which are determined by attitudes of secrecy on the part of the same toward other elements . . . .

The first internal relation that is essential to a secret society is the reciprocal *confidence* of its members. This element is needed in a peculiar degree, because the purpose of maintaining the secrecy is, first of all, protection. Most radical of all the protective provisions is certainly that of invisibility. At this point the secret society is distinguished in principle from the individual who seeks the protection of secrecy. This can be realized only with respect to specific designs or conditions; as a whole, the individual may hide himself temporarily, he may absent himself from a given portion of space; but, disregarding wholly abstruse combinations, his existence cannot be a secret. In the case of a societary unity, on the contrary, this is entirely possible. Its elements may live in the most frequent commerce, but that they compose a society—a conspiracy, or a band of criminals, a religious conventicle, or an association for sexual extravagances—may remain essentially and permanently a secret. This type, in which not the individuals but their combination is concealed, is sharply distinguished from the others, in which the social formation is unequivocally known, but the membership, or the purpose, or the special conditions of the combination are secrets; as, for instance, many secret bodies among the nature peoples, or the Freemasons. The form of secrecy obviously does not afford to the latter types the same unlimited protection as the former, since what is known about them always affords a point of attack for further intrusion. On the other hand, these *relatively* secret societies always have the advantage of a certain variability. Because they are from the start arranged on the basis of a certain degree of publicity, it is easier for them to accommodate themselves to further betrayals than for those that are as societies entirely unavowed. The first discovery very often destroys the latter, because their secret is apt to face the alternative, whole or not at all. It is the weakness of secret societies that secrets do not remain permanently guarded. Hence we say with truth: "A secret that two know is no longer a secret." Consequently, the protection that such societies afford is in its nature, to be sure, absolute, but it is only temporary, and, for contents of positive social value, their commitment to the care of secret societies is in fact a transitional condition, which they no longer need after they have developed a certain degree of strength. Secrecy is finally analogous only with the protection which one secures by evading interruptions. It consequently serves only provisionally, until strength may be developed to cope with interruptions. Under these circumstances the secret society is the appropriate social

form for contents which are at an immature stage of development, and thus in
a condition peculiarly liable to injury from opposing interests. Youthful
knowledge, religion, morality, party, is often weak and in need of defense.
Hence also there is a predestination of secret societies for periods in which new
life-contents come into existence in spite of the opposition of the powers that
be. The eighteenth century affords abundant illustrations. For instance, to cite
only one example, the elements of the liberal party were present in Germany
at that time. Their emergence in a permanent political structure was post-
poned by the power of the civic conditions. Accordingly, the secret association
was the form in which the germs could be protected and cultivated, as in the
case of the orders of the *Illuminati*. The same sort of protection which secrecy
affords to ascending movements is also secured from it during their decline.
Refuge in secrecy is a ready resort in the case of social endeavors and forces
that are likely to be displaced by innovation. Secrecy is thus, so to speak, a
transition stadium between being and not-being. As the suppression of the
German communal associations began to occur, at the close of the Middle
Ages, through the increasing power of the central governments, a wide-
reaching secret life developed within these organizations. It was characterized
by hidden assemblies and conferences, by secret enforcement of law, and by
violence—somewhat as animals seek the protection of concealment when near
death. This double function of secrecy as a form of protection, to afford an
intermediate station equally for progressing and for decaying powers, is
perhaps most obvious in the case of religious movements. So long as the Christian communities were persecuted by the state, they were often obliged to
withdraw their meetings, their worship, their whole existence, from public
view. So soon, however, as Christianity had become the state religion, nothing
was left for the adherents of persecuted, dying paganism than the same hiding
of its cultus which it had previously forced upon the new faith. As a general
proposition, the secret society emerges everywhere as correlate of despotism
and of police control. It acts as protection alike of defense and of offense
against the violent pressure of central powers. This is true, not alone in
political relations, but in the same way within the church, the school, and the
family.

Corresponding with this protective character of the secret society, as an
external quality, is, as already observed, the inner quality of reciprocal confidence between the members. This is, moreover, a quite specific type of confidence, viz., in the ability to preserve silence. Social unities may rest, so far as
their content is concerned, upon many sorts of presumption about grounds of

confidence. They may trust, for example, to the motive of business interest, or to religious conviction, to courage, or to love, to the high moral tone, or—in the case of criminal combinations—to the radical break with moral imperatives. When the society becomes secret, however, there is added to the confidence determined by the peculiar purposes of the society the further formal confidence in ability to keep still—evidently a faith in the personality, which has, sociologically, a more abstract character than any other, because every possible common interest may be subsumed under it. More than that, exceptions excluded, no kind of confidence requires so unbroken subjective renewal; for when the uncertainty in question is faith in attachment or energy, in morality or intelligence, in sense of honor or tact, facts are much more likely to be observable which will objectively establish the degree of confidence, since they will reduce the probability of deception to a minimum. The probability of betrayal, however, is subject to the imprudence of a moment, the weakness or the agitation of a mood, the perhaps unconscious shading of an accentuation. The keeping of the secret is something so unstable, the temptations to betrayal are manifold, in many cases such a continuous path leads from secretiveness to indiscretion, that unlimited faith in the former contains an incomparable preponderance of the subjective factor. For this reason those secret societies whose rudimentary forms begin with the secret shared by two, and whose enormous extension through all times and places has not even yet been appreciated, even quantitatively—such societies have exerted a highly efficient disciplinary influence upon moral accountability among men. For there resides in confidence of men toward each other as high moral value as in the companion fact that this confidence is justified. Perhaps the former phenomenon is freer and more creditable, since a confidence reposed in us amounts almost to a constraining prejudice, and to disappoint it requires badness of a positive type. On the contrary, we "give" our faith in another. It cannot be delivered on demand, in the same degree in which it can be realized when spontaneously offered.

Meanwhile the secret societies naturally seek means psychologically to promote that secretiveness which cannot be directly forced. The oath, and threats of penalties, are here in the foreground and need no discussion. More interesting is the frequently encountered technique for teaching novices the art of the silence. In view of the above-suggested difficulties of guarding the tongue absolutely, in view especially of the tell-tale connection which exists on primitive social planes between thought and expression—among children and many nature peoples thinking and speaking are almost one—there is need at the outset of learning silence once for all, before silence about any particular matter can be expected. . . .

In connection with these questions about the technique of secrecy, it is not to be forgotten that concealment is by no means the only means under whose protection promotion of the material interests of the community is attempted. The facts are in many ways the reverse. The structure of the group is often with the direct view to assurance of keeping certain subjects from general knowledge. This is the case with those peculiar types of secret society whose substance is an esoteric doctrine, a theoretical, mystical, religious gnosis. In this case secrecy is the sociological end-unto-itself. The issue turns upon a body of doctrine to be kept from publicity. The initiated constitute a community for the purpose of mutal guarantee of secrecy. If these initiates were merely a total of personalities not interdependent, the secret would soon be lost. Socialization affords to each of these individuals a psychological recourse for strengthening him against temptations to divulge the secret. While secrecy . . . works toward isolation and individualization, socialization is a counteractive factor. If this is in general the sociological significance of the secret society, its most clear emergence is in the case of those orders . . . in which secrecy is not a mere sociological technique, but socialization is a technique for better protection of the secrecy, in the same way that the oath and total silence, that threats and progressive initiation of the novices, serve the same purpose. All species of socialization shuffle the individualizing and the socializing needs back and forth within their forms, and even within their contents, as though promotion of a stable combining proportion were satisfied by introduction of quantities always qualitatively changing. Thus the secret society counterbalances the separatistic factor which is peculiar to every secret by the very fact that it is *society*.

Secrecy and individualistic separateness are so decidedly correlatives that with reference to secrecy socialization may play two quite antithetical roles. It can, in the first place . . . be directly sought, to the end that during the subsequent continuance of the secrecy its isolating tendency may be in part counteracted, that *within* the secret order the impulse toward community may be satisfied, while it is vetoed with reference to the rest of the world. On the other hand, however, secrecy in principle loses relative significance in cases where the particularization is in principle rejected. Freemasonry, for example, insists that it purposes to become the most universal society, "the union of unions," the only one that repudiates every particularistic character and aims to appropriate as its material exclusively that which is common to all good men. Hand in hand with this increasingly definite tendency there grows up indifference toward the element of secrecy on the part of the lodges, its restriction to the merely formal externalities. That secrecy is now promoted by socialization, and now abolished by it, is thus by no means a contradiction. . . .

The above-mentioned gradual initiation of the members belongs, moreover, to a very far-reaching and widely ramifying division of sociological forms, within which secret societies are marked in a special way. It is the principle of the hierarchy, of graded articulation, of the elements of a society. The refinement and the systematization with which secret societies particularly work out their division of labor and the grading of their members, go along with another trait to be discussed presently; that is, with their energetic *consciousness* of their life. This life substitutes for the organically more instinctive forces an incessantly regulating will; for growth from within, constructive purposefulness. This rationalistic factor in their upbuilding cannot express itself more distinctly than in their carefully considered and clear-cut architecture. I cite as example the structure of the Czechic secret order, *Omladina*, which was organized on the model of a group of the *Carbonari*, and became known in consequence of a judicial process in 1893. The leaders of the *Omladina* are divided into "thumbs" and "fingers." In secret session a "thumb" is chosen by the members. He selects four "fingers." The latter than choose another "thumb," and this second "thumb" presents himself to the first "thumb." The second "thumb" proceeds to choose four more "fingers;" these, another "thumb;" and so the articulation continues. The first "thumb" knows all the other "thumbs," but the remaining "thumbs" do not know each other. Of the "fingers" only those four know each other who are subordinate to one and the same "thumb." All transactions of the *Omladina* are conducted by the first "thumb," the "dictator." He informs the other "thumbs" of all proposed undertakings. The "thumbs" then issue orders to their respective subordinates, the "fingers." The latter in turn instruct the members of the *Omladina* assigned to each. The circumstance that the secret society must be built up from its base by calculation and conscious volition evidently affords free play for the peculiar passion which is the natural accompaniment of such arbitrary processes of construction, such foreordaining programs. All schematology—of science, of conduct, of society—contains a reserved power of compulsion. It subjects a material which is outside of thought to a form which thought has cast. If this is true of all attempts to organize groups according to *a priori* principles, it is true in the highest degree of the secret society, which does not grow, which is built by design, which has to reckon with a smaller quantum of ready-made building material than any despotic or socialistic scheme. Joined to the interest in making plans, and the constructive impulse, which are in themselves compelling forces, we have in the organization of a society in accordance with a preconceived outline, with fixed positions and ranks, the special stimulus of exercising a decisive influence over a future and ideally submissive circle of human beings. This impulse is decisively separated sometimes from every sort of utility, and revels in utterly fantastic construction of hierarchies. Thus, for example, in the "high degrees" of degenerate Freemasonry. . . .

Parallel with the development of the hierarchy, and with similar limitations, we observe within secret societies the structure of the ritual. Here also their peculiar emancipation from the prejudices of historical organizations permits them to build upon a self-laid basis extreme freedom and opulence of form. There is perhaps no external tendency which so decisively and with such characteristic differences divides the secret from the open society, as the valuation of usages, formulas, rites, and the peculiar preponderance and antithetic relation of all these to the body of purposes which the society represents. The latter are often guarded with less care than the secret of the ritual. Progressive Freemasonry emphasizes expressly that it is not a secret combination; that it has no occasion to conceal the roll of its members, its purposes, or its acts; the oath of silence refers exclusively to the forms of the Masonic rites. . . .

That which is striking about the treatment of the ritual in secret societies is not merely the precision with which it is observed, but first of all the anxiety with which it is guarded as a secret—as though the unveiling of it were precisely as fatal as betrayal of the purposes and actions of the society, or even the existence of the society altogether. The utility of this is probably in the fact that, through this absorption of a whole complex of external forms into the secret, the whole range of action and interest occupied by the secret society becomes a well-rounded unity. The secret society must seek to create among the categories peculiar to itself, a species of life-totality. Around the nucleus of purposes which the society strongly emphasizes, it therefore builds a structure of formulas, like a body around a soul, and places both alike under the protection of secrecy, because only so can a harmonious whole come into being, in which one part supports the other. That in this scheme secrecy of the external is strongly accentuated, is necessary, because secrecy is not so much a matter of course with reference to these superficialities, and not so directly demanded as in the case of the real interests of the society. . . . One of its essential characteristics is that, even when it takes hold of individuals only by means of partial interests, when the society in its substance is a purely utilitarian combination, yet it claims the whole man in a higher degree, it combines the personalities

more in their whole compass with each other, and commits them more to reciprocal obligations, than the same common purpose would within an open society. Since the symbolism of the ritual stimulates a wide range of vaguely
bounded feelings, touching interests far in excess of those that are definitely
apprehended, the secret society weaves these latter interests into an aggregate
demand upon the individual. Through the ritual form the specific purpose of
the secret society is expanded into a comprehensive unity and totality, both sociological and subjective. Moreover, through such formalism, just as through
the hierarchical structure above discussed, the secret society constitutes itself a
sort of counterpart of the official world with which it places itself in antithesis.
Here we have a case of the universally emerging sociological norm; viz., structures, which place themselves in opposition to and detachment from larger
structures in which they are actually contained, nevertheless repeat in
themselves the forms of the greater structures. Only a structure that in some
way can count as a whole is in a situation to hold its elements firmly together.
It borrows the sort of organic completeness, by virtue of which its members are
actually the channels of a unifying life-stream, from that greater whole to
which its individual members were already adapted, and to which it can most
easily offer a parallel by means of this very imitation.

The same relation affords finally the following motive for the sociology of
the ritual in secret societies. Every such society contains a measure of freedom,
which is not really provided for in the structure of the surrounding society.
Whether the secret society, like the *Vehme*, complements the inadequate judi-
cature of the political area; or whether, as in the case of conspiracies or
criminal bands, it is an uprising against the law of that area; or whether, as in
the case of the "mysteries," they hold themselves outside of the commands and
prohibitions of the greater area—in either case the apartness
(*Heraussonderung*) which characterizes the secret society has the tone of a
freedom. In exercise of this freedom a territory is occupied to which the norms
of the surrounding society do not apply. The nature of the secret society as
such is autonomy. It is, however, of a sort which approaches anarchy.
Withdrawal from the bonds of unity which procure general coherence very
easily has as consequences for the secret society a condition of being without
roots, an absence of firm touch with life (*Lebensgefuhl*), and of restraining res-
ervations. The fixedness and detail of the ritual serve in part to counter-
balance this deficit. . . .

With the ritual the secret society voluntarily imposes upon itself a formal
constraint, which is demanded as a complement by its material detachment

and self-sufficiency. It is characteristic that, among the Freemasons, it is precisely the Americans—who enjoy the largest political freedom—of whom the severest unity in manner of work, the greatest uniformity of the ritual of all lodges, are demanded; while in Germany—where the otherwise sufficient quantum of bondage leaves little room for a counterdemand in the direction of restrictions upon freedom—more freedom is exercised in the manner in which each individual lodge carries on its work. The often essentially meaningless, schematic constraint of the ritual of the secret society is therefore by no means a contradiction of its freedom bordering on anarchy, its detachment from the norms of the circle which contains it. Just as widespread existence of secret societies is, as a rule, a proof of public unfreedom, of a policy of police regulation, of police oppression; so conversely, ritual regulation of these societies from within proves a freedom and enfranchisement in principle for which the equilibrium of human nature produces the constraint as a counter-influence.

These last considerations have already led to the methodological principle with reference to which I shall analyze the still outstanding traits of secret societies. The problem is, in a word, to what extent these traits prove to be in essence quantitative modifications of the typical traits of socialization in general. In order to establish this manner of representing secret societies, we must again review their status in the whole complex of sociological forms.

The secret element in societies is a primary sociological fact, a definite mode and shading of association, a formal relationship of quality in immediate or mediate reciprocity with other factors which determine the habit of the group-elements or of the group. The secret society, on the other hand, is a secondary structure; i.e., it arises always only within an already complete society. Otherwise expressed, the secret society is itself characterized by its secret, just as other societies, and even itself, are characterized by their superiority and subordination, or by their offensive purposes, or by their initiative character. That they can build themselves up with such characteristics is possible, however, only under the presupposition of an already existing society. The secret society sets itself as a special society in antithesis with the wider association included within the greater society. This antithesis, whatever its purpose, is at all events intended in the spirit of exclusion. Even the secret society which proposes only to render the whole community a definite service in a completely unselfish spirit, and to dissolve itself after performing the service, obviously regards its temporary detachment from that totality as the unavoidable technique for its purpose. Accordingly, none of the narrower groups which are circumscribed by larger groups are compelled by their sociological constellation to insist so strongly as the secret society upon their formal self-sufficiency. Their secret encircles them like a boundary, beyond which there is nothing but the materially, or at least formally, antithetic, which therefore shuts up the society within itself as a complete unity. In the groupings of every other sort, the *content* of the group-life, the actions of the members in the sphere of rights and duties, may so fill up their consiousness that within it the formal fact of socialization under normal conditions plays scarcely any role. The secret society, on the other hand, can on no account permit the definite and emphatic consiousness of its members that they constitute a society to escape from their minds. The always perceptible and always to-be-guarded pathos of the secret lends to the form of union which depends upon the secret, as contrasted with the content, a predominant significance, as compared with other unions.

In the secret society there is complete absence of organic growth, of the character of instinct in accumulation, of all unforced matter of course with respect to belonging together and forming a unity. No matter how irrational, mystical, impressionistic (*gefuhlsmassig*) their contents, the way in which they are constructed is always conscious and intentional. Throughout their derivation and life *consciousness of being a society* is permanently accentuated. The secret society is, on that account, the antithesis of all genetic (*triebhaft*) societies, in which the unification is more or less only the expression of the natural growing together of elements whose life has common roots. Its socio-psychological form is invariably that of the teleological combination (*Zweckverband*). This constellation makes it easy to understand that the specifications of form in the construction of secret societies attain to peculiar definiteness, and that their essential sociological trains develop as mere quantitative heightenings of quite general types of relationship.

One of these latter has already been indicated; viz., the characterization and the coherence of the society through closure toward the social environment. To this end the often complicated signs of recognition contribute. Through these the individual offers credentials of membership in the society. Indeed, in the times previous to the general use of writing, such signs were more imperative for this use than later. At present their other sociological uses overtop that of mere identification. So long as there was lack of documentary credentials, an order whose subdivisions were in different localities utterly lacked means of excluding the unauthorized, of securing to rightful claimants only the enjoyment of its benefits or knowledge of its affairs, unless these signs were employed. These were disclosed only to the worthy, who were pledged to keep them secret, and who could use them for purposes of legitimation as members of the order wherever it existed. . . .

This significance of secret associations, as intensification of sociological exclusiveness in general, appears in a very striking way in political aristocracies. Among the requisites of aristocratic control secrecy has always had a place. It makes use of the psychological fact that the unknown as such appears terrible, powerful, and threatening. In the first place, it employs this fact in seeking to conceal the numerical insignificance of the governing class. . . . On the other hand, the democratic principle is bound up with the principle of publicity, and, to the same end, the tendency toward general and fundamental laws. The latter relate to an unlimited number of subjects, and are thus in their nature public. Conversely, the employment of secrecy within the aristocratic regime is only the extreme exaggeration of that social exclusion and exemption for the sake of which aristocracies are wont to oppose general, fundamentally sanctioned laws. . . .

The bar against all external to the circle, which, as universal sociological form-fact, makes use of secrecy as a progressive technique, gains a peculiar coloring through the multiplicity of degrees, through which initiation into the last mysteries of secret societies is wont to occur, and which threw light above upon another sociological trait of secret societies. As a rule, a solemn pledge is demanded of the novice that he will hold secret everything which he is about to experience, before even the first stages of acceptance into the society occur. Therewith is the absolute and formal separation which secrecy can effect, put into force. Yet, since under these conditions the essential content or purpose of the order is only gradually accessible to the neophyte—whether the purpose is the complete purification and salvation of the soul through the consecration of the mysteries, or whether it is the absolute abolition of all moral restraint, as with the *Assassins* and other criminal societies—the separation in material respects is otherwise ordered; i.e., it is made more continuous and more relative. When this method is employed, the initiate is in a condition nearer to that of the outsider. He needs to be tested and educated up to the point of grasping the whole or the center of the association. Thereby, however, a protection is obviously afforded to the latter, an isolation of it from the external world, which goes beyond the protection gained from the entrance oath. Care is taken. . . . that the still untried shall also have very little to betray if he would, inasmuch as, within the secret principle which surrounds the society as a whole, graduated secrecy produces at the same time an elastic zone of defense for that which is inmost and essential. The antithesis of the exotic and the esoteric members, as we have it in the case of the Pythagoreans, is the most striking form of this protective arrangement. The circle of the only partially initiated constitutes to a certain extent a buffer area against the totally uninitiated. As it is everywhere the double function of the "mean" to bind and to separate—or, rather, as it plays only one role, which we, however, according to our apperceptive categories, and according to the angle of our vision, designate as uniting and separating—so in this connection the unity of activities which externally clash with each other appears in the clearest light. Precisely because the lower grades of the society constitute a mediating transition to the actual center of the secret, they bring about the gradual compression of the sphere of repulsion around the same, which affords more secure protection to it than the abruptness of a radical standing wholly without or wholly within could secure. . . .

In spite of the actual quantitative delimitation of every real society, there is still a considerable number the inner tendency of which is: Whoever is not excluded is included. Within certain political, religious, and class peripheries, everyone is reckoned as of the association who satisfies certain conditions, mostly involuntary, and given along with his existence. Whoever, for example, is born within the territory of a state, unless peculiar circumstances make him an exception, is a member of the highly complex civic society. The member of a given social class is, as a matter of course, included in the conventions and forms of attachment pertaining to the same, if he does not voluntarily or involuntarily make himself an outsider. The extreme is offered by the claim of a church that it really comprehends the totality of the human race, so that only historical accidents, sinful obduracy, or a special divine purpose excludes any persons from the religious community which ideally anticipates even those not in fact within the pale. Here is, accordingly, a parting of two ways, which evidently signify a differentiation in principle of the sociological meaning of societies in general, however they may be confused, and their definiteness toned down in practice. In contrast with the fundamental principle: Whoso is not expressly excluded is included, stands the other: Whoever is not expressly included is excluded. The latter type is presented in the most decisive purity by the secret societies. The unlimited character of their separation, conscious at every step of their development, has, both as cause and as effect, the rule that whoever is not expressly adopted is thereby expressly excluded. The Masonic fraternity could not better support its recently much emphasized assertion that it is not properly a secret order, than through its simultaneously published ideal of including all men, and thus of representing humanity as a whole. . . .

Since the secret society occupies a plane of its own—few individuals belonging to more than one secret society—it exercises a kind of absolute sovereignty over its members. This control prevents conflicts among them which easily arise in the open type of co-ordination. The "King's peace" (*Burgfriede*) which should prevail within every society is promoted in a formally unsurpassed manner within secret societies through their peculiar and exceptional limitations. It appears, indeed, that, entirely apart from this more realistic ground, the mere form of secrecy as such holds the associates safer than they would otherwise be from disturbing influences, and thereby make concord more feasible. An English statesman has attempted to discover the source of the strength of the English cabinet in the secrecy which surrounds it. Everyone who has been active in public life knows that a small collection of people may be brought to agreement much more easily if their transactions are secret.

Corresponding with the peculiar degree of cohesion within secret societies is the definiteness of their centralization. They furnish examples of an unlimited and blind obedience to leaders, such as occurs elsewhere of course; but it is the more remarkable here, in view of the frequent anarchical and negative character toward all other law. The more criminal the purposes of a secret society, the more unlimited is likely to be the power of the leaders, and the more cruel its exercise. The *Assassins* in Arabia; the *Chauffeurs*, a predatory society with various branches that ravaged in France, particularly in the eighteenth century; the *Gardunas* in Spain, a criminal society that, from the seventeenth to the beginning of the nineteenth century, has relations with the Inquisition— all these, the nature of which was lawlessness and rebellion, were under one commander, whom they sometimes set over themselves, and whom they obeyed without criticism or limitation. To this result not merely the correlation of demand from freedom and for union contributes, as we have observed it in case of the severity of the ritual, and in present instance it binds together the extremes of the two tendencies. The excess of freedom, which such societies possessed with reference to all otherwise valid norms, had to be offset, for the sake of the equilibrium of interests, by a similar excess of submissiveness and resigning of the individual will. More essential, however, was probably the necessity of centralization, which is the condition of existence for the secret society, and especially when, like the criminal band, it lives off the surrounding society, when it mingles with this society in many radiations and actions, and when it is seriously threatened with treachery and diversion of interests the moment the most invariable attachment to one center ceases to prevail. It is consequently typical that the secret society is exposed to peculiar dangers, especially when, for any reasons whatever, it does not develop a powerfully unifying authority. . . .

It is nothing but an exaggeration of this formal motive when, as is often the case, secret societies are led by unknown chiefs. It is not desirable that the lower grades should know whom they are obeying. This occurs primarily, to be sure, for the sake of guarding the secret. . . . This, however, is by no means the only utility of the secret headship. It means rather the most extreme and abstract sublimation of centralized coherence. The tension between adherent and leader reaches the highest degree when the latter withdraws from the range of vision. There remains the naked, merciless fact, so to speak, modified by no personal coloring, of obedience pure and simple, from which the super-ordinated subject has disappeared. If even obedience to an impersonal authority, to a mere magistracy, to the representative of an objective law, has the character of unbending severity, this obedience mounts still higher, to the level of an uncanny absoluteness, so soon as the commanding personality remains in principle hidden. For if, along with the visibility of the ruler, and acquaintance with him, it must be admitted that individual suggestion, the force of the personality, also vanish from the commanding relationship; yet at the same time there also disappear from the relationship the limitations, i.e., the merely relative, the "human," so to speak, which are attributes of the single person who can be encountered in actual experience. In this case obedience must be stimulated by the feeling of being subject to an intangible power, not strictly defined, so far as its boundaries are concerned; a power nowhere to be seen, but for that reason everywhere to be expected. The sociologically universal coherence of a group through the unity of the commanding authority is, in the case of the secret society with unknown headship, shifted into a *focus imaginarius*, and it attains therewith its most distinct and intense form. . . .

Anonymous

Reception of a Carbonaro

The *Preparatore* (preparer) leads the *Pagan* (uninitiated) who is to become a member, blindfold, from the closet of reflextion to the door of the Baracca. He knocks irregularly; the *Copritore* (coverer) says to the second assistant, "A Pagan knocks at the door." The second assistant repeats this to the first, who repeats it to the Grand Master; at every communication the Grand Master strikes a blow with an axe.

> GRAND MASTER.   See who is the rash being, who dares to trouble our sacred labours.

This question having passed through the assistants and *Copritore* to the *Preparatore,* he answers through an opening in the door.

> PREPARATORE.   It is a man whom I have found wandering in the forest.
>
> GR. M.   Ask his name, country and profession.

Reprinted from Anonymous (perhaps Bertoldi), *Memoirs of the Secret Societies of the South of Italy, Particularly the Carbonari.* London: John Murray, 1821, pp. 194–202.

The secretary writes the answer.

> GR. M.   Ask him his habitation—his religion.

The secretary notes them.

> GR. M.   What is it he seeks among us?
>
> PREP.   Light; and to become a member of our society.
>
> GR. M.   Let him enter.

(The Pagan is led into the middle of the assembly; and his answers are compared with what the Secretary had noted.)

> GR. M.   Mortal, the first qualities which we require, are
>   frankness, and contempt of danger. Do you feel that
>   you are capable of practising them?

After the answer, the Grand Master questions the candidate on morality and benevolence; and he is asked, if he has any effects, and wishes to dispose of them, being at the moment in danger of death; after being satisfied of his conduct, the Grand Master continues, "Well, we will expose you to trials that have some meaning—let him make the first journey." He is led out of the Baracca—he is made to journey through the forest—he hears the rustling of leaves—he is then led back to the door, as at his first entrance.

> GR. M.   What have you remarked during this first journey?

(The Pagan relates accordingly.)

> GR. M.   The first journey is the symbol of human virtue: the
>   rustling of leaves, and the obstacles you have met in
>   the road, indicate to you, that weak as we are, and
>   struggling in this vale of tears, we can only attain
>   virtue by good works, and under the guidance of
>   reason, &c. &c. Let him make the second journey.

(The Pagan is led away, and is made to pass through fire; he is made acquainted with the chastisement of perjury; and, if there is an opportunity, he is shown a head severed from the body, &c. &c. He is again conducted into the Baracca.)

GR. M.   The fire through which you have passed is the symbol of that flame of charity, which should be always kindled in our hearts, to efface the stains of the seven capital sins, &c. &c.

Make him approach the sacred throne, &c.

GR. M.   You must take an irrevocable oath; it offends neither religion nor the state, nor the rights of individuals; but forget not, that its violation is punished with death.

The Pagan declares that he will submit to it; the Master of the Ceremonies leads him to the throne, and makes him kneel on the white cloth.

GR. M.   Order!

The Oath.

I, N. N. promise and swear, upon the general statutes of the order, and upon this steel, the avenging instrument of the perjured, scrupulously to keep the secret of Carbonarism; and neither to write, engrave, or paint any thing concerning it, without have obtained a written permission. I swear to help my Good Cousins in case of need, as much as in me lies, and not to attempt any thing against the honour of their families. I consent, and wish, if I perjure myself, that my body may be cut in pieces, then burnt, and my ashes scattered to the wind, in order that my name may be held up to the execration of the Good Cousins throughout the earth. So help me God.

GR. M.   Lead him into the middle of the ranks (this is done). What do you wish? The Master of the Ceremonies suggests to the Pagan, to say *Light.*

GR. M.   It will be granted to you by the blows of my axe.

The Grand Master strikes with the axe—this action is repeated by all the apprentices—the bandage is removed from the eyes of the Pagan—the Grand Master and the Good Cousins hold their axes raised.

GR. M.   These axes will surely put you to death, if you become perjured. On the other hand, they will all strike in your defence, when you need them, and if you remain faithful. (*To the Master of the Ceremonies.*) Bring him near the throne, and make him kneel.

GR. M.   Repeat your oath to me, and swear to observe exactly the private institutions of this respectable Vendita.

THE CANDIDATE.   I ratify it and swear.

GR. M.   Holding the specimen of wood in his left hand, and suspending the axe over the head of the candidate with his right, says, To the great and divine Grand Master of the universe, and to St. Theobald, our protector—In the name and under the auspices of the Supreme Vendita of Naples, and in virtue of the power which has been conferred upon me in this respectable Vendita, I make, name and create you an apprentice Carbonaro.

The Grand Master strikes the specimen which is held over the Apprentice's head, thrice; he then causes him to rise, and instructs him in the sacred words and touch.

GR. M.   Master of the Ceremonies, let him be acknowledged by the apprentices.

The Assistants anticipate the execution of this order, by saying to the Grand Master, All is according to rule, just and perfect.

GR. M.   Assistants, tell the respective orders to acknowledge, henceforth, the Good Cousin N. N. as an active member of this Vendita, &c. &c.

The Symbolical Picture is explained to the new apprentice.

GR. M.   At what hour do the Carbonari terminate their sacred labours?

FIRST ASSISTANT.	As soon as the Sun no longer enlightens our forest.
GR. M.	What hour is it?
SECOND ASSISTANT.	The Sun no longer enlightens our forest.
GR. M.	Good Cousins, as the Sun no longer enlightens our forest, it is my intention to terminate our sacred labours. First, let us make a triple salutation (Vantaggio), to our Grand Master, divine and human, (Jesus Christ).
	——To St. Theobald, our protector, who has assisted us and preserved us from the eyes of the pagans—Order! To me,——&c.

The signs and salutations (Vantaggi) are performed.

GR. M.	I declare the labours ended; retire to your Baracche—retire in peace.

Reception to the Second Rank. The signs of the Masters are made, and they arrange themselves in order.

The Grand Master on this occasion is called the President—The assistants, Counsellors of the College of R. (Respectable) Carbonarism.

THE PRESIDENT.	At what hour do the Counsellors meet?
FIRST COUNSELLOR.	When the cock crows.
PRESIDENT.	Second Counsellor, what hour is it?
SECOND COUNSELLOR.	Noon by the Sun.

The Counsellors make the triple salutation to the Grand Master, divine and human, and to St. Theobald, and invoke their blessing on their labours.

The President puts on a robe, and takes the name of Pilate; the First Counsellor that of Caiaphas; the second that of Herod; the Adept (Esperto) calls himself the chief of the guards; the Master of the Ceremonies, the Godfather; the Good Cousins generally are called the *People.*

The Godfather blinds the eyes of the novice, and makes him journey through the forest; he afterwards leads him towards the President, who causes his crown of thorns, and specimen, to be brought, and questions him on the catechism of the apprentices.

THE PRESIDENT.	Good Cousin, your trials as a novice are not sufficient

to raise you to an equality with us; you must undergo more important trials; reflect upon it, and tell us your intention.

The Apprentice declares that he is ready to undergo the trials.

PRESIDENT.   Conduct him to the Olives.

He is led to the place so called—he is placed in a supplicating attitude, his hands lifted towards heaven—the Godfather causes him to repeat aloud:

If the pains I am about to suffer can be useful to mankind, I do not ask to be delivered from them. Thy will be done, and not mine.

PILAT.   Let him drain the cup of bitterness.

He is made to drink, and he is then led bound to Pilate.

PILAT.   Who is this you bring me?

CHIEF OF THE GUARDS. One accused of sedition; we found him in the midst of wretches who listened to him, and who are witnesses of his wicked precepts.

THE PEOPLE.   He is a seducer of the people, who, to govern despotically, and to overthrow our religion, calls himself the living God.

PILAT.   The crime is heavy; I cannot judge him alone. Take him to Caiaphas.

The Chief of the Guards accompanies him.

CHIEF OF THE GUARDS. Pilate sends you this man, to judge him according to his crimes.

CAIAP.   From what I have heard, he is guilty; his punishment belongs to the Sovereign. Lead him to Herod.

HEROD.   Who art thou?

The Godfather instructs the novice to say,

I am the Son of God.

THE PEOPLE. You hear him, he blasphemes, and deserves the severest punishment.

HEROD. Is it true that thou art the Son of the living God?

The Godfather instructs the novice to say,

Thou sayest it.

HEROD. People! This is a man who is beside himself; put a white robe upon him, and lead him to Pilate, to judge the man as he thinks fit.

The tunic is put upon the novice, he is led to Pilate who shows him to the people.

PILAT. The Prince sends me this man; what will you that I shall do to him?

THE PEOPLE. Condemn him.

PILAT. I will not condemn him without having heard him. Who are you? The Godfather for the novice—Jesus of Nazareth, King of the Jews.

PILAT. If he is a king, let a crown of thorns be put upon his head, and a sceptre in his hand: (turning towards the people) Are you satisfied?

THE PEOPLE. No; he deserves a greater punishment.

PILAT. Strip him, bind him to this column, and scourge him.

Pilate causes him to be again clothed, in a red robe; shows him to the people, and says,

PILAT. Are you satisfied: Behold the man.

THE PEOPLE. No, let him be crucified.

PILAT. I have done my duty; you wish his death; I give him up to you; I wash my hands of the deed; the innocent blood be upon you and on your children [After Pilate has washed his hands, the novice is delivered over to the people, who make him carry his cross to Calvary; his pardon is asked; he is made to kneel upon the white cloth; the President takes off the red robe, and says,

PRESIDENT.   Do you consent to take your second oath? [If he
                    consents, the bandage is taken from his eyes; he is
                    made to kneel on his left knee, with his right hand on
                    the axe. All the Good Cousins arrange themselves in
                    order.

Form of the Oath.

I, N. N. promise and swear before the Grand
Master of the universe, upon my word of honour,
and upon this steel, the avenging instrument of the
perjured, to keep scrupulously and inviolably the
secrets of Carbonarism; never to talk of those of the
Apprentices before the Pagans, nor of those of the
Masters before the Apprentices. As also, not to
initiate any person, nor to establish a Vendita,
without permission, and in a just and perfect
number—not to write or engrave the secrets—to help
even with my blood, if necessary, the Good Cousins
Carbonari, and to attempt nothing against the
honour of their families. I consent, if I perjure
myself, to have my body cut in pieces, then burnt,
and the ashes scattered to the wind, that my name
may remain in execration with all the Good Cousins
Carbonari spread over the face of the earth. So help
me God.

James Dewar

Masonic Ceremony

The drama of the third initiation ceremony is the most powerful of the Craft degrees. The candidate is made to represent the hero figure of Masonry, the principal architect of King Solomon's temple, Hiram Abiff. After being symbolically slain by a blow with a maul, the candidate is lowered into a mock grave and later 'raised' from it by the lodge Master. The Masonic legend does not, however, include the resurrection theme: the story says merely that Hiram Abiff's body was disinterred for a more honourable burial. The allegorical instruction of the third degree drama is that all Master Masons are raised from a 'figurative death' to a new way of life.

Before examining this aspect of the degree more fully, it should be said again that the entry of the Hiramic legend into Freemasonry cannot be traced. Hiram is mentioned in Old Testament accounts of the building of King Solomon's temple (I Kings 5 and 7 and II Chronicles 2, 3, and 4). Both accounts, however, tell of Hiram a metal-worker; although the name Hiram becomes Huram in Chronicles. So there is no Biblical source for Hiram, the principal architect of the temple; nor, of course, for his murder after refusal to part with the secrets of a master mason.

From James Dewar, *The Unlocked Secret, Freemasonry Examined,* London: William Kimber & Co., 1966, pp. 98–102, 158–160. Reprinted by permission of William Kimber & Co. Limited.

Consequently, many ideas to account for the rise of the Legend have been suggested. Among the favoured sources are both medieval operative masons and speculative Freemasons who could have brought to the craft a Rosicrucian influence. The Graham Manuscript is evidence that medieval masons had a similar legend concerning Noah's death and the attempts of his sons to lift their father's body from its grave in the hope of discovering secrets; and the Rosicrucian legend embraces the discovery of the tomb of Rosenkreuz, a tomb decorated with secret signs and containing documents.

Whatever the origin, or origins, of the Hiramic legend it belongs to those expressing the life-death cycle of the sun which in many ancient religions finds expression in a hero-figure whose noble death is followed by miraculous resurrection. Here the Masonic ritual shows how incomplete it is by comparison with that of religion. Hiram Abiff is not a figure who triumphs physically over death, nor does he belong to a Holy Family which, in the Christian religions, fulfils the deepest spiritual and psychological needs. The Masonic degree achieves, however, the central symbolism of rebirth for the Master Mason candidate, and, because the circumstances of Hiram's legendary death (a direct result of his tight-lipped steadfastness) it hammers home an important part of the philosophy of any secret society; better death than betrayal and dishonour.

There are embellishments upon the third-degree ceremony in Scotland and America which extend the play-acting of the Hiramic legend. In English lodges, after the candidate has been raised from his mock grave, instructed in the secret signs and word of the degree, and presented with his Master Mason's apron, the background to the murder of Hiram Abiff is explained to him. He is told that Hiram is first missed because plans and designs fail to appear. King Solomon orders a general muster of workmen and finds three are missing. Twelve other craftsmen who had been involved in the conspiracy but withdrew confess their part in the plot and King Solomon sends fifteen Fellow Crafts to search for Hiram. The Fellow Crafts find the grave and mark the spot with a sprig of acacia at its head.

Much of this part of the legend is enacted in some Scottish lodges where the ritual requires the candidate to retire before his mock death. When he returns to the lodge, sometimes blindfolded, the candidate is asked in turn by the Wardens and the Master for the secrets of a Master Mason. He refuses and is 'slain,' his body being lowered on to a sheet upon the lodge floor and covered. Once the candidate is in his mock grave, the lodge members act out the search for Hiram, the discovery of the 'grave' and the capture of the three murderers. Only then is the candidate 'raised.'

The American third-degree working offers similar dramatic elaboration, and more. Several candidates are taken together for the first part of the ceremony, then they all retire and return individually, in ignorance, of course, of the ceremony which is still to follow. When the candidate comes back into the lodge he is wearing a Master Mason's apron with a Junior Warden's collar (the collar being an allusion to Hiram Abiff, who was Junior Warden to King Solomon), and he is told that although he wears the uniform of a Master Mason the ceremony has not been completed. He is taken to the altar, which in American lodges is usually in the centre of the floor, and invited to pray, say 'Amen' when he has finished. On the word 'Amen,' the lodge members sing 'Nearer My God to thee', and he is blindfolded. Three lodge members play the parts of the murderers and are called Jubela, Jubelo and Jubelum. They ask the candidate for the secrets of a Master Mason and when he resists them, ill-treat him during a knock-about scene. Finally, he is 'murdered' in the traditional manner. There is the same play-acting of the roll call of workmen ordered by King Solomon, the search by fifteen Fellow Crafts and the eventual discovery of the 'body' and the 'killers.' Jubela, Jubelo and Jebelum are 'executed' in accordance with the Masonic penalties and with suitable cries from them.

After he has been 'raised,' the candidate is read a charge and a lecture and can then take a rest while he watches the ceremony repeated with the remaining candidates. All American candidates for the degree must know the obligations of the earlier degrees and are examined in them. They are also called upon to demonstrate the secret signs of their degrees before being presented with the membership certificate of a Master Mason.

The candles of the Master and his Wardens are referred to by Masons as 'the three lesser lights' of the lodge, the three 'great though emblematical lights in Freemasonry' being the Volume of the Sacred Law, the square and the compasses. In English lodges the third-degree ceremony is carried out by the light of the Master's candle only and when the candidate is lowered into the mock grave a clock may strike twelve or the hour be sounded on a gong. Often the Dead March from *Saul* is played upon the organ and the last chapter of Ecclesiastes ('Remember now thy Creator. . . .') is recited. Some Scottish lodges offer a funeral prayer over the mock grave and in the American ritual the lodge members walk around it three times, singing a funeral hymn.

All ritual owes much to play-acting. The first plays were performed as part of religious services and often the actors were members of trade guilds simply projecting themselves and their work. The use of drama helps to achieve the aim of ritual, which is to impress. If the amount of play-acting is reduced, so is the impact of the ritual, because long speeches of description and instruction are needed to replace dialogue and action. In this way, not only is the ritual often made less effective, but it can speak only to the highly literate, for it is a common experience that as speeches become longer and more formal so do both the words and the language.

The loss of colour and theatrical elements from religious rituals appears to have left many Protestant men with a deep, if often unrecognised, sense of deprivation. Dr. David Steel, a Minister of the Church of Scotland who became a Freemason during 1952 while in East Africa, said in a television interview:

> The Church in Scotland, I think largely through the Puritan influence of the eighteenth century, has become somewhat barren of imagery, somewhat suspicious of ritual. . . . I think myself that this subconsciously is one of the attractions of Freemasonry to men in Scotland. They find in it this richness of symbol and imagery which articulates deep feelings which they may have, not in any rational sense, but in an imaginative way.

The basic effect on the individual of the drama and ceremonial of the three Craft degrees is, nevertheless, that sought by all initiation rites—the closest possible identification of the new-comer with the group. Freemasonry spreads this process over three ceremonies, each separated by a minimum of a month's waiting, and throughout the ceremonial it is emphasised that within the lodge the initiate can slowly progress to higher ranks.

The dark suits and ties, aprons, the passwords and secret signs, all speak of a special and closed group, but rank is declared by the uniform of Masonry. The apron and other regalia denote various levels of authority within it. The apron is a garment particularly appropriate to Masonry not only for its association with working craftsmen but also because it was worn by candidates seeking admission to some of the ancient mysteries. Once Freemasons enjoyed considerable freedom about the decoration, shape and size of aprons. Today the Grand Lodges have their rules about Masonic clothing.

The initiate is presented with a plain white apron of lambskin from fourteen to sixteen inches wide, twelve to fourteen inches deep, rectangular and with a pointed flap, bib, or fall. The strings are white. The apron of the Fellow Craft is the same, with the addition only of two sky-blue rosettes at the lower corners. The Master Mason's apron is the same size, but with sky-blue lining and edging of the same colour not more than two inches wide around apron and flap; also in the centre of the flap is placed a third sky-blue rosette and from beneath the flap extend two bands, or strings, of the same colour, attached to silver tassels.

The Master and past Masters wear, in place of the three rosettes on the Master Mason's apron, perpendicular lines upon horizontal lines, thereby forming three sets of two right-angles, the length of the horizontal lines to be two inches and a half each and of the perpendicular lines one inch each. These emblems which replace the sky-blue rosettes are to be of silver or of sky-blue ribbon. The collars of the lodge officers are of light blue ribbon four inches broad and from them hang the jewels of office. A past Master's collar incorporates a central band of silver braid a quarter of an inch wide.

In many American lodges only a white apron is worn by all ranks, but grades are denoted by the way in which it is worn. An Entered Apprentice has the flap of his apron pointing upwards, the Fellow Craft one of the lower corners tucked under his belt, and the Master Mason both corners tucked up. It is still customary for the Master Masons's apron to have a narrow edging of blue.

White is the colour of purity, but the source and possible associations of the blue of the Master Mason's apron continue to cause speculation. It has been suggested that the sky-blue was adopted from the ribbon of the Order of the Garter. This was a light blue upon the Order's institution by Edward III in 1348 and remained so until the early eighteenth century when the present darker shade was adopted. The suggestions finds support in the fact that England's Grand Lodge officers wear regalia of garter blue, with the exception of the Grand Stewards, whose regalia is red—the colour of the ribbon of the Order of the Bath. Scotland's Grand Lodge officers have adopted the green of the ribbon of the Order of the Thistle and the Irish Grand Lodge and light blue of the Order of St. Patrick. Another explanation for the blue edging of the Master Mason's apron may be suggested by Numbers 15:37–39:

And the Lord spake unto Moses, saying, 'Speak unto the children of Israel, and bid them that they make them fringes in the borders of their garments throughout their generation, and that they put upon the fringe of the borders a ribband of blue: And it shall be unto you for a fringe, that ye may look upon it, and remember all the commandments of the Lord, and do them; and that ye seek not after your own heart and your own eyes, after which ye used to go a whoring.'

The initiation ceremonies instruct the candidate in the roles of the principal lodge officers and bring him into physical contact with them as he is accompanied on perambulations around the lodge and exchanges hand grips. No satisfying explanation can be found for the derivation of the title of the first officer he meets, the Tyler; the medieval lodges of working masons had Wardens and, in Scotland, Deacons. The use of both titles is made the more reminiscent of church officers by the wands the Deacons carry as symbols of office.

Freemasonry's initiation ceremonies conspire in their ritual to satisfy deep longings for drama and brotherhood by using the trappings of religion. They achieve their purposes, for the majority of Masons take membership seriously and have a loyalty strong enough to protect the secrecy of the movement. There remain the dangers associated with almost any ritual; it may cease to speak to men in terms that they can understand or relate to contemporary experiences; and its practice may become an end in itself more important than the ideas it seeks to express.

Ceremony of Raising to the Third Degree. (The Lodge is opened in the Second Degree, and the Candidate examined according to the following catechism.)

WORSHIPFUL MASTER. Brethren, Brother John Smith is this evening a Candidate to be raised to the Third Degree, but it is first requisite that he give proofs of proficiency in the Second. I shall therefore proceed to put the necessary questions. How were you prepared to be passed to the Second Degree?

CANDIDATE. In a manner somewhat similar to the former, save that in this Degree I was not hoodwinked. My left arm, breast, and right knee were made bare, and my left heel was slipshod.

WORSHIPFUL MASTER. On what were you admitted?

CANDIDATE. The Square

WORSHIPFUL MASTER. What is a Square?

CANDIDATE. An angle of ninety degrees, or the fourth part of circle.

WORSHIPFUL MASTER. What are the peculiar objects of research in this Degree?

CANDIDATE. The hidden mysteries of Nature and Science.

WORSHIPFUL MASTER. As it is the hope of reward that sweetens labour, where did our ancient Brethren go to receive their wages?

CANDIDATE. In the middle chamber of King Solomon's temple.

WORSHIPFUL MASTER. How did they receive them?

CANDIDATE. Without scruple or diffidence.

WORSHIPFUL MASTER. Why in this peculiar manner?

CANDIDATE. Without scruple, well knowing they were justly entitled to them; and without diffidence, from the great reliance they placed on the integrity of their employers in those days.

WORSHIPFUL MASTER. What were the names of the two great pillars which were placed at the porchway or entrance of King Solomon's temple?

CANDIDATE. That on the left was called Boaz, and that on the right, Jachin.

WORSHIPFUL MASTER. What are their separate and conjoint significations?

CANDIDATE. The former denotes in strength, the latter, to establish; and when conjoined, stability, for God said, 'In strength will I establish this Mine house to stand firm for ever.'

WORSHIPFUL MASTER. There are the usual questions. I will put others if any Brother wishes me to do so. (*They seldom do.*)

Do you pledge your honour as a man and your fidelity as a Craftsman that you will steadily persevere through the ceremony of being raised to the sublime Degree of a Master Mason?

CANDIDATE. I do.

WORSHIPFUL MASTER. Do you likewise pledge yourself, under the penalty of both your Obligations, that you will conceal what I shall now impart to you with the same strict caution as the other secrets in Masonry?

CANDIDATE. I do.

WORSHIPFUL MASTER. Then I will entrust you with a test of merit, which is a pass grip and a pass word, leading to the Degree to which you seek to be admitted. The pass grip is given by a distinct pressure of the thumb between the second and third joints of the hand. This pass grip demands a pass word, which is TUBAL CAIN.

Tubal Cain was the first artificer in metals. The import of the word is wordly possessions. You must be particularly careful to remember this word, as without it you cannot gain admission into a Lodge in a superior Degree. Pass, Tubal Cain.

(Senior Deacon leads Candidate to door, where he salutes the Worshipful Master with signs of first two Degrees. He retires to be prepared for the ceremony. Both arms, breast, and knees are bared and both feet slippered. He wears the Fellow Crafts apron. Meanwhile, the Lodge is opened in the Third Degree. The Deacons lay a sheet upon the floor near to the Worshipful Master's pedestal. On the sheet is drawn an 'open grave', surrounded by skulls and cross-bones. The Tyler gives the Second Degree knocks.)

INNER GUARD. *(Step and Penal sign of Third Degree—right thumb to the left of the navel, thumb at right-angle to hand held palm down.)* Brother Junior Warden, there is a report.

JUNIOR WARDEN. *(Step and sign.)* Worshipful Master, there is a report.

WORSHIPFUL MASTER. Brother Junior Warden, inquire who wants admission.

JUNIOR WARDEN. *(Cuts sign.)* Brother Inner Guard, see who wants admission.

INNER GUARD. *(Cuts sign, opens the door.)* Whom have you there?

TYLER. Brother John Smith, who has been regularly initiated into Freemasonry, passed to the Degree of a Fellow Craft, and has made such further progress as he hopes will entitle him to be raised to the sublime Degree of a Master Mason, for which ceremony he is properly prepared.

INNER GUARD. How does he hope to obtain the privileges of the Third Degree?

TYLER. By the help of God, the united aid of the Square and Compasses, and the benefit of a pass word.

INNER GUARD. Is he in possession of the pass word?

TYLER. Will you prove him? *(Inner Guard offers right hand,*

and receives pass grip and pass word from Candidate.)

INNER GUARD. Halt, while I report to the Worshipful Master. *(Closes door, takes step and sign.)* Worshipful Master, Brother John Smith, who has been regularly initiated into Freemasonry, passed to the Degree of Fellow Craft, and has made such further progress as he hopes will entitle him to be raised to the sublime Degree of a Master Mason, for which ceremony he is properly prepared.

WORSHIPFUL MASTER. How does he hope to obtain the privileges of the Third Degree?

INNER GUARD. By the help of God, united aid of the Square and Compasses, and the benefit of a pass word.

WORSHIPFUL MASTER. We acknowledge the powerful aid by which he seeks admission; do you, Brother Green, vouch that he is in possession of the pass word?

INNER GUARD. I do, Worshipful Master.

WORSHIPFUL MASTER. Then let him be admitted in due form. Brother Deacons.

(All lights are put out except the candle by the Worshipful Master's pedestal. Junior Deacon puts kneeling stool in position, and both Deacons go to door. Inner Guard opens it and places the points of an open pair of compasses to the Candidate's breasts. He holds the compasses aloft to show that he has done so. Senior Deacon leads Candidate to kneeling stool.)

SENIOR DEACON. Advance as a Fellow Craft, first as an Entered Apprentice.

(Candidate takes step and gives First Degree sign, then another step and makes Second Degree sign.)

WORSHIPFUL MASTER. Let the Candidate kneel while the blessing of Heaven is invoked on what we are about to do. . . .

Abner Cohen

The Politics of Ritual Secrecy

There are about six million men in the world today who are the members of what has been described as the largest secret society on earth—Freemasonry. The overwhelming majority of these men live in the highly industrialised societies of western Europe and America and almost all are members of the wealthy and professional classes.

In Britain alone there are about three-quarters of a million Freemasons (see Dewar 1966: 46–47). They are organised within local lodges which are ritually, ideologically and bureaucratically supervised by the grand lodges of England, Scotland and Ireland. They meet periodically in their local centres and, behind the locked and well-guarded doors of their temples, they wear the colourful and elaborately embroidered regalia, carry the jewels, swords and other emblems of office, and perform their 'ancient' secret rituals.

The bulk of these rituals is concerned with the initiation of new members or the promotion of existing members to higher degrees. These rites of passage involve the enactment of lengthy dramas, in the course of which candidates go through phases of death and rebirth, are entrusted with new secret signs, passwords and hand-clasps, and are made to take oaths, under the threat of

Abner Cohen, "The Politics of Ritual Secrecy," *Man,* **6** (September, 1971), 427–448. Reprinted with permission by the Royal Anthropological Institute, London, and the author.

horrifying sanctions, not to betray these secrets to outsiders. Recurring within these rites of passage are episodes from the life and career of a mythological hero, Hiram Abiff, who is said to have designed the Temple of Solomon. In the face of continual criticism and opposition from the Church, Freemasons go out of their way to emphasise their faith in the Supreme Being, to whom they refer as 'The Great Architect of the Universe' or, at times, 'The Grand Geometrician', and prominently display the Holy Book[1] in all their meetings.

There is a vast literature on Freemasonry. A large part of it is concerned with controversies about the origins of the cult or the sources of its mythology and rituals. The long essay in the *Encyclopedia Britannica* is purely historical. Another section of this literature consists of attacks, particularly by Roman Catholic clergymen, against the movement, or of apologetic reactions by Masons against these attacks. A third section consists of speculations or disclosures about the secret rituals of the craft.

Although a great deal is now known about its history and rituals, very little is known about its social significance, or its involvement in the system of the distribution and exercise of power in our society. Our ignorance is only partly due to the secrecy in which the movement is enveloped. Freemasons repeatedly point out that they are not a secret society but a society with secret rituals. By this they mean that it is only their rituals that are secret, but that membership is not secret. But the anomalous situation today is that while these rituals are no longer secret, hardly anything is known about membership. Legally, every lodge is obliged by law to submit a list of its members to the local Clerk of the Peace. But neither clerks of the peace, nor the Masonic authorities are obliged to make public the full list of members (see Dewar 1967:103–104). Some scanty bits of information appear in the newspapers every now and then about individual Masons and some Masons may also in one way or another reveal to friends their membership, but on the whole the majority do not go out of their way to make their membership known.

A great deal of this reluctance to disclose membership is probably the result, not of the teachings of Freemasonry as such, but of the general tendency of members of the middle and upper classes, from which Masons are recruited, to be highly individualistic and to value privacy in their lives. This is indeed one of the main reasons why so little sociological research in general has been carried out in Britain among these classes.

Added to this difficulty is the immensity of the scale of our social groups and settlements, with the result that amidst our massive and highly impersonal urban milieux, it is too difficult to identify and locate members or to be acquainted with their circles or to know much about their economic, political or other social roles.

Finally, it must be remembered that sociologists are often so immersed in the very culture of which Freemasonry is a part, that some of them are hardly aware even of its existence or of the significance of its informal symbolism.

Some of these epistemological and methodological difficulties can be overcome if Freemasonry is studied as it is practised in a totally different social and cultural context from that of our own, within relatively small-scale societies. I believe that we can learn a great deal about our own culture generally when we study its forms in foreign lands. Most anthropologists working in preindustrial societies have so far, for a variety of reasons, shied away from investigating the functions of Western cultural forms in these societies.

Even a casual look through the pages of the year books of the Masonic grand lodges will be sufficient to show that relatively large numbers of Masonic lodges exist in nearly all the new states of Africa and Asia. (There are 44 in Nigeria, 43 in Ghana, and well over 100 in India, to take only random examples.) There is practically nothing whatever known about the social significance of these Masonic lodges.

I shall discuss here the organisation and functioning of Freemasonry in Sierra Leone, west Africa. The interplay between individual motives and structural constraints in the local development and functioning of this cult will be analysed. In conclusion some observations about the social significance and political potentialities of Freemasonry within industrial societies will be made.

The Creoles. There are today seventeen Masonic lodges in Sierra Leone, all in Freetown, the capital. Seven of these follow the English Constitution of Freemasonry. They are organised under a District Grand Lodge and are ultimately supervised by the Grand Lodge of England. The remaining ten lodges follow the Scottish Constitution of Freemasonry, are organised under a separate District Grand Lodge, and are ultimately supervised by the Grand Lodge of Scotland (see table 1). There are no Masonic Lodges in Sierra Leone which follow the third 'sister' Constitution of Ireland.

I estimate that there are about 2,000 members in these lodges. Only a handful of these are Europeans, mainly British, although it was originally British officials in the colonial administration who established Freemasonry in Sierra Leone.[2] Most of these Europeans are today concentrated in one particular lodge, along with other Africans. Some of the British members have been in the movement in Britain before going to Sierra Leone and want to

Table 1 The Freemasonic Lodges in Freetown by Name, Year of Consecreation, and Constitution

English Constitution		Scottish Constitution	
Name	Year of Consecration	Name	Year of Consecration
Freetown	1882*		
St. George	1894*		
Rokell	1899*	S. L. Highland	1905*
Loyal	1914	Academic	1914*
About thirty years with no change			
Progressive	1947		
Wilberforce	1947		
		Tranquility	1949
		Harmony	1950*
		Travellers	1950
Granville	1952		
About thirteen years with no change			
		Mount Aureol	1965
		Sapiens	1966
		Delco	1966
		Leona	1968
		Earl of Eglington and Winton	1968

* Lodges with asterisk have been granted Royal Arch Status.

continue their membership through affiliation within a Freetown lodge. A few have joined in Sierra Leone mainly in order to become part of the movement in Britain when they return home. These find joining much easier in Sierra Leone than in Britain. My impression is that on the whole these European Masons play no significant role in the activities of the local lodges at present and at least some of them seem to be lukewarm in their attendance at the regular meetings of the movement.

The bulk of the Masons in Freetown are thus Africans, and the Grand Masters and the other important office-bearers in both district grand lodges are African.

With very few individual exceptions, all the Africans in the Masonic lodges are Creoles, the descendants of the slaves who were emancipated by the British between the 1780's and 1850's, and were duly settled in the 'Province of Freedom', the Freetown Peninsula, which was bought for the purpose from the local Temne chiefs (see Fyfe 1962; Porter 1963; Peterson 1969). The Creoles are predominantly literate, highly educated, and occupationally differentiated. They number only 41,783 in the whole of Sierra Leone, with 37, 560 of them concentrated in the Freetown Peninsula, and 27,730 in the city of Freetown itself. The remaining 4,223 are scattered among the provincial towns and are mostly civil servants and teachers whose homes are in Freetown. (For census details, see Central Statistics Office, 1965.) The Creoles are thus essentially metropolitan. Although they comprise only 1.9 per cent of the total population, they dominate the civil service, the judiciary and the other major professions of medicine, law, engineering, university and high school teaching. A relatively substantial number of them have completed university training in Britain or in the U.S.A.

From the very beginning of their settlement in Sierra Leone, the Creoles made a bid to have a new start in their cultural life. They adopted English names, English styles of dress, education, religion, etiquette, art, music, and a general English style of life. Even today they can truly be said to be in many ways more English than the English. I have indeed heard Creole men who have visited 'swinging Britain' recently express personal shock and disillusionment at the departure of the English from their 'proper' tradition which, in the Creole ideology, is synonymous with civilisation and enlightenment. It is certainly no exaggeration that has led them so often to be called 'The Black Englishmen'.

After a period of interaction with the Creoles on the basis of equality and comradeship, the British administrators turned their backs on them and began to resent their attempts to be equal partners in British civilisation and in the sharing of political power with them. The British administrators gradually segregated themselves from Creole company and British writers and travellers poured scorn and ridiculed their 'rubbishy' White culture and their 'aping' of English customs and ways of life. But, as Banton (1957: 96–120) points out, their culture is very far from being merely the blind result of any superficial aping of English ways. On the contrary, it represents a unique and highly sophisticated culture combining different traits, both English and non-English, in a new way. Anyone who has had close personal contacts with the Creoles would know that their style of life is genuine and natural and is deeply rooted in their personality structure and entrenched in their thinking and in their way of life. It is a culture well worth investigating in its own right.

Although they originally hailed from different parts of west Africa (principally from Nigeria) and carried different cultural traditions, the Creoles managed in the course of only a few decades to develop a homogenous culture of their own and to set themselves sharply apart, both culturally and socially, from the rest of the population of Sierra Leone, to whom they referred derisively as the 'Aboriginies'. (For a detailed account, see Peterson 1969). During the second half of the nineteenth century and the early decades of the present century they attempted to control the Natives,[3] but the British colonial administration, for a variety of considerations, thwarted that attempt (see Fyfe 1962: 614–620). If it had not been for this British policy, the Creoles would have probably succeeded in achieving the same degree of overall domination that has been accomplished by the Americo-Liberians, a similar minority with a similar origin, in neighbouring Liberia (see Libenow 1969).

Until about the end of the first world war, the Creoles were prominent in business. But since then a number of factors have led to the rapid decline of their businesses and to the transfer of their resources and of their energies into the training and recruitment of civil servants and professionals (see Porter 1963). Extensive biographical evidence shows how one successful businessman after another spent his fortune, not on the development of his business, but on giving his children higher education in Britain or America. Almost invariably the succeeding generation preferred the highly lucrative, stable, and socially esteemed positions of the professions and government service, so Creole businesses virtually died out, to be taken over by Lebanese, British, and Indian business firms who are still dominant today.

Creole power today stems from two major resources. The first is the extensive property in land and in housing in Freetown and in the rest of the Freetown Peninsula which they control. This property has greatly appreciated in value since the end of the second world war, more particularly so since independence, because of an increasing demand by foreign diplomatic missions, by wealthy Sierra Leoneans from the interior of the country, and by the rapidly expanding government administration. This property is freehold, while all the land in the other provinces of the country, in what was formerly referred to as the Protectorate, is still 'tribal' land which cannot be sold. Their second source of power is their predominance in the civil service and in the professions.

Both these strongholds are now being seriously challenged by the tribesmen of the provinces, particularly by the Mende (30.9 per cent of the population) and the Temne (29.8 per cent of the population; see Central Statistical Office 1965). By their sheer voting power, these non-Creole Sierra Leoneans completely dominate the executive and the legislature and their politicians have been frequently harassing the Creoles and denouncing them as foreigners. The Temne maintain that the very land on which the Creoles have developed their society and culture, the Freetown Peninsula is theirs and that their forefathers were tricked into selling it to the British for a trivial price for the purpose of settling the Creoles (see Fyfe 1964: 112–113). It is significant that even now, the Creoles are still legally referred to as 'Non-Native'. And, as rapidly increasing numbers of 'Natives' are becoming educated and trained, Creole predominance in the civil service and in the professions is becoming increasingly more precarious.

The cleavage between the Creoles and the Natives has dominated Sierra Leone politics throughout this century. This cleavage is symbolically represented in the very flag of the state. The committee which designed the flag chose blue to represent 'those who came from across the seas', namely the Creoles, green for the native inhabitants, and white, signifying peace—or rather, the wish for peace—separating them. But the cleavage is becoming deeper, though its processes are operating behind new slogans and new identities. Many Creoles today claim that they are facing not just the threat of losing their property and their positions, but virtual physical annihilation and they quote in support of this claim various pronouncements by politicians and others, particularly in the provinces.

From the figures quoted earlier, it should be evident that nearly one in every three Creole men in Freetown is a Mason. Creole Masons do not hide the fact that Masonry in Sierra Leone is overwhelmingly Creole. But they argue at length that this is not the result of any kind of policy of exclusion. They invariably mention some names of non-Creole Sierra Leoneans who are Masons. The name of one man in particular was mentioned to me over and over again by different Creole Masons. A creole Mason will eagerly tell you that there are many non-Creole Sierra Leoneans in the movement. But when you ask specifically whether there are such members in his own lodge, the answer will often be that: 'It so happens that there is no one in our own lodge, but there are many in the other lodges'. There is no doubt that there are a few Natives in the lodges but their number is insignificant and for a variety of reasons which will become clear later their membership is only nominal. It is a fact that all the important figures in the Masonic movement, including the two Grand District Masters, are Creole. No native name is ever mentioned in the newspapers in connexion with Freemasonry and all the announcements of funerals and obituaries of deceased Masons which I have been able to see or hear include no Natives.

I do not myself think that there is any consciously formulated policy of excluding non-Creole Sierra Leoneans from membership. Many Masons think that non-Creoles are rare in the movement either because they are not interested, or because they are Muslims, or because they cannot afford the expense, or simply that they are not sufficiently educated. Many Creoles would also add that the Natives have their own secret society, the 'Poro', to which they are always affiliated. The Natives do not in fact need to become members in the Masonic movement. More than that, while there is a good deal of pressure on Creole men to join the movement, there is a good deal of pressure on Natives *not* to join it.[4]

The Incidence of Membership.   As with every other cult, individual Masons mention a wide variety of motives for joining the movement and remaining within it. Some join because they personally want to, but others join because of pressure. Often a man may join initially for one motive, but develop others after joining. The same man may emphasise different motives for being a Mason at different times. A man who joined as a result of pressure may develop motives or sentiments that are individual and personal. If we consider the sentiments, motives, and circumstances of each individual membership, we will find that each is a unique case and, when questioned, Masons often offer conscious and rational considerations for their membership.

   This, of course, is only one side of the story and it will fail by itself to tell us anything about Freemasonry as an institution in its own right or about the structural circumstances which keep it alive as a going concern. The structural consequences of Freemasonic activity are certainly largely unintended by individual Masons, as each individual's first concern is his own interests. There is thus a dialectical relation between the individual and the group. In other words, although individual members seem to be acting freely and rationally, their action is nevertheless conditioned largely unconsciously by structural factors which to some extent constrain a man to behave in certain ways. Thus, the collective and the individual are closely related, though for analytical purposes they should be kept apart if we are to understand the social significance of the movement. I want to avoid at this stage discussing this problem in the abstract and will thus proceed to consider briefly the multiplicity and complexity of factors underlying membership.

   Like many other ritual systems, Freemasonry offers a body of beliefs and practices which have intrinsic value. It provides a world view which includes the place of man in the universe. The literature of speculative Freemasonry contains a large number of treatises on metaphysics and theology written by men who are passionate in their search for what they believe to be the truth. In Freetown I met young Masons who spent a good deal of their spare time reading Masonic literature for sheer intellectual satisfaction.

Some men join the movement in the belief that the secrets which they will acquire contain vital intellectual and mystical formulae. This belief is sustained for long after joining as more and more secrets and rituals are unfolded to the Mason when he passes to higher degrees within the order.

Many of the Masons in Freetown with whom I talked stressed the personal satisfaction which they derived from the regular, frequent and extensive rituals and ceremonies of the lodge. Some of these Masons said, in explanation, that after all they were Africans and thus fond of the type of drama that the movement provided. A particularly powerful sentiment in this respect is Freemasonic ceremonial connected with the death of a 'brother'. The Creoles are intensely concerned with death, and funerals are great public events, often attended by thousands of people, depending on the status of the deceased. Deaths and funerals are regularly announced on the national radio in special bulletins, and often the lodge or lodges connected with a deceased man are summoned to the funeral by a special announcement on the radio. Lodges under the English Masonic constitution are prohibited by special rules of the Grand Lodge of England from going out in regalia to attend a public funeral, although they are allowed by special permission to appear in regalia within the church for the funeral service of a brother. But this prohibition does not exist within the Scottish constitution to which the greater number of Freetown lodges belong. Many of the members of English lodges are however also affiliated within Scottish lodges, so that their funerals are often attended formally by their lodges of affiliation, in regalia. The deceased man is 'laid out' in his formal black suit, with his full Masonic regalia decorating him, for hours before the funeral service and large numbers of people file past. When the coffin is finally covered, the regalia is taken off the body and placed on top. Masons under the Scottish constitution proceed in their regalia to the burial ground and when the Christian burial service is over, the Masons perform a special service at the grave to send their deceased brother off to the 'Highest Lodge'. It is indeed the dream of many Creole men with whom I talked to be buried with all the pomp and colour of the Masonic ceremonial, and I have no doubt that this is an important source of satisfaction for members of the movement. Some of the obituaries in the newspapers also carry photographs of the deceased in their Masonic regalia.

A second body of intrinsic values that men find in Freemasonry is the

'system of morality' that it offers. A great deal of the organisation and ceremonial of the movement is concerned with the development and maintenance
of a true brotherhood among its members. Members are asked specifically to
'fraternise' with one another, and a good deal of the time and resources of the
lodges is devoted to this end. The regular ritual sessions of the lodge are
followed by institutionalised, lavish banqueting and drinking. The Creoles
generally drink heavily and many cynics in Freetown say that men take to
Masonry primarily for 'boozing'. The lodge is indeed very much an exclusive
club.

One important aspect of Freemasonry as a brotherhood is the elaborate
organisation of mutual help which it develops, and there is no doubt that the
welfare and social security benefits that it offers attract some to the movement.
Freemason welfare services in Britain are indeed among the most lavish and
efficient. Many of their benevolent institutions are patronised by members of
the Royal Family. In the United States this aspect of the movement is even
more pronounced. In Freetown, no formal benevolent institutions have been
established yet. Such institutions take time to develop and nearly all Masons
have a network of kin who are under customary obligations to help in the hour
of need. Nevertheless, the lodges have provided help in many instances and
their care for aged members is particularly pronounced. Every lodge has an al-
moner who attends to cases of need and has for the purpose a special welfare
fund to which each member contributes regularly at a fixed rate. Thus, although a Creole may expect help in the time of need from his kin, he may still
join in order to secure for himself and for his family an additional measure of
support or security without the burden of kin obligations.

Some Masons mentioned also the importance of contacting brothers in
foreign lands. The Creoles travel very frequently to Britain and the U.S.A. in
the course of their educational and professional careers and they see in
Freemasonry an organisation that enables them to find helping and welcoming
brothers wherever they go. These brothers abroad tend to be at the same time
people of means and influence and their help can be substantial. I met a young
Creole on his way to Britain for the first time to study who told me that he
was a member of a Scottish lodge but that shortly before he left he affiliated
himself within one of the English Lodges in order to be able to make contacts
with brothers in both England and Scotland.

Freemasons are required by special rules to harbour no enmity against one
another and to settle any misunderstanding or tension between brothers
promptly and amicably. This must be particularly significant for many Creole

Masons who, in ordinary secular life, are caught by the tensions of competition for appointments and promotions and by the estrangement resulting from involvement in the hierarchical bureaucratic structures of the civil service or the professions.

One of the moral principles of the Freemasonic brotherhood which is particularly stressed by Creole Masons in Freetown is that no brother should flirt or commit adultery with the wife of another brother. This 'private' piece of morality is one of the mechanisms meant to reduce potential sources of tension and enmity between members, and is widely used in the organisation of many kinds of fraternities. Women are seen in many contexts as a source of tension between men. This is probably the main reason why Freemasonry and other secret societies of this kind are exclusively male organisations. Indeed one of the indirect consequences of Freemasonic membership among the Creoles is that it serves as a mechanism institutionalising the weaning of men from their wives. Wives and female relatives are invited only once a year to a Ladies' Night which each lodge holds. Even if a man belongs to only one lodge, he can spend two or three nights a week in ceremonial sessions, meetings of committees, or visiting other lodges, away from his wife. A substantial proportion of the members of a lodge are Office Bearers and their various duties necessitate frequent meetings. And, as many Creoles in Freetown are not only members in one lodge but are affiliated to one or more other lodges, their absence from their wives is indeed frequent and prolonged. Most Masonic meetings in Freetown start about 6:30 p.m. and go on in ceremonial and in banqueting until about 2 a.m. While often sharing with their husbands some of the benefits of Freemasonry, wives are annoyed by it. Many wives think that their husbands use lodge meetings as an alibi for visiting other women.

The Creoles are devout Christians and pride themselves on being monogamous. Also, Creole marriage is governed by British law, so that while a Mende or a Temne can marry according to customary law more than one wife, a Creole man would be prosecuted for bigamy if he married another wife. But it is an established 'customary' institution that most Creole men take 'outside women', support them, and have children by them. One of the peculiarities of the demography of the Creoles is that within the age group of twenty-five to forty-five, women substantially outnumber men. The effect of this numerical imbalance between the sexes is aggravated by the fact that men marry late. As there is a very strong pressure on Creoles to marry Creoles, the result is that there are many more unmarried women than men, and hence the institution of the 'outside woman'. The wealthier and the more eminent a man is the more outside wives he has. This is true even of eminent clergymen with the Church hierarchy, and is certainly an integral part of Creole culture (see Fashole-Luke 1968). Its functioning has required a good deal of 'distance' or avoidance between man and wife and from my observation I can say that Freemasonry serves indirectly as a mechanism for bringing about this avoidance.

Apart from these ritual and moral values, some individual Creoles find in Freemasonry more 'practical' and mundane advantages. Non-Mason cynics in Freetown claim that men join in order to establish informal links with their superiors in the civil service or the professions, as the case may be. It must be remembered that many of the most eminent judges, lawyers, permanent secretaries, heads of departments, doctors, engineers and others are members of the Masonic lodges in Freetown. In a society where rank and patronage count for a great deal, this must indeed be an important factor attracting men to join. One often hears gossip in Freetown society to the effect that all appointments and promotions in certain establishments are 'cooked' in the lodges. Similar charges have also been made against Freemasonry in Britain, America and elsewhere. But one need not assume the validity of these charges in order to appreciate the fact that men should seek to establish primary relations with their superiors, irrespective of possible material gain. Many of the Masons are involved in bureaucratic hierarchies, as superiors and subordinates, outside the movement, and a great deal of tension arises between them in various situations. It is natural that they should welcome an institution which alleviates the effects of this tension.

Association with the 'high-ups' through Masonry leads many non-Masons in Freetown to complain that Masons are snobs and behave in a superior manner. Masonry is certainly synonymous with high class in Freetown for the simple reason that a man cannot become a Mason if he cannot afford to pay the high expenses of membership and of the very frequent and lavish banqueting. The annual cost of membership for an initiate into the Entered Apprentice degree is about £ 50, excluding the cost of a black suit, transport, and so on. At promotion to a second degree the cost will be higher. When he is eventually 'raised' to the Third degree, that of a Master Mason, the cost during the year when he is 'reigning' in the lodge is between £ 400 and £ 500. Although both kin and lodge brothers contribute towards this expense, the bulk of the cost will be borne by the man himself. The regular payments that members make annually include fees for registration, contribution to benevolent funds, and some other minor items. The regalia for the initiate costs over £ 25 and as the Mason rises in degrees so does the cost of his regalia. Most of the lodges in Freetown include the basic cost of banqueting for the whole year in their annual fees, so that whether a man attended a banquet or not he would have paid the costs. Quite apart from the expenses of membership, a man must also have the right connexions if he wants to join the order. Freemasons do not proselytise and candidates are nearly always introduced by kin and friends who are already members. There is an initial period of investigation by a Committee of Membership during which inquiries are made about the candidate, and the candidate himself is interviewed and questioned at length. When the Committee is satisfied, the candidate is proposed for election in a general meeting of the lodge. Election is by secret balloting. If more than one black-ball were cast the candidate would not be admitted. This means that only 'the right people', who are acceptable to nearly the whole lodge will be admitted. Membership is thus taken as a privilege and Masons are to a great extent proud of it.

Perhaps largely unconsciously, the Creoles generally see in Masonry a mechanism for the development and maintenance of a 'mystique' which marks and enhances their distinctiveness and superiority vis-à-vis the Natives. This is becoming increasingly necessary in recent years as native Sierra Leoneans, backed by the political power of their sheer numbers, which they have enjoyed since the early 1950's, are challenging the Creoles on their own grounds of claims to superiority—education. One myth which you hear over and over again in conversation with Creoles is that no matter how highly educated a Native may be, he will never have the same kind of 'mentality', 'civilisation', or cultural sophistication as the Creoles. These elite qualities, the Creoles maintain, are the outcome of centuries of 'civilisation' and can never be achieved by money or by formal education. There are various symbolic mechanisms for the development of this 'mystique' among the Creoles, and Freemasonry, through its association with Western civilisation, is seen as the hall-mark of superiority, in contrast to the 'bush' secret societies of the Mende, the Temne, and others. For the Creoles, Freemasonry is in this respect an organisation within which they share ritual and moral values with eminent Europeans on the bases of equality and 'brotherhood'. Freemasonry requires a good deal of literacy and education and of sophistication in dress and etiquette. Freemasonry probably serves the same kind of need in Britain and America for the development of a mystique of superiority which is created not so much to convince others as to convince the actors themselves.

Structural Constraints.   But by far the most important factor driving Creole men to Freemasonry is pressure from kin, from friends, and from wider groupings. Indeed many of the benefits that individual Masons are said to gain from membership are elaborations or rationalisations developed after joining. A great deal of insight into the structural forces that constrain Creole men to join Freemasonry can be gained from talking to men who are not yet Masons.

Some men join because their fathers are or were Masons. A Mason regards it as a duty and a source of pride to bring his sons into membership, often within the same lodge. As sons reach the age of twenty-one their fathers begin to press them to join. I know of at least one case where a man who is eminent in both Freemasonry and in the political organisation of the state in Sierra Leone, took the trouble to ask the higher Masonic authorities in Britain for special permission to have his eighteen-year-old son admitted as a member. I talked to men in their twenties and a few in their thirties who told me they had been putting off joining the movement by telling their fathers or other related Masons that they were not yet 'really old enough' for it. Even when a father is dead, older brothers or other relatives urge their younger brothers that it was their father's wish that the sons should join. Pressure also comes from other kin who are already within the movement or who are not.

Most important of all is the pressure of friends. Friendship ties are significant among the Creoles. It must be remembered that we are discussing here a few thousand men who were born, brought up, had their schooling and most of their university education within a relatively small town. Men spend most of their leisure time in cliques of friends and when most of a man's peers join Masonry, one after the other and become absorbed within its activities, a great deal of pressure is exerted on him to join. If he does not, he is likely to lose his friends. A young engineer told me that his Masonic friends would sometimes request him to leave the room so that they could say something in the confidence of Masonic brothers. He was in fact not sure, as he was telling me this, that this was not done deliberately by his friends in order to induce him to join.

Although only about a third of Creole men are full members of the Masonic lodges, the other two-thirds are to a large extent structurally involved within the movement. The Creoles on the whole are the highest and the most privileged status group in Sierra Leone. But they are themselves internally stratified. A few scores of households command a great deal of power derived from property and from professional standing and high prestige which they have held for many generations. Below these are the other professionals, and the senior civil servants. Below these are the clerks, the salesmen, teachers. At the bottom are the relatively poorer households whose members are mainly skilled and some unskilled workers. Only men from the two top sectors tend to be in the lodges. But the Creoles are organised in 'families' whose structure combines kinship relations and patronage. The Creoles are bilateral in their kinship organisation, and patrilateral, matrilateral as well as affinal kin and sometimes even friends, are included within what a Creole would call his 'family'. From this it is obvious that all the Creoles are potentially related to one another, and that what a person would call his 'family' tends to be an ego-centric entity. Nevertheless, a degree of permanence and discreteness is given to a set of kin through the system of patronage. Each eminent man becomes the patron of a large number of kinsmen some of whom will even adopt the name of the patron, whether they are related to him patrilaterally, matri-laterally or affinally. Even a preliminary study of the structure of these 'families' is sufficient to show that each includes men and women from all classes of Creoldom. Although there is at the same time a tendency for the wealthy and eminent to seek close social relations with their equals in status, there are strong economic, political, moral and ritual forces that link the members together. Thus although only the relatively well-to-do are in the lodges, these are in fact the patrons of those who are not members. Patronage involves both privileges and obligations and it is difficult for a man to remain in this position without keeping in close relationship with the other patrons who occupy strategic positions in the society. Masonic membership is an im-portant feature of the style of life of any Creole of importance. It is a collective representation without which a man will not be able to partake in the network of privilege. A patron is indeed under strong pressure to join if he does not want to forfeit his role and his power.

On deeper analysis, it will become evident that this pressure by relatives, friends, and status groups, operating on the individual, is itself a mechanism of constraint whose source is the wide cleavage between Creoles and non-Creoles, within the Sierra Leone polity. To appreciate the nature of this structural constraint, we must view it developmentally. I have drawn for this purpose a list of the Freemasonic lodges in Freetown, each by name, year of consecration and constitution. The establishment, consecration, and continuity of a lodge are supervised and administered by the 'mother' Grand Lodge in Britain. No lodge can be formed unless it gets a special charter from the Grand Lodge to certify that the lodge is formed in accordance with all the regulations of the movement. This charter must be displayed in every lodge at every one of its meetings and without it the meeting is invalid. The charter must be renewed annually. Each lodge has a special serial number within the constitution and its name, address and other details are formally listed in the Year Book of the Mother Constitution (see table 1).

The first point to be noticed from the list is that the proliferation of the lodges has not been a gradual process but has occurred in bouts. We can divide the development of Masonry in Freetown into three major periods. The first phase is from 1882 to 1914, when six lodges were formed, four under the English constitution and two under the Scottish constitution. Most of the members of those lodges were British officials. I am not concerned in this article with that period. For the following three decades, from 1914 to 1946, no new lodges were established. This was roughly the period of indirect rule in British West Africa, which came to an,end in most British colonies shortly after the second world war.

Then in the course of four to five years, from 1947 to 1952, the number of lodges in Freetown doubled, from six to twelve. This was the beginning of new political developments leading to independence in 1961.

There followed a standstill period of about thirteen years which roughly coincided with the stable premiership of Sir Milton Margai, ending in 1964 with his death, and the succession to the premiership of his brother, Sir Albert Margai. This ushered in a turbulent time which came to an end with the *coups d'etat* of 1967 and 1968. In the course of less than three years the number of lodges leapt by nearly 50 per cent. From twelve to seventeen, with all the increase occurring within the Scottish constitution, the number of whose daughter lodges thus doubled.

We thus have two phases of concentrated and intensified 'freemasonisation', the 1947–1952 period, and the 1965–1968 period. What is significant in both periods is that each involved a direct and serious threat to Creoldom. This emerges clearly from the wealth of documentation of all sorts, and from the detailed studies of the politics of Sierra Leone since the second world war by political scientists and other scholars (see particularly Cartwright 1970; Kilson 1966; Fisher 1969). I can here give only a brief outline of the relevant events.

The developments of the 1947–52 period still remain the most traumatic experience in the psychology of the Creoles. Until then the Creoles were securely entrenched in the Colony—despite the British policy of restraining them from dominating the natives from the Protectorate. Their ascendance in the civil service and in the professions was overwhelming. Even as late as 1950 there were at least seventy Creole doctors as against three from the Protectorate (Cartwright 1970: 24). In 1953, 92 per cent of the civil servants were

Creoles. In 1947 the British government presented proposals for constitutional reform in Sierra Leone aiming at unifying the Colony and the Protectorate and setting the whole country on the path to independence. The proposals at that stage were not revolutionary for the country as a whole but they dramatically affected the balance of power between Colony and Protectorate. Among other things they stipulated that the fourteen African members of the new Legislative Council should be elected by the people. This virtually meant the beginning of the end of Creole political influence even within what they had hitherto regarded as their own home: the Colony.

Their reaction was frantic. In 1948 all the major Creole political groupings, including the Combined Rate Payers Association and the Sierra Leone Socialist Party presented a petition to the Secretary of State for the Colonies attacking the colonial government for intending to give power to illiterate 'foreigners'; i.e. the people of the Protectorate. The Creoles demanded that only the literate should be given the right to vote.

There were bitter exchanges across the deepening cleavage between the Creoles and the Natives. Dr. H. C. Bankole-Bright, the Creole political leader at the time, described the Creoles and the Natives as 'two mountains that can never meet'. In a letter published by the Creole *Sierra Leone Weekly News* (26 August, 1950) he recalled that the Protectorate had come into being 'after the massacre of some of our fathers and grandfathers . . . in Mendeland because they were described as "Black Englishmen"'. For the other camp, Milton Margai, who was soon to become the Prime Minister of Sierra Leone, described the Creoles (see *Protectorate Assembly* 1950:28–31) as a handful of foreigners to whom 'our forefathers' had given shelter and who imagined themselves to be superior because they aped Western modes of living but who had never breathed the true spirit of independence.

What is important to note here is that although the more conservative Creole elements fought a desperate battle for a long time and continue to do so still trying to put the clock back, most of the Creole moderates and intellectuals recognised the futility of this stand and tried to adjust to the times and make the most out of the new opportunities. They soon recognised that any attempt by the Creoles to organise politically on formal lines would be disastrous because of their hopeless numerical weaknesses. It should be emphasised that in their determination to leave Sierra Leone, the British pursued a consistent policy in the Africanisation of their administration. This entailed the replacement of British officials by Africans, and as few Natives were educated enough to qualify, it was inevitable that the bulk of the new recruits should come from among the Creoles. The British did their best to educate Africans particularly from the Protectorate for the new jobs, by giving them scholarships for study overseas. But even so and despite all pressure, 60 per cent of the holders of these scholarships between 1951 and 1956 were Creoles (Cartwright 1970:24). Also, as holders of land property in the Colony, the Creoles began to reap the benefits of the impending independence by the rise in the value of their property. All this meant that the Creoles would lose everything if they stood as a formal solid political bloc within the new state structure, while, if they co-operated in the maintenance of a liberal regime on the basis of individual equality they would gain a great deal because of their superior education and cultural sophistication. The Creoles who were think-ing along these lines, eventually co-operated with the Native-dominated Mil-ton Margai government. Milton Margai, who was a shrewd politician, rec-ognised that he could not establish a government without the Creoles and he also recognized the immense contribution that the Creoles had made and could still make to the country. He therefore included many Creoles in his Party's representation and retained Creole men in key administrative positions. Thus, despite the grumbling of some Creoles every now and then, a period of co-operation and stability prevailed throughout Milton Margai's regime, ending with his death in 1964.

His brother, Albert Margai who succeeded him, was different in character and in style of government. Within a short time he made a serious attempt to change the constitution in order to establish officially a One-Party system. He could not do this without the close co-operation of the civil service, the judi-ciary as well as the legislature. But his attempt was immediately opposed by almost all the Creoles who now shifted their support to the opposition party. Opposition papers began to agitate against Albert and to expose his alleged corruption. The government brought the agitators to court. But the courts were presided over by Creole judges and verdicts were in the hands of juries who, because of the demand that they should be literate, were also Creole and most of the accused were acquitted. This outraged Albert Margai who began to attack ominously in his speeches the 'doctors, lawyers, and lecturers of Freetown' who were wilfully refusing to see the blessings of the one party system.

Events during the following one or two years show what an influential small minority elite can do against an established government supported by a large section of the population. Creole heads of trade unions, clergymen, lawyers, doctors, teachers, and university students used every shred of influence they had to bring about the downfall of Albert Margai. An opportunity presented itself in the 1967 general elections when the majority of Creole men and women threw their influence and their organisational weight behind the op-position party. The governing party, the SLPP, was defeated though by a nar-row majority (for details see Cartwright 1970; Fisher 1969).

Thus in both the 1947–1952 and 1965–1968 periods there was a sharp dramatic turn of events which brought about a serious threat to the continuity of Creole power and privilege. The very men whose power was most threatened in this way, mainly the civil servants and members of the professions, were those who filled the Freemasonic lodges in Freetown. Unless we assume that these men had split personalities, we can easily see that the two processes of change, i.e. the developing threat to Creole power and the increase in Freemasonic membership, are significantly interrelated. Nearly all the names of the Creoles who were involved in the struggle against Albert Margai in 1966 and in 1967 are those of well-known Freemasons. The varied forms that Creole action took to bring about the downfall of Albert Margai showed a remarkable degree of overall co-ordination which no formal political party or association was at the time capable of achieving.

An Exclusive Organisation.   Largely without any conscious policy or design, Freemasonic rituals and organisation helped to articulate an informal organisation, which helped the Creoles to protect their position in the face of increasing political threat. It did this in a number of ways, the most important being in providing an effective mechanism for regular communication, deliberation, decision-making, and for the development of an authority structure and of an integrated ideology. Although the members are divided into two constitutions and further, within each, into several lodges, there is a very great deal of intensive interaction between the whole membership. This is done through the manipulation of some of the institutions of Freemasonic organisation.

A Mason can become a Member in only one lodge, his 'lodge of birth', into which he is initiated. But he can seek 'affiliation' within other lodges, whether from his own constitution or from the other constitution. Many Masons are affiliated to one or more lodges, depending on their ability to meet the high expense in both time and money. Affiliation within a lodge costs only slightly less than membership. When you are affiliated within a lodge you enjoy the same privileges and share in the same activities as the members of that lodge. I know of some men who are affiliated within five lodges. On the individual level, men seek affiliation for the same reasons mentioned above in connexion with membership. They may want to associate with eminent men who are the members of other lodges, to interact socially, to enjoy eating and drinking more frequently. Other Masons seek affiliation within other lodges where they have better prospects for earlier promotion to the degree of Master Mason.

Another institution, which is probably even more important in establishing channels of communication between the lodges is that of visiting. A Mason can visit other lodges, where he may or may not have friends. All except the Royal Arch lodges are open to members from all degrees. Royal Arch lodges however are open to only reigning or past Master Masons. I understood from Masons in Freetown with whom I talked that on average nearly a quarter to a third of those present in any lodge meeting are visitors from other lodges.

Sociologically, the most important feature of lodge ceremonials is not the formal rituals of the order but the banqueting following their performance. It is here, amidst heavy drinking and eating, that Masons are engaged in the process of true 'fraternising'. In my view this informal institution within Masonry, whose procedure is neither planned nor consciously pursued, is the most fundamental mechanism in welding the members of all the lodges into a single, highly interrelated organisation. It must be remembered that we are dealing here with a small and limited community of a few thousand men who were born and brought up within a relatively small town. Indeed the seventeen lodges meet within less than one square mile. In some cases many lodges have their temples in the same building in the centre of the town. These are also the men who are related to one another as relatives, affines or friends, and who attend one another's weddings, funerals, and other family occasions.

It is obvious that the wealthier a man is the more mobile he becomes within the lodges, and this brings us to a second and a most fundamental structural function of Masonic organisation. This is that although there is a emphasis in Masonry on equality and true brotherhood, Masonic organisation provides effective and efficient mechanisms for the establishment of a strong authority structure. Formally, this is achieved through the ritual promotion within the three degrees of the Craft, the Entered Apprentice, Fellow of the Craft, and Master Mason. These degrees are the same under both the English and the Scottish Constitutions. But the English Constitution has further degrees within what is known as the Royal Arch.

Initiation into the First Degree, and then promotion to the Second, 'raising' to the Third, and further promotion in the Royal Arch Degrees, are marked by very elaborate ritual dramas. Each stage is also marked by new regalia with additional signs of office. It is also marked by the acquisition of further secrets, by new duties and new privileges. Apart from these ritual degrees there is also in each lodge a large number of Office Bearers of all sorts, who are concerned with the running and organisation of the lodge. And at the top of the lodges within each Constitution there is a District Grand Lodge, headed by a District Grand Master, his Deputy and Secretary. A Master is always addressed as 'Worshipful Master'. A Grand Master is addressed as the 'Most Worshipful Master'. The higher a Mason's degree the greater his mobility within, and access to, the lodges. A Master Mason can enter, without permission or invitation, even the Royal Arch Lodges.

All promotions are formally on the basis of attainment in Freemasonic theology and ritual and require devotion to the movement in regular attendance. But as each promotion to a higher degree necessitates spending more money in fees, in regalia and, more especially in providing banquets, only those Masons who can meet these expenses and who have the necessary backing in the lodges will seek or accept promotion. Promotion usually takes time and sometimes it can take a man over ten years to become a Master Mason. But the process can be greatly speeded up, and there are cases in Freetown of men being raised to the Third Degree within three years.

In this respect, the Scottish Constitution is more helpful than the English. Promotion can be quicker. Masons from Scottish lodges in Freetown told me they thought the Scottish constitution was more democratic than the English, which they described as conservative. In a Scottish lodge it is the members of the lodge who decide who will be raised to the position of Master and his Deputy while in English lodges the decision comes from above. On the whole, the Scottish constitution seems to be more easily adaptable to changing situations than the English one, and I believe that this is the main reason why, as the table above shows, it is now more predominant among the Creoles than the English one. In a rapidly changing situation it is important for a group to have a more flexible articulating ideology and organisation. For the Creoles, this is indeed crucial.

Within the hierarchy of degrees and offices in the Freemasonic organisation there is thus a close relationship between wealth and position in the non-Masonic sphere on the one hand, and ritual authority within the order on the other. The prominent men in the Masonic order are indeed the prominent men in Sierra Leone in general. There is a close relation between the two spheres.

Individual Masons often manipulate various factors to gain authority and power within the movement. A man who has just joined a lodge and who will probably have to take his place in the queue behind many other 'brothers' in order to be raised to the coveted status of Master Mason, will seek either affiliation to another lodge in which more opportunities exist, or will group with other members, who should include at least seven Masters, in order to drive an application through for the foundation of a new lodge. If he is a member of an English lodge he may discover that his chances are better in affiliation within a Scottish Lodge. And within the lodge he will try to gain the affection and support of various cliques of friends.

Even at the level of District Lodges, the two Masonic organisations are closely interrelated, and, taken together, they indeed merge in effect to articulate one unified Masonic hierarchy. The present District Grand Master of the Scottish constitution for example was originally initiated into an English constitution lodge, was then affiliated to other lodges from both constitutions, and became founding Master of a Scottish lodge. Other eminent Masons in Freetown had similar careers within the order.

The integrated hierarchy of authority is of immense significance for the Creoles as a corporate interest group. Like the middle classes in many countries, the Creoles are in general notoriously individualistic and no sooner does a leader begin to assume leadership than a number of other men begin to contest his claim in the spirit of 'why he, not me?' It must be emphasised that during the Colonial period, while the Temne, Mende, and the other tribes of Sierra Leone had their own local and paramount chiefs whose authority was upheld by the Colonial administration, the Creoles were without traditional leadership. Up to the present, the Creoles are treated legally as non-Natives and their family and social life is regulated under British civil law, while the Natives are treated mainly according to customary law. The Creoles have for long identified strongly with the British and do not have any kind of tribal structure.

The difficulty in developing a unified leadership and a system of authority was further increased by the fact that, outside the formal political arena, the Creoles had several, often competing, hierarchies of authority within different groupings. One was the church hierarchy, the others were within each one of the major professions, including the teachers, as well as property holders. Furthermore, there was intensive strife within each grouping characterised by intense competition for promotion into high positions and by perpetual tension between superior and subordinate within the bureaucratic structure. But when the members of all these groupings became incorporated within the Masonic lodges, they became integrated within an all-encompassing authority structure in which members from the higher positions of the different non-Masonic hierarchies were included. The different types and bases of power within those groupings were expressed in terms of the symbols and ideology of Freemasonry. A unified system of legitimation for a unified authority structure was thus created. This has been of course, not a once-and-for-all development, but a continuing process of interaction between the ritual authority within the order and the various authority systems outside it.

Freemasonry has thus provided the Creoles with the means for the articulation of the organisational functions of a political group. The organisation that has emerged is efficient and effective and is thus in sharp contrast with the loose and feeble political organisations in Sierra Leone generally. As Cartwright (1970) points out, the political parties of Sierra Leone are loose alliances between various groups, many of which shift their allegiance from one party to another unpredictably. But Freemasonic organisation is strictly supervised by the two Grand Lodges in Britain who enforce the same strict standards of organisation that have been evolved in an advanced and highly industrialised society. This is why, in my view, Freemasonic organisation in Sierra Leone today is one of the most efficient and effective organisations in the whole country. It has thus partly made up for Creole numerical weakness. A small group can indeed greatly enhance its power through rigorous organisation.

In adopting Freemasonry in this way, the Creoles are making use of a novel kind of ideology and organisation in Sierra Leone politics. For it is well known that Sierra Leone and some of her neighbouring countries constitute an ethnographic area which is especially characterised by the variety and multiplicity of its secret societies. The role of the Poro secret society of the Mende in organising and staging the so-called Hut Tax War against the British and the Creoles in 1898 is well documented (see Chalmers 1899; Little 1965; 1966; Scott 1960; 173–174). As Kilson point out (1966: 256–258) the Poro has ever since been used in modern political contexts down to the present. Its symbols, ideology, and organisation have been used by the SLPP, the major, Mende-backed party of Milton Margai, to mobilise votes and support its elections. A similar use of the symbols and organisation of secret societies in the modern politics of neighbouring Liberia has also been reported (see Libenow 1969).

Although I have been discussing here the political functions of a ritual organisation, I am not implying any kind of reductionism which aims at explaining, or rather explaining away, the ritual in terms of political or economic relations. Nor am I imputing conscious and calculated political design on the part of men who observe the beliefs and the symbolic codes of such an organisation. Like many other ritual systems, Freemasonry is a phenomenon *sui generis*. It is a source of values in its own right, and individuals often look at it as an end in itself and not as a means to an end. A Creole Mason will be genuinely offended if he is told that he is joining the movement for political considerations. More fundamentally, the Freemasonic movement is officially and formally opposed to the discussion of political issues in the course of its formal meetings. There is certainly no conscious and deliberate use of Freemasonry in political maneuvering.

But all this does not mean that the movement has no political aspects or political consequences. Although man in contemporary society plays different roles in different fields of social life, these roles are nevertheless related to one another within one 'self', 'ego' or psyche. A normal man has his identity, his 'I', which is developed only through the integration of the disparate roles that he plays. To achieve selfhood at all, a man's role as a Mason must be brought into relation with his role as a professional, a politician, a husband, a father.

The Creoles generally have been under severe pressure and strain during the past twenty-five years or so. During this period they have had to put up with threats of various sorts, in the street, in the courtroom, in parliament. These men are conscious of and worried about these problems and they talk about them all the time. When they meet in the Masonic temples, they meet to perform the prescribed formal rituals. But when they adjourn to banqueting, or when they meet informally altogether outside the framework of Freemasonry, what do they discuss?

I addressed this question to several Masons. Almost invariably the reply was that they talked about 'the usual ordinary current problems', which people usually talk about. There is no doubt whatsoever that this is so. But it is not unreasonable to conjecture that these men do talk about their current problems and about their anxieties, hopes, and also deliberate about solutions. They do not even need to talk about these problems exclusively within the lodges or while banqueting. Through the sharing of the same sign language, the same system of beliefs, the same secret rituals, and the same organisation, and through frequent banqueting, strong moral bonds develop between them which often transcend, become stronger than, many other bonds, so that when they meet outside the lodge framework they talk together more confidentially and more intimately than if they were not brothers within the same movement. Attend any of the frequent ceremonials staged by the Creoles in the ordinary social life, such as weddings, christenings, or graduation, and you will not fail to see that while the women are busy dancing on their own to the wild beat of the Gumbe band, the men sit quietly in cliques on the side drinking and talking. If you ask the women what their men were doing they will say 'they are talking lodge'. Indeed the phrase 'talking lodge' which is frequently heard in Freetown society, has the connotation of 'talking politics'.

Through these intimate and exclusive gatherings, within and outside the framework of the lodge, men pool their problems, deliberate about them, try to find solutions to them and eventually develop formulae for appropriate action. It is because of all this deliberation, communication, and co-ordination of decisional formulations, that there is a remarkable unanimity of opinion among the Creoles over major current problems. Talk about any public issue on any day with a number of Creoles in Freetown and you will most probably hear in comment the same statements, using almost the same phrases and words. Many expatriates in Sierra Leone have remarked on this uniformity of response to major issues on the part of the Creoles. In the course of a few months I followed a number of public issues, concentrating particularly on two of them. One issue was raised by three different men in different situations within two to four days of each other, including one article in a daily newspaper. On enquiry all three men turned out to be members of the same lodge. In a few days' time the statements about that issue became stereotyped and truly became the 'collective representation', of a whole group of men and, later, of their women.

Freemasonry is, of course, not the only cultural institution which helps to articulate the corporate organisation of Creole interests. In my view, it is best to study an interest group in terms of two interconnected, though analytically separated dimensions: the political and the symbolic. The symbolic consists of all the patterns of normative behaviour within a number of institutions such as the church, the family, friendship, art and literature. Most of these patterns of symbolic behaviour have consequences affecting the organisational functions of the group, although some will have more direct effects in articulating certain functions than others. A single institution, like Freemasonry, will contribute to the articulation of different organisational functions, such as communications and decision-making. On the other hand, a number of institutions will jointly help in the articulation of a single function such as that of distinctiveness (for details, see Cohen 1969: 201–211). To study Creoldom in this way would require a complete monograph. What I have attempted here is simply to isolate the structural consequences of Freemasonry.

Throughout this discussion I have referred to the Creoles as if they were a discrete ethnic group. They indeed *are* such a group, having their own distinct culture and their own history. What is more, they are still regarded legally as 'non-Native'. They see themselves and are seen by others as a distinct culture group. But this is to some extent a false picture because it entails, among other things, the strict observance of a rigid principle of descent, and hence of recruitment. But the Creoles are bilateral and a man will often include within what he regards as his 'family' both patrilateral, matrilateral, and affinal relatives as well as friends. Throughout the history of the Creoles in Sierra Leone men and wome of Native descent were Creolised through various processes (see Banton 1957; Porter 1963). By acquiring the symbols and style of life of Creoldom and by being incorporated within the Creole social network, these Natives became in effect Creole. On the other hand, there is evidence of an opposite process going on all the time whereby Creoles became Natives and came to identify themselves with different ethnic groups. More recently, some Creoles have publicly renounced their English names which they changed into African names and advocated complete integration with the Natives. Creole men today, and certainly almost all the Freemasons among them, declare publicly they are opposed to 'tribalism', and play down their distinctive identity as Creoles.

Creoldom within the modern Sierra Leone polity is essentially a status group marked off from other social groups by a special style of life and by a dense network of relationships and co-operation. Although they are internally stratified, they stand as a group on their own within the wider society. There is no doubt that Freemasonry has helped them to co-ordinate their struggle to preserve their high status. It must be remembered that the Creoles are essentially professionals and wage earners. They are not exploiters. They have been the main factor in keeping the country's institutions liberal. Until very recently Sierra Leone was one of the few states in the Third World which was still democratic.[5] The Creoles want the country to remain liberal not only because of their ideological zeal, but also because they realise that, as long as there is free competition for jobs in the civil service and the professions they, with their advanced schooling system, their Western style of life, and the advantages they have had over other groups in the fields for over a century and a half, are likely to win and to maintain their present high social status.

One of the sociological lessons we can learn from the study of a group like the Creoles for the understanding of Western industrial societies is the study of class—particularly the higher class—as groups which are informally organised for action through a variety of institutions like Freemasonry. The association between Freemasonry and the higher social classes in Britain and the U.S.A. has been known for a long time now. What I have tried to do in this article is to indicate how this cult operates in articulating a corporate organisation for a group of highly individualistic people. An analysis of this type can perhaps supplement that by for example Lupton and Wilson (1959) in their well-known study of decision-makers in Britain.

Freemasonry offers two major functions to its members: an exclusive organisation and a mechanism for the creation of a brotherhood. Through upholding the principle of secrecy, or rather of the monopoly of secrets, Freemasons are able to develop, maintain and run a vast, intricate, efficient, and highly complex organisation, with its symbols of distinctiveness, channels of exclusive communication, structure of authority, ideology, and frequent socialisation through ceremonials. Through its networks of lodges, its ritual degrees and hierarchial structure, its institutions of affiliation and visiting, and existence of three different constitutions, it is particularly suited to operate in the highly differentiated and complex structure of our industrial society. For it is capable of articulating the groupings of different occupational and social categories of people, allowing both unity and diversity.

As men join the organisation, the impersonal character of a social category like class gives way to the rapid development of moral bonds that link its individuals. Through the sharing of common secrets and of a common language of signs, passwords, and hand-clasps, through sharing the humilities of the ceremonials of initiation, through mutual aid, the frequent communion in worshipping and eating together, and the rules to settle disputes amicably between them, the members are transformed into a true brotherhood. This combination of strict, exclusive organisation, with the primary bonds of a brotherhood, makes Freemasonry a powerful organisation in contemporary society.

Freemasonry has different structural functions under different social conditions, and in its history in Europe it has served to organise a conservative as well as progressive movements. Its functions are determined neither by its doctrine nor by its formal organisation. But it is definitely an organisation especially suited for the well-to-do. What is more, because of its secrecy and its rules of recruitment, it is such that once it is captured or dominated by a strong interest group, or by a number of related interest groups, it tends to become the exclusive vehicle for promoting the interests of that group. Through secret balloting and the requirement of almost complete consensus for admitting new members, it can easily exclude the members of other groups from joining it. Sociologically, the question of whom it excludes becomes as significant as that of whom it includes.

NOTES

The field study on which this article is based was carried out in Freetown, Sierra Leone, between September 1969 and September 1970. It was financed by the School of Oriental and African Studies, University of London. During that period I was given the status of Visiting Research Fellow by Fourah Bay College, University of Sierra Leone. I would like to record my thanks to both institutions for their generous help.

I am grateful to Dr. Humphrey Fisher for his detailed and critical comment on an earlier draft of the article.

1. According to Freemasonic principles, the Holy Book can be either the Bible or the sacred book of any other universal religion. To my knowledge, all Freetown lodges display the Bible only.

2. According to Fyfe (1962:146) the first lodge was opened in Freetown in 1821, but was abolished, together with other dormant lodges, in 1864 by order of the Grand Lodge of England. Freemasonry was revived in 1882 (1962:437) with Creoles and Europeans joining the same lodge.

3. I am using the term Native for non-Creole Sierra Leoneans in the same way as it is used when one writes of the natives of France, for example.

4. In its agitation against the APC government in 1970, an opposition paper claimed that the Prime Minister of Sierra Leone had made history by being the first Prime Minister of the country to join Freemasonry. This was to imply that the Prime Minister had been under the influence of the Creoles.

5. I left Freetown in September 1970. For some of the political developments since then, see Dalby 1971.

REFERENCES

Banton, M.
   1957   *West African city*. London: Oxford Univ. Press.

Cartwright, John R.
   1968   Shifting forces in Sierra Leone. *Africa Rep.* **13**, 26–30.
   1970   *Politics in Sierra Leone 1947–1967*. Toronto: Univ. Press.

Central Statistics Office, Freetown
   1965   *1963 population census of Sierra Leone*, vol. **2**. Freetown: Central Statistics Office.

Chalmers, David
   1899   *Report by Her Majesty's Commissioner and correspondence on the subject of the insurrection in the Sierra Leone Protectorate 1898. I–II Cmd.* 9388, 9391. London: H.M.S.O.

Cohen, A.
   1969   *Custom and politics in urban Africa*. London: Routledge & Kegan Paul.

Dalby, David
   1971   Africa in a new era of intervention. *New Society* **22 April 1971**, 670–671.

Dewar, James
   1966   *The unlocked secret: Freemasonry examined*. London: William Kimber.

Fashole-Luke, E. W.
    1968   Religion in Freetown. In *Freetown: a symposium*. (eds) C. Fyfe & E. Jones, Freetown: Sierra Leone Univ. Press.

Fisher, Humphrey J.
    1969.   Elections and coups in Sierra Leone, 1967, *J. mod. Afr. Stud.* **7,** 611–636.

Fyfe, Christopher
    1962   *A history of Sierra Leone*. London: Oxford Univ. Press.
    1964   *Sierra Leone inheritance*. London: Oxford Univ. Press.

Jones, Mervyn
    1967   Freemasonry. In *Secret societies* (ed.) Norman MacKenzie. London: Aldous Books.

Kilson, Martin
    1967   *Political change in a west African state*. Cambridge, Mass.: Harvard Univ. Press.

Libenow, J. Gus
    1969   *Liberia: the evolution of privilege*. Ithaca, London: Cornell Univ. Press.

Little, K.
    1965   The political functions of the Poro, I. *Africa* **35,** 349–365.
    1966   The political functions of Poro, 2. *Africa* **36,** 62–72.
    1967   *The Mende of Sierra Leone*. London: Routledge & Kegan Paul.

Lupton, T. & S. Wilson
    1959   Background and connections of top decision-makers. *Manchester School* 30–51.

Peterson, John
    1969   *Province of freedom*. London: Faber & Faber.

Porter, Arthur
    1963   *Creoldom: a study of the development of Freetown society*. London: Oxford Univ. Press.

Protectorate Assembly
    1950   *Proceedings of the Seventh Meeting*. 26 September 1950.

Scott, D. J. R.
    1960   The Sierra Leone election, May 1957. In *Five elections in Africa* (eds) W. J. M. Mackenzie & K. Robinson, London: Oxford Univ. Press.

Francis Bacon (1561–1626)

Selections From *New Atlantis*

... The next day, about ten of the clock, the Governor came to us again, and after salutations, said familiarly, that he was come to visit us; and called for a chair, and sat him down; and we, being some ten of us (the rest were of the meaner sort, or else gone abroad), sat down with him; and when we were set, he began thus: 'We of this island of Bensalem (for so they called it in their language) have this: that by means of our solitary situation, and of the laws of secrecy, which we have for our travellers, and our rare admission of strangers, we know well most part of the habitable world, and are ourselves unknown. Therefore because he that knoweth least is fitted to ask questions, it is more reason, for the entertainment of the time, that ye ask me questions, than that I ask you.' . . .

The next day, the same Governor came again to us, immediately after dinner, and excused himself, saying, that the day before he was called from us

Bacon's *New Atlantis* was first posthumously published in 1627. For a recent comparative study of utopias, of which *New Atlantis* is one of the most important, see Nell Eurich, *Science in Utopia,* Cambridge: Harvard University Press, 1967. *Editor's Note.*

somewhat abruptly, but now he would make us amends, and spend time with us, if we held his company and conference agreeable. We answered, that we held it so agreeable and pleasing to us, as we forgot both dangers past, and fears to come, for the time we heard him speak; and that we thought an hour spent with him was worth years of our former life. He bowed himself a little to us, and after we were set again, he said, 'Well, the questions are on your part.'

One of our number said, after a little pause, that there was a matter we were no less desirous to know than fearful to ask, lest we might presume too far. But encouraged by his rare humanity towards us (that could scarce think ourselves strangers, being his vowed and professed servants), we would take the hardness to propound it; humbly beseeching him, if he thought it not fit to be answered, that he would pardon it, though he rejected it. We said, we well observed those his words, which he formerly spake, that this happy island, where we now stood, was known to few, and yet knew most of the nations of the world, which we found to be true, considering they had the languages of Europe, and knew much of our state and business; and yet we in Europe (notwithstanding all the remote discoveries and navigations of this last age) never heard any of the least inkling or glimpse of this island. This we found wonderful strange; for that all nations have interknowledge one of another, either by voyage into foreign parts, or by strangers that come to them; and though the traveller into a foreign country doth commonly know more by the eye than he that stayeth at home can by relation of the traveller; yet both ways suffice to make a mutual knowledge, in some degree, on both parts. But for this island, we never heard tell of any ship of theirs that had been seen to arrive upon any shore of Europe; no, nor of either the East or West Indies, nor yet of any ship of any other part of the world, that had made return from them. And yet the marvel rested not in this; for the situation of it (as his lordship said) in the secret conclave of such a vast sea mought cause it. But then, that they should have knowledge of the languages, books, affairs of those that lie such a distance from them, it was a thing we could not tell what to make of; for that it seemed to us a condition and propriety of divine powers and beings, to be hidden and unseen to others, and yet to have others open, and as in a light to them.

At this speech the Governor gave a gracious smile and said, that we did well to ask pardon for this question we now asked, for that it imported, as if we thought this land a land of magicians, that sent forth spirits of the air into all parts, to bring them news and intelligence of other countries. It was answered by us all, in all possible humbleness, but yet with a countenance taking knowledge, that we knew he spake it but merrily; that we were apt enough to think there was somewhat supernatural in this island, but yet rather as angelical than magical. But to let his lordship know truly what it was that made us tender and doubtful to ask this question, it was not any such conceit, but because we remembered he had given a touch in his former speech that this land had laws of secrecy touching strangers. . . .

'Ye shall understand, my dear friends, that amongst the excellent acts of that king,[1] one above all hath the pre-eminence. It was the erection and institution of an order, or society, which we call Salomon's House; the noblest foundation, as we think, that ever was upon the earth, and the lantern of this kingdom. It is dedicated to the study of the works and creatures of God. Some think it beareth the founder's name a little corrupted, as if it should be Solamona's House. But the records write it as it is spoken. So as I take it to be denominate of the king of the Hebrews, which is famous with you, and no stranger to us; for we have some parts of his works which with you are lost; namely, that Natural History which he wrote of all plants, from the cedar of Libanus to the moss that groweth out of the wall; and of all things that have life and motion. This maketh me think that our king finding himself to symbolize, in many things, with that king of the Hebrews (which lived many years before him) honoured him with the title of this foundation. And I am the rather induced to be of this opinion, for that I find in ancient records, this order or society is sometimes called Salomon's House, and sometimes the College of the Six Days' Works; whereby I am satisfied that our excellent kind had learned from the Hebrews that God had created the world, and all that therein is, within six days: and therefore he instituting that house, for the finding out of the true nature of all things (whereby God mought have the more glory in the workmanship of them, and men the more fruit in the use of them), did give it also that second name. . . .

'We have also engine-houses, where are prepared engines and instruments for all sorts of motions. There we imitate and practise to make swifter motions than any you have, either out of your muskets or any engine that you have; and to make them and multiply them more easily and with small force, by wheels and other means, and to make them stronger and more violent than yours are, exceeding your greatest cannons and basilisks. We represent also ordnance and instruments of war and engines of all kinds; and likewise new mixtures and compositions of gunpowder, wild-fires burning in water and unquenchable, also fire-works of all variety, both for pleasure and use. We imitate also flights of birds; we have some degrees of flying in the air. We have ships and boats for going under water and brooking of seas, also swimming-girdles and supporters. We have divers curious clocks, and other like motions of return, and some perpetual motions. We imitate also motions of living creatures by images of men, beasts, birds, fishes, and serpents; we have also a great number of other various motions, strange for equality, fineness and subtilty.

'We have also a mathematical-house, where are represented all instruments, as well of geometry as astronomy, exquisitely made.

'We have also houses of deceits of the senses, where we represent all manner of feats of juggling, false apparitions, impostures and illusions, and their fallacies. And surely you will easily believe that we, that have so many things truly natural which induce admiration, could in a world of particulars deceive the senses if we would disguise those things, and labour to make them seem more miraculous. But we do hate all impostures and lies, insomuch as we have severely forbidden it to all our fellows, under pain of ignominy and fines, that they do not show any natural work or thing adorned or swelling, but only pure as it is, and without all affectation of strangeness.

'These are, my son, the riches of Salomon's House.

'For the several employments and offices of our fellows, we have twelve that sail into foreign countries under the names of other nations (for our own we conceal), who bring us the books and abstracts, and patterns of experiments of all other parts. These we call Merchants of Light.

'We have three that collect the experiments which are in all books. These we call Depredators.

'We have three that collect the experiments of all mechanical arts, and also of liberal sciences, and also of practises which are not brought into arts. These we call Mystery-men.

'We have three that try new experiments, such as themselves think good. These we call Pioneers or Miners.

'We have three that draw the experiments of the former four into titles and tables, to give the better light for the drawing of observations and axioms out of them. These we call compilers.

'We have three that bend themselves, looking into the experiments of their fellows, and cast about how to draw out of them things of use and practice for man's life and knowledge, as well for works as for plain demonstration of causes means of natural divinations, and the easy and clear discovery of the virtures and parts of bodies. These we call dowry-men or Benefactors.

'Then after divers meetings and consults of our whole number, to consider of the former labours and collections, we have three that take care out of them to direct new experiments, of a higher light, more penetrating into Nature than the former. These we call Lamps.

'We have three others that do execute the experiments so directed, and report them. These we call Inoculators.

'Lastly, we have three that raise the former discoveries by experiments into greater observations, axioms, and aphorisms. These we call Interpreters of Nature.

'We have also, as you must think, novices and apprentices, that the succession of the former employed men do not fail; besides a great number of servants and attendants, men and women. And this we do also: we have consultations, which of the inventions and experiences which we have discovered shall be published, and which not: and take all an oath of secrecy for the concealing of those which we think fit to keep secret: though some of those we do reveal sometimes to the State, and some not.

'For our ordinances and rites, we have two very long and fair galleries: in one of these we place patterns and samples of all manner of the more rare and excellent inventions: in the other we place the statues of all principal inventors. There we have the statue of your Columbus, that discovered the West Indies: also the inventor of ships: your Monk that was the inventor of ordnance and gunpowder: the inventor of music: the inventor of letters: the inventor of printing: the inventor of observations of astronomy: the inventor of works in metal: the inventor of glass: the inventor of silk of the worm: the inventor of wine: the inventor of corn and bread: the inventor of sugars: and all these by more certain tradition than you have. Then we have divers inventors of our own, of excellent works, which since you have not seen, it were too long to make descriptions of them; and besides, in the right understanding of those descriptions you might easily err. For upon every invention of value we erect a statue to the inventor, and give him a liberal and honourable reward. These statues are some of brass, some of marble and touchstone, some of cedar and other special woods gilt and adorned; some of iron, some of silver, some of gold.

'We have certain hymns and services, which we say daily, of laud and thanks to God for His marvellous works. And forms of prayer, imploring His aid and blessing for the illumination of our labours, and the turning of them into good and holy uses.

'Lastly, we have circuits or visits, of divers principal cities of the kingdom; where, as it cometh to pass, we do publish such new profitable inventions as we think good. And we do also declare natural divinations of diseases, plagues, swarms of hurtful creatures, scarcity, tempests, earthquakes, great inundations, comets, temperature of the year, and divers other things; and we give counsel thereupon, what the people shall do for the prevention and remedy of them.' . . .

NOTES

1. The Governor is referring to King Solamon, the wise lawgiver of the "island" of Bensalem. Editor's note.

Max Heindel (1865–1919)

The Order of Rosicrucians

The Order of Rosicrucians is not merely a secret society; it is one of the Mystery Schools, and the Brothers are Hierophants of the lesser Mysteries, Custodians of the Sacred Teachings and a spiritual Power more potent in the life of the Western World than any of the visible Governments, though they may not interfere with humanity so as to deprive them of their free will.

As the path of development in all cases depends upon the temperament of the aspirant, there are two paths, *the mystic* and *the intellectual*. The Mystic is usually devoid of intellectual knowledge; he follows the dictates of his heart and strives to do the will of God as he *feels* it, lifting himself upward without being conscious of any definite goal, and in the end he attains to knowledge. In the middle ages people were not as intellectual as we are nowadays, and those who felt the call of a higher life usually followed the mystic path. But in the last few hundred years, since the advent of modern science, a more *intellectual* humanity has peopled the earth; the head has completely overruled the heart, materialism has dominated all spiritual impulse and the majority of thinking

From Max Heindel, *The Rosicrucian Cosmo-Conception,* Mt. Ecclesia, Oceanside, California; The Rosicrucian Fellowship. Selection is an abridgement of pp. 520–530, reprinted by permission of The Rosicrucian Fellowship.

people do not believe anything they cannot touch, taste or handle. Therefore, it is necessary that appeal should be made to their intellect in order that the heart may be allowed to believe what the intellect has sanctioned. As a response to this demand the Rosicrucian Mystery teachings aim to correlate scientific facts to spiritual verities.

In the past these have been kept secret from all but a few Initiates, and even today they are among the most mysterious and secret in the Western World. All so-called "discoveries" of the past which have professed to reveal the Rosicrucian secrets, have been either fraudulent, or the result of treachery upon the part of some outsider who may, accidentally or otherwise, have overhead fragments of conversation, unintelligible to all but those who have the key. It is possible to live under the same roof and on terms of the closest intimacy with an Initiate of any school, yet his secret will always remain hidden in his breast until the friend has reached the point where he can become a Brother Initiate. The revealing of secrets does not depend upon the Will of the Initiate, but upon the qualifications of the aspirant.

Like all other Mystery Orders, the Order of Rosicrucians is formed on cosmic lines: If we take balls of even size and try how many it will take to cover one and hide it from view, we shall find that it will require 12 to conceal a thirteenth ball. The ultimate division of physical matter, the true atom, found in interplanetary space, is thus grouped in twelve around one. The twelve signs of the Zodiac enveloping our Solar System, the twelve semi-tones of the musical scale comprising the octave, the twelve Apostles who clustered around the Christ, etc., are other examples of this grouping of 12 and 1. The Rosicrucian Order is therefore also composed of 12 Brothers and a 13th.

There are other divisions to be noted, however. We have seen that of the Heavenly Host of twelve Creative Hierachies who were active in our scheme of evolution, five have withdrawn to liberation, leaving only seven to busy themselves with other further progress. It is in harmony with this fact that the man of today, the indwelling Ego, the microcosm, works outwards through seven visible orifices in his body: 2 eyes, 2 ears, 2 nostrils and a mouth, while five other orifices are wholly or partially closed, the mammae, the umbilicus and the two excretory organs.

The seven roses which garnish our beautiful emblem and the five pointed radiating star behind, are emblematical of the twelve Great Creative Hierarchies which have assisted the evolving human spirit through the previous conditions as mineral, plant and animal, when it was devoid of self-consciousness and unable to care for itself in the slightest degree. Of these twelve hosts of

Great Beings, three classes worked upon and with man of their own free wills and without any obligation whatever.

These are symbolized by the three points in the star upon our emblem which point upwards. Two more of the Great Hierarchies are upon the point of withdrawal and these are pictured in the two points of the star which radiate downward from the center. The seven roses reveal the fact that there are still seven Great Creative Hierarchies active in the development of the beings upon earth, and as all of these various classes from the smallest to the greatest are but parts of One Great Whole whom we call God, the whole emblem is a symbol of God in manifestation.

The Hermetic axiom says: "As above so below," and the lesser teachers of mankind are also grouped upon the same cosmic lines of 7, 5 and 1. There are upon earth seven schools of the lesser Mysteries, five of the Greater and the whole is grouped under one Central Head Who is called the Liberator.

In the Order of Rosicrucians seven Brothers go out into the World whenever occasion requires; appearing as men among other men or working in their invisible vehicles with or upon others as needed; yet it must be strictly kept in mind that they never influence people against their will or contrary to their desires; but only strengthen good wherever found.

The remaining five Brothers never leave the temple; and though they do possess physical bodies all of their work is done from the inner Worlds.

The Thirteenth is Head of the Order, the link with a higher Central Council composed of the Hierophants of the Greater Mysteries, who do not deal with ordinary humanity at all, but only with graduates of the lesser Mysteries.

The Head of the Order is hidden from the outside world by the twelve Brothers, as the central ball mentioned in our illustration. Even the pupils of the School never see him, but at the nightly Services in the Temple His presence is *felt* by all, whenever He enters, and is the signal for the commencement of the ceremony.

Gathered around the Brothers of the Rose Cross, as their pupils, are a number of "lay brothers"; people who live in various parts of the Western World, but are able to leave their bodies consciously, attend the services and participate in the spiritual work at the temple; they having each and every one been "initiated" in the method of so doing by one of the Elder Brothers. Most of them are able to remember all that happens, but there are a few cases where the faculty of leaving the body was acquired in a previous life of well-doing and where a drug habit or a sickness contracted in the present existence has unfitted the brain to receive impression of the work done by the man when away.

. . . We know well, that when a boy has graduated from grammar school he is not therefore fitted to teach. He must first go through high school and college, and even then he may not feel the call to be a school teacher. Similarly in the school of life, because a man has graduated from the Rosicrucian Mystery School he is not even then a Rosicrucian. Graduates from the various schools of the lesser mysteries advance into five schools of the greater mysteries. In the first four they pass the four Great Initiations and at last reach the Liberator, where they receive a knowledge concerning other evolutions and are given the choice of remaining here to assist their brothers or enter other evolutions as Helpers. Those who elect to stay here as helpers are given various positions according to their tastes and natural bent. The Brothers of the Rose Cross are among those Compassionate Ones, and it is a sacrilege to drag the Rosicrucian name in the mire by applying it to ourselves when we are merely students of their lofty teachings.

During the past few centuries the Brothers have worked for humanity in secret; each night at midnight there is a Service at the temple where the Elder Brothers, assisted by the lay brothers who are able to leave their work in the World (for many of them reside in places where it is yet day when it is midnight in the location of the temple of the Red Cross), gather up from everywhere in the Western World the thoughts of sensuality, greed, selfishness and materialism. These they seek to transmute into pure love, benevolence, altruism and spiritual aspirations sending them back to the World to uplift and encourage all Good. Were it not for this potent source of spiritual vibration materialism must long ago have totally squelched all spiritual effort, for there has never been a darker age from the spiritual standpoint than the last three hundred years of materialism.

Now the time has come, however, when the method of secret endeavor is to be supplemented with a more direct effort to promulgate a definite, logical and sequential teaching concerning the origin, evolution and future development of the World and man, showing both the spiritual and the scientific aspect: a teaching which makes no statements that are not supported by reason and logic; a teaching which is satisfying to the mind, for it holds out a reasonable solution to all mysteries; it neither begs nor evades questions and its explanations are both profound and lucid.

But, and this is a very important "But," *the Rosicrucians do not regard an intellectual understanding of God and the Universe as an end in itself;* far from it! The greater the intellect, the greater the danger of its misuse. Therefore, *this scientific, logical and exhaustive teaching is given in order that man may believe in his heart that which his head has sanctioned and start to live the religious life.*

Rudolf Steiner (1861–1925)

Experiences of Initiation in the Northern Mysteries

. . . To-day we will turn our minds to the other path that a man may take, not by descending into his inner self at the moment of waking, but by consciously experiencing the moment of going to sleep, consciously experiencing the condition during which he is given over to sleep. We have heard how man has then expanded as it were into the Macrocosm, whereas in his waking state he has plunged into his own being, into the Microcosm. We also heard that what a man would experience if his Ego were to pour consciously into the Macrocosm, would be so dazzling, so shattering, that it must be regarded as a wise dispensation that at the moment of going to sleep man forgets his existence altogether and consciousness ceases.

What man can experience in the Macrocosm opening out before him, provided he retains a certain degree of consciousness, was described as a state of

Abridgement from Lecture Six of Rudolf Steiner, *Macrocosm and Microcosm,* London Rudolf Steiner Press, 1968, pp. 97–115. The translation from the sixth lecture of Rudolf Steiner's *Macrocosm and Microcosm* is printed by permission of Rudolf Steiner Press, London, and the Rudolf Steiner-Nachlassverwaltung, Dornach, Switzerland, the holders of the original copyright.

ecstasy. But it was said at the same time that in ecstasy the Ego is like a tiny drop mingling in a large volume of water and disappearing in it. Man is in the state of being outside himself, outside his ordinary nature; he lets his Ego flow out of him. Ecstasy, therefore, can by no means be considered a desirable way of passing into the Macrocosm, for a man would lose hold of himself and the Ego would cease to control him. Nevertheless in bygone times, particularly in certain parts of Europe, a candidate who was to be initiated into the mysteries of the Macrocosm was put into a condition comparable with ecstasy. This is no longer part of the modern methods for attaining Initiation, but in olden times, especially in the Northern and Western regions of Europe, including our own, it was entirely in keeping with the development of the peoples living there that they should be led to the secrets of the Macrocosm through a form of ecstasy. Thereby they were also exposed to what might be described as the loss of the Ego, but this condition was less perilous in those times because men were still imbued with a certain healthy, elemental strength; unlike people to-day their soul-forces had not been enfeebled by the effects of highly developed intellectuality. They were able to experience with far greater intensity all the hopefulness connected with Spring, the exultation of Summer, the melancholy of Autumn, the death-shudder of Winter, while still retaining something of their Ego—although not for long. In the case of those who were to become initiates and teachers of men, provision had to be made for this introduction to the Macrocosm to take place in a different way. The reason for this will be evident when it is remembered that the main feature in this process was the loss of the Ego. The Ego became progressively weaker, until finally man reached the state when he lost himself as a human being.

How could this be prevented? The force that became weaker in the candidate's own soul, the Ego-force, had to be brought to him from outside. In the Northern Mysteries this was achieved by the candidate being given the support of helpers who in their turn supported the officiating initiator. The presence of a spiritual initiator was essential, but helpers were necessary as well.

Twelve individuals—three Spring-helpers, three Summer-helpers, three Autumn helpers and three Winter-helpers were necessary; they transmitted their specialised Ego-forces to the candidate for Initiation and he, when he had risen into higher worlds, was able to give information about those worlds from his own experience. A team or 'college' of twelve men worked together in the Mysteries in order to help a candidate for Initiation to rise into the Macrocosm. A reminiscence of this has been preserved in certain societies existing to-day, but in an entirely decadent form. As a rule in such societies special functions are also carried out by twelve members; but this is only a last and moreover entirely misunderstood echo of acts once performed in the Northern Mysteries for the purposes of Initiation.

If, then, a man endowed with an Ego-force artificially maintained in him, penetrated into the Macrocosm, he actually ascended through worlds. The first world through which he passed was the one that would be revealed to him if he did not lose consciousness on going to sleep. We will therefore now turn our attention to this moment of going to sleep as we did previously to that of waking.

The process of going to sleep is in very truth an ascent into the Macrocosm. Even in normal human consciousness it is sometimes possible, through particularly abnormal conditions, to become conscious to a certain extent of the processes connected with going to sleep. This happens in the following way.—The man feels a kind of bliss and can distinguish this consciousness of bliss quite clearly from the ordinary waking consciousness. It is as though he became lighter, as though he were growing out beyond himself. Then this experience is connected with a certain feeling of being tortured by remembrance of the personal faults inhering in the character during life. What arises here as a painful remembrance of personal faults is a very faint reflection of the feeling a man has when he passes the Lesser Guardian of the Threshold and can perceive how imperfect he is and how trivial in face of the great realities and Beings of the Macrocosm. This experience is followed by a kind of convulsion—indicating that the inner man is passing out into the Macrocosm. Such experiences are unusual but known to many people when they were more or less conscious at the moment of going to sleep. But a person who has only the ordinary, normal consciousness loses it at the moment of going to sleep. All the impressions of the day—colours, light, sounds, and so on— vanish, and the man is surrounded by dense darkness instead of the colours and other impressions of daily life. If he were able to maintain his consciousness—as the trained Initiate can do—at the moment when the impressions of the day vanish, he would perceive what is called in spiritual science the *Elementary* or *Elemental World,* the *World of the Elements.*

This World of the Elements is, to begin with, hidden from man while he is in process of going to sleep. Just as man's inner being is hidden on waking through his attention being diverted to the impressions of the outer world, so, when he goes to sleep, the nearest world to which he belongs, the first stage of the Macrocosm, the Elementary World, is hidden from his perception. He can learn to gaze into it when he actually ascends into the Macrocosm in the way indicated. To begin with, this Elementary World makes him conscious that everything in his environment, all sense-perceptions and impressions, are an emanation, a manifestation of the spiritual, that the spiritual lies behind everything material. When a man on the way to Initiation—not, therefore, losing consciousness while passing into sleep—perceives this world, no doubt any longer exists for him that spiritual Beings and spiritual realities lie behind the physical world. Only as long as he is aware of nothing except the physical world does he imagine that behind this world there exist all kinds of conjectured material phenomena—such as atoms and the like. For the man who penetrates into the Elementary World there can no longer be any question of whirling, clustering atoms of matter. He knows that what lies behind colours, sounds and so forth is not material but the *spiritual*. Certainly, at this first stage of the World of the Elements the spiritual does not yet reveal itself in its true form as spirit. Man has before him impressions which, although in a different form from those known in waking consciousness, are not yet the spiritual facts themselves. It is not yet anything that could be called a true spiritual manifestation but to a considerable degree it is something that might be described as a kind of new veil over the spiritual Beings and facts.

The form in which this world reveals itself is such that the designations, the names, which since olden times have been used for the Elements are applicable to it. We can describe what is there seen by choosing words used for qualities otherwise perceived in the physical world: solid, liquid or fluid, airy or aeriform, or warmth; or: earth, water, air, fire. These expressions are taken from the physical world for which they are coined. Our language is after all a means of expression for the physical world. If there the spiritual scientist has to describe the higher worlds, he must borrow the words from the language that was coined for the things of ordinary life. He can speak only in similes, endeavouring so to choose the words that little by little an idea is evoked of what is perceived by spiritual vision. In depicting the Elementary World we must not take the terms and expressions that are used for circumscribed objects in the physical world but those used for certain qualities common to a category of objects. Otherwise we shall lose our bearings. Things in the physical world reveal themselves to us in certain states which we call solid, liquid, aeriform; and in addition there is also what we become aware of when we touch the surfaces of objects or feel a current of air which we call warmth.

Things in the everyday world are revealed to us in these states or conditions: solid, liquid, aeriform or gaseous, or as warmth. These, however, are always qualities of some external body, for an external body may be solid in the form of ice or also be liquid or gaseous when the ice melts. Warmth permeates all three states. So it is in the case of everything existing in the outer world of the senses. . . .

Then there is something in the Elementary World comparable with what we call 'airy' or 'aeriform' in the physical world. This is designated as 'air' in the Elementary World. Then, further, there is 'fire' or 'warmth,' but it must be realised that what is called 'fire' in the physical world is only a simile. 'Fire' as it is in the Elementary World is easier to describe than the other three states for these can really only be described by saying that water, air and earth are similes of them. The 'fire' of the Elementary World is easier to describe because everyone has a conception of *warmth of soul* as it is called, of the warmth that is felt, for example, when we are together with someone we love. What then suffuses the soul and is called warmth, or fire of excitement, must naturally be distinguished from ordinary physical fire which will burn the fingers if they come into contact with it. In daily life, too, man feels that physical fire is a kind of symbol of the fire of soul which, when it lays hold of us, kindles enthusiasm. By thinking of something midway between an outer, physical fire that burns our fingers, and fire of soul, we reach an approximate idea of what is called 'elemental fire.' When in the process of Initiation a man rises into the Elementary World, he feels as if from certain places something were flowing towards him that pervades him inwardly with warmth, while at another place this is less the case. An added complication is that he feels as if he were within the being who is transmitting the warmth to him. He is united with this elementary being and accordingly feels its fire. Such a man is entering a higher world which gives him impressions hitherto unknown to him in the world of the senses.

When a man with normal consciousness goes to sleep his whole being flows out into the Elementary World. He is within everything in that world; but he takes his own nature, what he is as man, into it. He loses his Ego as it pours forth, but what is *not* Ego—his astral qualities, his desires and passions, his sense of truth or the reverse—all this is carried into the Elementary World. He loses his Ego which in everyday life keeps him in check, which brings order and harmony into the astral body. When he loses the Ego, disorder prevails among the impulses and cravings in his soul and they make their way into the Elementary World together with him; he carries into that world everything that is in his soul. If he has some bad quality, he transmits it to a being in the Elementary World who feels drawn towards this bad quality. Thus with the loss of his Ego he would, on penetrating into the Macrocosm, transmit his whole astral nature to evil beings who pervade the Elementary World. Because he contacts these beings who have strong Egos, while he himself, having lost his Ego, is weaker than they, the consequence is that they will reward him in the negative sense for the sustenance with which he supplies them for his astral nature. When he returns into the physical world they transmit to him, for his Ego, qualities they have received from him and made particularly their own; in other words they strengthen his propensity for evil.

So we see that it is a wise dispensation for man to lose consciousness when he enters the Elementary World and to be safeguarded from passing with his Ego into that world. Therefore one who in the ancient Mysteries was to be led into the Elementary World had to be carefully prepared before forces were poured into him by the helpers of the Initiator. This preparation consisted in the imposition of rigorous tests whereby the candidate acquired a stronger moral power of self-conquest. Special value was attached to this attribute. In the case of a mystic, different attributes—humility, for example—were considered particularly valuable.

Accordingly upon a man who was to be admitted to an Initiation in these Mysteries, tests were imposed which helped him to rise above disasters of every kind even in physical existence. Formidable dangers were laid along his path. But by overcoming these dangers his soul was to be so strengthened that he was duly prepared when beings confronted him in the Elementary World; he was then strong enough not to succumb to any of their temptations, not to let them get the better of him but to repel them. Those who were to be admitted into the Mysteries were trained in fearlessness and in the power of self-conquest. . . .

When the candidate in those ancient Mysteries, after long experiences connected with the Elementary World, had become capable of realising that 'earth,' 'water,' 'air,' 'fire'—everything he perceives in the material world—are the revelations of spiritual beings, when he had learned to discriminate between them and to find his bearings in the Elementary World, he could be led a stage further to what is called the *World of Spirit* behind the Elementary World. Those who were initiates—and this can only be described as a communication of what they experienced—now realised that in very truth there are beings behind the Physical and the Elementary Worlds. But these beings have no resemblance at all to men. Whereas men on the Earth live together in a social order, in certain forms of society, under definite social conditions, whether satisfactory or the reverse, the candidate for Initiation passes into a world in which there are spiritual beings—beings who naturally have no external body but who are related to each other in such a way that order and harmony prevail. It is now revealed to him that he can understand the order and harmony he perceives in that world only by realising that what these spiritual beings do is an external expression of the heavenly bodies in the solar system, of the relationship between the Sun and the planets in their movements and positions. Thereby these heavenly bodies give expression to what the beings of the spiritual world are doing.

It has already been said that our solar system may be conceived as a great cosmic clock or timepiece. Just as we infer from the position of the hands of a clock that something is happening, we can do the same from the relative positions of the heavenly bodies. Anyone looking at a clock is naturally not interested in the hands or their position *per se,* but in what this indicates in the outer world. The hands of a clock indicate, for example, what is happening here in Vienna or somewhere in the world at this moment. A man who has to go to his daily work looks at the clock to see if it is time to start. The position of the hands is therefore the expression of something lying behind. And so it is in the case of the solar system. This great cosmic clock can be regarded as the expression of spiritual happenings and of the activity of spiritual beings behind it.

At this stage the candidate for the Initiation we have been describing comes to know the spiritual beings and facts. He comes to know the World of Spirit and realises that this World of Spirit can best be understood by applying to it the designations used in connection with our solar system; for there we have an outer symbol of this World of Spirit. For the Elementary World the similes are taken from the qualities of earthly things—solid, liquid, airy, fiery. But for the World of Spirit other similes must be used, similes drawn from the starry heavens.

And now we can realise that the comparison with a clock is by no means far fetched. We relate the heavenly bodies of our solar system to the twelve constellations of the Zodiac, and we can find our bearings in the World of Spirit only by viewing it in such a way as to be able to assert that spiritual Beings and events are realities; we compare the *facts* with the courses of the planets but the spiritual *Beings* with the twelve constellations of the Zodiac. If we contemplate the planets in space and the zodiacal constellations, if we conceive the movements and relative positions of the planets in front of the various constellations to be manifestations of the activities of the spiritual Beings and the twelve constellations of the Zodiac as the spiritual Beings themselves, then it is possible to express by such an analogy what is happening in the World of Spirit.

We distinguish seven planets moving and performing deeds, and twelve zodiacal constellations at rest behind them. We conceive that the spiritual facts—the courses of the planets—are brought about by twelve Beings. Only in this way is it possible to speak truly of the World of Spirit lying behind the Elementary World. We must picture not merely twelve zodiacal constellations, but Beings, actually categories of Beings, and not merely seven planets, but spiritual facts.

Twelve Beings are acting, are entering into relationship with one another and if we describe their actions this will show what is coming to pass in the World of Spirit. Accordingly, whatever has reference to the *Beings* must be related in some way to the number *twelve*; whatever has reference to the *facts* must be related to the number *seven*. Only instead of the names of the zodiacal constellations we need to have the names of the corresponding Beings. In Spiritual Science these names have always been known. At the beginning of the Christian era there was an esoteric School which adopted the following names for the Spiritual Beings corresponding to the zodiacal constellations: Seraphim, Cherubim, Thrones, Kyriotetes, Dynameis, Exusiai, then Archai (Primal Beginnings or Spirits of Personality), then Archangels and Angels. The tenth category is Man himself at his present stage of evolution. These names denote ten ranks. Man, however, develops onwards and subsequently reaches stages already attained by other Beings. Therefore one day he will also be instrumental in forming an eleventh and a twelfth category. In this sense we must think of twelve spiritual Beings.

If we wanted to describe the World of Spirit we should have to attribute the origin of the spiritual universe to the co-operation among these twelve categories of Beings. Any description of what they *do* would have to deal with the planetary bodies and their movements. Let us assume that the Spirits of Will (the Thrones) co-operate with the Spirits of Personality (Archai) or with other Beings—and Old Saturn comes into existence. Through the co-operation of other Spirits the planetary bodies we call Old Sun and Old Moon come into existence.

We are speaking here of the deeds of these spiritual Beings. A description of the World of Spirit must include the Elementary World, for that is the last manifestation before the physical world; fire, air, water, earth, must also be considered. On Old Saturn, everything was fire or warmth; during the Old Sun evolution, air was added; during the Old Moon evolution, water. In describing the World of Spirit we must begin with the *Beings*. We call them the Hierarchies and pass on to their *deeds* which come to expression through the planets in their courses. And to have a picture of how all this manifests in the Elementary World we must describe it by using terms derived from this world. Only in this way is it possible to give a picture of the World of Spirit lying behind the Elementary World and our physical world of sense.

The Beings, the spiritual Hierarchies, their correspondences with the zodiacal constellations, the planetary embodiments of our Earth described by using expressions connected with the Elementary World—all this is presented in detail in the chapter on the evolution of the world in the book *Occult Science—an Outline,* and we can now understand the deeper reasons for that chapter having been written in the way it has. It describes the Macrocosm as it should be described. Any real description must go back to the spiritual Beings. I tried in the book *Occult Science* to give guiding lines for the right kind of description of the World of Spirit—the world entered when there has been an actual ascent into the Macrocosm.

This ascent into the Macrocosm can of course proceed to still higher stages, for the Macrocosm has by no means been exhaustively portrayed by what has here been said. Man can ascend into even higher worlds; but it becomes more and more difficult to convey any idea of these worlds. The higher the ascent, the more difficult this becomes. If we want to give an idea of a still higher world it must be done rather differently. An impression of the world that is reached after passing beyond the World of Spirit may be obtained in the following way.—In describing man as he stands before us we may say that his existence was only made possible through the existence of these higher worlds. Man has become the being he is because he has evolved out of the physical world but above all out of the higher, spiritual worlds. Only a fantasy-ridden, materialistic mind can believe that it would be possible for a man to originate from the nebula described by the Kant-Laplace theory. Such a nebula could have produced only an automaton—never a man!

Around us, we have, firstly, the physical world. The physical body of man belongs to the world we perceive with our senses. With ordinary consciousness we perceive it only from outside. To what world do the more deeply lying, invisible members of man's nature belong? They all belong to the higher worlds. Just as with physical eyes we see only the material aspect of man, so too we see of the great outer world only what the senses perceive; we do not see those supersensible worlds of which two—the Elementary World and the World of Spirit—have been described. But man, with his inner constitution, has issued from these higher worlds. The whole of man's being, his external, bodily nature too, has become possible only because certain invisible spiritual Beings have worked on him. If the etheric body alone had worked on man, he would be like a plant, for a plant has a physical and an etheric body. Man has in addition the astral body; but so too has the animal. If man had only these three members (physical body, etheric body, astral body) he would be an animal. It is because man has his Ego as well that he towers above these lower creatures of the mineral, plant and animal kingdoms of nature. All the higher members of man work on his physical body; the physical body could not be what it is unless man also possessed these higher members. A plant would be a mineral if it had no etheric body. Man would have no nervous system if he had no astral body; he would not have his present structure, his upright gait, his overarching brow, if he had not an Ego. If he had not his invisible members in higher worlds, he could not confront us as the figure he is. . . .

One who has attained Initiation recognises that if only the Elementary World and the World of Spirit existed, man's organ of intelligence could never have come into being. The World of the Spirit is indeed a lofty world but the forces which have formed the physical organ of thinking must have streamed into man from a yet higher world in order that intelligence might manifest outwardly, in the physical world. Spiritual science has not without reason figuratively expressed this frontier of the world we have described as the world of the Hierarchies, by the word "Zodiac." Man would be at the level of the animal if only the two worlds that have been described were in existence. In order that man could become a being able to walk upright, to think by means of the brain and to develop intelligence, an instreaming of even higher forces was necessary, forces from a world *above* the World of Spirit. Here we come to a world designated by a word that is totally misused to-day because of the prevailing materialism. But in a past by no means very distant the word still conveyed its original meaning. The faculty man unfolds here in the physical world when he thinks, was called 'Intelligence' in the spiritual science of that earlier period. It is from a world lying *beyond* both the World of Spirit and the Elementary World that forces stream down through these two worlds to build our brain. Spiritual Science has also called it the World of Reason (*Vernunftwelt*). It is the world in which there are spiritual Beings who are able to send down their power into the physical world in order that a shadow-image of the Spiritual may be produced in the physical world in man's intellectual activity. Before the age of materialism no one would have used the word "reason" for thinking; thinking would have been called intellect, intelligence. "Reason" (*Vernunft*) would have been spoken of when those who were initiates had risen into a world even higher than the World of Spirit and had direct perception there. In the German language "reason" is connected with perception (*Vernehmen*), with what is directly apprehended, perceived as coming from a world still higher than the one denoted as the World of Spirit. A faint image of this world exists in the shadowy human intellect. The architects and builders of our organ of intellect must be sought in the *World of Reason*.

It is only possible to describe a still higher world by developing a spiritual faculty transcending the physical intellect. There is a higher form of consciousness, namely, *clairvoyant consciousness*. If we ask: how is the organ evolved which enables us to have clairvoyant consciousness?—the answer is that there must be worlds from which emanate the forces necessary for the development of this clairvoyant consciousness. Like everything else, it must be formed from a higher world. The first kind of clairvoyant consciousness to develop is a picture-consciousness, Imaginative Consciousness. This Imaginative Consciousness remains mere phantasy only for as long as the organ for it is not formed by forces from a world lying beyond even the World of Reason. As soon as we admit the existence of clairvoyant consciousness we must also admit the existence of a world from which emanate the forces enabling the organ for it to develop. This is the *World of Archetypal Images (Urbilderwelt)*. Whatever can arise as true Imagination is a reflection of the World of Archetypal Images.

Thus we rise into the Macrocosm through four higher worlds: the Elementary World, the World of Spirit, the World of Reason and the World of Archetypal Images. In the next lectures I will deal with the World of Reason and the World of Archetypal Images and then describe the methods by which, in line with modern culture, the forces from the World of Archetypal Images can be brought down in order to make possible the development of clairvoyant consciousness.

W. B. Yeats (1865–1939)

Invoking the Irish Fairies

This article appeared in the first issue (October, 1892) of the *Irish Theoso-phist*. The initials signed at the end, "D.E.D.I.," represent the Latin phrase "Demon est deus inversus," or in English, "A demon is an inverted god." These initials are known to have been those assumed by Yeats when he joined the Order of the Golden Dawn in March, 1890, a short time before he was ex-pelled from the esoteric Section of Madame Blavatsky's Theosophical Society in London.

This account of a trance is filled with learning which Yeats would have been acquiring as he passed through the first stages of initiation in the Golden Dawn. His companion, "D. D.," may have been either Florence Farr ("S.S.D.D." in the Golden Dawn) or Maud Gonne (whose initials were "P.I.A.L." in this society).

The *Irish Theosophist* was the magazine of the Dublin Theosophical So-ciety. A. E. was the guiding spirit of this branch of the society, and the magazine was edited by David M. Dunlop. Yeats, though never formally a

Reprinted from *Uncollected Prose by W. B. Yeats,* vol. 1, collected and edited by John P. Frayne. New York: Columbia University Press, 1970, pp. 245–247. Introduction to the text and footnotes are by John P. Frayne. Reprinted by permission of Columbia University Press and the Estate of William Butler Yeats.

member, took part in some of their activities. For another account of a trance
attended by Yeats, see "The Sorcerers" in *The Celtic Twilight*.

The Occultist and student of Alchemy whom I shall call D.D. and myself
sat at opposite sides of the fire one morning, wearied with symbolism and
magic. D.D. had put down a kettle to boil. We were accustomed to meet every
now and then, that we might summon the invisible powers and gaze into the
astral light; for we had learned to see with the internal eyes. But this morning
we knew not what to summon, for we had already on other mornings invoked
that personal vision of impersonal good which men name Heaven, and that
personal vision of impersonal evil, which men name Hell.[1] We had called up
likewise, the trees of knowledge and of life, and we had studied the hidden
meaning of the Zodiac, and enquired under what groups of stars, the various
events of the bible story were classified by those dead Occultists who held all
things, from the firmament above to the waters under the Earth, to be but
symbol and again symbol. We had gone to ancient Egypt, seen the burial of
her dead and heard mysterious talk of Isis and Osiris. We had made the invisible powers interpret for us the mystic tablet of Cardinal Bembo,[2] and we
had asked of the future and heard words of dread and hope. We had called up
the Klippoth[3] and in terror seen them rush by like great black rams, and now
we were a little weary of shining colours and sweeping forms. "We have seen
the great and they have tried us," I said; "let us call the little for a change.
The Irish fairies may be worth the seeing; there is time for them to come and
go before the water is boiled."

I used a lunar invocation and left the seeing mainly to D.D. She saw first a
thin cloud as though with the ordinary eyes and then with the interior sight, a
barren mountain crest with one ragged tree. The leaves and branches of the
tree were all upon one side, as though it had been blighted by the sea winds.
The Moon shone through the branches and a white woman stood beneath
them. We commanded this woman to show us the fairies of Ireland marshalled
in order. Immediately a great multitude of little creatures appeared, with
green hair like sea-weed and after them another multitude dragging a car
containing an enormous bubble. The white woman, who appeared to be their
queen, said the first were the water fairies and the second the fairies of the air.
The first were called the Gelki and the second the Gieri (I have mislaid my
notes and am not quite certain if I give their names correctly). They passed on

and a troop who were like living flames followed and after them a singular multitude whose bodies were like the stems of flowers and their dresses like the petals. These latter fairies after a while, stood still under a green bush from which dropped honey like dew and thrust out their tongues, which were so long, that they were able to lick the honey-covered ground without stooping. These two troops were the fairies of the fire and the fairies of the earth.

The white woman told us that these were the good fairies and that she would now bring D.D. to the fairies of evil. Soon a great abyss appeared and in the midst was a fat serpent, with forms, half animal, half human, polishing his heavy scales. The name of this serpent was Grew-grew and he was the chief of the wicked goblins. About him moved quantities of things like pigs, only with shorter legs, and above him in the air flew vast flocks of cherubs and bats. The bats, however flew with their heads down and the cherubs with their foreheads lower than their winged chins.—I was at the time studying a mystic system that makes this inversion of the form a mark of certain types of evil spirits, giving it much the same significance as is usually given to the inverted pentegram [sic]. This system was unknown to D.D. whose mind was possibly, however, overshadowed for the moment by mine; the invoking mind being always more positive than the mind of the seer.—Had she been invoking the conditions would have been reversed.

Presently the bats and cherubs and the forms that a moment before had been polishing the scales of Grew-grew, rushed high up into the air and from an opposite direction appeared the troops of the good fairies, and the two kingdoms began a most terrible warfare. The evil fairies hurled burning darts but were unable to approach very near to the good fairies, for they seemed unable to bear the neighbourhood of pure spirits. The contest seemed to fill the whole heavens, for as far as the sight could go the clouds of embattled goblins went also. It is that contest of the minor forces of good and evil which knows no hour of peace but goes on everywhere and always. The fairies are the lesser spiritual moods of that universal mind, wherein every mood is a soul and every thought a body.[4] Their world is very different from ours, and they can but appear in forms borrowed from our limited consciousness, but nevertheless, every form they take and every action they go through, has its significance and can be read by the mind trained in the correspondence of sensuous form and supersensuous meaning.

D.E.D.I.

NOTES

1. Yeats liked the phrase "which men name . . . ." See "The Secret Rose":—". . . heavy with the sleep/men have named beauty."

2. Pietro, Cardinal Bembo (1460–1547), Italian Renaissance historian and man of letters. I have not located any mystical writings of Cardinal Bembo. Yeats may have meant an eleventh-century Cardinal Benno who was interested in diabolism. Benno claimed that between Popes John XII (965–972) and Gregory VII (1073–1085) there had been an unbroken line of eighteen popes who had practiced black magic (E.M. Butler, *The Myth of the Magus*, London and New York, 1948).

3. "Klippoth" is the Hebrew word for demons. Literally "the world of shells," in Kabalistic cosmology it is formed from emanations of the Yetzirah or world of the gods.

4. By 1895 this doctrine of the moods as spiritual emanations of the world soul was to become an essential part of Yeats's aesthetic. . . .

Louis Pauwels and Jacques Bergier

Theosophy and Nazism

The Earth is hollow. We are living inside it. The stars are blocks of ice. Several Moons have already fallen on the Earth. The whole history of humanity is contained in the struggle between ice and fire.

Man is not finished. He is on the brink of a formidable mutation which will confer on him the powers the ancients attributed to the gods. A few specimens of the New Man exist in the world, who have perhaps come here from beyond the frontiers of time and space.

Alliances could be formed with the Master of the World or the King of Fear who reigns over a city hidden somewhere in the East. Those who conclude a pact will change the surface of the Earth and endow the human adventure with a new meaning for many thousands of years.

Such are the "scientific" theories and "religious" conceptions on which Nazism was originally based and in which Hitler and the members of his groups believed—theories which, to a large extent, have dominated social and political trends to recent history. This may seem extravagant. Any explanation, even partial, of contemporary history based on ideas and beliefs of this kind may seem repugnant. In our view, nothing is repugnant that is in the interests of the truth.

It is well known that the Nazi party was openly, and even flamboyantly anti-intellectual; that it burned books and relegated the theoretical physicists among its "Judaeo-Marxist" enemies. Less is known about the reasons which led it to reject official Western science, and still less with regard to the basic conception of the nature of man on which Nazism was founded—at any rate in the minds of some of its leaders. If we knew this it would be easier to place the last World War within the category of great spiritual conflicts: history animated once again by the spirit of *La Légende des Siècles*.

Hitler used to say: "We are often abused for being the enemies of the mind and spirit. Well, that is what we are, but in a far deeper sense than bourgeois science, in its idiotic pride, could ever imagine."

This is very like what Gurdjieff said to his disciple Ouspensky after having condemned science: "My way is to develop the hidden potentialities of man; a way that is against Nature and against God."

This idea of the hidden potentialities of Man is fundamental. If often leads to the rejection of science and disdain for ordinary human beings. On this level very few men really exist. To be, means to be something different. The ordinary man, "natural" man is nothing but a worm, and the Christians' God nothing but a guardian for worms.

Dr. Willy Ley, one of the world's greatest rocket experts, fled from Germany in 1933. It was from him that we learned of the existence in Berlin shortly before the Nazis came to power, of a little spiritual community that is of great interest to us.

This secret community was founded, literally, on Bulwer Lytton's novel *The Coming Race*. The book describes a race of men psychically far in advance of ours. They have acquired powers over themselves and over things that make them almost godlike. For the moment they are in hiding. They live in caves in the center of the Earth. Soon they will emerge to reign over us.

This appears to be as much as Dr. Ley could tell us. He added with a smile that the disciples believed they had secret knowledge that would enable them to change their race and become the equals of men hidden in the bowels of the Earth. Methods of concentration, a whole system of internal gymnastics by which they would be transformed. They began their exercises by staring fixedly at an apple cut in half. . . . We continued our researches.

This Berlin group called itself *The Luminous Lodge*, or *The Vril Society*. The vril[1] is the enormous energy of which we only use a minute proportion in our daily life, the nerve-center of our potential divinity. Whoever becomes master of the vril will be the master of himself, of others round him and of the world.

This should be the only object of our desires, and all our efforts should be directed to that end. All the rest belongs to official psychology, morality, and religions and is worthless.

The world will change: the Lords will emerge from the center of the Earth. Unless we have made an alliance with them and become Lords ourselves, we shall find ourselves among the slaves, on the dung-heap that will nourish the roots of the New Cities that will arise.

The *Luminous Lodge* had associations with the theosophical and Rosicrucian groups . . . .

The reader will recall that the writer, Arthur Machen, we discovered was connected with an English society of Initiates, the *Golden Dawn*. This neopagan society, which had a distinguished membership, was an offshoot of the English Rosicrucian Society, founded by Wentworth Little in 1867, Little was in contact with the German Rosicrucians. He recruited his followers, to the number of 144, from the ranks of the higher-ranking Freemasons. One of his disciples was Bulwer Lytton.

Bulwer Lytton, a learned man of genius, celebrated throughout the world for his novel *The Last Days of Pompeii*, little thought that one of his books, in some ten years' time, would inspire a mystical pre-Nazi group in Germany. Yet in works like *The Coming Race* or *Zanoni*, he set out to emphasize the realities of the spiritual world, and more especially, the infernal world. He considered himself an Initiate. Through his romantic works of fiction he expressed the conviction that there are beings endowed with superhuman powers. These beings will supplant us and bring about a formidable mutation in the elect of the human race.

We must beware of this notion of a mutation. It crops up again with Hitler, and is not yet extinct today.[2]

We must also beware of the notion of the "Unknown Supermen." It is found in all the "black" mystical writings both in the West and in the East. Whether they live under the Earth or came from other planets, whether in the form of giants like those which are said to lie encased in cloth of gold in the crypts of Thibetan monasteries, or of shapeless and terrifying beings such as Lovecraft describes, do these "Unknown Supermen," evoked in pagan and Satanic rites, actually exist? When Machen speaks of the World of Evil, "full of caverns and crepuscular beings dwellings therein," he is referring, as an adept of the *Golden Dawn*, to that other world in which man comes into contact with the "Unknown Supermen." It seems certain that Hitler shared this belief, and even claimed to have been in touch with these "supermen."

We have already mentioned the *Golden Dawn* and the German Vril Society. We shall have something to say later about the *Thule* Group. We are not so foolish as to try to explain history in the light of secret societies. What we shall see, curiously enough, is that it all "ties up," and that with the coming of Nazism it was the "other world" which ruled over us for a number of years. That world has been defeated, but is not dead, either on the Rhine or elsewhere. And there is nothing alarming about it: only our ignorance is alarming.

. . . Samuel Mathers was the founder of the *Golden Dawn*. Mathers claimed to be in communication with these "Unknown Supermen" and to have established contact with them in the company of his wife, the sister of Henri Bergson. Here follows a page of the manifesto addressed to "Members of the Second Order" in 1896:

"As to the Secret Chiefs with whom I am in touch and from whom I have received the wisdom of the Second Order which I communicated to you, I can tell you nothing. I do not even know their Earthly names, and I have very seldom seen them in their physical bodies. . . . They used to meet me physically at a time and place fixed in advance. For my part, I believe they are human beings living on this Earth, but possessed of terrible and superhuman powers. . . . My physical encounters with them have shown me how difficult it is for a mortal, however 'advanced,' to support their presence. . . . I do not mean that during my rare meetings with them I experienced the same feeling of intense physical depression that accompanies the loss of magnetism. On the contrary, I felt I was in contact with a force so terrible that I can only compare it to the shock one would receive form being near a flash of lightning during a great thunder-storm, experiencing at the same time great difficulty in breathing. . . . The nervous prostration I spoke of was accompanied by cold sweats and bleeding from the nose, mouth and sometimes the ears."

Hitler was talking one day to Rauschning, the Governor of Danzig, about the problem of a mutation of the human race. Rauschning, not possessing the key to such strange preoccupations, interpreted Hitler's remarks in terms of a stock-breeder interested in the amelioration of German blood.

"But all you can do," he replied, "is to assist Nature and shorten the road to be followed! It is Nature herself who must create for you a new species. Up til now the breeder has only rarely succeeded in developing mutations in animals—that is to say, creating himself new characteristics."

"The new man is living amongst us now. 'He is here'." exclaimed Hitler, triumphantly. "Isn't that enough for you? I will tell you a secret. I have seen the new man. He is intrepid and cruel. I was afraid of him."

"In uttering these words," added Rauschning, "Hitler was trembling in a kind of ecstasy." . . .

We leave it to the reader to compare the statement of Mathers, head of a small neo-pagan society at the end of the nineteenth century, and the utterances of a man who, at the time Rauschning recorded them, was preparing to launch the world into an adventure which caused the death of twenty million men. We beg him not to ignore this comparison and the lesson to be drawn from it on the grounds that the *Golden Dawn* and Nazism, in the eyes of a "reasonable" historian, have nothing in common. The historian may be reasonable, but history is not. These two men shared the same beliefs: their fundamental experiences were the same, and they were guided by the same force. They belong to the same trend of thought and to the same religion. This religion has never up to now been seriously studied. Neither the Church nor the Rationalists—that other Church—have allowed it. We are now entering an epoch in the history of knowledge when such studies will become possible because now that reality is revealing its fantastic side, ideas, and techniques which seem abnormal, contemptible or repellent will be found useful in so far as they enable us to understand a "reality" that becomes more and more disquieting.

We are not suggesting that the reader should study an affiliation Rosy Cross-Bulwer Lytton-Little-Mathers-Crowley-Hitler, or any similar association which would include also Mme. Blavatsky and Gurdjieff. Looking for affiliations is a game, like looking for "influences" in literature; when the game is over, the problem is still there. In literature it's a question of genius; in history, of power.

The *Golden Dawn* is not enough to explain the *Thule* Group, or the *Luminous Lodge*, the *Ahnenherbe*. Naturally there are cross-currents and secret or apparent links between the various groups, which we shall not fail to point out. Like all "little" history, that is an absorbing pastime. But our concern is with "big" history.

We believe that these societies, great or small, related or unrelated, with or without ramifications, are manifestations, more or less apparent and more or less important, of a world other than the one in which we live. Let us call it the world of Evil, in Machen's sense of the word. The truth is, we know just as little about the world of Good. We are living between two worlds, and pretending that this "no-man's-land" is identical with our whole planet. The rise of Nazism was one of those rare moments in the history of our civilization, when a door was noisily and ostentatiously opened on to something "Other." What is strange is that people pretend not to have seen or heard anything apart from the sights and sounds inseparable from war and political strife.

All these movements: the modern Rosy-Cross, *Golden Dawn*, the German Vril Society (which will bring us to the *Thule* Group where we shall find Haushofer, Hess and Hitler) were more or less closely associated with the powerful and well organized Theosophical Society. Theosophy added to neo-pagan magic an oriental setting and a Hindu terminology. Or, rather, it pro-vided a link between a certain oriental Satanism and the West.

Theosophy was the name finally given to the whole vast renaissance in the world of magic that affected many thinkers so profoundly at the beginning of the century.

In his study *Le Théosophisme, histoire d'une pseudo-religion*, published in 1921, the philosopher René Guénon foresaw what was likely to occur. He realized the dangers lurking behind theosophy and the neo-pagan Initiatory groups that were more or less connected with Mme. Blavatsky and her sect.

This is what he wrote:

"The false Messiahs we have seen so far have only performed very inferior miracles, and their disciples were probably not very difficult to convert. But who knows what the future has in store? When you reflect that these false Messiahs have never been anything but the more or less unconscious tools of those who conjured them up, and when one thinks more particularly of the series of attempts made in succession by the theosophists, one is forced to the conclusion that these were only trials, experiments as it were, which will be renewed in various forms until success is achieved, and which in the meantime invariably produce a somewhat disquieting effect. Not that we believe that the theosophists, any more than the occultist and the spiritualists, are strong enough by themselves to carry out successfully an enterprise of this nature. But might there not be, behind all these movements, something far more dangerous which their leaders perhaps know nothing about, being themselves in turn the unconscious tools of a higher power?"

It was at this time, too, that that extraordinary personage, Rudolf Steiner, founded in Switzerland a research society based on the idea that the entire Universe is contained in the human mind, and that this mind is capable of activities outside the scope or range of official psychology. It is a fact that some of Steiner's discoveries in biology (fertilizers that do not harm the soil), medicine (use of metals that affect metabolism) and especially in pedagogy (there are numerous Rudolf Steiner schools in Europe today) have rendered considerable service to humanity. Steiner thought that there are both black and white forms of "magic," and believed that theosophism and the various neo-pagan societies sprang from the great subterranean world of Evil and heralded the coming of a Satanic, or demoniac age. In his own teaching he was careful to embody a moral doctrine binding the "initiates" to work only for good. He wanted to create a society of "do-gooders."

We are not concerned with the question whether Steiner was right or wrong. What does seem to us very striking is that the Nazis from the beginning seem to have looked upon Steiner as Enemy No. 1.

From the very beginning the Nazis' armed gangs broke up meetings of Steiner's followers by force, threatened his disciples with death, forced them to flee from Germany and, in 1924, burned down the Rudolf Steiner center at Dornach in Switzerland. The archives were destroyed. Steiner was unable to continue his works and died of grief a year later.

Up til now we have been describing the first signs of approach of Hitlerism. . . . Two theories were current in Nazi Germany: the theory of the frozen world, and the theory of the hollow Earth.

These constitute two explanations of the world and humanity which link up with tradition, are in line with mythology and in keeping with some of the "truths" proclaimed by groups of Initiates, from the theosophists to Gurdjieff. Moreover, these theories have had the backing of important politico-scientific circles, and almost succeeded in banishing from Germany what we call modern science. A great many people came under their influence; they even affected some of Hitler's military decisions, influenced the course of the war and doubtless contributed to the final catastrophe. It was through his enslavement to these theories, and especially the notion of the sacrificial deluge, that Hitler wished to condemn the entire German race to annihilation.

We do not know why these theories, which have been so strongly proclaimed and held by scores of men, including some superior intellects, and which have called for great sacrifices, both human and material, have not yet been studied in our countries and to this day are still unknown.

NOTES

1. The notion of the "vril" is mentioned for the first time in the works of the French writer Jacolliot, French Consul in Calcutta under the Second Empire.

2. Hitler's aim was neither the founding of a race of supermen, nor the conquest of the world; these were only means towards the realization of the great work he dreamed of. His real aim was to perform an act of creation, a divine operation, the goal of a biological mutation which would result in an unprecedented exaltation of the human race and the "apparition of a new race of heroes and demi-gods and god-men." (Dr. Achille Delmas.)

Part Two

The Social Setting of the Occult: Witchcraft

The phenomenon of witchcraft, with its horror and fascination, is found in nearly every society. Magic always has two aspects, its benevolent ("white") aspect and its malevolent ("black") aspect, or witchcraft. A small place in theological studies is devoted to "demonology." Priests of traditional Christianity were familiar with the techniques of exorcism. Witchcraft has been the subject of extensive anthropological studies of non-Western societies, where witchcraft beliefs, practices, and accusations have been seen as an important source of information about social structure, including its cleavages and tensions.

Witchcraft illustrates the social aspects of the occult. It places in relief various dimensions of social organization as well as changes in social values. Those who practice witchcraft form a deviant community, perhaps the most deviant of communities. What are society's religious, political, and legal responses to this community? What do the responses to this deviant community tell us about variations in social cohesion? If witchcraft is so condemned, how does it perpetuate itself in its recruitment process? What accounts for a waxing and waning of public arousal and interest in witchcraft? The selections here are concerned with such considerations.

The selections in this part present aspects of witchcraft spanning seven centuries. The historian Jeffrey B. Russell discusses the first recrudescence of witchcraft in the West after the institutionalization of Christianity; charges of witchcraft were levelled against a religious sect of Southern France, the Cathars, who, branded with the charge of heresy, became the object of the first Crusade officially proclaimed against Christians. The selections by sociologists Elliott P. Currie and Kai T. Erikson provide materials on the relationship of witchcraft to social structure in Western Europe and North America three centuries ago.

In the past five years witchcraft has come to life again in the urban centers of the United States, a country where one might least expect it to happen. The selection by Marcello Truzzi provides a sociological accounting of this unexpected phenomenon in American society. The companion piece by Moody offers descriptive materials obtained in the course of urban anthropological field work.

Jeffrey B. Russell

Medieval Witchcraft and Medieval Heresy

Between 500 and 1500 A.D., some tens of thousands of alleged witches in Catholic Europe were condemned to death by burning or hanging or lynching. These victims, and the hundreds of thousands of victims of the persecution of witches from 1500 to 1750, make it impossible to treat the history of witchcraft as a joke or pastime. Witchcraft is an important chapter in the history of human evil, evil in the warped will of the witches, and even greater evil in the vindictive nature of their persecutors.

The many problems that the serious historian finds in the study of witchcraft include the relationship of witchcraft to movements of social rebellion; the ascription of witchcraft to women in particular; witchcraft as a manifestation of psychological projection; the analysis of witchcraft in terms of the sociology of collective behavior, that is, as a "craze" or a "panic." The

This article was presented as a paper to the American Historical Association during 1969 annual meeting in Washington, D.C. The paper's thesis that witchcraft and heresy are closely united is a main theme of my book, *Witchcraft in the Middle Ages* (Ithaca, N.Y.: Cornell University Press, 1972), which analyzes the phenomenon in Europe from the fourth to the fifteenth century.

most important aspect of medieval witchcraft is, I believe, its relationship to medieval heresy.

I should make it clear at the outset what it is that I mean by witchcraft. I do not use the term as a synonym of sorcery or magic. In spite of the efforts of anthropologists to compare the two, there are only limited analogies between European witchcraft and the sorcery of Africa or Oceania. Still less do I mean to dignify modern occultists by adopting the Murrayite view that witchcraft is an ancient religion that has preserved a marvelous continuity to the present day. Such a continuity is indeed marvelous to the historian, who knows there is no evidence for it. On the other hand, I depart sharply from the nineteenth-century liberal school, graced by such great scholars as Lea, Hansen, Burr, and Kittredge and today ably represented by Rossell Hope Robbins. One must not permit one's reverence for these names to obscure the limitations of their position. Liberal and anticlerical—in some cases even antireligious—in their views, these scholars allowed their justifiable outrage at inquisitorial proceedings to cause them to assume that there never were any witches in the world. So convincing have they been that today the smallest child can tell you that "there is no such things as a witch." The position I adopt here is that there were indeed witches in the world. By this I do not mean there were people who changed into beasts or flew through the air. What I mean is that there were people who believed that they did such things, who worshipped the powers of evil, and who practiced rites less ludicrous than abominable. The historian cannot judge whether witchcraft existed in objectivity, but the *phenomenon* of witchcraft did exist. The idea of witchcraft was a reality in the minds of those who practiced as well as those who prosecuted it: it was not simply an invention of fiendish inquisitors or crabbed scholastics.

But, even if you grant the *principium* that the phenomenon of witchcraft was real, I am still obliged to define what exactly it was, and how, historically, it came to be. The best method for this purpose was established by the great archivist of Cologne, Joseph Hansen, in 1900 and 1901 with the publication of two books: *Zauberwahn, Inquisition, und Hexenprozess im Mittelalter und die Entstehung der grossen Hexenverfolgung,* and *Quellen und Untersuchungen zur Geschichte des Hexenwahns und der Hexenverfolgung im Mittelalter.* These remain the best studies of medieval witchcraft, and although the book I am now working on departs from Hansen in many respects and will, I believe, add new facts and new dimensions to his interpretations, I follow him gratefully on many trails he was the first to scout. Basically, Hansen's method was to accept the characteristics of witchcraft as defined by the inquisitors and theoreticians of the second half of the fifteenth century, and then trace each of the elements as far back to its origins as possible. For example, the fifteenth-century witch passed through walls or closed doors, rode through the air, met in secret places at night to hold sexual revels, ritually slaughtered and ate children, had intercourse with the Devil who took various shapes, and offered him obscene homage with ritual kisses. It must then be determined whence each of these characteristics was derived and how all were synthesized in the witch phenomenon.

Speaking crudely, there are four important sources of medieval witchcraft. The first is folklore, including tales of bloodsucking screech owls, fairies, or kobolds. The most important element of witchcraft folklore is sorcery. Simple magic or sorcery existed in medieval Europe as it has in almost all societies. Evilly inclined sorcerers might do harm—*maleficium*—to others, and the concept of *maleficium* was eventually applied to witches. But the influence of simple sorcery on witchcraft has been exaggerated. In fact only a small proportion of witch beliefs were derived from sorcery and folklore. A second source was inquisitional fabrication, which has also been much exaggerated, especially by historians of the liberal school. The Inquisition helped increase the magnitude of witchcraft and to fix it firmly in the popular mind. Equally responsible for the repression of witchcraft were canon law, the episcopal courts, and the secular courts. No witch doctrine was invented by the Inquisition alone. Indeed, it is impossible that the Inquisition should have created witchcraft, for almost all the elements of classical witchcraft had appeared and coalesced before the foundation of the papal Inquisition in the 1220's and 1230's. A third source is scholasticism. Though the scholastics were not, except for William of Auvergne, much concerned with witchcraft, they accepted it, and their intellectual prestige helped legitimize the phenomenon in the minds of scholars and, more importantly, canon lawyers. Again, Hansen and Lea exaggerated the role of scholastics. Among intellectuals, lawyers and, even more, popular preachers were more influential than the scholastics. Thomas Aquinas' views on witchcraft, for example, were very much in line with those of his predecessors. As a whole, they said little about witchcraft that had not already been said by the Fathers or by the lawyers.

The fourth source was heresy. The relationship between witchcraft and heresy was close. First, as Robbins emphasizes, witchcraft was defined as a heresy by the lawyers and inquisitors. In the thirteenth century, Pope Alexander IV had repeatedly forbidden the inquisitors to waste their time and magic with *maleficium* unless it smacked clearly of heresy (*sapere heresim manifeste*). In the early fourteenth century, abetted by the fanatical fear of both sorcery and heresy manifested by Pope John XXII, the inquisitors increased their power by defining *maleficium* as heresy. To this end they argued the following syllogism: All those cut off from communion with the pope are heretics. John XXII has excommunicated all sorcerers. Therefore, sorcerers are heretics. Or, more commonly, and with the authority of some scholastics behind them, the inquisitors maintained that all sorcery which sought the aid of demons involved at least an implicit pact with Satan, and pact, whether implicit or explicit, was heresy because it offered worship to someone other than God.

The second aspect of the relationship between heresy and witchcraft is that the derivation of most doctrines of classical witchcraft is not from folklore, sorcery, canon law, inquisition, or scholasticism, but from the heresy trials. The relationship is so close as to make any history of medieval witchcraft absolutely dependent upon medieval heresy. Lea saw this more clearly than any other historian, but he did not live to develop the idea. Hundreds of incidents and trials from about 700 to 1500 bear out this contention. I shall here offer only three examples: one from the period before the introduction of Catharism; one that shows strong Catharist influence; and one that shows the influence of the antinomian heresies of the later Middle Ages.

The trial at Orléans in 1022.[1]   From 700 to the introduction of Catharism in the 1140's, Western European heresy was predominantly Reformist in character: that is to say, it sought a return to pristine apostolic simplicity and honesty and tended to reject the structure of the Church and its sacraments. Reformism was often touched by eccentric teaching and behavior, some of which, like Aldebert's litany of uncanonical angels in the eighth century, lent themselves to the development of witchcraft. The trial at Orléans is deservedly famous as being the first in the Middle Ages in which heretics were judicially executed. It also deserves fame as the trial whose accounts introduce a number of witch beliefs into the medieval West, beliefs that would be repeated over and over until they became an unalterable part of the witch phenomenon. The heretics professed such ordinary Reformist beliefs as rejection of the authority of the bishop, of the sacraments, and of the communion of Saints, and they held the Reformist belief that what the Holy Spirit spoke to their hearts was greater than any or all of these.

In addition to such unexceptional doctrines, the heretics were accused of holding orgies at night in secret places, underground or in abandoned buildings. The devotees entered bearing torches, and they chanted the names of demons until one appeared, after which the lights were put out, and the sectaries seized for their pleasure whoever lay closest to hand, whether mother, sister, or nun. The children conceived at these orgies were burned to death shortly after their birth and their ashes made into an edible substance that was then used in a blasphemous parody of Christian communion. The heretics adored the Devil, who appeared to claim his homage in the form of a beast, of an angel of light, or of a black man.

Obviously the reliability of the sources must be questioned. Herbert Grundmann, the most eminent living authority on medieval heresy, has long argued, as does Walter Wakefield and many other historians, that all such charges in medieval chronicles must be dismissed from our serious consideration as meaningless clichés. Grundmann claimed that the Orléans accusations must have had a literary origin rather than a factual one. This contention is greatly strengthened by the fact that the Byzantine statesman and scholar Michael Psellos uses, in his treatise *On the Function of Demons*,[2] almost precisely the same language to describe the sex orgies as Paul of Saint Père de Chartres in his account of the Orléans incident. At least one common literary ancestor of Michael and Paul turns out to be very distinguished and well-known indeed. In his treatises *De Haersibus* and *De Moribus Manchaeorum*, St. Augustine uses much the same ideas and language that the later writers were to adopt. Similar notions appear before Augustine in the pages of Origen, Justin Martyr, and others. They were used by the pagans against Jews and Christians and by the Christians against the Jews.

This should not lead us to dismiss Paul's account as a fabric of meaningless clichés. Of all the sources relating to the Orléans trial, it is generally admitted that his is the best. Not only is it clear and unconfused, but its author is the only one of those reporting the trial who was personally acquainted with at least one of the principals. It is probable that he borrowed from Augustine, but the question remains: why, of all the varied and extensive remarks that the Fathers made about heretics, should Paul have chosen these in particular? Is it not possible that some truth lies beneath the clichés?

Not every historian has accepted the notion that all charges of sexual orgies are mere clichés. The eminent Marxist scholar Ernst Werner, and his late colleague, the brilliant young Gottfried Koch, have both contended that we have been too cavalier in our dismissal of the sources. There is nothing improbable in such stories, up to a limit, they argue, for we are aware of the existence of ritual orgies in many cults at different times and places. Werner even suggests that the similar accusations lodged against the early Christians may have had some truth in them, not as regards orthodox Christians, but at least as regards gnostics.[3] Second, the eccentric behavior of other Western heretics, like Tanchelm, who distributed his bath water as a holy relic, or like Alberic of Brittany, who slaughtered animals on the altar and sold the blood, makes it not inconceivable that the Orléans heretics themselves had odd rites. But what could Reformist heretics have to do with such practices? Again, I argue that the eccentricities of other Reformists are well established. As with the Catharists or the pantheists later, rebellion against the Church and society, even in the name of purity, can produce some odd side effects.

But the Gordian knot is more easily cut. It will probably be forever uncertain just how many of the charges against the heretics were true. What is certain is that these ideas now appeared in the West and were frequently repeated. People believed them, and the belief constitutes an historical phenomenon. At Orléans, in a trial for heresy, some of the major components of the witchcraft phenomenon were established.

Catharism and witchcraft.   Eastern dualism arrived in the West in the first half of the twelfth century and spread rapidly thereafter, following the roads already constructed by the Reformist heretics. Witchcraft was encouraged by the rejection of Catholic Church and Catholic society that characterized both Catharists and Reformists. But the connection between Catharism and witchcraft was closer, both logically and historically, than that between Reformism and witchcraft. In the first place, witchcraft was particularly strong in those areas where Catharism was strong: southern France, northern Italy, and the Rhineland and Low Countries. The term *Gazari*, a corruption of *Cathari* frequently employed from the thirteenth century, was later applied to the witches. The doctrines, alleged or real, of the Catharists had implications important to witchcraft: the orgies and infanticide of the witches may have been encouraged by the violent condemnation of marriage and procreation inherent in Catharism.

These external connections are by no means conclusive evidence, but they are reinforced by internal considerations, primarily the underlining by Catharism of the presence and power of the Devil in the world. The Catharists taught that this world, the world of matter, was created, and is ruled, by the Devil. The true, good God, the Lord of spirit, is hidden from our souls, encased as they are in matter. The Catharists, of course, strove rigorously to free themselves from matter and to worship the good God. But some people, impressed with the Catharist doctrine that the Devil is Lord of the world, his powers nearly equal to God's, and his presence vividly and everywhere felt, chose to propitiate and worship him, rather than struggle against him. Both Germanic and Greco-Roman pagans had endeavored to placate the chthonic powers by worship, and there is no reason why medieval people under the influence of Catharism should not have acted in the same way. Moreover, if one accepted the identification of the Devil with the God of the Old Testament but had been brought up as a Christian to venerate that God, there is an actual consistency in worshiping the Devil. The conception of a mighty struggle between God and Satan impressed itself on many a mind, and for some it was convenient to forget that Catharism promised the ultimate victory of God and to hope instead for the triumph of Satan.

The kind of thinking, twisted from the Catharist as well as from the Catholic points of view, that might lead to such conclusions appears in this statement of Catharist beliefs by an anonymous writer in Southern France about 1208–1213.[4]

> [Some heretics say] that the malign god exists without beginning or end, and rules as many and as extensive lands, heavens, people, and creatures as the good God. The present world, they say, will never pass away or be depopulated. . . . God himself, they say, has two wives, Collam and Colibam, and from them He engendered sons and daughters, as do humans. On the basis of this belief, some of them hold there is no sin in man and woman kissing and embracing each other, or even lying together in intercourse, nor can one sin in doing so for payment. . . . [They] await the general resurrection which they shall experience, so they say, in the land of the living, with all their inheritance which they shall recover by force of arms. For they say that until then they shall possess that land of the malign spirit and shall make use of the clothing of the sheep, and shall eat the good things of the earth, and shall not depart thence until all Israel is saved.

To follow the Devil, and to enter with him the kingdom of his delights, this is the belief and hope *par excellence* of the witch.

The Rhenish heretics.[5]   Catharism, under the pressures first of Crusade and then of Inquisition, declined in the thirteenth century. At the same time, new heresies, antinomian in nature, were gaining wide support. One of the sources of medieval Antinomianism was the pantheism of the Parisian theologian Amalric of Bena, who taught that "God is all things in all things." Another was the millennarianism of Joachim of Flora, who argued that the world was about to enter a third age, the age of the Spirit, when both laws and faith would yield to a direct revelation of God to all men. These two streams of thought merged, producing the heresy of the Amalricians, who claimed that Joachim's third age was imminent and that there was no need for law, civil government, or the Church, for there was no distinction between God and themselves. If God is all things, they argued, then I am God and unable to sin. I can do wrong only when I forget that I am God. These pantheist-millennarian ideas found reinforcement in some of the contemporary movements of apostolic piety, the Beguines and the Fraticelli, for example, who also distrusted power, authority and wealth, and who claimed that the visible Church had defaulted in its responsibility and that God spoke directly to the hearts of the poor. From the nexus of Almalrician, Joachite, and apostolic ideas, sprang a number of unrelated or loosely related heretical movements: Free Spirit and the Freedom of the Spirit; the Apostolici or Dolcinisti; the Guglielmites; and, ultimately, the Luciferans and Adamites. Some Brethen of the Free Spirit, for example, argued that since all things are God, there is no evil. What is called evil, like what is called good, comes from God and is God. They themselves are the Holy Spirit and therefore need obey no law. Urges to lust, greed, or other so-called sins must be fulfilled as soon as possible, since they come from God: the only evil is to *resist* these feelings. In a curious reversal of Catharist custom, some of the Brethen often practiced asceticism as "neophytes" but when fully initiated as "men of freedom" they became the same as God, were incapable of sin, and were permitted all things.

Just as the Catharists had encouraged witchcraft by magnifying the awesome power of the Devil, the antinomians, by arguing that all action was virtuous and that Satan was God, advanced the cause of rebellion, libertinism, and Satanism. But so close to classical witchcraft did some of these heretics become that it is fair to say that in fact they were witches—that, in other words, the phenomenon of antinomian heresy became indistinguishable from that of witchcraft.

The first papal inquisitor in Germany, Konrad of Marburg, who was appointed by Gregory IX in 1233, did not take long to produce a crop of witches more diabolical than any that had before been seen. That Konrad did not, in spite of his deservedly evil reputation, invent the heresies out of whole cloth is evident from the alleged witches' doctrines, which are partly Catharist and partly antinomian. In 1224 there had already been a synod at Hildesheim in which a Dominican named Heinrich Minneke was condemned for having written that matrimony was useless and that the Devil would one day be restored to grace. In 1231, heretics at Trier were said to have held strange rites, kissing the face of a pale man or the anus of a cat. One of them, a woman named Luckard, claimed that Lucifer had been unjustly cast down from heaven and would ultimately, she hoped, regain his rightful place. On June 13, 1223, Gregory IX, terrified by the accounts Konrad sent him, issued his bull *Vox in Rama* detailing the witch habits of the Rhenish heretics.

Connected with the tradition of Konrad, is a confession made by a heretic named Lepzet, probably in the 13th century.[6] When a person is initiated into their sect, Lepzet reported, he must renounce the sacraments of the Church. A pale-faced man in black and of terrifying appearance arrives, and the postulant kisses him. Then a huge frog, as big as a pot, and with a gaping eye, materializes, and this also he kisses. He is now considered initiated and returns to the house of the master of the sect. When the sectaries wish to practice their religion, they go secretly into a cave beneath the master's cellar. There the master bares his buttocks, into which he inserts a silver spoon, with which he offers an oblation. The congregation kiss the master's backsides. After this, they all stand or sit round a pillar, up which a hugh cat climbs until he reaches the top, where a lamp has been placed. There the animal clings, lifting up his tail so that everyone may kiss his backsides. Then the cat puts out the light, and each person carnally embraces the one next him, men men and women women. The God of heaven, the heretics claim, is the evil God who unjustly cast Lucifer out of heaven. They call Lucifer their father and say that he was the creator of all visible things including human bodies (scarcely an orthodox Catharist point of view). At the end of the world, Lucifer will regain his power with the help of the Antichrist, who will be engendered by the carnal union of the sun and the moon.

Lepzet confessed publicly that for five years he had worn a hair shirt in mourning for Lucifer's exile. He also was in the habit of hiding the host in his mouth and taking it home and burning it. He had personally killed thirty people in accordance with the sect's teachings that murder is a sacrifice pleasing to their God, that is, Lucifer. He and his friends also accepted as virtues other deeds that Christians call sins. They condemned marriage but approved incest. If a man wishes to sleep with his mother, he must pay 18d., 6d. for having conceived him, 6d. for bearing him, and 6d. for nursing him. A man might sleep with his daughter for 9d., but the best bargain was a sister, who cost only 6d. Sodomy was of course perfectly acceptable. Others of Lepzet's doctrines were closer to more standard Catharist or antinomian beliefs.

It is tempting to dismiss this confession as a farrago invented by the Inquisition. Yet it was made to a secular court. Nor is the confession wholly impossible: aside from the apparition of huge toads and obscene cats there is nothing that is physically impossible or morally without precedent. Even the pallid or hairy men can be explained without recourse to the supernatural if we remember the long-lived European custom of dressing in the clothes of animals for ritual purposes: a manuscript of 1280, for example, shows pictures of maskers dressed as stags, donkeys, hares, or bulls. The other witch concepts are easily explained as offshoots of heretical tradition, Catharist or antinomian. It is believable and natural that discontented individuals coming under the influence of heretical teachings could agree that this world was created by an evil God, and that God's enemy, Lucifer, is consequently good. They would accept with the greatest pleasure the idea that Lucifer would triumph at the end of the world and lead them with him into his kingdom. And they would then quite naturally decide that in order to obtain this reward they must worship him here on earth in the way he wishes. Much of what the witches were accused had been thought of done earlier by heretics, and very little was not done later by modern Satanists of one kind or another. There is no reason that the phenomenon should not have existed in the minds of the accused as well as in those of the accusers.

The most important point, though, is that the phenomenon of witchcraft had sprung out of the medieval heresy trials. The formal renunciation of God, the longing for the triumph of Satan, the homage and obscene worship paid him, the secret meetings at night for orgiastic purposes, and the ritual slaying of children: all these characteristics of classical witchcraft had their origins, not in sorcery, but in medieval heresy.

NOTES

1. See Jeffrey B. Russell, *Dissent and Reform in the Early Middle Ages* (Berkeley, Cal.: University of California Press, 1965), pp. 27–35; Walter L. Wakefield and Austin P. Evans, *Heresies of the High Middle Ages* (New York: Columbia University Press, 1969), pp. 74–81.

2. Michael Psellos, *De Demonum operatione*, J. P. Migne, *Patrologia Graeca*, CCXXII, 819–834.

3. Theodora Büttner and Ernst Werner, *Circumcellionen und Adamiten* (Berlin, Akademie Verlag, 1959), pp. 73–134; Gottfried Koch, *Frauenfrage und Ketzertum im Mittelalter* (Berlin, Akademie Verlag, 1962), pp. 113–121.

4. Translation by Walter Wakefield in Wakefield and Evans, *op. cit.*, pp. 232–234.

5. On the Brethren of the Free Spirit, see Martin Erbstösser and Ernst Werner, *Ideologische Probleme des mittelalterlichen Plegjertums. Die freigeistige Häresie und ihre sozialen Wurzeln* (Berlin, Akademie Verlag, 1960); Gordon Leff, *Heresy in the Later Middle Ages*, 2

vols. (Manchester, Manchester University Press, 1967), I, 303–407; and Robert Lerner, *The Heresy of the Free Spirit* (Berkeley, Cal.: University of California Press, 1972). Professor Lerner and I have amicably agreed to disagree on the disputed and, I believe, unresolvable question of the extent to which the practices associated with the Free Spirit actually occurred. My contention is that orgiastic patterns in other instances in the Middle Ages and in other societies, including our own (e.g., the Manson "family"), indicate that the charges are not inherently improbable and there is therefore no compelling reason to dismiss the evidence. Lerner, however, is convincing in his argument that the Free Spirit was, like Catharism, essentially a movement of spiritual purity. The paradox will not surprise students of myth or psychology: the principle of the *coincidentia oppositorum* is that great light is usually accompanied by great darkness.

6. Lepzet's confession appears in Ignaz Döllinger, *Beiträge zur Sektengeschichte des Mittelalters*, 2 vols. (Munich, 1890), II 295–296, from MS Munich CLM, 7714 f64a. An offset reproduction of this edition has been published by Burt Franklin, New York, 1960. I am indebted to Walter Wakefield for his help in identifying the manuscript sources.

Elliott P. Currie

Crimes Without Criminals: Witchcraft and Its Control in Renaissance Europe

The sociological study of deviant behavior has begun to focus less on the deviant and more on society's response to him.[1] One of the several implications of this perspective is that a major concern of the sociology of deviance should be the identification and analysis of different kinds of systems of social control. Particularly important is the analysis of the impact of different kinds of control systems on the way deviant behavior is perceived and expressed in societies.

By playing down the importance of intrinsic differences between deviants and conventional people, and between the social situation of deviants and that of nondeviants, the focus on social response implies much more than the commonplace idea that society defines the kinds of behavior that will be considered

Reprinted and excerpted from Elliot P. Currie, "Crimes Without Criminals: Witchcraft and its Control in Renaissance Europe," *Law & Society Review,* 3 (August, 1968), pp. 7–32. *Law & Society Review* is the official publication of the Law and Society Association. Reprinted by permission of the author and the Law and Society Association.

odd, disgusting, or criminal. It implies that many elements of the behavior system of a given kind of deviance, including such things as the rate of deviance and the kinds of people who are identified as a deviant, will be significantly affected by the kind of control system through which the behavior is defined and managed.

In this paper, I attempt to add to the rather small body of research on kinds of social control systems and their impact.[2] The subject is witchcraft in Renaissance Europe, and in particular, the way in which the phenomenon of witchcraft differed in England and in continental Europe,[3] as a result of differences in their legal systems. I will show that the English and the continental legal systems during this period represented the two ends of a continuum along which different social control systems may be placed, and I will suggest some general ways in which each kind of control system affects the deviant behavior systems in which it is involved. Along the way, however, I will also suggest that the *degree* to which a social control system can influence the character of a deviant behavior system is variable and depends in part on the *kind* of behavior involved and the particular way it is socially defined.

Witchcraft as Deviance.   Something labeled witchcraft can be found in many societies, but the particular definition of the crime of witchcraft which emerged in Renaissance Europe was unique. It consisted of the individual's making, for whatever reason and to whatever end, a pact or covenant with the Devil, thereby gaining the power to manipulate supernatural forces for anti-social and un-Christian ends. What was critical was the pact itself; not the assumption or use of the powers which it supposedly conferred, but the willful renunciation of the Faith implied by the act of Covenant with the Devil. Thus, on the Continent, witchcraft was usually prosecuted as a form of heresy, and in England as a felony whose essence was primarily mental.[4] Witchcraft, then, came to be defined as a sort of thought-crime. It was not necessarily related to the practice of magic, which was widespread and had many legitimate forms. There were statutes forbidding witchcraft before the Renaissance, but the new conception of witchcraft involved important changes in both the nature and the seriousness of the crime. Early legislation, throughout Europe, had tended to lump witchcraft and magic in the same category, and to deal with them as minor offenses. In ninth-century England, the Law of the Northumbrian Priests held that if any " . . . in any way love witchcraft, or worship idols, if he be a king's thane, let him pay X half-marks; half to Christ, half to the king. We are all to love and worship one God, and strictly hold one Christianity, and renounce all heathenship."[5]

Similar mildness is characteristic of other early English legislation, while the Catholic Church itself, in the 13th century, explicitly took the position that the belief in witchcraft was an illusion.[6] In no sense were witches considered by ecclesiastical or secular authorities to be a serious problem, until the 15th century.

I cannot speculate here on the process through which the early conception of witchcraft as, essentially, the witch's delusion evolved to the point where the witch was believed to have actual powers. Suffice it to say that such a shift in definition did take place:[7] that during the 15th and 16th centuries a new theological and legal conception of witchcraft emerged, which amounted to an official recognition of a hitherto unknown form of deviance. In 1484, Pope Innocent IV issued a Bull recognizing the seriousness of the crime of witchcraft, affirming its reality, and authorizing the use of the Holy Inquisition to prosecute it with full force. . . .

A few years later, the new conception of witchcraft was given practical impetus with the publication of a manual known as the *Malleus Maleficarum,* or Witch-Hammer, written by two German Inquisitors under Papal authorization, which set forth in systematic form the heretofore diffuse beliefs on the nature and habits of witches, means for their discovery, and guidelines for their trial and execution.[8] At this point, the witch persecutions in continental Europe entered a peak phase which lasted into the 18th century. Estimates of the number of witches executed in Western Europe vary, but half a million is an average count.[9] Although there were consistently dissident voices both within and outside of the Church, the prevalence of witches was a fact widely accepted by the majority, including a number of the most powerful intellects of the time. Luther and Calvin were believers, as was Jean Bodin, who wrote an extremely influential book on witches in which he argued, among other things, that those who scoffed at the reality of witches were usually witches themselves.[10] Witchcraft was used as an explanation for virtually everything drastic or unpleasant that occurred; leading one Jesuit critic of the persecutions to declare: "God and Nature no longer do anything; witches, everything." . . .[11]

Once officially recognized, the crime of witchcraft presented serious problems for those systems of control through which it was to be hunted down and suppressed. The fact that no one had ever been seen making a pact with the Devil made ordinary sources of evidence rather worthless. Ordinary people, indeed, were in theory unable to see the Devil at all; as an eminent jurist, Sinistrari, phrased the problem, "There can be no witness of that crime, since the Devil, visible to the witch, escapes the sight of all beside."[12] The attendant acts—flying by night, attending witches' Sabbaths, and so on—were of such nature that little reliable evidence of their occurrence could be gathered through normal procedures. The difficulty of proving that the crime had ever taken place severely taxed the competence of European legal institutions and two different responses emerged. In England, the response to witchcraft took place within a framework of effective limitations on the suppressive power of the legal order and a relatively advanced conception of due process of law; on the Continent, the response took place within a framework of minimal limitations on the activity of the legal system, in which due process and legal restraint tended to go by the board.

Continental Europe: Repressive Control.   In continental Europe, people accused of witchcraft were brought before the elaborate machinery of a specialized bureaucratic agency with unusual powers and what amounted to a nearly complete absence of institutional restraints on its activity. Originally, the control of witchcraft was the responsibility of the Inquisition. After the disappearance, for practical purposes, of the Inquisition in most of Western Europe in the 16th century, witches were tried before secular courts which retained for the most part the methods which the Inquisition had pioneered.[13] This was as true of the Protestant sectors of Europe—England excepted—as it was of those which remained Catholic.[14] The methods were effective and extreme.

Ordinary continental criminal procedure approximated the "inquisitorial" process, in which accusation, detection, prosecution and judgment are all in the hands of the official control system, rather than in those of private persons; and all of these functions reside basically in one individual.[15] The trial was not, as it was in the "accusatorial" procedure of English law, a confrontative combat between the accuser and the accused, but an attack by the judge and his staff upon the suspect, who carried with him a heavy presumption of guilt. Litigation was played down or rejected. . . .[16] Above and beyond the tendencies to repressive control visible in the inquisitorial process generally, the establishment of the Holy Inquisition in the 13th century as a weapon against heresy ushered in a broadening of the powers of the control system vis-à-vis the accused. Ecclesiastical criminal procedure had always been willing to invoke extraordinary methods in particularly heinous crimes, especially those committed in secret. With the coming of the Inquisition a good many procedural safeguards were systematically cast aside, on the ground that the Inquisition was to be seen as "an impartial spiritual father, whose functions in the salvation of souls should be fettered by no rules."[17] Thus, in the interest of maintaining the ideological purity of Christendom, the legal process became conceived as a tool of the moral order, whose use and limits were almost entirely contingent on the needs of that order.

Nevertheless, certain powerful safeguards existed, in theory, for the accused. Chief among these was a rigorous conception of proof, especially in the case of capital crimes. In general, continental criminal procedure, at least from the 15th century onward, demanded a "complete proof" as warrant for capital punishment. "Complete proof" generally implied evidence on the order of testimony of two eyewitnesses to the criminal act or, in the case of certain crimes which otherwise would be difficult to establish, like heresy or conspiracy against the Prince, written proofs bound by rigorous standards of authenticity.[18] In most cases of heresy and of witchcraft generally, proof of this order was hard, if not impossible, to come by, for obvious reasons. As a result, it was necessary to form a complete proof through combining confession, which was strong but not complete evidence, with another indication, such as testimony by one witness.[19] The result was tremendous pressure for confession at all costs, as well as a pressure for the relaxation of standards for witnesses and other sources of lesser evidence. The pressure for confession put a premium on the regular and systematic use of torture. In this manner, the procedural safeguard of rigorous proof broke down in practice through the allowance of extraordinary procedures which became necessary to circumvent it.[20]

In theory, there were some restraints on the use of torture, but not many. One 16th-century German jurist argued that it could not be used without sufficient indication of guilt, that it could not be used "immoderately," and that it should be tempered according to the strength, age, sex and condition of the offender. German officials, when approving the use of torture, usually added the phrase *Doch Mensch-oder-Christlicher Weise,*—roughly, "In humane or Christian fashion."[21] In theory, confessions under torture had to be reaffirmed afterward by the accused; but torture, though it could not lawfully be repeated, could be "continued" indefinitely after interruption, and few accused witches could maintain a denial of their confession after several sessions.[22]

Besides being virtually required for the death penalty, confession was useful in two other important ways, which consequently increased the usefulness of torture. First, confession involved the denunciation of accomplices, which assured a steady flow of accused witches into the courts. Secondly, confessions were publicly read at executions, and distributed to the populace at large, which reinforced the legitimacy of the trials themselves and recreated in the public mind the reality of witchcraft itself. If people *said* they flew by night to dance with the devil, then surely there was evil in the land, and the authorities were more than justified in their zeal to root it out. In extorting confessions from accused witches, the court also made use of means other than torture. Confession was usually required if the accused were to receive the last sacraments and avoid damnation,[23] and the accused, further, were frequently promised pardon if they confessed, a promise which was rarely kept.[24]

In line with the tendency to relax other standards of evidence, there was considerable weakening of safeguards regarding testimony of witnesses. Heretics could testify, which went against established ecclesiastical policy; so could excommunicates, perjurors, harlots, children and others who ordinarily were not allowed to bear witness. Witnesses themselves were liable to torture if they equivocated or appeared unwilling to testify; and, contrary to established procedure in ordinary continental courts, names of witnesses were withheld from the accused.[25]

In general, prisoners were not provided with information on their case.[26] Most of the proceedings were held in secret.[27] The stubborn prisoner who managed to hold to a denial of guilt was almost never released from custody and frequently spent years in prison. Acquittal, in witchcraft and heresy cases, was virtually impossible. Lacking enough evidence for conviction, the court could hold an accused in prison indefinitely at its discretion. In general, innocence was virtually never the verdict in such cases; the best one could hope for was "not proven." . . .[28]

Lesser indications of guilt were supplied through the court's use of impossible dilemmas. If the accused was found to be in good repute among the populace, he or she was clearly a witch, since witches invariably sought to be highly thought of; if in bad repute, then he or she was also clearly a witch, since no one approves of witches. If the accused was especially regular in worship or morals, it was argued that the worst witches made the greatest show of piety.[29] Stubbornness in refusing to confess was considered a sure sign of alliance with the Devil, who was known to be taciturn. Virtually the only defense available to accused witches was in disabling hostile witnesses on the grounds of violent enmity; this provision was rendered almost useless through the assumption that witches were naturally odious to everyone, so that an exceptionally great degree of enmity was required.

A final and highly significant characteristic of the continental witch trial was the power of the court to confiscate the property of the accused, whether or not he was led to confess.[30] The chief consequence of this practice was to join to a system of virtually unlimited power a powerful motive for persecution. This coincidence of power and vested interest put an indelible stamp on every aspect of witchcraft in continental Europe.

All things considered, the continental procedure in the witch trials was an enormously effective machine for the systematic and massive production of confessed deviants. As such, it approximates a type of deviance-management which may be called repressive control. Three main characteristics of such a system may be noted, all of which were present in the continental legal order's handling of the witch trials:

1. Invulnerability to restraint from other social institutions;
2. Systematic establishment of extraordinary powers for suppressing deviance, with a concomitant lack of internal restraints;
3. A high degree of structured interest in the apprehension and processing of deviants.

The question at hand is what the effects of this type of control structure are on the rate of deviance, the kinds of people who become defined as deviant, and other aspects of the system of behavior that it is designed to control. This will be considered after a description of the English approach to the control of witchcraft, which, having a very different character, led, to very different results.

England: Restrained Control.   There was no Inquisition in Renaissance England, and the common law tradition provided a variety of institutional restraints on the conduct of the witch trials. As a consequence, there were fewer witches in England, vastly fewer executions, and the rise of a fundamentally different set of activities around the control of witchcraft.

Witchcraft was apparently never prosecuted as a heresy in England, but after a statute of Elizabeth in 1563 it was prosecuted as a felony in secular courts.[31] The relatively monolithic ecclesiastical apparatus, so crucial in the determination of the shape of witch trials on the Continent, did not exist in England; the new definition of witchcraft came to England late and under rather different circumstances.[32] English laws making witchcraft a capital crime, however, were on the books until 1736 although executions for witchcraft ceased around the end of the 17th century.[33] Nevertheless, the English laws were enforced in a relatively restrained fashion through a system of primarily local courts of limited power, accountable to higher courts and characterized by a high degree of internal restraint.

With a few exceptions, notably the Star Chamber, English courts operated

primarily on the accusatory principle, stressing above all the separation of the
functions of prosecution and judgment, trial by jury, and the presumption of
the innocence of the accused.[34] Accuser and accused assumed the role of equal
combatants before the judge and jury; prosecution of offenses generally required a private accuser. The English trial was confrontative and public, and
the English judge did not take the initiative in investigation or prosecution of
the case. Again unlike the situation on the Continent, the accused witch could
appeal to high authority from a lower court, and could sue an accuser for defa-
mation; such actions frequently took place in the Star Chamber.[35] Reprieves
were often granted. From the middle of the 17th century, the accused in
capital cases could call witnesses in their defense. In general, the English
courts managed to remain relatively autonomous and to avoid degeneration
into a tool of ideological or moral interests: Voltaire was to remark, in the
18th century, that "In France the Criminal Code seems framed purposely for
the destruction of the people, in England it is their safeguard."[36]

There were, nevertheless, important limitations to this picture of the
English courts as defenders of the accused. Accusatory ideals were not always
met in practice, and many elements of a developed adversary system were only
latent. Defendants were not allowed counsel until 1836.[37] In general, since the
defendant entered court with a presumption of innocence, the English courts
did not demand such rigorous proofs for conviction as did the continental
courts. Testimony of one witness was usually sufficient for conviction in felony
cases; children were frequently allowed to testify. In practice, however, this
worked out differently than might be expected. The lack of complex, rigid
standards of proof in English courts meant that there was little pressure to
subvert the series of safeguards surrounding the accused through granting the
court extraordinary powers of interrogation, and it went hand-in-hand with a
certain care on the part of the courts for the rights of the defendant. Torture,
except in highly limited circumstances as an act of Royal prerogative, was
illegal in England, and was never lawfully or systematically used on accused
witches in the lower courts.[38]

Given the nature of the crime of witchcraft, witnesses were not always easily
found; given the illegality of torture, confessions were also relatively rare. In
this difficult situation, alternative methods of obtaining evidence were required. As a consequence, a variety of external evidence emerged.

Three sources of external evidence became especially significant in English
witch trials. These are pricking, swimming, and watching.[39] Pricking was
based on the theory that witches invariably possessed a "Devil's Mark,"

which was insensitive to pain. Hence, the discovery of witches involved searching the accused for unusual marks on the skin and pricking such marks with an instrument designed for that purpose. If the accused did not feel pain, guilt was indicated. Often pricking alone was considered sufficient evidence for conviction.

Swimming was based on the notion that the Devil's agents could not sink in water, and was related to the "ordeal by water" common in early European law. . . .[40]

The third source of evidence, watching, reflected the theory that the Devil provided witches with imps or familiars which performed useful services, and which the witch was charged with suckling. The familiars could therefore be expected to appear at some point during the detention of the suspected witch, who was therefore placed in a cell, usually on a stool, and watched for a number of hours or days, until the appointed watchers' observed familiars in the room. . . .

These methods were called for by the lack of more coercive techniques of obtaining evidence within the ambit of English law. In general, the discovery and trial of English witches was an unsystematic and inefficient process, resembling the well-oiled machinery of the continental trial only remotely. The English trial tended to have an ad hoc aspect in which new practices, techniques and theories were continually being evolved or sought out.

Finally, the confiscation of the property of suspected witches did not occur in England, although forfeiture for felony was part of English law until 1870. As a consequence, unlike the continental authorities, the English officials had no continuous vested interest in the discovery and conviction of witches. Thus, they had neither the power nor the motive for large-scale persecution. The English control system, then, was of a "restrained" type, involving the following main characteristics:

1.   Accountability to, and restraint by, other social institutions;

2.   A high degree of internal restraint, precluding the assumption of extraordinary powers;

3.   A low degree of structured interest in the apprehension and processing of deviants.

The English and continental systems, then, were located at nearly opposite ends of a continuum from restrained to repressive control of deviance. We may now look at the effect of these differing control systems on the character of witchcraft in the two regions.

Witchcraft Control as Industry: The Continent. On the Continent, the convergence of a repressive control system with a powerful economic motive created something very much like a large-scale industry based on the mass stigmatization of witches and the confiscation of their property. This gave distinct character to the *rate* of witchcraft in Europe, the kinds of people who were convicted as witches, and the entire complex of activities which grew up around witchcraft.

The Inquisition, as well as the secular courts, were largely self-sustaining; each convicted witch, therefore, was a source of financial benefit through confiscation.[41] "Persecution," writes an historian of the Inquisition, "as a steady and continuous policy, rested, after all, upon confiscation. It was this which supplied the fuel to keep up the fires of zeal, and when it was lacking the business of defending the faith languished lamentably."[42]

The witchcraft industry in continental Europe was a large and complex business which created and sustained the livelihoods of a sizable number of people. As such, it required a substantial income to keep it going at all. As a rule, prisoners were required to pay for trial expenses and even for the use of instruments of torture. Watchmen, executioners, torturers and others, as well as priests and judges, were paid high wages and generally lived well.[43] A witch-judge in 17th century Germany boasted of having caused 700 executions in three years, and earning over 5,000 gulden on a per-capita basis. . . .[44] A total of 720,000 florins were taken from accused witches in Bamberg, Germany in a single year. Usually, the goods of suspected witches were sold after confiscation to secular and ecclesiastical officials at low prices. . . .

Like any large enterprise, the witchcraft industry was subject to the need for continual expansion in order to maintain its level of gain. A mechanism for increasing profit was built into the structure of the trials, whereby, through the use of torture to extract names of accomplices from the accused, legitimate new suspects became available.

The creation of a new kind of deviant behavior was the basis for the emergence of a profit-making industry run on bureaucratic lines, which combined nearly unlimited power with pecuniary motive and which gave distinct form to the deviant behavior system in which it was involved.

Its effect on the scope or rate of the deviance is the most striking at first glance. Several hundred thousand witches were burned in continental Europe during the main period of activity, creating a picture of the tremendous extent of witchcraft in Europe. The large number of witches frightened the population and legitimized ever more stringent suppression. Thus, a cycle developed in which rigorous control brought about the appearance of high rates of deviance, which were the basis for more extreme control, which in turn sent the rates even higher, and so on.

A second major effect was the selection of particular categories of people for accusation and conviction. A significant proportion of continental witches were men, and an even more significant proportion of men and women were people of wealth and/or property. This is not surprising, given the material advantages to the official control apparatus of attributing the crime to heads of prosperous households.

In trials of Offenburg, Germany, in 1628, witnesses noted that care was taken to select for accusation "women of property."[45] A document from Bamberg at about the same time lists the names and estimated wealth of twenty-two prisoners, nearly all of whom are propertied, most male, and one a burgher worth 100,000 florins.[46] In early French trials, a pattern developed which began with the conviction of a group of ordinary people, and then moved into a second stage in which the wealthy were especially singled out for prosecution.[47] In German trials, the search for accomplices was directed against the wealthy, with names of wealthy individuals often supplied to the accused under torture.[48] At Trier, a number of burgomasters, officials, and managers of large farms were executed as witches. An eyewitness to the trials there in the late 16th century was moved to lament the fact that [b]oth rich and poor, of every rank, age and sex, sought a share in the accursed crime." Apparently, resistance or dissent, or even insufficient zeal, could open powerful officials to accusation and almost certain conviction.

Thus, though it was not the case that all continental witches were well-to-do or male, a substantial number were. The witch population in England, to be considered shortly, was strikingly different.

The mass nature of the witchcraft industry, the high number of witches in Europe, and the upper-income character of a sufficient proportion of them,[49] were all due to the lack of restraints on court procedure—especially, of the systematic use of torture—coupled with the legal authority to confiscate property, which added material interest to unrestrained control. That the prevalence of witches in continental Europe was a reflection of the peculiar structure of legal control is further implied by the fact that when torture and/or confiscation became from time to time unlawful, the number of witches decreased drastically or disappeared altogether. In Hesse, Phillip the Magnificent forbade torture in 1526 and, according to one witness, "nothing more was heard of witchcraft till the half-century was passed."[50] In Bamberg, pressure from the Holy Roman Emperor to abandon confiscation resulted in the disappearance of witchcraft arrests in 1630. The Spanish Inquisitor Salazar Frias issued instructions in 1614 requiring external evidence and forbidding confiscation; this move marked the virtual end of witchcraft in Spain.[51] It was not until criminal law reform began in earnest in the 18th century that witches disappeared, for official purposes, from continental Europe.

A form of deviance had been created and sustained largely through the efforts of a self-sustaining bureaucratic organization dedicated to its discovery and punishment, and granted unusual powers which, when removed, dealt a final blow to that entire conception of deviant behavior. In England too, witches existed through the efforts of interested parties,[52] but the parties were of a different sort.

Witchcraft Control as Racket: England. The restrained nature of the English legal system precluded the rise of the kind of mass witchcraft industry which grew up on the Continent. What the structure of that system did provide was a context in which individual entrepreneurs, acting from below, were able to profit through the discovery of witches. Hence, the England, there developed a series of rackets through which inviduals manipulated the general climate of distrust, within the framework of a control structure which was frequently reluctant to approve of their activities. Because of its accusatorial character, the English court could not systematically initiate the prosecution of witches; because of its limited character generally, it could not have processed masses of presumed witches even had it had the power to initiate such prosecutions; and because of the absence of authority to confiscate witches' property, it had no interest in doing so even had it been able to. Witch prosecutions in England were initiated by private persons who stood to make a small profit in a rather precarious enterprise. As a result, there were fewer witches in England than on the Continent, and their sex and status tended to be different as well.

Given the lack of torture and the consequent need to circumvent the difficulty of obtaining confessions, a number of kinds of external evidence, some of which were noted above, became recognized. Around these sources of evidence there grew up a number of trades, in which men who claimed to be expert in the various arts of witchfinding—pricking, watching, and so on—found a ready field of profit. They were paid by a credulous populace, and often credulous officials, for their expertise in ferreting out witches. In the 17th century, the best-known of witchfinders was one Matthew Hopkins, who became so successful that he was able to hire several assistants. Hopkins, and many others, were generalists at the witchfinding art; others were specialists in one or another technique. Professional prickers flourished. A Scottish expert who regularly advertised his skill was called to Newcastle-upon-Tyne in 1649 to deal with the local witch problem, with payment guaranteed at twenty shillings per convicted witch. His technique of selecting potential witches was ingenious and rather efficient, and indicates how the general climate of fear and mistrust could be manipulated for profit. He sent bell-ringers through the streets of Newcastle to inquire if anyone had a complaint to enter against someone they suspected of witchcraft. This provided a legitimate outlet for grievances, both public and private, against the socially marginal, disapproved, or simply disliked, and was predictably successful; thirty witches were discovered, most of whom were convicted. . . . [53]

An essential characteristic of all these rackets was their precariousness. To profess special knowledge of the demonic and its agents opened the entrepreneur to charges of fraud or witchcraft; money could be made, but one could also be hanged, depending on the prevailing climate of opinion. The Scottish pricker of Newcastle was hanged, and many other prickers were imprisoned, the witchfinder Hopkins continually had to defend himself against charges of wizardry and/or fraud, and may have been drowned while undergoing the "swimming" test.[54] People who professed to be able to practice magic—often known as "cunning folk"—frequently doubled as witchfinders, and were especially open to the charge of witchcraft.

The peculiar and restrained character of the English control of witches led to characteristic features of the behavior system of English witchcraft. The lack of vested interest from above, coupled with the absence of torture and other extraordinary procedures, was largely responsible for the small number of witches executed in England from 1563 to 1736.[55] Of those indicted for witchcraft, a relatively small percentage was actually executed—again in contrast to the inexorable machinery of prosecution in continental Europe. In the courts of the Home Circuit, from 1558 to 1736, only 513 indictments were brought for witchcraft; of these, only 112, or about 22 per cent, resulted in execution.[56]

Further, English witches were usually women and usually lower class. Again, this was a consequence of the nature of the control structure. English courts did not have the power or the motive to systematically stigmatize the wealthy and propertied; the accusations came from below, specifically from the lower and more credulous strata or those who manipulated them, and were directed against socially marginal and undesirable individuals who were powerless to defend themselves. The process through which the witch was brought to justice involved the often reluctant capitulation of the courts to popular sentiment fueled by the activities of the witchfinders; the witches were usually borderline deviants already in disfavor with their neighbors. Household servants, poor tenants, and others of lower status predominated. Women who worked as midwives were especially singled out, particularly when it became necessary to explain stillbirths. Women who lived by the practice of magic—cunning women—were extremely susceptible to accusation. Not frequently, the accused witch was a "cunning woman" whose accusation was the combined work of a witchfinder and a rival "cunning woman." In the prevailing atmosphere, there was little defense against such internecine combat, and the "cunning" trade developed a heavy turnover. In general, of convicted witches in the Home Circuit from 1564–1663, only 16 of a total of 204 were men,[57] and there is no indication that any of these were wealthy or solid citizens.

The decline of witchcraft in England, too, was the result of a different process from that on the Continent, where the decline of witchcraft was closely related to the imposition of restraints on court procedure. In England, the decline was related to a general shift of opinion, in which the belief in witchcraft itself waned, particularly in the upper strata, as a result of which the courts began to treat witchcraft as illusory or at best unprovable. English judges began refusing to execute witches well before the witch laws were repealed in 1736; and although there were occasional popular lynchings of witches into the 18th century, the legal system had effectively relinquished the attempt of control witchcraft. With this shift of opinion, the entire structure of witchcraft collapsed, for all practical purposes, at the end of the 17th century.[58]

Conclusion. If one broad conclusion emerges from this discussion, it is that the phenomenon of witchcraft in Renaissance Europe strongly reinforces on one level the argument that deviance is what officials say it is, and deviants are those so designated by officials. Where the deviant act is nonexistent, it is necessarily true that the criteria for designating people as deviant do not lie in the deviant act itself, but in the interests, needs, and capacities of the relevant official and unofficial agencies of control, and their relation to extraneous characteristics of the presumptive deviant. Witchcraft was invented in continental Europe, and it was sustained there through the vigorous efforts of a system of repressive control; in England it was sustained, far less effectively, through the semi-official efforts of relatively small-time entrepreneurs. In both cases, witchcraft as a deviant behavior system took its character directly from the nature of the respective systems of legal control. On the Continent, the system found itself both capable of and interested in defining large numbers of people, many of whom were well-to-do, as witches; therefore, there *were* many witches on the Continent and many of these were wealthy and/or powerful. In England, the control system had little interest in defining anyone as a witch, and consequently the English witches were those few individuals who were powerless to fend off the definition supplied by witchfinders on a base of popular credulity. Witches were, then, what the control system defined them to be, and variation in the behavior system of witchcraft in the two regions may be traced directly to the different legal systems through which that definition was implemented. . . .

NOTES

1. This approach is presented in the following works, among others; H. S. Becker, *Outsiders* (1963); K. T. Erikson, *Wayward Puritans* (1966); J. I. Kitsuse, "*Societal Response to Deviance; Some Problems of Theory and Method*," 9 *Social Problems* 247–56 (Winter 1962); E. Goffman, *Stigma* (1963); and *Asylums* (1962). Earlier general statements in a similar vein can be found in E. M. Lemert, *Social Pathology* (1951); and F. Tannenbaum, *Crime and the Community* (1951).

2. One interesting study along these lines is E. M. Schur, *Narcotic Addiction in England and America; The Impact of Public Policy* (1963).

3. Erikson, *supra* note 1, discusses some aspects of witchcraft in America, which unfortunately cannot be discussed here without unduly lengthening the paper. For the curious, though, it should be noted that the American experience was in general much closer to the English than to the continental experience, particularly in terms of the small number of witches executed. For anyone interest in American witchcraft, Erikson's discussion and bibliography is a good place to start.

4. Elizabeth's statute of 1563 made witchcraft punishable by death only if it resulted in the death of the bewitched; witchcraft unconnected with death was a lesser offense. However, in 1604 James I revised the statute to invoke the death penalty for witchcraft regardless of result. On this point see R. T. Davies, *Four Centuries of Witch Beliefs* 15, 41–42 (1947).

5. Quoted in M. Murray, *The Witch-Cult in Western Europe* 22 (1962). Other early legislation is also quoted by Murray, and can also be found in C. L'Estrange Ewen, *Witch Hunting and Witch Trials 1–5* (1929).

6. This position was formulated in a document known as the Capitulum Episcopi, apparently written in 1215, which molded Church policy for over 200 years. . . . Quoted in 3 H. C. Lea, *A History of the Inquisition in the Middle Ages 493* (1888), and in Murray, *supra* note 5, at 22.

7. The shift, however, did not take place all at once, nor did it take place without important ideological struggles both within and beyond the Church; a number of important figures

remained skeptical throughout. Interesting materials on this process can be found 1 H. C. Lea, *Materials Toward a History of Witchcraft* (1939).

8. This remarkable work has been translated. J. Sprenger and H. Kramer, *Malleus Maleficarum* (M. Summers transl. 1948).

9. This estimate is from G. L. Kittredge, *Notes on Witchcraft* 59 (1907).

10. Davies, *supra* note 4, at 25, 5–9.

11. Father Friedrich Spee, quoted in Kittredge, *supra* note 10, at 47.

12. Quoted in G. Parrinder, *Witchcraft: European and African* 76 (1958).

13. Lea, *supra* note 7, at 244.

14. G. L. Burr, *The Fate of Dietrich Flade, Papers of the American Historical Association*, pt. 3, 11 (July 1891).

15. *See* A. Esmein, *A History of Continental Criminal Procedure* 8 *passim* (1913).

16. *Id.* at 9.

17. 1 H. C. Lea, *A History of the Inquisition in the Middle Ages* 405 (1958).

18. Esmein, *supra* note 15, at 655–23.

19. *Id.* at 625. It would still, of course, have been difficult to get even one reliable witness to an act of witchcraft; in practice, the testimony of one accused, under torture, was used for this purpose.

20. *See* Esmein, *supra* note 17, at 625. . . . It should be noted that the employment of torture by the Inquisition was a retrograde step in continental criminal procedure. . . . It was early laid down as an accepted rule of Canon Law that no confession should be extracted by torment; but the elimination of trials by ordeal in the 13th century, coupled with the rise of powerful heretical movements, put strong pressure on the Church to modify its approach. Originally, torture was left to the secular authorities to carry out, but a Bull of Pope Alexander IV in 1256 authorized Inquisitors to absolve each other for using it directly, and to grant each other dispensation for irregularities in its use. *See* Lea, *supra* note 1, at 421.

21. Lea, *supra* note 7, at 854–55.

22. Lea, *supra* note 1, at 427–28; Esmein, *supra* note 17, at 113–14.

23. 3 Lea, *supra* note 6, at 506.

24. *Id.* at 514; 2 Lea, *supra* note 7, at 895. . . .

25. Esmein, *supra* note 15, at 91–94; Lea, *supra* note 17, at 434–37.

26. Esmein, *supra* note 15, at 129.

27. Lea, *supra* note 17, at 406.

28. *Id.* at 453. . . .

29. 2 Lea, *supra* note 7, at 858.

30. 2 Lea, *supra* note 7, at 808–11; Lea, *supra* note 17, at 529.

31. . . . Before that, too, there were occasional trials for witchcraft or sorcery, and witchcraft of a sort, as I have shown, appears in the earliest English law. But this was the older conception of witchcraft, blurring into that of magic; and it was not until Elizabeth's statute that witch trials began in earnest. *See* W. Notestein, *A History of Witchcraft in England* ch. 1 (1911).

32. Two of these circumstances may be mentioned. One was the general atmosphere of social and political turmoil surrounding the accession of Elizabeth to the throne; another was the return to England, with Elizabeth's crowning, of a number of exiled Protestant leaders who had been exposed to the witch trials in Geneva and elsewhere and had absorbed the continental attitudes toward witchcraft. . . .

33. *See* Ewen, *supra* note 5, at 43. On the repeal of the witch laws, *see* 2 Sir J. F. Stephen, *History of the Criminal Law in England* 436 (1883).

34. *See* Esmein, *supra* note 15, at Introduction. Esmein notes the similarity between the politically-oriented Star Chamber and the typical continental court. A few cases of witchcraft, notably those with political overtones, were processed there; *see* C. L'Estrange Ewen, *Witchcraft in the Star Chamber* esp. 11 (1938).

35. *Cf.* Ewen, *supra* note 46.

36. Quoted in Esmein, *supra* note 15, at 361.

37. *Id.* at 342.

38. Torture may have been used on some witches in the Star Chamber. Notestein, *supra* note 31, at 167, 204 suggests that it may have been used illegally in a number of cases; nevertheless, torture was not an established part of English criminal procedure, except in the limited sense noted above. . . . It was allowed in Scotland, where, predictably, there were more executions; several thousand witches were burned there during this period. *See* G. F. Black, *A Calendar of Cases of Witchcraft in Scotland, 1510–1727,* 13–18 (1938); Notestein, *supra* note 31 at 95–96.

39. This discussion is taken from Ewen, *supra* note 5, at 60–71, and from remarks at various places in Notestein, *supra* note 31.

40. *See* M. Hopkins, *The Discovery of Witches* 38 (1928).

41. Self-sustaining control systems often view presumptive deviants as a source of profit. On a smaller scale, it has been noted that some jurisdictions in the American south have been known to make a practice of arresting Negroes en masse in order to collect fees. *See* G. B. Johnson, *"The Negro and Crime,"* in *The Sociology of Crime and Delinquency* (M. Wolfgang, L. Savitz, and N. Johnson, 1962).

42. Lea, *supra* note 21, at 529.

43. Lea, *supra* note 7, at 1080.

44. *Id.* at 1075.

45. 3 Lea, *supra* note 7, at 1163.

46. *Id.* at 1177–78.

47. Lea, *supra* note 17, at 523–27.

48. Lea, *supra* note 7, at 235.

49. That a greater percentage of wealthy witches did not appear is due in part to the fact that wealthy families often paid a kind of "protection" to local officials to insure that they would not be arrested. *See* 3 Lea, *supra* note 7, at 1080.

50. *Id.* at 1081.

51. Parrinder, *supra* note 12, at 79.

52. It should be stressed that quite probably, a number of people, both in England and on the Continent, did in fact believe themselves to be witches, capable of doing all the things witches were supposed to be able to do. Some of them, probably, had the intent to inflict injury or unpleasantness on their fellows, and probably some of these were included in the executions. This does not alter the fact that the designation of witches proceeded independently of such beliefs, according to the interests of the control systems. Some students of witchcraft have suggested that the promotion of witch beliefs by the official control systems provided a kind of readymade identity, or role, into which some already disturbed people could fit themselves. . . .

53. Ewen, *supra* note 5, at 62.

54. Hopkins, *supra* note 40, at 45. Summers, the editor of Hopkins' work, denies that Hopkins was drowned in this fashion. . . .

55. *Cf.* Ewen, *supra* note 5, at 112; Kittredge, *supra* note 9, at 59.

56. Ewen, *supra* note 5, at 100.

57. Ewen, *supra* note 5, at 102–108. Also, *cf.* the list of English witches in Murray, *supra* note 5, at 255–70.

58. An incident supposedly involving the anatomist, William Harvey, is indicative of this change of opinion. Harvey, on hearing that a local woman was reputed to be a witch, took it upon himself to dissect one of her familiars, which took the shape of a toad; he found it to be exactly like any other toad, and a minor blow was struck for the Enlightenment. *See* Notestein, *supra* note 31, at 111.

Kai T. Erikson

The Witches of Salem Village

Historically, there is nothing unique in the fact that Massachusetts Bay should have put people on trial for witchcraft. As the historian Kittredge has pointed out, the whole story should be seen "not as an abnormal outbreak of fanaticism, not as an isolated tragedy, but as a mere incident, a brief and transitory episode in the biography of a terrible, but perfectly natural, superstition."[1]

The idea of witchcraft, of course, is as old as history; but the concept of a malevolent witch who makes a compact with Satan and rejects God did not appear in Europe until the middle of the fourteenth century and does not seem to have made a serious impression on England until well into the sixteenth. The most comprehensive study of English witchcraft, for example, opens with the year 1558, the first year of Elizabeth's reign, and gives only passing attention to events occurring before that date.[2]

In many ways, witchcraft was brought into England on the same current of change that introduced the Protestant Reformation, and it continued to draw

From Kai. T. Erikson, *Wayward Puritans* (New York: John Wiley and Sons, 1966), pp. 153–159. Copyright ©1966 by John Wiley & Sons, Inc. Reprinted by permission of John Wiley & Sons, Inc.

nourishment from the intermittent religious quarrels which broke out during the next century and a half. Perhaps no other form of crime in history has been a better index to social disruption and change, for outbreaks of witchcraft mania have generally taken place in societies which are experiencing a shift of religious focus—societies, we would say, confronting a relocation of boundaries. Throughout the Elizabethan and early Stuart periods, at any rate, while England was trying to establish a national church and to anchor it in the middle of the violent tides which were sweeping over the rest of Europe, increasing attention was devoted to the subject. Elizabeth herself introduced legislation to clarify the laws dealing with witchcraft, and James I, before becoming King of England, wrote a textbook on demonology which became a standard reference for years to come.

But it was during the Civil Wars in England that the witchcraft hysteria struck with full force. Many hundreds, probably thousands of witches were burned or hung between the time the Civil Wars began and Oliver Cromwell emerged as the strong man of the Commonwealth, and no sooner had the mania subsided in England than it broke out all over again in Scotland during the first days of the Restoration. Every important crisis during those years seemed to be punctuated by a rash of witchcraft cases. England did not record its last execution for witchcraft until 1712, but the urgent witch hunts of the Civil War period were never repeated.

With this background in mind, we should not be surprised that New England, too, should experience a moment of panic; but it is rather curious that this moment should have arrived so late in the century.

During the troubled years in England when countless witches were burned at the stake or hung from the gallows, Massachusetts Bay showed but mild concern over the whole matter. In 1647 a witch was executed in Connecticut, and one year later another woman met the same fate in Massachusetts.[3] In 1651 the General Court took note of the witchcraft crisis in England and published an almost laconic order that "a day of humiliation" be observed throughout the Bay,[4] but beyond this, the waves of excitement which were sweeping over the mother country seemed not to reach across the Atlantic at all. There was no shortage of accusations, to be sure, no shortage of the kind of gossip which in other days would send good men and women to their lonely grave, but the magistrates of the colony did not act as if a state of emergency was at hand and thus did not declare a crime wave to be in motion. In 1672, for example, a curious man named John Broadstreet was presented to the Essex County Court for "having familiarity with the devil," yet when he admitted the charge the court was so little impressed that he was fined for telling a lie.[5] And in 1674, when Christopher Brown came before the same court to testify that he had been dealing with Satan, the magistrates flatly dismissed him on the grounds that his confession seemed "inconsistent with truth."[6]

So New England remained relatively calm during the worst of the troubles in England, yet suddenly erupted into a terrible violence long after England lay exhausted from its earlier exertions.

In many important respects, 1692 marked the end of the Puritan experiment in Massachusetts, not only because the original charter had been revoked or because a Royal Governor had been chosen by the King or even because the old political order had collapsed in a tired heap. The Puritan experiment ended in 1692, rather, because the sense of mission which had sustained it from the beginning no longer existed in any recognizable form, and thus the people of the Bay were left with few stable points of reference to help them remember who they were. When they looked back on their own history, the settlers had to conclude that the trajectory of the past pointed in quite a different direction than the one they now found themselves taking: they were no longer participants in a great adventure, no longer residents of a "city upon a hill," no longer members of that special revolutionary elite who were destined to bend the course of history according to God's own word. They were only themselves, living alone in a remote corner of the world, and this seemed a modest end for a crusade which had begun with such high expectations.

In the first place, as we have seen, the people of the colony had always pictured themselves as actors in an international movement, yet by the end of the century they had lost many of their most meaningful contacts with the rest of the world. The Puritan movement in England had scattered into a number of separate sects, each of which had been gradually absorbed into the freer climate of a new regime, and elsewhere in Europe the Protestant Reformation had lost much of its momentum without achieving half the goals set for it. And as a result, the colonists had lost touch with the background against which they had learned to assess their own stature and to survey their own place in the world.

In the second place, the original settlers had measured their achievements on a yardstick which no longer seemed to have the same sharp relevance. New England had been built by people who believed that God personally supervised every flicker of life on earth according to a plan beyond human comprehension, and in undertaking the expedition to America they were placing themselves entirely in God's hands. These were men whose doctrine prepared them to accept defeat gracefully, whose sense of piety depended upon an occasional moment of failure, hardship, even tragedy. Yet by the end of the century, the Puritan planters could look around them and count an impressive number of accomplishments. Here was no record of erratic providence; here was a record of solid human enterprise, and with this realization, as Daniel Boorstin suggests, the settlers moved from a "sense of mystery" to a "consciousness of mastery,"[7] from a helpless reliance on fate to a firm confidence in their own abilities. This shift helped clear the way for the appearance of the shrewd, practical, self-reliant Yankee as a figure in American history, but in the meantime it left the third generation of settlers with no clear definition of the status they held as the chosen children of God.

In the third place, Massachusetts had been founded as a lonely pocket of civilization in the midst of a howling wilderness, and as we have seen, this idea remained one of the most important themes of Puritan imagery long after the underbrush had been cut away and the wild animals killed. The settlers had lost sight of their local frontier, not only in the sense that colonization had spread beyond the Berkshires into what is now upper state New York, but also in the sense that the wilderness which had held the community together by pressing in on it from all sides was disappearing. The original settlers had landed in a wilderness full of "wild beasts and wilder men"; yet sixty years later, sitting many miles from the nearest frontier in the prosperous seaboard town of Boston, Cotton Mather and other survivors of the old order still imagined that they were living in a wilderness—a territory they had explored as thoroughly as any frontiersmen. But the character of this wilderness was unlike anything the first settlers had ever seen, for its dense forests had become a jungle of mythical beasts and its skies were thick with flying spirits. In a sense, the Puritan community had helped mark its location in space by keeping close watch on the wilderness surrounding it on all sides; and now that the visible traces of the wilderness had receded out of sight, the settlers invented a new one by finding the shapes of the forest in the middle of the community itself.[8]

And as the wilderness took on this new character, it seemed that even the Devil had given up his more familiar disguises. He no longer lurked in the underbrush, for most of it had been cut away; he no longer assumed the shape of hostile Indians, for most of them had retreated inland for the moment; he no longer sent waves of heretics to trouble the Bay, for most of them lived quietly under the protection of toleration; he no longer appeared in the armies of the Counter-Reformation, for the old battlefields were still and too far away to excite the imagination. But his presence was felt everywhere, and when the colonists began to look for his new hiding places they found him crouched in the very heart of the Puritan colony. Quite literally, the people of the Bay began to see ghosts, and soon the boundaries of the New England Way closed in on a space full of demons and incubi, spectres and evil spirits, as the settlers tried to find a new sense of their own identity among the landmarks of a strange, invisible world. Cotton Mather, who knew every disguise in the Devil's wardrobe, offered a frightening catalogue of the Devil's attempts to destroy New England.

> I believe, there never was a poor Plantation, more pursued by the wrath of the Devil, than our poor New-England. . . . It was a rousing alarm to the Devil, when a great Company of English Protestants and Puritans, came to erect Evangelical Churches, in a corner of the world, where he had reign'd without control for many ages; and it is a vexing Eye-sore to the Devil, that our Lord Christ should be known, and own'd and preached in this howling wilderness. Wherefore he has left no Stone unturned, that so he might undermine his Plantation, and force us out of our Country.
>
> First, the Indian Powawes, used all their Sorceries to molest the first Planters here; but God said unto them, Touch them not! Then, Seducing spirits came to root in this Vineyard, but God so rated them off, that they have not prevail'd much farther than the edges of our Land. After this, we have had a continual blast upon some of our principal Grain, annually diminishing a vast part of our ordinary Food. Herewithal, wasting Sicknesses, especially Burning and Mortal Agues, have Shot the Arrows of Death in at our Windows. Next, we have had many Adversaries of our own Language, who have been perpetually assaying to deprive us of those English Liberties, in the encouragement whereof these Territories have been settled. As if this had not been enough; the Tawnies among whom we came have watered our Soil with the Blood of many Hundreds of Inhabitants. . . . Besides all which, now at last the Devils are (if I may so speak) in Person come down upon us with such a Wrath, as is justly much, and will quickly be more, the Astonishment of the World.[9]

And this last adventure of the Devil has a quality all its own.

> Wherefore the Devil is now making one Attempt more upon us; and Attempt more Difficult, more Surprising, more snarl'd with unintelligible Circumstances than any that we have hitherto Encountered.

...An Army of Devils is horribly broke in upon the place which is the center, and after a sort, the First-born of our English Settlements: and the Houses of the Good People there are fill'd with the doleful shrieks of their Children and Servants, Tormented by Invisible Hands, with Tortures altogether preternatural.[10]

The witchcraft hysteria occupied but a brief moment in the history of the Bay. The first actors to take part in it were a group of excited girls and a few of the less savory figures who drifted around the edges of the community, but the speed with which the other people of the Bay gathered to witness the encounter and accept an active role in it, not to mention the quality of the other persons who were eventually drawn into this vortex of activity, serves as an index to the gravity of the issues involved. For a few years, at least, the settlers of Massachusetts were alone in the world, bewildered by the loss of their old destiny but not yet aware of their new one, and during this fateful interval they tried to discover some image of themselves by listening to a chorus of voices which whispered to them from the depths of an invisible wilderness.

NOTES

1. George L. Kittredge, *Witchcraft in Old and New England* (New York: Russell E. Russell, 1956), p. 329.

2. Wallace Notestein, *History of Witchcraft in England* (Washington, D.C.: The American Historical Society, 1911).

3. Winthrop, Journal, II, pp. 323, 344–345. Altogether, five or possibly six persons were executed for witchcraft in New England prior to the outbreak of 1692.

4. Massachusetts Records, IVa, pp. 52–53.

5. Essex County Records, I, p. 265.

6. Essex County Records, V, pp. 426–427.

7. Daniel Boorstein, *The Genius of American Politics* (Chicago: University of Chicago Press, 1953).

8. See . . . the very interesting paper by Alan Heimert, "Puritanism, The Wilderness and the Frontier," *New England Quarterly,* 26 (1953), pp. 361–382.

9. Cotton Mather, "Wonders of the Invisible World," in Samuel G. Drake, editor, *The Witchcraft Delusion,* (Roxbury, Mass.: W. Elliot Woodward, 1866) pp. 94–95.

10. *Ibid.,* pp. 16–17.

Marcello Truzzi

Witchcraft and Satanism

Witchcraft and Satanism follow astrology as the second most popular focus of current attention in occultism. The large number of recent popular books and articles dealing with these subjects attests to this upsurge of interest in them. (Often these publications are reprints of much older volumes.) Although witchcraft and Satanism are commonly linked together, they actually represent very different belief-systems, and each has an existing variety of forms.

The alleged difference between so-called *white* versus *black* magic is one major distinction discussed in much of the occult literature. While white magic is supposed to be the use of magic for socially beneficent ends, black magic is supposed to be the use of magic for malevolent ends. Even though some ritual forms of black magic clearly involve calling upon such malevolent forces as the Devil or his demons, most magicians basically view magic as a value-free "technology-of-the-supernatural" (or *super-normal*, a term preferred by many magicians). They believe that their own motives really determine whether their use of magic is for good (white), or for evil (black). Most contemporary

Reprinted and excerpted from Marcello Truzzi, "The Occult Revival as Popular Culture," *Sociological Quarterly,* 13 (Winter 1972), pp. 16–36, by permission of the author. Copyright © 1970 by Marcello Truzzi.

witches stress that they perform only white magic (e.g., Leek, 1968:3-5; or Holzer, 1969:19) as an attempted antidote for the stereotypes usually portraying them as evil workers of the devil. The distinction between black and white magic is essentially a matter of the user's intent rather than of his technique.

Contemporary witches usually do not consider themselves to be Satanists. Satanism is basically a worship of the Judaeo-Christian Devil, which is, at times, only a symbol and, at other times, very literally real. (Varying degrees of fundamentalism exist among Satanists. For these varieties, see Truzzi, 1974; and Lyons, 1970.) Practitioners in witchcraft do not usually view themselves as an heretical off-shoot of Christianity, but Satanists do view themselves, either literally or symbolically (since many Satanists are atheists), as members in league with the Christian's Devil. Most witches perceive witchcraft as a folk tradition of magical beliefs. Many, if not most of them, further perceive it as an ancient, pre-Christian fertility religion that the Christian churches sought to suppress: primarily through the Catholic inquisitions and the Protestant witch trials. They believe that their religion became misrepresented and distorted as an heretical worship of the Devil. [For the early Catholic image, see Kramer and Sprenger, 1948. Most Catholics no longer accept the orthodox picture of the witch, but some Catholic scholars do; e.g., see Pratt, 1915, and Cristiani, 1962. The leading writer presenting the strictly orthodox (medieval) Catholic viewpoint in recent years was the late Montague Summers (1946, 1956, and 1958).] On the other hand, Satanists do often constitute a kind of inverted Christian sect. (Most of the presently vast literature on Satanism is quite unreliable. Some reliable sources include Hartland, 1921; Spence, 1960:123-124; Carey, 1941; and Murray, 1962. For the official views of the Church of Satan, centered in San Francisco, see LaVey, 1969. For good historical commentaries, see Carus, 1969; Langston, 1945; Coulange, 1930; and Garcon and Vinchon, 1929. And for the classic occult view on Satanism, see Huysmans, 1958; and Waite, 1896.) Oddly enough, most of history's Satanisms seemed to be direct outgrowths of the Christian churches' misrepresentations of early witchcraft practices. The inquisitors so impressed some individuals with the fantastic and blasphemous picture of Satanism that they apparently decided that they also would "rather reign in hell than serve in heaven."

Several different varieties seem to depict the non-heretical, non-Satanic or white witches. The major division of great importance to the sociologist is between those witches who are individual practitioners and those who belong to organized witch groups or *covens*. Most frequently encountered, the former variety represents the independent or solitary witches. This variety can be further subdivided into two, somewhat oversimplified, classes: (1) one represents those who, having learned the secrets of the art through some special kinship-relation to another solitary witch, practice witchcraft as a culturally inherited art from kin; (2) the other represents those who, having invented their own techniques or having obtained their practices from the occult literature, practice witchcraft as self-designated witches. My investigations show that the vast majority of witches are in the second class: they belong to no organized group and have obtained their knowledge from their readings and conversations with others uninitiated into coven-held secrets. The typical person of this class is a young high-school or college-age girl who, for a variety of reasons, self-designates herself as a witch to her peers; because her status is attractive to her friends but elicits fear in her enemies, it produces many social rewards for her. Yet this type of witch is "illegitimate" in terms of the very criteria that she herself may accept for being a witch. Most of the major works on witchcraft state that before one becomes a true practitioner of the craft, he must obtain initiation into a coven and learn the group (coven) secrets. These secrets, however, are not available in such public works as the occultism-volumes in most public libraries or occult bookstores.

A number of varieties exist among the organized white witch groups. A rather clear division seems to exist between the witch coven formed before and after the 1951 repeal of witchcraft-laws in England or, especially, after the 1954 publication of the late Gerald Gardner's first book on witchcraft (also, see Gardner, 1959, and Bracelin's biography on Gardner, 1960). Gardner's works were influential in British occult circles, and many contemporary witches, sometimes called Gardnerites, received their credentials through Gardner's Witchcraft Museum on the Isle of Man. The question of legitimacy among British witches is still raging, each accusing the other of concocting his own rituals. *Pentagram: A Witchcraft Review,* the publication of the Witchcraft Research Association in London, prominently featured this debate in its first five issues (for an example of a lively exchange, see issue number 5, December 1965:18–19). The much publicized witch, Monique Wilson, who with her husband inherited Gardner's museum, has stated that she holds a secret register of covens existing around the world (Wilson, 1968). This, however, seems to include only the Gardnerite covens, which, according to Mrs. Wilson, numbered several hundred at that time. In 1969, another well publicized witch, Mrs. Sybil Leek, estimated to me that approximately 300 covens were then operating in the United States. The facts are that covens, especially those in existence before 1951, have little communication with one another. Members sometimes migrate from an area and join or begin a new coven, but no central hierarchy or witchcraft-organization actually exists. Except for Mrs. Wilson and Mrs. Leek, most witches know little about those in the other parts of the country. These women are somewhat unusual because their extensive publicity and travel about the world have brought them into contact with a great many witches wanting interaction with them. It is, therefore, impossible to obtain any sort of accurate estimate of the number of covens now in operation. Because a great number of new covens did begin after 1951, they certainly appear to represent the bulk of the *known* witchcraft-groups about which we read today. Even though more could exist, I did locate three pre-1951 covens in Michigan. I thus estimate that at least 150 such traditional covens probably exist in Great Britain and the United States.

According to Murray, the maximum number of persons in a coven is thirteen: Thus, Great Britain and the United States probably can claim no more than 1950 coven members. These cultists represent a rather small part of the mass market currently devouring the many marketable witchcraft items and books. Coupling the number of coven members with that of the solitary witches (many of whom are really not very serious about witchcraft) still leaves us with a relatively small number of witches in the United States, the maximum being probably less than 3000.Like their interest with astrology, the popular interest of the general public toward this form of occultism is very superficial. From my observations of many people's reactions toward witches during public occasions, I know that most people show interest in meeting a witch for the novelty rather than for any occult enlightenment. Like astrology, witchcraft also represents a play-function for the major portion of its current popular audience.

Like the witches, the Satanists also represent two distinct types of individuals: those acting as solitary agents and those operating in groups. We know next to nothing about the former. If some individuals in the world believe that they have made contractual arrangements with the Devil, then they probably would prefer that this not be widely known: this seems likely, especially if they are really doing evil things. Much diversity exists among the Satanic groups; these groups have at least four major varieties. Probably the least frequent, the first variety represents Satanic groups who follow some non-heretical (to them) interpretation of Christianity in which Satan is perceived as an angel still to be worshipped. These may represent some sort of Gnostic tradition which the members claim to follow.

A second variety about which one can read a great deal in the "soft-core" pornographic literature (e.g., Moore, 1969) consists of sex clubs that incorporate Satanism and some of its alleged rituals. Here we find, as an attraction or embellishment, the celebrated but usually artificial "black mass" (for the best work on this topic, see Rhodes, 1954). Many of these groups are sado-masochist clubs or flagellation societies.

Probably more frequent than the previous two, a third variety of Satanic group is an outgrowth of the current narcotics or "acid-culture" now found in various parts of the country [even though the author seems to confuse it with traditional Satanism, Burke (1970) presents a good description of one of these groups]. Epitomized by the much publicized Charles Manson group that allegedly killed Sharon Tate in 1969, this sort of group has received much publicity. It is, however, much more rare than the newspaper headlines would imply. More importantly, most of these groups are almost completely untraditional, and they make up their brand of Satanism as they go along (Burke, 1970; and Kloman, 1970). Like the sex club, their central focus is not occultism at all; in their case, it is narcotics. Ironically enough, many traditional Satanists commonly complain that the sex and acid cultists give a "bad name" to "real Satanism."

Clearly dominant today, the fourth variety of Satanic group consists of members of the Church of Satan in San Francisco. High Priest Anton Szandor LaVey founded this church, which is, in fact, a church, not a cult.[1] Only LaVey knows the exact number of members in the Church of Satan, but on numerous occasions he has stated that over 7000 were contributing members.[2] He gave this figure before mid-1969: since then, LaVey's book *The Satanic Bible* has had national circulation (125,000 copies in its first of now four printings), and two movies that prominently feature the Church of Satan have been released nationally. The figure of 7000 appears reasonable, if not conservative, for several reasons; because LaVey does remarkable public relations works and because *Rosemary's Baby,* the movie with which he was associated, has been a great success, the Church of Satan has received vast international publicity over the past five years.

The church has been remarkably successful during its short life. Although it still depends heavily upon the charisma of its founder, it is hierarchically governed[3] and now has two churches (Grottos) in the Bay Area plus a number of still secret (to the general public) branches scattered around the country. By the end of 1971, LaVey hopes that Grottos will exist in every state of the Union. At the current rate of growth, achievement of his goal is not impossible. Because contributing members pay an initial fee of twenty dollars for their lifetime membership, the church has a relatively prosperous economic beginnning.

Although the Church of Satan believes in the practice of magic, it simply defines magic as "obtaining changes in accordance with one's will."[4] The church perceives magic not as supernatural (i.e., forever scientifically inexplicable), but simply as supernormal (i.e., not yet fully understood by science but amenable to eventual scientific explanation). The church actively rejects spirituality and mysticism of any sort; it espouses an elitist, materialist, and basically atheistic philosophy. Satan constitutes a worship of one's own ego. Unlike most atheisms, the position of the Church of Satan is that these symbolic entities are powerful and indispensable forces in man's emotional life and that these forces are necessary conditions for the success of greater (Ritual) Magic.

In its major features, the Church of Satan takes the position of Extreme Machiavellianism and cynical-realism toward the nature of man. It has many philosophical parallels with philosophies as divergent in sophistication as the Superman views of Friedrich Nietzsche and the Objectivist ideals of Ayn Rand. Its major feature, however, is its emphasis upon the importance of myth and magic and upon their impact in a world of people who can still be manipulated through such beliefs and emotions. This Satanist, then, is the *ultimate pragmatist.*[5]

This predominant form of Satanism does not represent a new mysticism at all. It not only denies the existence of anything supernatural or spiritual, but it even condemns any narcotics, hallucinogens, or other agents that might act to separate rational man from his material environment. This Satanist does not seek escape from reality; he wishes full control of reality and is even willing to use all forces—including irrational elements—that help him in achieving his desired ends. Unlike the acid-culture Satanist who seeks identity through mysticism and other levels of "consciousness," this Satanist is very much opposed to the hippie culture of acid and altruism.[6]

Thus, I argue that the major followers of Satanism represent not a search for a new spiritual meaning, but only a disenchantment with religious orthodoxy. . . .

REFERENCES

Bracelin, J. L.
    1960   *Gerald Gardner: Witch.* London: Octagon Press.
Burke, T.
    1970   "Princess Leda's castle in the air." *Esquire,* March, p. 104.

Carus, Paul
    1969   *The History of the Devil and the Idea of Evil.* New York: Land's End Press.
Casey, R. P.
    1941   "Transient cults." *Psychiatry* 4 (November):525-535.
Coulange, Louis
    1930   *The Life of the Devil.* S. H. Guest (trans.) New York: Alfred A. Knopf.
Cristiani, Leon
    1962   *Evidences of Satan in the Modern World.* New York: Macmillan.
Crowley, Aleister
    1929   *Magick in Theory and Practice.* Paris: Lecram Press.
Garcon, Maurice and Jean Vinchon
    1929   *The Devil: An Historical Critical and Medical Study.* S. H. (trans.). London: Victor
            Gollancz, Ltd.
Gardner, Gerald
    1959   *The Meaning of Witchcraft.* London: Aquarian Press.
    1954   *Witchcraft Today.* London: Rider and Co.
Hartland, Widney E.
    1921   "Satanism." Pp. 203-207 in James Hastings (ed.), *Encyclopedia of Religion and
            Ethics,* Vol. 11. New York: Charles Scribner's Sons.
Holzer, Hans
    1969   *The Truth about Witchcraft.* Garden City, N.Y.: Doubleday.
Huysmans, Joris-Karl
    1958   *Down There.* Keene Wallis (trans.). New Hyde Park, N.Y.: University Books.
Kloman, W.
    1970   "Banality of the new evil." *Esquire,* March, p. 115.
Kramer, Heinrich and James Sprenger
    1948   *Malleus Maleficarum.* Montague Summers (trans.). London: Pushkin Press.
Langston, Edward
    1945   *Satan, A Portrait.* London: Skeffington and Sons.
LaVey, Anton Szandor
    1970   *Letters from the Devil,* 14 February, p. 5.
    1969   *The Satanic Bible.* New York: Avon Books.
    1968   Personal communication.
Leek, Sybil
    1968   *Diary of a Witch.* Englewood Cliffs, N.J.: Prentice-Hall.
Lyons, Arthur
    1970   *The Second Coming: Satanism in America.* New York: Dodd, Mead and Co.
Moore, Martin
    1969   *Sex and Modern Witchcraft.* Los Angeles: Echelon Book Publishers, Impact Library.
Murray, H. A.
    1962   "The personality and career of Satan." *Journal of Social Issues* 18 (October):36-54.
Nelson, G. K.
    1968   "The concept of cult." *The Sociological Review* 16 (November):351-362.
Pratt, Antoinette Marie
    1915   *The Attitude of the Catholic Church towards Witchcraft and the Allied Practices of
            Sorcery and Magic.* Washington, D.C.: National Capital Press.

Rhodes, H. T. F.
    1954   *The Satanic Mass*. London: Rider and Co.
Spence, Lewis
    1960   *Encyclopedia of Occultism*. New Hyde Park, N.Y.: University Books.
Summers, Montague
    1958   *The Geography of Witchcraft*. New Hyde Park, N.Y.: University Books.
    1956   *The History of Witchcraft*. New Hyde Park, N.Y.: University Books.
    1946   *Witchcraft and Black Magic*. London: Rider and Co.
Truzzi, Marcello
    1974   "Towards a sociology of the occult: notes on modern witchcraft." In I. I. Zaretsky
            and M. P. Leone (eds.). *Religious Movements in Contemporary America*. Princeton,
            N.J.: Princeton University Press, forthcoming.
    1969   *Caldron Cookery*. New York: Meredith Press.
Waite, Arthur E.
    1896   *Devil Worship in France*. London: George Redward.
Wilson, Monique
    1968   Interview with Johnny Carson on NBC-TV, the Tonight Show, 31 October.

NOTES

1. Four sociological criteria determine that the Church of Satan is not a cult but a church: (1) it
    is very large; (2) it is bureaucratically organized and hierarchically governed; (3) people be-
    come members of the church only through complex testings and initiations; and (4) the suc-
    cess of the church no longer centers around its founder's charisma. The government also has
    given the Church of Satan legal recognition of its church status for tax and other purposes.
    (For an excellent discussion of the distinction between cult and church, see Nelson, 1968.)

2. Contributing members belong to the lowest membership-level in the Church of Satan. Al-
    though they receive their membership-card, they are not involved in the rituals or ceremonies
    of the church. The six hierarchical levels of membership in the church include (1)
    Contributing Member, (2) Active Member, (3) Witch or Warlock, (4) Wizard or
    Enchantress, (5) Satanic Master or Sorcerer or Sorceress, and (6) Magus (High Priest). (Cf.,
    LaVey, 1970.)

3. The secret governing body of the Church of Satan is called the Order of the Trapezoid. Pas-
    tors or priests of the Church of Satan are called Magister Cavernus or Master or Mistress
    of the Grotto, (Cf., LaVey, 1970.)

4. This agrees with the definition of the well-known 20th Century magician, Aleister Crowley,
    whom others often mistakenly accused of being a Satanist. (Cf., Crowley, 1929:xii.)

5. It is not insignificant that a magical ritual is usually termed a working.

6. As a result, many conservative, anti-hippie persons have been strongly attracted to Satanism.
    The Church of Satan is elitist, but it has no political ideology or preference for a particular
    economic system. Some authoritarian personalities are especially attracted to the Church of
    Satan; in some of the recent church literature, a rising note of appeals to patriotism has oc-
    curred.

Edward J. Moody

Urban Witches

Every Friday evening just before midnight, a group of men and women gathers
at a home in San Francisco; and there, under the guidance of their high priest,
a sorcerer or magus sometimes called the "Black Pope of Satanism," they
study and practice the ancient art of black magic. Precisely at midnight they
begin to perform Satanic rituals that apparently differ little from those
allegedly performed by European Satanists and witches at least as early as the
seventh century. By the dim and flickering light of black candles, hooded
figures perform their rites upon the traditional Satanic altar—the naked body
of a beautiful young witch—calling forth the mysterious powers of darkness to
do their bidding. Beneath the emblem of Baphomet, the horned god, they
engage in indulgences of flesh and sense for whose performance their forebears
suffered death and torture at the hands of earlier Christian zealots.

Many of these men and women are, by day, respected and responsible
citizens. Their nocturnal or covert practice of the black art would, if exposed,

make them liable to ridicule, censure, and even punishment. Even though we live in an "enlightened" age, witches are still made a focus of a community's aggression and anxiety. They are denounced from the pulpit, prosecuted to the limit of the law, and subjected to extralegal harassment by the fearful and ignorant.

Why then do the Satanists persist? Why do they take these risks? What benefits do they derive from membership in a Satanic church, what rewards are earned from the practice of witchcraft? What indulgences are enjoyed that they could not as easily find in one of the more socially acceptable arenas of pleasure available in our "permissive" society?

The nearly universal allegation of witchcraft in the various cultures of the world has excited the interest of social scientists for years and the volume of writing on the topic is staggering. Most accounts of witchcraft, however, share the common failing of having been written from the point of view of those who do not themselves practice the black art. Few, if any, modern authors have had contact with witches, black magicians, or sorcerers, relying instead on either the anguished statements of medieval victims of inquisition torture, or other types of secondhand "hearsay" evidence for their data. To further confuse the issue, authoritative and respected ethnologists have reported that black magic and witchcraft constitute an imaginary offense because it is impossible—that because witches cannot do what they are supposed to do, they are nonexistent.

Witches and Magicians.   But the witches live. In 1965 while carrying out other research in San Francisco, California, I heard rumors of a Satanic cult which planned to give an All-Hallows Eve blessing to a local chamber of horrors. I made contact with the group through its founder and high priest and thus began over two years of participant-observation as a member of a contemporary black magic group. As a member of this group I interacted with my fellow members in both ritual and secular settings. The following description is based on the data gathered at that time.

The witches and black magicians who were members of the group came from a variety of social class backgrounds. All shades of political opinion were represented from Communist to American Nazi. Many exhibited behavior identified in American culture as "pathological," such as homosexuality, sadomasochism, and transvestism. Of the many characteristics that emerged from psychological tests, extensive observations, and interviews, the most common trait, exhibited by nearly all Satanic novices, was a high level of general anxiety related to low self-esteem and a feeling of inadequacy. This syndrome appears to be related to intense interpersonal conflicts in the nuclear family during socialization. Eighty-five percent of the group, the administrative and magical hierarchy of the church, reported that their childhood homes were split by alcoholism, divorce, or some other serious problem. Their adult lives were in turn marked by admitted failure in love, business, sexual, or social relationships. Before entering the group each member appeared to have been battered by failure in one or more of the areas mentioned, rejected or isolated by a society frightened by his increasingly bizarre and unpredictable behavior, and forced into a continuing struggle to comprehend or give meaning to his life situation.

Almost all members, prior to joining the group, had made some previous attempt to gain control over the mysterious forces operating around them. In order to give their environment some structure, in order to make it predictable and thus less anxiety-provoking, they dabbled in astrology, the Tarot, spiritualism, or other occult sciences, but continued failure in their everyday lives drove them from the passive and fatalistic stance of the astrologer to consideration of the active and manipulative role of sorcerer or witch. In articles in magazines such as *Astrology* and *Fate*, the potential Satanist comes into direct contact with magic, both white and black. Troubled by lack of power and control, the pre-Satanist is frequently introduced to the concept of magic by advertisements which promise "Occult power . . . now . . . for those who want to make real progress in understanding and working the forces that rule our Physical Cosmos . . . a self-study course in the practice of Magic." Or, Ophiel will teach you how to "become a power in your town, job, club, etc. . . . ," how to "create a familiar [a personal magic spirit servant] to help you through life," how to "control and dominate others." "The Secret Way" is offered free of charge, and the Esoteric Society offers to teach one how herbs, roots, oils, and rituals may be used, through "white magic," to obtain love, money, power, or a peaceful home. They will also teach one self-confidence and how to banish "unwanted forces." The reader is invited to join the Brotherhood of the White Temple, Inc.; the Monastery of the Seven Rays (specializing in sexual magic); the Radiant School; and numerous other groups that promise to reveal the secrets of success in business, sex, love, and life—the very secrets the potential or pre-Satanist feels have eluded him. Before joining the group, the pre-Satanist usually begins to perform magic ceremonies and rituals whose descriptions he receives for a fee from one of the various groups noted above, from magical wholesale houses, or from occult book clubs. These practices reinforce his "magical world view," and at the same time bring him in contact with other practitioners of the magical arts, both white and black.

Although most of the mail-order magic groups profess to practice "white" magic—benevolvent magic designed only to benefit those involved and never aggressive or selfish, only altruistic—as opposed to "black," malevolent, or selfish magic, even white magic rituals require ingredients that are rare enough so they can be brought only at certain specialty stores. These stores, usually known to the public as candle shops although some now call themselves occult art supply houses, provide not only the raw materials—oils, incenses, candles, herbs, parchments, etc.—for the magical workings, but serve as meeting places for those interested in the occult. A request for some specific magic ingredient such as "John the Conqueror oil," "Money-come" powder, "crossing" powder, or black candles usually leads to a conversation about the magical arts and often to introductions to other female witches and male warlocks. The realization that there are others who privately practice magic, white or black, supports the novice magician in his new-found interest in magical manipulation. The presence of other witches and magicians in his vicinity serves as additional proof that the problems he has personally experienced may indeed be caused by witchcraft, for the pre-Satanist has now met, firsthand, witches and warlocks who previously were only shadowy figures, and if there are a few known witches, who knows how many there might be practicing secretly?

Many witches and magicians never go beyond the private practice of white or black magic, or at most engage in a form of magic "recipe" swapping. The individual who does join a formal group practicing magic may become affiliated with such a group in one of several ways. In some cases he has been practicing black magic with scant success. Perhaps he has gone no further than astrology or reading the designs on the ancient Tarot cards, a type of socially acceptable magic which the leader of the Satanic church disparagingly calls "god in sport clothes." But the potential Satanist has come to think of the cosmos as being ordered, and ordered according to magical—that is, imperceptible—principles. He is prompted by his sense of alienation and social inadequacy to try to gain control of the strange forces that he feels influence or control him and, hearing of a Satanic church, he comes to learn magic.

Others join because of anxiety and inadequacy of a slightly different nature. They may be homosexual, nymphomaniac, sadist, or masochist. They usually have some relatively blatant behavioral abnormality which, though they personally may not feel it wrong, is socially maladaptive and therefore disruptive.

As in many "primitive" societies, magic and witchcraft provide both the "disturbed" persons and, in some cases, the community at large with a ready and consistent explanation for those "forces" or impulses which they themselves have experienced. Seeking control, or freedom, the social deviants come ultimately to the acknowledged expert in magic of all kinds, the head of the Satanic church, to have their demons exorcised, the spells lifted, and their own powers restored.

Others whose problems are less acute come because they have been brought, in the larger religious context, to think of themselves as "evil." If their struggle against "evil" has been to no avail, many of the individuals in question take this to mean that the power of "evil" is greater than the power of "good"—that "God is dead"—and so on. In their search for a source of strength and security, rather than continue their vain struggle with that "evil" force against which they know themselves to be powerless, they seek instead to identify themselves with evil, to join the "winning" side. They identify with Satan—etymologically the "opposition"—and become "followers of the left-hand path," "walkers in darkness."

Finally, there are, of course, those who come seeking thrills or titillation, lured by rumors of beautiful naked witches, saturnalian orgies, and other strange occurrences. Few of these are admitted into the group.

Black Magic. For the novice, initial contact with the Satanists is reassuring. Those assisting the "Prince of Darkness" who heads the church are usually officers in the church, long-term members who have risen from the rank and file to positions of trust and authority. They are well-dressed, pleasant persons who exude an aura of confidence and adequacy. Rather than having the appearance of wild-eyed fanatics or lunatics, the Satanists look like members of the middle-class, but successful middle-class. The Prince of Darkness himself is a powerfully built and striking individual with a shaven head and black, well-trimmed beard. Sitting among the implements of magic, surrounded by books that contain the "secrets of the centuries," he affirms for those present what they already know: that there is a secret to power and success which can and must be learned, and that secret is black magic.

All magic is black magic according to the Satanists. There is no altruistic or white magic. Each magician intends to benefit from his magical manipulation, even those workings performed at someone else's behest. To claim to be performing magic only for the benefit of others is either hypocrisy—the cardinal sin in Satanic belief—or naiveté, another serious shortcoming. As defined by the Satanists, magic itself is a surprisingly common-sense kind of phenomenon: "the change in situations or events in accordance with one's will, which would, using normally accepted methods, be unchangeable." Magic can be divided into two categories: ritual (ceremonial) and nonritual (manipulative).

Ritual, or "the greater magic," is performed in a specified ritual area and at a specific time. It is an emotional, not an intellectual act. Although the Satanists spend a great deal of time intellectualizing and rationalizing magic power, they state specifically that "any and all intellectual activity must take place *before* the ceremony, not during it."[1]

The "lesser magic," nonritual (manipulative) magic, is, in contrast, a type of transactional manipulation based upon a heightened awareness of the various processes of behavior operative in interaction with others, a Satanic "games people play." The Satanist in ritual interaction is taught to analyze and utilize the motivations and behavioral Achilles' heels of others for his own purposes. If the person with whom one is interacting has masochistic tendencies, for example, the Satanist is taught to adopt the role of sadist, to "indulge" the other's desires, to be dominant, forceful, and even cruel in interaction with him.

Both the greater and the lesser magic is predicated upon a more general "magical" world view in which all elements of the "natural world" are animate, have unique and distinctive vibrations that influence the way they relate to other natural phenomena. Men, too, have vibrations, the principal difference between men and inanimate objects being that men can alter their pattern of vibrations, sometimes consciously and at will. It is the manipulation and the modification of these vibrations, forces, or powers that is the basis of all magic. There are "natural magicians," untrained and unwitting manipulators of magic power. Some, for example, resonate in harmony with growing things; these are people said to have a "green thumb," gardeners who can make anything grow. Others resonate on the frequency of money and have the "Midas touch" which turns their every endeavor into a profit-making venture. Still others are "love magnets"; they automatically attract others to them, fascinate and charm even though they may be physically plain themselves. If one is a "natural magician," he does some of these things unconsciously, intuitively, but because of the intellectual nature of our modern world, most people have lost their sensitivity to these faint vibrations. Such individuals may, if they become witches, magicians or Satanists, regain contact with that lost world just as tribal shamans are able to regain contact with another older world where men communicated with animals and understood their ways. It is this resensitization to the vibrations of the cosmos that is the essence of magical training. It takes place best in the "intellectual decompression chamber" of magical ritual, for it is basically a "subjective" and "nonscientific" phenomenon.

Those who have become members of the inner circle learn to make use of black magic, both greater and lesser, in obtaining goals which are the antithesis of Christian dogma. The seven deadly sins of Christian teaching—greed, pride, envy, anger, gluttony, lust, and sloth—are depicted as Satanic virtues. Envy and greed are, in the Satanic theology, natural in man and the motivating forces behind ambition. Lust is necessary for the preservation of the species and not a Satanic sin. Anger is the force of self-preservation. Instead of denying natural instincts the Satanist learns to glory in them and turn them into power.

Satanists recognize that the form of their ritual, its meanings and its functions are largely determined by the wider society and its culture. The novitiate in the Satanic cult is taught, for example, that the meaning of the word "Satan" etymologically is "the opposition," or "he who opposes," and that Satanism itself arose out of opposition to the demeaning and stultifying institutions of Christianity. The cult recognizes that had there been no Christianity there would be no Satanism, at least not in the form it presently takes, and it maintains that much of the Satanic ritual and belief is structured by the form and content of Christian belief and can be understood only in that larger religious context. The Satanists choose black as their color, not white, precisely because white is the symbol of purity and transcendence chosen by Christianity, and black therefore has come to symbolize the profane earthy indulgences central to Satanic theodicy. Satanists say that their gods are those of the earth, not the sky; that their cult is interested in making the sacred profane, in contrast to the Judeo-Christian cults which seek to make the profane sacred. Satanism cannot, in other words, be understood as an isolated phenomenon, but must be seen in a larger context.

The Satanic belief system, not surprisingly, is the antithesis of Christianity. Their theory of the universe, their cosmology, is based upon the notion that the desired end state is a return to a pagan awareness of the mystical forces inhabiting the earth, a return to an awareness of their humanity. This is in sharp contrast to the transcendental goals of traditional Christianity. The power associated with the pantheon of gods is also reversed: Satan's power is waxing; God's, if he still lives, waning. The myths of the Satanic church pur-

230 THE CASE OF WITCHCRAFT

port to tell the true story of the rise of Christianity and the fall of paganism, and there is a reversal here too. Christ is depicted as an early "con man" who tricked an anxious and powerless group of individuals into believing a lie. He is typified as "pallid incompetence hanging on a tree."[2] Satanic novices are taught that early church fathers deliberately picked on those aspects of human desire that were most natural and made them sins, in order to use the inevitable transgressions as a means of controlling the populace, promising them salvation in return for obedience. And finally, their substantive belief, the very delimitation of what is sacred and what is profane, is the antithesis of Christian belief. The Satanist is taught to "be natural; to revel in pleasure and in self-gratification. To emphasize indulgence and power in this life."

The opposition of Satanists to Christianity may be seen most clearly in the various rituals of greater magic. Although there are many different types of rituals all aimed at achieving the virtues that are the inverted sins of the Christian, we shall examine briefly only two of these: blasphemy and the invocation of destruction. By far the most famous of Satanic institutions, the Black Mass and other forms of ritual blasphemy serve a very real and necessary function for the new Satanist. In many cases the exhortations and teachings of his Satanic colleagues are not sufficient to alleviate the sense of guilt and anxiety he feels when engaging in behavior forbidden by Judeo-Christian tradition. The novice may still cower before the charismatic power of Christian symbols; he may still feel guilty, still experience anxiety and fear in their presence. It is here that the blasphemies come into play, and they take many forms depending on the needs of the individuals involved.

A particular blasphemy may involve the most sacred Christian rituals and objects. In the traditional Black Mass powerful Christian symbols such as the crucifix are handled brutally. Some Black Masses use urine or menstrual flow in place of the traditional wine in an attempt to evoke disgust and aversion to the ritual. If an individual can be conditioned to respond to a given stimulus, such as the communion wafer or wine, with disgust rather than fear, that stimulus's power to cause anxiety is diminished. Sexuality is also used. A young man who feared priests and nuns was deliberately involved in a scene in which two witches dressed as nuns interacted with him sexually; his former neurotic fear was replaced by a mildly erotic curiosity even in the presence of real nuns. The naked altar—a beautiful young witch—introduces another deliberate note of sexuality into a formerly awe-inspiring scene.

By far the most frequently used blasphemy involves laughter. Awe-inspiring or fear-producing institutions are made the object of ridicule. The blasphemous rituals, although still greater magic, are frequently extremely informal. To the outsider they would not seem to have any structure; the behavior being exhibited might appear to be a charade, or a party game. The Satanists decide ahead of time the institution to be ridiculed and frequently it is a Christian ritual. I have seen a group of Satanists do a parody of the Christmas manger scene, or dress in clerical garb while performing a satire or priestly sexual behavior. The target of the blasphemy depends upon the needs of the various Satanists. If the group feels it is necessary for the well-being of one member, they will gladly, even gleefully, blaspheme anything from psychiatry to psychedelics.

In the invocation of destruction black magic reaches its peak. In some cases an individual's sense of inadequacy is experienced as victimization, a sense of powerlessness before the demands of stronger and more ruthless men. The Satanic Bible, in contrast to Christian belief, teaches the fearful novice that "Satan represents vengeance instead of turning the other cheek." In the Third Chapter of the Book of Satan, the reader is exhorted to "hate your enemies with a whole heart, and if a man smite you on one cheek, SMASH him on the other . . . he who turns the other cheek is a cowardly dog."[3]

One of the most frequently used rituals in such a situation is the Conjuration of Destruction, or Curse. Contrary to popular belief, black magicians are not indiscriminately aggressive. An individual must have harmed or hurt a member of the church before he is likely to be cursed. Even then the curse is laid with care, for cursing a more powerful magician may cause one's curse to be turned against oneself. If, in the judgment of the high priest and the congregation, a member has been unjustly used by a non-Satanist, even if the offender is an unaffiliated witch or magician, at the appropriate time in the ritual the member wronged may step forward and, with the aid and support of the entire congregation, ritually curse the transgressor. The name of the intended "sacrifice" is usually written on parchment made of the skin of unborn lamb and burned in the altar flame while the member speaks the curse; he may use the standard curse or, if he so desires, prepare a more powerful, individualistic one. In the curse he gives vent to his hostility and commands the legions of hell to torment and sacrifice his victim in a variety of horrible ways. Or, if the Satanist so desires, the High Priest will recite the curse for him, the entire group adding their power to the invocation by spirited responses.

The incidence of harmful results from cursing is low in the church of Satan because of two factors: first, one does not curse other members of the church for fear that their superior magic might turn the curse back upon its user;

second, victims outside the congregation either do not believe in the power of black magic or do not recognize the esoteric symbols that should indicate to them they are being cursed.

On only one occasion was I able to see the effect of a curse on a "victim." A member attempted to use the church and its members for publicity purposes without their permission. When the leader of the group refused to go along with the scheme, the man quit—an action that would normally have brought no recrimination—and began to slander the church by spreading malicious lies throughout San Francisco social circles. Even though he was warned several times to stop his lies, the man persisted; so the group decided to level the most serious of all curses at him, and a ritual death rune was cast.

Casting a death rune, the most serious form of greater magic, goes considerably beyond the usual curse designed to cause only discomfort or unhappiness, but not to kill. The sole purpose of the death's rune is to cause the total destruction of the victim. The transgressor's name is written in blood (to the Satanist, blood is power—the very power of life) on special parchment, along with a number of traditional symbols of ceremonial magic. In a single-minded ritual of great intensity and ferocity, the emotional level is raised to a peak at which point the entire congregation joins in ritually destroying the victim of the curse. In the case in question, there was an orgy of aggression. The lamb's-wool figurine representing the victim was stabbed by all members of the congregation, hacked to pieces with a sword, shot with a small calibre pistol, and then burned.

A copy of the death rune was sent to the man in question, and every day thereafter an official death certificate was made out in his name and mailed to him. After a period of weeks during which the "victim" maintained to all who would listen that he "did not believe in all that nonsense," he entered the hospital with a bleeding ulcer. Upon recovery he left San Francisco permanently.

In fairness, I must add that the "victim" of the curse had previously had an ulcer, was struggling with a failing business, and seemed hypertense when I knew him. His knowledge of the "curse" may have hastened the culmination of his difficulties. The Satanic church, however, claimed it as a successful working, a victory for black magic, and word of it spread among the adherents of occult subculture, enhancing the reputation of the group.

Conclusion. Contemporary America is presently undergoing a witchcraft revival. On all levels, from teenagers to octogenarians, interest in, or fear of, witchcraft has increased dramatically over the past two years. It is hardly possible to pass a popular magazine rack without seeing an article about the revival of the black arts. Covens and cults multiply, as does the number of exorcisms and reconsecrations. England, France, Germany, and a host of other countries all report a rebirth of the black art. Why? Those who eventually become Satanists are attempting to cope with the everyday problems of life, with the here and now, rather than with some transcendental afterlife. In an increasingly complex world which they do not fully understand, an anxiety-provoking world, they seek out a group dedicated to those mysterious powers that the sufferers have felt moving them. Fearful of what one calls "the dark powers we all feel moving deep within us," they come seeking either *release* or *control*. They give various names to the problems they bring, but all, anxious and afraid, come to the Satanic cult seeking help in solving problems beyond their meager abilities. Whatever their problem—bewitchment, business failure, sexual impotence, or demonic possession—the Satanists, in the ways I have mentioned and many more, *can* and *do* help them. Witchcraft, the witches point out, "is the most practical of all beliefs. According to its devotees, its results are obvious and instantaneous. No task is too high or too lowly for the witch." Above all, the beliefs and practices provide the witch and the warlock with a sense of power, a feeling of control, and an explanation for personal failure, inadequacy, and other difficulties.

Moreover, a seeker's acceptance into the Inner Circle provides a major boost for his self-esteem; he has, for the first time, been accepted into a group as an individual despite his problems and abnormalities. Once within the Inner Circle that support continues. The Satanic group is, according to the cultural standards of his society, amoral, and the Satanist frequently finds himself lauded and rewarded for the very impulses and behavior that once brought shame and doubt.

Each Satanist is taught, and not without reason, that the exposure of his secret identity, of the fact that he is a powerful and adequate black magician, means trouble from a fearful society. Therefore, in keeping with the precepts of lesser magic, he learns to transform himself magically by day (for purposes of manipulation) into a bank clerk, a businessman, or even a college professor. He wears the guise and plays the role expected by society in order to manipulate the situation to his own advantage, to reach his desired goals. Members of society at large, aware only of his "normal" role behavior and unaware of the secret person within, respond to him positively instead of punishing him or isolating him. Then, in the evening, in the sanctity of his home, or when surrounded by his fellow magicians, he reverts to his "true" role, that of Satanic priest, and becomes himself once again. Inadequate and anxious persons, guilty because of socially disapproved impulses, are accepted by the Satanists and taught that the impulses they feel are natural and normal, but must be contained within certain spatial and temporal boundaries—the walls of the ritual chamber, the confines of the Inner Circle.

NOTES

1. The official doctrine of several Satanic groups within the continental United States is contained in the *Satanic Bible* by Anton Szandor LaVey (New York: Avon Books, 1969), p. 111.
2. LaVey 1969: 31.
3. LaVey 1969: 33.

Part Three

Sociological Perspectives and Research on the Esoteric and the Occult

This section presents a variety of sociological perspectives, analyses, and interpretations of the esoteric and the occult as components of social life. Most of the essays may be thought of as responding, directly or indirectly, to the recent "occult revival" in modern society.

The initial selection by Hubert and Mauss, two French sociologists of the Durkheimian school, was written seventy years ago. It was during that period, around the start of the century, that France and other countries in the West witnessed their own "occult revivals". The revivals had two branches. The first was in avant-garde culture, with the pronounced interest in the occult on the part of Romantic, post-Romantic, and Symbolist writers in France such as Gérard de Nerval, Baudelaire, Lautréamont, and Verlaine, continuing with Jarry, Artaud, and Breton. Outside the literary world, the study of occultism and esotericism had been renovated by Alphonse Louis Constant (1810–1875), known as Eliphas Lévi, and by Stanislas de Guaita (1860–1897). Their work was carried on by Oswald Wirth, Gérard Encausse (Papus), and René Guénon, contemporaries of Hubert and Mauss. The interest in the esotericism of Wirth, Papus, and Guénon was partly motivated by the desire to restore the meaning and vitality of the *symbolic* aspects of Freemasonry in France, as Albert Pike (1809–1891) had sought to do for Freemasonry in the United States after the Civil War, and as Arthur Edward Waite (1875–1942) had undertaken for late and post-Victorian England. The emphasis of the Durkheimian school on rituals and symbols is thus an interesting sociological echo of the renewed interest in rituals and symbolism that took place at about the same time in Masonic intellectual quarters.

235

The recent "occult revival," however, has been more a phenomenon of mass society or "popular culture" than one localized in small study groups of fraternal associations. It is this aspect, at least, that has caught the attention of the public and many sociologists. The essays by contemporary sociologists in this section indicate various approaches to the social significance of the esoteric and the occult.

The selection by Truzzi is an analytical and typological approach to the occult, with the focus on how the occult relates to anomalies. The article by Tiryakian raises a different question, the relationship of esoteric culture to Western cultural changes. The first contribution by Greeley relates the occult revival to the sociology of religion and questions the "secularization" model of religion in modern society. The contribution by Greeley and McCready is a preliminary report of their study on mysticism and ecstasy from a nation-wide sample of the American population, and challenges the assumption that "occult" experiences are dysfunctional for mental health. The essay by Fischler provides materials, based on survey research and interviews conducted in France, on the social meaning and the adherents of astrology. Finally, a different, interpretive sociological approach based on ethnomethodology is formulated by Eglin in an original study of alchemy.

Henri Hubert and Marcel Mauss

Magic, Technology, and Science

Magic is thus a social phenomenon. We need now indicate how it relates to other social phenomena, holding aside for the time being religious ones. Its relationships to law and mores, to economy and aesthetics, and also to language, however intriguing they may be, are not of present interest. Between these phenomena and magic there are only exchanges of influence. Magic has real affinity only with religion, on the one hand, and with technology and science, on the other.

We have stated that magic tended to be like techniques as it became over time individualized and specialized in seeking its various ends. But there exists between these two orders of facts more than an outward similarity; there is an

This selection represents the "Conclusion" of Hubert and Mauss, "Esquisse d'une Théorie Générale de la Magie," *L'Année Sociologique*, VII (1902–1903), pp. 143–146. The editor has prepared the translation. A translation of nearly the whole of the monograph, prepared by Robert Brain, was published in 1972 by Routledge and Kegan Paul, Ltd. (London); although the original carried a joint authorship, the 1972 translation, based on Levi-Strauss' 1950 edition of collected works of Mauss (*Sociologie et Anthropologie*), lists only Mauss as the author. Hubert and Mauss collaborated on several works in the general area of the sociology of religion (e.g., "Essai sur la nature et la fonction du Sacrifice," *L'Année Sociologique*, II (1897–1898), published in English in 1964 by the University of Chicago Press). Their monograph on magic reflects their long-term interest in the relation of rituals to social structure.

identity of function, since . . . both strive for the same ends. While religion
tends toward metaphysics and becomes incorporated in the creation of images
of the ideal, magic leaves through numerous slits the mystical life from whence
it draws its energy, becomes part of mundane life, and provides services for it.
Magic tends toward the concrete while religion tends toward the abstract.

Magic operates in the way that our techniques, industries, medicine,
chemistry, mechanics, etc., operate. Magic is essentially an art of doing, and
magicians have utilized with care their know-how, their knack, their manual
dexterity. Magic is the domain of pure production, *ex nihilo*; it produces with
words and gestures what techniques do with labor. Fortunately, magical art
has not always been vain gesticulation. It has actually treated materials, carried out real experiments, and even made discoveries.

Still, it may be said that magic is always the most facile technique. It avoids
effort because it succeeds in replacing reality with images. Magical art does
nothing or hardly anything, but it makes believe everything by placing
collective forces and ideas in the service of the imagination of the individual.
The art of the magician suggests means, augments the virtue of things, anticipates effects, and thereby amply satisfies desires whose hoped-for realiza-
tions have nourished entire generations. Magic gives a form to haphazard and
powerless gestures; by making these into rituals, magic renders such gestures
efficacious.

It might be pointed out that these gestures prefigure technology. Magic is
both an *opus operatum* from the point of view of the magical world and an
opus inoperans from the perspective of technology. Magic, being the most in-
fantile technique, is perhaps the oldest craft. Indeed, the history of technology
informs us of the genealogical tie between magic and crafts. It is by dint of its
mystical character that magic has assisted in their development. It has har-
bored them while they progressed. Magic gave the crafts its indubitable authority. It loaned its real efficacy to the practical but timorous early ventures
of craftsmen-magicians; the latter's experimentations would have been
branded as outright failures had it not been for the support of magic. Certain
techniques, such as those of pharmacy, medicine, surgery, metallurgy and ena-
meling (the latter two derive from alchemy), which have complex objectives
and an uncertain action as well as delicate procedures, could not have survived
without the assistance of magic; their near absorption [in their formative
stage] by magic enabled them to endure. We are justified in saying that
medicine, pharmacy, alchemy and astrology developed in a context of magic
and around a basic kernel of purely technical discoveries. We hazard the sup-

position that other crafts, older and more ancient perhaps, became equally mingled with magic in the beginnings of human society. Howitt[1] informs us concerning the Woivorung that the local clan which furnishes the tribe its magician-bards also own the flint quarry where neighboring tribes come for their tools. This fact may be a coincidence, but it seems to us that it is suggestive of the way the invention and manufacture of the first instruments have come about. For us, techniques are like seeds that have germinated in the terrain of magic, and they have subsequently displaced the latter. Techniques have progressively shorn themselves of everything they borrowed from the mystical. The procedures which remain have more and more changed in significance: formerly they were attributed a mystical virtue; today they are seen as having only a mechanical action. Thus, in our days the medical massage is no longer done under the spell of the bone-setter.

Magic is related to the sciences in the same way it is to the crafts. Magic is not only a practical art but also a storehouse of ideas. It gives great importance to knowledge, and the latter is one of its mainsprings. As we have seen in many instances, for magic, knowledge is power. But while religion, in its intellectual aspects, is drawn toward the metaphysical, magic, as we have interpreted it, is drawn towards the concrete and towards the knowledge of nature. Magic very early constitutes a sort of index of plants, metals, phenomena, beings in general; it constitutes an early catalogue of astronomical, physical, and natural science. Indeed, in Greece certain branches of magic, such as astrology and alchemy, were applied physical sciences. It was thus justified that magicians were called *physikoi* and that the word *physikos* was synonymous with magic.

Magicians have even tried at times to systematize their knowledge and to specify its principles. When such a theory becomes explicated in schools of magicians, it is by rational and individual procedures. In the course of this doctrinal enterprise, it happens that magicians are concerned with discarding the mystical, thus leading magic to take on the characteristic of genuine science. This is what took place in the late phase of Greek magic. "I want to represent the mind of the ancients," says Olympiodorus the alchemist,[2] "and tell you how, being philosophers, they have the language of philosophers and have applied philosophy to art by means of science [*sophias*]."

There is no doubt that, especially in primitive societies, a part of the sciences was elaborated by magicians. The alchemist-magicians, the astrologer-magicians, and the medical magicians were, in Greece, India and elsewhere, the founders and artisans of astronomy, physics, chemistry and natural history. One can venture, as we have previously done for technology, that other and more rudimentary sciences have had the same genealogical tie with magic. Mathematics certainly owes much to the research on magical squares and on magical properties of numbers and figures. This treasurehouse of ideas gathered by magic was for a long time the capital which science exploited. Magic has nurtured science, and magicians have served as scholars. In primitive societies only wizards (*sorciers*) had the leisure to observe nature, and to reflect or dream upon it. They did it as part of their social function. One may think that it is also in the colleges of magicians wherein developed a scientific tradition and a method of intellectual education. These schools were the first academies. In the lower rungs of civilization, magicians are the scientists and scientists are magicians. Scientists and magicians are the bards capable of metamorphosis in Australian tribes as well as in the Celtic literature (concerning the latter, Amairgen, Talieesin, Talhwiarn, Gaion, are prophets, astrologers, astronomers, physicians who seem to have drawn their knowledge of nature and its laws in the cauldron of the sorceress Ceridwen).[3]

Far removed as we think we are from magic, we are still involved in it. For example, notions of good luck and bad luck, as well as of quintessence, which are still familiar to us, are very close to the idea of magic itself. Neither technology, nor science, nor even the principles which guide our intellect have altogether rubbed off their original imprint. It isn't bold to venture that, for a major part, all that the notions of force, causality, effect, and substance still contain of a non-factual, mystical and poetic sort derives from ancient habits of the mind which gave birth to magic and which the human mind is slow to discard.

Consequently, we believe that we have found in the beginnings of magic the first form of collective representations which have since become the grounds of human understanding. Hence, our research is not simply . . . a chapter in the sociology of religion but indeed a contribution to the study of collective representations. It is to be hoped that general sociology can benefit from this, since we think we have shown, in dealing with magic, how a collective phenomenon can cloak individual forms.

NOTES

1. Alfred W. Howitt (1830–1908), specialist on Australian ethnography. Hubert and Mauss drew information from various articles of his appearing in the 1880's in the *Journal of the Anthropological Institute*. These were incorporated in his major work, *The Native Tribes of South-East Australia* (London and New York: Macmillan, 1904).—Editor's note.

2. Hubert and Mauss take this quote from Olympiodorus' *Commentary on Zosimos,* 18, in Marcellin Berthelot, *Collection des anciens Alchimistes grecs,* I, 86 (Paris, 1887–1888). Professor William Willis of the Classics Department at Duke University has pointed out to me problems in interpreting key terms in the original Greek text, one problem being that it is hard to know which Olympiodorus is the author and when this text was written. Moreover, although Hubert and Mauss use "science" for *sophias* (following Berthelot), it should be kept in mind that the French usage has a broader connotation, in the sense of "erudition", than in English.—Editor's note.

3. See Henri Hubert's posthumous two-volume study of the Celts (edited by Marcel Mauss): *The Rise of the Celts* (London: K. Paul, Trench, Trubner; New York: A. Knopf, 1934); and *The Greatness and Decline of the Celts* (London: K. Paul, Trench, Trubner, 1934).—Editor's note.

Marcello Truzzi

Definition and Dimensions of the Occult: Towards a Sociological Perspective

The first problem engaging anyone interested in the development of a sociological perspective on occultism is one of definition. The term "occult" has a variety of common designations, and one's choice of the properties will largely determine the results of any analysis. A typical dictionary definition of "occult" includes the following among its many meanings:

1. Beyond the range of ordinary knowledge; mysterious.
2. Secret; disclosed or communicated only to the initiated.
3. Of or pertaining to magic, astrology, and other alleged sciences claiming use or knowledge of secret, mysterious, or supernatural.[1]

Reprinted from the *Journal of Popular Culture*, v. 5, no. 3 (Winter, 1971), pp. 635/7–646/18, by permission of the *Journal of Popular Culture*.

Examination of the current social science literature on the occult reveals that it has emphasized different and sometimes contradictory elements in the above definition while eliminating others. Thus, John R. Staude has stressed the occult's anti-scientific and mystical aspects,[2] Robert Galbreath has distinguished occultism from mysticism and magic;[3] Andrew M. Greeley has emphasized the occult's "neo-sacral" or religious aspects,[4] as has Martin Marty;[5] Edward A. Tiryakian has emphasized its characteristic secrecy;[6] and I have stressed its mysterious but often very open and public elements.[7] Such varying definitions of the occult have led these analysts into somewhat different directions.

Unfortunately, examination of the term within the general literature calling itself occult does not clarify the picture substantially. The problem is not merely one of denotation but also one of connotation. As Arthur N. Foxe noted:

> The term occult has a variety of meanings. To many it is the antithesis of science, the bugbear of religion. To others it is the know all and believe all. It is often dismissed with not a little display of emotion as unworthy of intellectual consideration and is said to be akin to superstition and the unreal. On the other hand it may be used objectively merely to suggest that which is not entirely known.[8]

In general, the term tends to have the former, negative connotations among scientists, who tend to equate it with mystical and anti-naturalistic world views. Occultists, on the other hand, especially in recent years, have tended to secularize the term to make it more acceptable. Thus, the occult has become growingly interested in things supernormal or paranormal rather than supernatural. Emphasis has been placed on the occult as basically amenable to scientific investigation, and one often hears practitioners in the occult speak of the occult sciences. Claims are simply made of knowledge and techniques which science has yet to validate or investigate. This is further confounded by the fact that large segments of even modern occultism stress the *hidden* character of such wisdom. As W. B. Crow has noted: "It would be better to call these subjects *arcane sciences* to signify that they are secret rather than unknown."[9]

The claim to scientific status by most occultists presents several problems. It is clear from their general literature that most of the requirements of scientific method are not met by their investigations,[10] but it also seems true that some past claims of what were considered occult sources have more recently been accepted into Establishment science.[11] Aside from the lack of scientific rigor in most occultists' investigations, emphasis on the secrecy of such knowledge presents a major obstacle to such knowledge as scientific. Science, to most of us, implies public investigation, validation and solution whereas occultism usually suggests privacy and puzzlement. The very idea of a secret science represents what closely approximates a contradiction in terms. Yet occultists persist in speaking of their perspectives as scientific, and this would appear to be in large part a concern for credibility and legitimation by the attachment of their esoteric beliefs to the high status most of us give to our scientific institutions. In fact, once an occult viewpoint achieves a degree of scientific legitimacy (e.g., hypnosis or parapsychology), it will usually dissociate itself from the description of itself as an occultism. Thus, while most psychologists consider parapsychology to be about as much occultism as science, [12] parapsychology is most anxious to remove this label from itself.[13]

Review of the use of the term "occult" as a self-descriptive label reveals very mixed connotations about the term. Among the more mystical traditions of occultism, the term has a very positive connotation, and one often hears references to a persuasion of person being a "true occultism" or "true occultists."[14] At this end of the occult continuum, one hears of "pure" and "applied" occultism, just as one hears of pure and applied science. Occultism is very multi-dimensional and makes placement of its different forms quite difficult. There is little accord about what constitutes an occultism. Some occultists would call astrology an occultism (as would most scientists), but many would not (especially many astrologers). In many ways, the occult is a residual category, a wastebasket, for knowledge claims that are deviant in some way, that do not fit the established claims of science or religion. And once such a knowledge claim gains acceptance within establishment science or religion, it loses its status as an occultism. Thus, to many people, witchcraft is a religion and not an occultism, and graphology is not an occult study but a science. A question which must be considered in defining the occult, then, should at the outset be *who* is labelling the beliefs as occult, *where* the labelling is being done (the social context), and *at what time* the designation is made (the historical period).[15]

Given these complications, how can we develop a sociological analysis of the occult or occult movements? I have elsewhere proposed [16] that a common denominator for most (if not all) perspectives labelled occult (by anyone) is that they have in some way concerned themselves with things anomalous to our generally accepted cultural-storehouse of "truths." That is, we are here dealing with claims that contradict common-sense or institutionalized (scientific or religious) knowledge. This contradiction of accepted beliefs is the very thing which makes the occult somehow strange, mysterious and inexplicable. It is the very character of the occult that it deals with dissonant or contradicting knowledge claims.

At base, anomalies are of two kinds: (1) *anomalous objects* (things or events), and (2) *anomalous processes* (relationships). An anomalous object consists of the existence (or claimed existence) of some thing or event which is somehow a deviation from the usual, credible order of things, e.g., the sighting of an abominable snowman, a levitated fakir floating in the air, or a giant sea serpent. An anomalous process, however, can consist of quite ordinary things or events in some extraordinary conjunction. Thus, an occultist may believe that a pin placed in a wax image will lead to the death of someone (neither death nor wax images and pins themselves being extraordinary), or that the position of the planets at certain times can effect the personality development of children born at certain places on the earth at those times (planetary positions and children born with personalities in themselves being ordinary events).

Anomalies can be further classified as being *isolated* or *integrated* with one another. Thus, some anomalies are quite singular and disconnected from other anomalies. A typical example would be belief in the existence of an Unidentified Flying Object. Though some groups have turned belief in UFOs into an integrated anomaly by seeing flying saucers as vehicles piloted by angelic spacemen [17] most believers in UFOs see them as unexplained phenomena within an otherwise normal scientific world-view.

Integrated anomalies seem to more often consist of process anomalies than object anomalies. An occultist who believes in a set of magical processes is often likely to accept (or at least reserve judgment on) the credibility of someone else's claim about other magical processes, but a believer in UFOs is usually no more likely to accept the claims for a Loch Ness Monster than those who disbelieve in UFOs. Since anomalous processes are usually based on the inference of strange causalities among otherwise ordinary events (events the non-occultist would simply label as "coincidences"), the establishment of such anomalies requires more evidence to convince the skeptical than might the anomalous object. This has implications for the frequency of belief in such anomalies. Yet the relationship is not a simple one. For, on the one hand, seeing a demon or an abominable snowman is immediately validated for someone who believes he has seen such a creature; but such direct experiences (even of a mystical, personal kind) are had by only a minority of us.[18] On the other hand, unusual coincidences that seem meaningful but which are causally inexplicable (what C. G. Jung called synchronicity[19]) are commonplace to most of us at some time in our lives. Thus, the "raw materials" for occultism involving anomalous processes is more common than that involving anomalous objects.

In general, anomalous processes seem to be more likely to be integrated with other anomalies than are anomalous objects. It also seems to be the case that anomalous processes are more likely to be integrated with other anomalous processes than with anomalous objects. A network of beliefs in anomalous processes (with or without anomalous objects) constitutes an *occult system*.

As already noted, before a view can be labelled occult, consideration must be given to the source and context of the belief. Anomalies are relative to the existing picture of what constitutes the normal. An airplane is a commonplace phenomenon to most of us but an anomaly to a preliterate tribesman who sees one flying overhead for the first time. On the other hand, the commonplace fish eaten by the same native might be a still surviving prehistoric species that the zoologist pilot of our plane would find equally "impossible."

We can also differentiate between (1) *general* (common sense) *anomalies* and (2) *theoretical* (special) *anomalies*. A general anomaly is one which most people within a given culture would, under most circumstances, consider a strange or incredible event, e.g., an object vanishing into or appearing from nowhere. A theoretical anomaly is one which appears unusual only to one with special knowledge or training. Thus, the existence of an extinct animal or healing by some means inconsistent with current medical understanding (e.g., by acupuncture) might seem ordinary to those who live near the animal or use the healing method but would constitute an anomaly to the scientific investigator.

Recognizing the role of the anomalous in the definition of what is usually classified as occult, let us now turn to a consideration of some other principal dimensions of occultism of central relevancy for the development of its sociological understanding.

Dimensions of Occultism. We might ask five major questions about an occult belief: (1) What is alleged to be known? (2) Who claims to know it? (3) How or why do they know it to be so? (4) Where, under what conditions, do they learn it to be so and is the belief maintained? And (5) what use does this knowledge have for the believer?

The Substance of the Occult Belief. As regards what is known, I have argued that the basic claim is for the existence of some anomaly which can be dichotomized into the categories of object-process, isolation-integration, and general-theoretical. All combinations of these attributes can be empirically found. In general, an integrated set of anomalous processes which are contrary to general expectancies are most unequivocally called occult. Belief in theoretically isolated anomalous objects is least likely to be thus labelled by most occultists.

The Source of the Occult Label. I have also noted that the labelling source is a factor in occultism. If the believer wishes to gain scientific or establishment acceptance of his belief, he will avoid that label. The believer's status in the world of "normal knowledge" will often affect his being labelled an occultist. If a physicist states he believes in some anomaly, he is not as likely to be labelled an occultist. Much confusion results from such status differences and this is clearly reflected in the language of occultism which is full of semantic subtleties stemming from such factors. Thus, a physicist might speak of radiesthesia while our occultist simply speaks of dowsing or water divining. If one believes in "mind reading," one is an occultist; if one speaks of "psi phenomena," he is labelled a parapsychologist-scientist. Occultism is full of such "scientisms" which euphemize the language.

Rather than an Occult Establishment,[20] there is an occult hierarchy. Some occult beliefs are more "far out" or deviant than others, and as one gains respectability it (1) tends to dissociate itself from other occultisms, and (2) develops non-occult terminology to minimize its occult appearance. Thus, one can probably rank order occultisms according to their degree of integration into generally institutionalized knowledge. This is especially clear in the literature of occultism itself. Thus, hypnosis journals (now that hypnosis has established itself in psychology) avoid publication of articles relating hypnosis to extrasensory perception and leave such articles to the parapsychology journals. The latter seem to welcome such article,[21] thus relating their less legitimized anomalies (ESP variables) to newly accepted hypnosis. At the same time, the parapsychology journals apparently ignore publication of experiments by proponents of astrology, a form of "occultism" less legitimized among scientists than their own. In turn, astrology journals seem to welcome reference to ESP findings but generally ignore less "established" occultisms' claims. This is by no means a stable arrangement, however, since some forms of occultism have come into and out of fashion and have evidenced a kind of credibility mobility. Thus, astrology has been in the ascent in recent years so that it today is probably more generally credible than once "scientific" phrenology.

The Authority of Occult Claims. Occult claims can be categorized according to the criteria upon which the alleged knowledge is based. In general, claims to validity are based on the same sources of authority familiar to sociologists from the study of many social organizations, as first classified by Max Weber.[22] First, authority may rest on culturally inherited beliefs in *traditional authority*, as when a witch is told how to cast a spell by an older witch, possibly her mother. Or, second, an occult belief may be found on faith in the *charismatic authority* of an occult leader, as when a follower believes that knowledge has been psychically obtained by his spiritual superior. And third, an occult belief may rest on *rational-legal authority*, the criteria here being some pragmatic experience of the belief's effectiveness. Thus, an occultist may believe in magic because he thinks he has seen it work.

Sources of authority for occult beliefs are related to the criteria for validation of the claims. These criteria run along a continuum from scientific to purely mystical proofs. The central question here is whether the claim can be validated empirically and intersubjectively or merely existentially and subjectively. There are at least five major points along this scale which stand out in the occult literature.

A first form of occult criteria may be one very closely approximating the validational criteria of science. I would call this *proto-scientific occultism.* Parapsychology is a good example at this level. Essentially scientific criteria for demonstration of the anomalies is desired and attempted, but the claims have not been fully integrated into the scientific community (in this case, psychology[23]) due to a lack of sufficient evidence that might convince the skeptical established sciences.

A second form of occult criteria might be characterized as *quasi-scientific* in that a kind of "lip service" is paid the search for scientific criteria for validation, but the search for hard evidence is more a stated goal than an actuality. Astrology is an excellent example at this level. Though many writers on astrology have stated the need for good statistical evidence, only a minimum of such evidence has been forthcoming and that has been most unconvincing to the skeptical.[24] Both *proto-scientific* and *quasi-scientific occultism* tend to avoid the use of the term occultism to describe themselves, but scientific opponents of these views usually call them *pseudo-sciences.*

A third form of occult criteria consists of some *pragmatic* grounds close to those of science but without usually claiming any scientific status for the belief. Authority for the beliefs here, as with the proto- and quasi- scientific ones, tends to be rational-legal. Most magical practice is a good example of this level. The magician often believes his magic *works* in that he has seen it tried to good effect. A love potion may be believed to work because he has been successful in using it or has heard testimonials by satisfied users. Here, the basic attitude is that the method works and *could* be demonstrated to the skeptical scientist but that such demonstration is not part of the occultist's function. The magician is not a scientist trying to explain why magic works; he is merely one trying to find the most effective forms of magic in any way he can. I would label this *pragmatic occultism*.

A fourth form of occult criteria consists of consensual validation of existential experiences. Like pragmatic occultism, this form of belief centers around some personal demonstration of truth but without the possibility of empirical or truly intersubjective validation. Here one experiences a personal, essentially mystical truth, but this is in part communicable to another through language and others are told that they too can experience this same subjective truth if they perform appropriate acts. An example of this would be Transcendental Meditation. Here one can allegedly learn to have private experiences by following proper instructions. This mystical state is then validated not only by existential experience of it but also by the claim that others have had the same experience the same way. I would label this *shared mystical occultism*.[25]

A fifth form of occult criteria consists of purely private forms of occult validation. Here the believer must have a direct mystical experience of his "truth," and this is self-validating. Since this form of experience has little or no social support from others, it must be quite strong for the subject to remain convinced afterwards that he did not simply hallucinate or imagine the "message."The extreme examples here are revelations. Though revelations have usually been claimed as coming from divine or supernatural agencies, the "messages" that have been obtained by mediums in trance states from the "Spirit World" or, more recently, from extra-terrestrial spokesmen would fall into this class. I would call this form *private mystical occultism*.

These categories represent rather pure types which are not often found in such clear empirical cases. For example, many trance mediums claim to be unaware of the revelations they transmit to their listeners. The listeners, in turn, may not simply accept these revelations as authentic but may attempt to validate the "messages" by testing their accuracy, as when there is a prophetic statement transmitted that can be awaited. Most occultisms are some mixture of these pure types, but all of them can be meaningfully examined against this backdrop.

It should also be borne in mind that the criteria for validation are not simply related to the forms of authority. Although the more scientific forms of validational criteria tend to go with rational-legal authority, all combinations probably occur empirically. Many of us accept established scientific beliefs on a traditonal basis, sometimes even on the basis of the charisma of our scientific teachers, at least to some degree. The matter is not a simple one of objectivity versus subjectivity. Empirical examination of the various occultisms would probably reveal general relationships between these sources of authority.

The Source of Occult Knowledge. A distinction should be made between *elite* and *non-elite* occultism. Some writers[26] have placed great emphasis on the secretive and elite nature of occultism. Historically, this has been a prominent characteristic,[27] but in recent years, privacy hardly seems a defining characteristic of the occult. Nonetheless, much of even today's occult literature which appears prominently displayed in bookstores all over the country describes itself as "forbidden knowledge" of a very secret sort. Readers are often made to feel privy to *special* knowledge generally unavailable to the mass of mankind.

Presenting deviant forms of knowledge has distinct advantages. (1) The recipient feels he is special ("chosen") and superior for having been granted the difficulty to obtain "truth." (2) By being a private form of knowledge, a reason is given why the general community (which has not seen the "evidence") has not accepted the "truth." (3) Privacy insulates critical examination of the ideas by outsiders. And (4) privacy makes the deviant approach more attractive since this emphasizes the *difference* in the occult approach to the recipient's problem from those non-deviant, public approaches which probably earlier failed to meet his needs.

Given the character of occult ideas as deviant, there are numerous social pressures to cloak them in secrecy.[28] Following the ideas of Simmel, Lawrence E. Hazelrigg has noted that:

> As the members of a secret society increasingly emphasize universally valued ideas, objects, activities, or sentiments, the secret society tends to change in the direction of non-secret forms of organization.[29]

In terms of the criteria for validation which we have discussed, the more an occultism lies towards the proto-scientific end of our continuum, the less likely that occultism will emphasize secrecy.

Despite the importance of secrecy and secret societies in occultism, however, most of what we have termed the occult is quite public and much of it seeks a wider accepting audience. Wider audiences of believers mean greater power and better status for the existing occult believers in the form of money, prestige, and general social acceptance. But as J. L. Simmons has noted, the maintenance of divergent (occult) beliefs is facilitated by "differential associa- tion and identification with those who share one's beliefs, coupled with relative isolation from and disparagement of those whose beliefs differ."[30] Thus, as the occult beliefs have become more public and truly have had to engage in public debate, special problems have been created for the maintenance of the belief. This has forced the need for more public justification of the occult ideas which tends to move the occultism up the ladder of our continuum of verifiability from the mystical to the proto-scientific end if it is to survive. This, at least partially explains the move away from supernaturalistic elements in occultism and what I have termed the modern secularization of magic.[31]

The Functions of Occultism.   In light of the multi-dimensional character of the occult, there can be no simple or monistic description of its social and psychological functions. As Lawrence W. Littig has suggested, the reasons why people may believe in UFOs may be related to their need for affiliation,[32] but such an explanation seems to have little relevance for why another person might seek a conceptual scaffolding for his total world view in a mystical oc- cultism.[33] The various occultisms provide a great variety of need-fulfilling ele- ments (even within one form of occultism, usually) including claims of power, love, health, knowledge, and spiritual satisfactions. As I have noted elsewhere, even a single form of occultism usually spoken of as a single type, such as as- trology[34] or witchcraft,[35] in fact consists of many levels of belief and partici- pation, and these must be mapped before consideration of its functions can be seriously undertaken. Thus, to account for the current resurgence of occultism in the popular culture of America by means of any monistic psychological or sociological theory is to oversimplify the reality of the many movements. Even many of the attempts to explain upsurges in some of the analytic dimensions of occultism have generally proved premature and definitionally inadequate to deal with the complexity of the real world, e.g., witness the confusion in the many attempts to discuss the relations between magic, religion and science.[36]

Most of our terminology which has been used to discuss the occult has, from a sociological standpoint, been incredibly fuzzy. In this brief paper, an attempt has been made to "unpack" the term occult itself and to try to relate its definition to the broad spectrum of its actual use by those who claim an involvement with it. In so doing, the term has been broadened in its meaning in a manner which many occultists (especially those seeking scientific status for their esoteric beliefs) might resent. Yet, this search for a common denominator of meaning must strip the term of its connotations if an adequate denotative definition of analytic value is to be created.

This issue is further compounded by the obvious (some would say mediating) role of occultism between science and religion. Most of the literature on the occult has emphasized its religious emphases. But most occultisms make empirical claims about the real world. Because of the past over-emphasis on the religious elements in occultism, and the space limitations for this article, I have concentrated more upon the occult's parallels and integrations with science. But a sociology of the occult must ultimately be integrated with the sociologies of both science and religion if we are to obtain a full sociological understanding of this remarkable area of man's social and intellectual life.

NOTES

1. Laurence Urdang, editor in chief, *The Random House Dictionary of the English Language, College Edition* (New York: Random House, 1968), p. 919.

2. John R. Staude, "Alienated Youth and the Cult of the Occult," paper presented at the Annual Meeting of the Midwest Sociological Society, 1970.

3. Robert Galbreath, "Modern Occultism: A Thematic Analysis," paper presented at the Annual Meeting of the Popular Culture Association, 1971.

4. Andrew M. Greeley, "Implications for the Sociology of Religion of Occult Behavior in the Youth Culture," *Youth and Society* 2 (1970), 131–140. See also his: "There's a New Time Religion on Campus," *The New York Times Magazine* (June 1, 1969), 14ff.

5. Martin Marty, "The Occult Establishment," *Social Research*, 37 (1970), 212–230.

6. Edward A. Tiryakian, "Sociology in the Age of Aquarius," paper presented at the Annual Meeting of the American Sociological Association, 1971.

7. Marcello Truzzi, "Toward a Sociology of the Occult: Notes on Modern Witchcraft," in I. I. Zaretsky and M. P. Leone, eds., *Pragmatic Religions: Contemporary Religious Movements in America* (Princeton, N.J.: Princeton University Press, in press for 1972). See also my "The Occult Revival as Popular Culture: Some Random Observations on the Old and the Nouveau Witch," *Sociological Quarterly,* in press for 1972.

8. Arthur N. Foxe, "Occult Sensation," *Psychoanalytic Review*, 34 (1947), 443–448.

9. W. B. Crow, *A History of Magic, Witchcraft, and Occultism* (No. Hollywood, Calif.: Wilshire Book Co., 1968), p. 14.

10. For excellent discussion of some of these problems, see Martin Gardner, *Fads and Fallacies in the Name of Science* (New York: Dover Publications, 1957 edition).

11. The history of science is full of anomalies labelled "occult" by those who did not believe in

their existence but which were later accepted as factual. Among such things one can include hypnosis ("animal magnetism"), meteorites, and many herbal remedies in early witchcraft.

12. E.g., see D. H. Rawcliffe, *The Psychology of the Occult* (London: Derricke Ridgway, 1952; reissued under the title *Illusions and Delusions of the Supernatural and the Occult* by Dover Publications in 1959).

13. On this issue see J. B. Rhine's review of Rawcliffe's book in the *Journal of the American Society for Psychical Research*, 47 (1953), 125–127. For one attempt at such dissociation of parapsychology from the occult, see D. W. T. C. Vessey, "The Psychology of Occultism: Some Notes," *Journal of the Society for Psychical Research* 45 (Dec. 1969), 161–165.

14. Cf. Robert Galbreath, *op. cit.*

15. A very similar definitional problem surrounds the parallel term "superstition." For an excellent discussion, see Gustav Jahoda, *The Psychology of Superstition* (London: Penguin Press, 1969), pp. 1–16.

16. "Toward A Sociology of the Occult," *op. cit.*

17. Cf. H. Taylor Buckner, "The Flying Saucerians: An Open Door Cult," in Marcello Truzzi, ed., *Sociology and Everyday Life* (Englewood Cliffs, N.J.: Prentice-Hall, 1968), pp. 223–230.

18. George Gallup, Jr., "The Gallup Poll Report on Religious Experience," *Fate*, 16, 4 (April 1963), 31–37. For analysis of this poll, see Linda Brookover Bourque, "Social Correlates of Transcendental Experiences," *Sociological Analysis*, 30 (1969), 151–163.

19. C. G. Jung, "Synchronicity: An Acausal Connecting Principle," in *The Collected Works of C. G. Jung*, Volume 8: *The Structure and Dynamics of the Psyche* (2nd ed.; Princeton, N.J.: Princeton University Press, 1969), pp. 417–531.

20. Cf. Martin Marty, *op. cit.*

21. E.g., cf. Charles Honorton and Stanley Krippner, "Hypnosis and ESP Performance: A Review of the Experimental Literature," *Journal of the American Society for Psychical Research*, 63 (1969), 214–252.

22. Max Weber, "The Three Types of Legitimate Rule," translated by Hans Gerth in Marcello Truzzi, ed., *Sociology: The Classic Statements* (New York: Random House, 1971), pp. 169–179.

23. Re the problems of acceptance, see C. E. M. Hansel, *ESP: A Scientific Evaluation* (New York: Charles Scribner's Sons, 1966); and Champe Ransom, "Recent Criticisms of Parapsychology: A Review," *Journal of the American Society for Psychical Research*, 65 (1971), 289–307.

24. Cf. John Anthony West and Jan Gerhard Toonder, *The Case for Astrology* (New York: Coward-McCann, 1970); Michel Gauquelin, *The Scientific Basis of Astrology: Myth or Reality?* (New York: Stein and Day, 1969); and Doris Chase Doane, *Astrology: 30 Years Research* (Hollywood, Calif.: Professional Astrologers, Inc., 1956).

25. For an excellent study of one such occult group emphasizing the problem of non-falsifiability of the claims, see J. L. Simmons, "On Maintaining Deviant Belief Systems," *Social Problems*, 11 (1964), 250–256.

26. E.g., Edward A. Tiryakian, *op. cit,* and W. B. Crow, *op. cit.*

27. Cf. Charles W. Heckethorn, *The Secret Societies of All Ages and Countries*, 2 vols. (New Hyde Park, N.Y.: University Books, 1965 edition, original edition published in 1875); Norman MacKenzie ed., *Secret Societies* (New York: Collier Books, 1971 edition, original published in 1967); and Arkon Daraul, *A History of Secret Societies* (New York: Citadel Press, 1961).

28. Cf. Georg Simmel, "The Sociology of Secrecy and Secret Societies," translated by Albion W. Small, *American Journal of Sociology*, 11 (1906), 441–498.

29. Lawrence E. Hazelrigg, "A Reexamination of Simmel's 'The Secret and the Secret Society': Nine Propositions," *Social Forces*, 47 (1969), 329.

30. J. L. Simmons, *op. cit.*, p. 198.

31. For good examples of such secularization, see W. Michael A. Brooker, "Magic in Business and Industry: Notes Towards Its Recognition and Understanding," *Anthropologica*, N.S. 9 (1967), 3–20.

32. Lawrence W. Littig, "Affiliation Motivation and Belief in Extraterrestrial UFOs," *The Journal of Social Psychology*, 83 (1971), 307–308.

33. For excellent descriptions of some of these, see Jacob Needleman, *The New Religions* (New York: Doubleday and Co., 1970).

34. Cf. Marcello Truzzi, "The Occult Revival as Popular Culture," *op. cit.*

35. Cf. Marcello Truzzi, "Towards a Sociology of the Occult," *op. cit.*

36. For a recent good discussion of this problem, see Dorothy Hammond, "Magic: A Problem in Semantics," *American Anthropologist.* 72 (1970), 1349–1356.

Edward A. Tiryakian

Toward the Sociology of
Esoteric Culture

Among other bewildering aspects of the kaleidoscopic cultural scene of
Western societies in recent years is a complex of phenomena which, for lack of
a more precise label, has generally come to be designated as the "occult revival." Receiving public exposure in this context have been a variety of forms
of popular entertainment dealing with occult themes, for example, the musical
Hair with its "Age of Aquarius" hit song, movies such as *Rosemary's Baby* and
The Mephisto Waltz, and the television series "Bewitched." Clairvoyants
such as Jeanne Dixon in the United States and Madame Soleil in France have
become public figures and authors of best sellers, while self-designated practitioners of witchcraft or even devil worship (as in the respective cases of Sybil
Leek and Anton LaVey) have gotten public exposure in the mass media, along
with attention to the macabre Tate-Manson affair and other cases of pur-

Reprinted from *The American Journal of Sociology,* 78 (November, 1972), pp. 491–512. Copyright © 1972, by the University of Chicago. Reprinted by permission of the University of Chicago
Press.

   Revision of a paper presented at the 1971 meetings of the American Sociological Association. I
wish to thank Josefina Tiryakian for assistance in the preparation of the manuscript.

ported ritual homicides and suicides in which figured weird occult themes. Bookstores specializing in occult works of various kinds, frequently located in proximity to college campuses, are flourishing; sales of items bearing a Zodiac sign are booming and have even received in France, since 1969, a quasiofficial blessing in the form of a special monthly drawing of the National Lottery. Tottering ivory towers have been no refuge from the occult revival: seminars and courses, with or without credit, have taken up the new "in" study, with the logical extreme being the recent formation of an "Aquarian University" in Maryland, offering a full range of esoteric studies from alchemy to Zen Buddism.

The sociological response to this new cultural development is just beginning to emerge. One of the aims of this paper is to see what sociological interpretations of this phenomenon have been recently advanced. At the same time, we will seek to carry the discussion further by outlining how the present occult revival poses broader considerations for sociological inquiry, regardless of whether the revival is destined to be a short-term affair of no significance or one with more durability. What we shall seek to develop in these pages, then, is an initial formulation of the sociology of esoteric culture and its relation to the larger social context.

The Sociology of the Occult Revival.   One of the earliest and most extensive sociological treatments of the occult revival is that of Marcello Truzzi (1970), providing, in particular, much information on the spread and organization of witchcraft in contemporary urban American society. The perspective within which the materials are presented is that of the sociology of popular culture, with modern occultism taking on the significance of a "pop religion" (we might even say of coven adepts, "Have broomstick, will travel!"), which Truzzi regards as a "demystification process of what were once fearful and threatening cultural elements" Persons playing the role of witches, for example, are attacking some of the last cultural frontiers of Western psychic inhibitions; to engage in role taking of parts formerly publicly branded as odious and the object of extreme social repression is, in a sense, to demonstrate the final liberation of Western man (and woman) from traditional cultural prohibitions dealing with the supernatural. The occult revival, at least in terms of the receptivity of witchcraft among segments of the middle class, could thus be seen as another step in the modernization of Western society, in this context as a secularization of the demonic. Such a perspective would be consonant with the secularization hypothesis concerning the relation of religion to modern society (Wilson 1966).[1]

Supplementing Truzzi's linking of witchcraft to popular and mass culture, Marty (1970) has examined a variety of publications dealing with astrology and psychic phenomena, on the basis of which he differentiates an occult establishment, responsible for most of the widely circulated publications in this area, from an occult underground press. Marty gives most of his attention to the former and notes that it is predominantly intended for an audience of middle America. In this literature there is an absence of a social message, so that "like some forms of conservative orthodoxy, the occult establishment concentrates almost entirely on individual life and often on 'other-worldly concerns'" (Marty 1970, p. 228).

Evaluations contrasting with the above have been entertained by Staude (1970) and Greeley (1970a), 1970b). Staude views the current interest of youth in occult practices and mysticism as essentially a search for meaning and identity because "they feel alienated and disillusioned with the liberal progressivist ideology of their parents and with totalistic ideologies" (1970, p. 13); in this respect, he suggests, today's cultural setting is similar to the religious and cultural renewal of the Renaissance. More directly than Staude, Greeley has seen the import of current youth interest in occult behavior in its implications for the sociology of religion. Whereas Marty (1970, p. 228) had pointed to an absence of a communal impulse in the literature of the occult establishment, Greeley stresses such an impulse in the broad neosacral movement of today: "The young people who are involved do . . . assert that their sacred, or mystical, or occult interest do indeed provide them with meaning, with community, with a contact with the transcendent, and with norms by which to live" (1970a, p. 6).

Greeley, like Staude, sees the appeal of occult behavior on the college campus as symptomatic of the alienation of youth from the scientific-rationalist ethos of modern society, with the invocation of new gods: superstition, ecstasy, and "groupism" (Greeley 1970b).[2] He notes an affinity between those engaged in occult practices on the campus and the new left, not only in terms of the rejection of the dominant institutional ethos but also in terms of certain value orientations: the affirmation of the inherent goodness of human nature (an echo of both Rousseau and the much older Pelagian heresy) and the concern for transcendent power in human interaction (1970b, p. 208). Further characteristics of the new faiths, he suggests, are that they are millennialistic, charismatic, and liturgical. The thrust of Greeley's argument is that the occult revival is to be seen as a neosacral movement in contemporary culture, which by the significance of its presence is further evidence against the proposition that increasing secularization accompanies or is an integral aspect of modernization.[3]

Greeley's writings on the significance of occult behavior among youth, as well as his earlier empirical research (1968), constitute a major critique of the secularization hypothesis.[4] Additional testimony in the occult revival literature comes from a recent article of Shepherd (1972), who observes "a new mysticism emerging among the young in the developed countries, one not constrained by an already well-defined religious context" (p. 8). Arguing that the new religious life-style is analogous to the aesthetic experience of music—a theme which echoes the contention of Roszak (1969) that today's dissenting youth have returned to the archaic aesthetic vision of beauty of the shaman, a vision communally shared—Shepherd (1972) proposes that "the counter cultural young among Westerners . . . may be the agents in a process of "reorientalization' occurring within our own culture, and that they may be the harbinger of spring, of a new value consensus" (p. 8).

In this vein, one might argue that a function of occult practices is to provide a position against what is perceived as "Establishment" mentality with its structural apparatus of modern societies: the oppressive "technocracy," "reductive rationality," and "objective consciousness," to borrow terms from Roszak. Occult practices are appealing, among other reasons, because they are seemingly dramatic opposites of empirical practices of science and of the depersonalization of the industrial order. The appeal of the occult may thus be related to the new appeal of artisan work to many college youth, since it is nonindustrial work, affording a reintegration of personality with the product of one's labor.[5]

One last sociological study of the occult in modern society to be noted here is a recent French collaborative work on contemporary astrology (Defrance et al. 1971). It is not easy to present in a few words the contents of this work which, taken as a whole, is a sociology of astrology, but several of the themes discussed earlier are elaborated here. Edgar Morin (Defrance et al. 1971, pp. 110–25) sees the appeal of astrology among youth today as stemming from the cultural crisis of bourgeois society, with astrology offering symbols of identity as a science of subjectivity. Paradoxically, modern astrology has an antithetical function in modern society: in mass culture, the popularization of astrology in the mass media plays an integrative role in bourgeois civilization by reconciling individuals with their situation. Morin suggests that among counterculture youth astrology is also part of a new gnosis which has a revolutionary conception of a new age, the Age of Aquarius.

In his chapter "Astrology and Society," Fischler (Defrance et al. 1971, pp. 69–81) considers other latent functions of astrology. Modern society multiplies fragmentary contacts between strangers, without traditional norms to guide comportment; in the face of making an increased number of decisions, especially of an interpersonal kind, resort to astrology and other means of divination reduces the ambiguity of intersubjective conduct. Since astrology is subject oriented, it is a means for self-apprehension and self-grasping. Fischler also presents data initially gathered in 1963 by the French Institute of Public Opinion, which examined in a cross section of the French public just how widely diffused is adherence to astrology. The survey sought the social distribution of those respondents possessing three attributes, namely, they (a) knew their own Zodiac sign, (b) read their horoscopes fairly often, and (c) thought there was some truth to astrological character traits. The results are shown in table 1.

Noting the high incidence of astrological adherence among women and those under 35, Fischler suggests (Defrance et al. 1971, pp. 80 f.) that as these formerly segregated strata enter more and more in the modern *polis,* having been less stamped by the belief systems of the dominant culture, they are more prone to recourse to astrology in relating to the larger society.

What is of further interest are additional data presented by Fischler (Defrance et al. 1971, p. 75) indicating the social distribution of two groups: (a) those having consulted at least once a card reader, a clairvoyant, or a person predicting the future; and (b) those having consulted at least once an astrologer. On the whole ($N = 6,000$ in the national sample), the results were consistent with the first survey (the more populated the community, the higher incidence in each group, etc.), save that the category of those 18–25 years of age had a lower incidence (9% and 1.5%, respectively, in the two groups) than the other age categories (which all had practically the same incidence, about 13% and 3%). Although Fischler sees in this that older persons go in for more applied astrology and the young for a more speculative curiosity, it may also be the case that the young are their own practitioners of astrology (and other divinatory practices), for whom going to professional practitioners (part of the occult establishment) would defeat the purpose of a personal quest for meaning and certainty in an ambiguous world.

Although more suggestive than conclusive, the French data point to a

Table 1. Social Characteristics of Believers in Astrology (France)

Category	Percentage in Total Sample
Total believing in astrology	30
By sex	
Men	21
Women	39
By occupation*	
Professional, managers, and executives	34
Small business owners and artisans	36
("commerçants")	
Clerical and sales ("employés")	46
Manual workers ("ouvriers")	29
Farmers and farm workers	15
Not in the labor force or retired	30
By locality	
Under 2,000 inhabitants	21
2,000–5,000	27
5,000–20,000	37
20,000–100,000	34
Over 100,000	40
By age (years)	
20–34	38
35–49	33
50–64	24
65 and over	20

SOURCE. Defrance et al., *Le retour des astrologues*, p. 74, from survey data gathered in 1963 by the Institut Français d'Opinion Publique, at the request of *France-Soir*.

* Since occupational classification in France differs in some cases from that commonly used in the United States, we have given in parentheses the French category in those instances where the translation is approximate.

redrawing a certain sociological image of superstition/rationality as distributed in society. For the greatest spread of adherence to astrology is not to be found in the countryside among farmers or among the lower rungs of the occupational structure, but rather in the most densely populated urban centers and among white-collar workers. Moreover, although the French materials are silent on this, my own observations suggest that there is a higher incidence of belief and interest not only in astrology but also in other occult sciences among those of high educational achievement—college and university level—than among those who have not gone beyond high school or those who are still in high school. Obviously, this is a terrain for further empirical studies.

In examining various sociological writings dealing with the occult revival, a number of themes have been touched upon. Most significant, perhaps, is that this phenomenon has to be seen in terms of a broader social context of cultural change. As a spiritual reaction against the rationalistic-industrial-bureaucratic ethos of modern society, it is part of the counterculture. Similarly, it may also be seen as part of a new religious cultural revitalization, having an affinity with both the exuberant neoevangelical movement crossing denominational lines and the equally vigorous political movement of the new left in developed societies.

To take the sociological interpretation of the occult in modern society further along, there is need to develop a more articulated conceptualization. For one thing, we need to differentiate basic elements of the occult, and for another, to reexamine how the occult relates to modernization in its cultural aspect. This will be undertaken in the following section.

Components of Esoteric Culture. The previously discussed sociological literature on the occult revival has related it, on the one hand, to the sociology of mass society, and on the other, to the sociology of religion. Since we posit that the sociology of the occult is also germane to the study of cultural change and the dynamics of modernization, it may be located more broadly as part of the sociology of culture. It is at this point that I wish to explicate some basic terms of central importance to this essay: "occult," "esoteric," and "secret society." These are familiar terms, yet ones which have had little currency in standard sociological reference works.[6] It is necessary, before conceptualizing these terms, to have a preliminary understanding of "culture." The sense of culture which is followed here is, so to speak, that of a collective paradigm which provides the basic interpretations and justification of ongoing social existence. As the anthropologist Ward Goodenough has expressed it: "Culture then consists of the 'concepts' and 'models' which people have in their minds for organizing and interpreting their experiences." It should be noted that Goodenough takes into account nonlinguistic aspects of culture (which have a bearing on the significance of symbols in esoteric culture, since symbols and imagery are primary modes of relating to reality for the latter) when he adds: "nonlinguistic forms have systematic relationships to each other in paradigms" (quoted in Singer 1968, p. 538).

Equally pertinent here is the conceptualization of Parsons viewing culture as that integral component of systems of social action which provides the fundametal symbolic grounds of expression to the existential problem of meaning inherent in social existence. Although "meaning" has a cognitive and rational orientation, it also has a complex moral one as well, one involved in the evaluation of social action. As Parsons states: "The highest level of the problem of meaning is that of the conceptions of ultimate reality, in the religio-philosophical sense. This concerns the major premises in which the nonempirical components of a culture's total belief system are rooted" (1961, p. 970).

There is one qualification that needs to be introduced to the above conceptualization of culture, since it has a crucial bearing on the central thesis of this paper. It is that a given social complex, as in the case of modern Western society, may have more than one set of major premises present in its cultural matrix; that is, that there are several cultural paradigms offering the ground of meaning of social action, albeit one set may have dominance in the institutional fabric of society while another set remains covert or latent.[7] The cultural paradigm which is manifest in public institutions, a set of cognitive and evaluative orientations publicly recognized and legitimated in the network of social institutions, is what I propose to call "exoteric culture." Exoteric culture provides the ground of meaning and orientation for the everyday social world. It is the social basis of what the phenomenologist Husserl designated as "the natural attitude," in terms of which actors take the existence of the world for granted, that is, in a sociological sense they take as nonproblematic the institutionalized structures of the social world. It is implicitly in reference to exoteric culture that sociologists and anthropologists, for the most part, have formulated their conceptualizations regarding culture and society.

I wish to propose that a unitary conceptualization of the cultural system of Western civilization in its historical development via modernization has to be modified, and that to arrive at a more sophisticated understanding of cultural systems and societal change there is need to consider what, for heuristic purpose if nothing else, I will call "esoteric culture." It is at this juncture that we need to specify three major components of this esoteric culture, elements common to any cultural whole but taking specific forms in esoteric culture: a set of beliefs and doctrines (cognitive and moral orientations), a set of practices oriented to empirical action, and a social organization within which action is patterned or structured.

Although "esoterism" and "occultism" are often used interchangeably, and although there is no standard agreement as to their referents, it may still be fruitful to venture an analytic differentiation. Both, of course, refer to something which is not immediately given to the senses or to perception, to the nonempirical in this sense.

By "occult" I understand intentional practices, techniques, or procedures which (a) draw upon hidden or concealed forces in nature or the cosmos that cannot be measured or recognized by the instruments of modern science, and (b) which have as their desired or intended consequences empirical results, such as either obtaining knowledge of the empirical course of events or altering them from what they would have been without this intervention. Obviously, I exclude for the purpose of my analysis some broader considerations of occult phenomena, such as extrasensory perception and déjà vu experiences, because these are harder to integrate within a sociological scheme. To go on further, insofar as the subject of occult activity is not just any actor, but one who has acquired specialized knowledge and skills necessary for the practices in question, and insofar as these skills are learned and transmitted in socially (but not publicly available) organized, routinized, and ritualized fashion, we can speak of these practices as occult sciences or occult arts.[8]

Commonly recognized occult practices include a variety of phenomena, such as those designated as "magic"[9] and divinatory practices,[10] which are very numerous cross-culturally (astrology, the Tarot, and the I Ching having been particularly noted in the contemporary occult revival); they also include practices which are oriented to changing the physical nature of nonhuman objects by the active participation or ego involvement of the subject, as in the case of alchemy.

By "esoteric" I refer to those religiophilosophic belief systems which underlie occult techniques and practices; that is, it refers to the more comprehensive cognitive mappings of nature and the cosmos, the epistemological and ontological reflections of ultimate reality, which mappings constitute a stock of knowledge that provides the ground for occult procedures. By way of analogy, esoteric knowledge is to occult practices as the corpus of theoretical physics is to engineering applications. But a crucial aspect of esoteric knowledge is that it is a secret knowledge of the reality of things, of hidden truths, handed down, frequently orally and not all at once, to a relatively small number of persons who are typically ritually initiated by those already holding this knowledge. Moreover, it should be added, this knowledge is not of a detached or objective sort about an outer reality which stands against the observer as this page stands against the reader; esoteric knowledge is of a participatory sort, namely a knowledge (or gnosis) of the meaning of the world to human existence, in the progressive realization of which the subject develops internally and liberates himself from the strictures of everyday life.

Since esoteric knowledge is taken as knowledge of the real but concealed nature of things, of ultimate reality (a knowledge which therefore is divine, theosophic in the generic sense), it is important that its recipient be demonstrated worthy of receiving it; that is he must meet criteria of acceptance into the inner circle of true knowers. Hence the need of the candidate to submit at various stages to a series of trials and ordeals, in the course of which the adept becomes increasingly socialized into the esoteric culture and increasingly desocialized from the natural attitude of the exoteric culture.[11]

At the heart of esoteric knowledge is its concealment from public dissemination, from the gaze of the profane or uninitiated. To shield it from vulgarization, it is presented to the adept not directly but, typically, symbolically or metaphorically, so that it has to be deciphered progressively by the neophyte who uncovers layers of meaning in stages of initiation. As a correlate of this, the social organization and handling of esoteric culture tends to take the form of secret societies, societies whose modes and codes of organization and membership lists are not publicly disclosed and which may even be incompletely known to members who have not attained the highest stages of initiation and spiritual perfection.

The sociology of secrecy and secret societies, which is essential for any consideration of esoteric culture, has largely lain fallow since the seminal essay by Georg Simmel (1906). Yet secrecy is of general sociological interest since, as Simmel was quick to note, it is constitutive of social structure and social interaction. Even the most democratic countries, de jure or de facto, organize much of their affairs secretly and have agencies which specialize in concealed activities; all information about the doings of formal organization is not for public consumption but only to qualified insiders, some more than others. This leads to other outsiders seeking to obtain this information in specialized ways (private and governmental espionage activity seeking industrial, military, and state secrets), with such information-gathering activities being themselves secret.

To be sure, not all secret societies pertain to esoteric culture, nor are all social organizations that have secrets, secret societies. But those secret societies which are social forms of esoteric culture have common features. They typically have rituals of initiation and are hierarchically structured in terms of strata which correspond to different degrees of initiation. Leadership and authority are functions of stages of acquisition of esoteric knowledge, at least in theory. At the top echelon is a very small elite designated variously as "Magi," "Grand Masters," or other appropriate terms, and a council responsible for ultimate internal and external policies of the organization. The council is somewhat along the lines of an executive committee of formal organizations; an enlarged board of directors may include, as notably in the case of Freemasonry, persons holding high ranks in exoteric society, even including heads of state.[12] Although the hierarchic principle of organization is basic to secret societies, the higher rungs are accessible to all. Moreover, fraternal solidarity is greatly emphasized: irrespective of social standing in the larger society, all members are brothers (or sisters), and when in a situation of distress, a member is to be given every assistance possible by any other member at hand, even on the battlefield, if they belong to opposite forces.

These, then, are major components of esoteric culture. It would go beyond this essay to articulate specific belief systems or to discuss the details of organization of specific secret societies. More relevant is to indicate that esoteric culture is not concretely disjoint from exoteric culture, that it coexists, albeit unobtrusively with the latter,[13] or stated differently, that there are many interchanges between them.

The esoteric culture often uses as referents publicly known cultural materials such as religious texts and figures (e.g., the Torah, the Book of Revelations, Adam, Christ, etc.), but it considers that the meaning of these is not exhausted by their public definition and recognition; rather, the esoteric group sees itself as the true repository of the ultimate reality manifest in the materials in question. Only a select few, initiated into the mysteries can decipher and pass on in an unbroken chain the real meaning of what underlies the figurative. Only a few, thus, can be permitted to attain knowledge of the secret name of God which Moses learned on Mount Sinai and which has been transmitted orally to those who can correctly understand the Kabbalah; only a few can learn the secret teachings of Christ to His chosen disciples, etc.

Since these secrets are those that reveal the ultimate nature of reality, the concealed forces of the cosmic order, it means that esoteric knowledge is an ultimate source of power, which must be shared and utilized by a relatively small group of initiates. Such power is never justifiable in terms of the enhancement of the material conditions of the esoteric knowers but rather in terms of broad impersonal ends, humanitarian ideals, etc. Consequently, much of the parlance of esoteric culture is necessarily obscure, that is, designed to put off members of the larger society; this is in some ways similar to the argot of the underworld or even to the language of some psychotics used as a shield from public deciphering. Exoteric language glosses over the esoteric source of such expressions as "third degree" (from Masonic initiation), "magnum opus" (from alchemy), or "sub rosa" (from Rose Croix), just as other items originating in the esoteric culture have been absorbed, for example, card games (the major suits trace back to the Tarot, the esoteric depiction of human existence seen as a dialectical process).

Esoteric Culture and Sociocultural Changes.   It is the relation of esoteric culture to various facets of Western modernization that is of particular interest to this article. We wish to argue that much of what is modern, even the ideology of modernization at its source, has originated in esoteric culture; paradoxically, the value orientation of Western exoteric society, embodied in rationalism, the scientific ethos, and industrialism, has forced esoteric culture into the role of a marginal or underground movement. That is, modern Western civilization (dating it back to the Renaissance and Reformation) has increasingly given to esoteric culture the mantle of a counterculture, while at the same time coopting many of its values and products.

I would like to suggest that the conceptions of ultimate reality in the esoteric tradition may be conceptualized as part of the latency subsystem of Western society, following Parsons's model of structural differentiation of social systems of action (Parsons 1969). Further, we contend that in the Western case, at least, (*a*) such esoteric conceptions and modes of interpreting reality form a cultural paradigm which provides leverage against the institutionalized paradigm, hence function as a seat of inspiration for new systems of social action; and (*b*) that at various historical points these conceptions and modes have come into play in the larger society so as to provide vehicles of social and cultural change.

Moreover, albeit to document this point would require much more space than here available, the basic cognitive model of hidden, underlying reality central to esoteric thought, is that of a reality moved by forces, by energies constantly in motion and in tension with one another; it is a model opposed to the static, stable, or harmonious view of things inherent in the natural attitude. Hence, we suggest, at the very heart of the ideology of modernization, or modernism, is an esoteric influence. This ideology, which positively evaluates what is new as against what is old, which sees the unfolding present as a time of liberation and freedom from the yoke of the stagnating past, is an ideology of a new order of things to come and of a this-worldly salvation by human means—an ideology which at least one author (Voegelin, 1952, p. 133) has seen as a product of esoteric (gnostic in this instance) symbolism manifested in the development of the Puritan Revolution.

Of relevance here is to discuss the relation between esoteric culture and avant-garde culture, for the esoteric apprehensions, depictions, and interpretations of reality find a ready-made terrain of expression in artistic products (literature, painting, architecture, even music) whose esoteric significance escapes the larger public. To the initiates such symbols are more than artistic: they also convey a message, and hence are expressive symbols in the fullest sense.

In a recent article pointing out the antithetical relation of the social structures of industrial-technological society and modern culture, Daniel Bell (1970) has noted in the latter the prevalence of a dominant impulse "towards the new and the original . . . so that the *idea* of change and novelty overshadows the dimensions of actual change" (1970, p. 17). This ideology of change, of modernism per se, is one which Bell locates in the cultural tradition of avant-garde art that appeared in the 19th century as a counterculture to the rising bourgeois culture of industrial society.[14]

Bell does not examine any linkage of occultism and the formation of avant-garde in the 19th century, although he proposes in passing (1970, p. 34) that what avant-garde values stand for—antistructure, antihistory, radical freedom, in brief, values of nihilism and anarchism—are part of an older Western tradition, that of gnostic esotericism.[15]

In a complementary article, Vytautas Kavolis has explored recently (1970) the sociopsychological nexus between avant-garde culture and what he calls "Satanic" and "Promethean" personality modes, the former characterized by a "resentment-destruction mechanism," the latter by a "sympathetic concern for the needs of others."[16] These personality orientations are manifested in the activist and nihilistic aspects of avant-garde culture, oriented to both the destruction of the established order of things and to a perpetual innovation and renovation of forms. Moreover, Kavolis sees avant-garde culture as giving positive value to the symbols of the satanic psychological mode of orientation, symbols treated as the epitome of antisocial values in the established order of society: "To some extent, the avant-garde culture could be interpreted as an attempt to legitimate much of what used to be illegitimized in the Satanic mythology" (1970, p. 27).

The influence of occult themes, particularly those dealing with the demonic and the satanic, is a striking aspect in the historical development of modern avant-garde culture, which is viewed here as both a literary and a political protest against the institutionalization of a rationalistic-industrial bourgeois social order. This protest against modernization was a major common denominator in the Romantic movement, and esoteric culture provided much of the materials for the protest against the new social order, though neither esoteric culture nor avant-garde culture sought a return to the *ancien régime*. Ritual magic, "forces of darkness," Satan himself, became symbols of identification, rallying points, in brief, revolutionary forces drawn from the counterculture of the occult,[17] in the fight against bourgeois values. The occult as a source of inspiration abounds, then, in writings of well-known and lesser-known Romantics, such as Goethe (Lepinte, 1957), Novalis, Gautier, Nerval, Byron, Lautréamont, and Baudelaire (Bays 1964).[18]

Such themes of the occult were continued by later generations of the avant-garde culture,[19] notably the "accursed" symbolist poets such as Rimbaud and Verlaine (Senior 1959), but also Yeats and Thomas Mann, and finally, André Breton, the crucial figure of surrealism, a movement of particular sociological significance since it represents a clear articulation of artistic protest and political radicalism.[20] Many of the surrealists (Breton himself, Aragon, Eluard, Naville) were or are politically committed to the radical left, and the influence of surrealism is even to be found in the writings of A. Césaire, one of the founders of *Négritude*, the cultural arm of black liberation. Breton drew upon various sources of inspiration (including Marx, Freud, and occultism) to formulate a revolutionary consciousness aimed against the bourgeois world (of utility, reason, realism, and technological society), a consciousness whose intention "is always to allow the *irruption* of 'wild' images that will disturb the sensibility by shattering the coherence of those 'stable' images that make up, for each individual, the objective world (Willener 1970, p. 224).

The contemporary significance of surrealism as a source of inspiration for the May 1968 revolutionary movement in France has been fully discussed in an excellent sociological study by Willener (1970).[21]

In the political development of modern society, both in the West and in the Westernization (including imperial domination) of the "Third World," esoteric culture has also had an influence in avant-garde political movements and ideologies which have pitted themselves against established regimes. A major social vehicle of such protest have been secret societies: Weishaupt's Bavarian Illuminati in the 18th century, Freemasonry in France in the 18th and 19th centuries, the Carbonari in Italy and France, Mazzini's Young Italy, the Sinn Fein in Ireland, and many others. For the most part, the ideology of such

secret societies was nationalistic, republican, anticlerical, even interna-
tionalistic. All these drew upon the imagery and expressive symbols of esoteric
conceptions of reality, especially symbols of the liberation of man from the
yoke of darkness (politically interpreted as the yokes of traditional political institutions or alien oppressors) into the realm of light, of freed humanity. For
the most part, these movements succeeded in establishing political regimes
which at least partly satisfied their aspirations.[22]

Assuredly, not all secret societies drawing upon esoteric symbols, rituals,
and interpretations can be classified as progressive, for there is the minority
case of those having a reactionary image, such as the Ku Klux Klan in the
United States, the Cagoule in the France of the 1930s, and even, in the light of
the discussion provided by Pauwels and Bergier (1968), there were esoteric influences operative in secret societies (such as the Thulé order) that played a
covert role in the formation of nazism. This is perhaps indicative of the fact
that esoteric culture, with its fantastic wealth of imagery and symbolism, is
multivalent in terms of political expressions that can be derived from it. Yet,
whatever the specific instance, it may be said that esoteric culture provides leverage against the existing order by grounding political reflection and action in
a reality that transcends that of everyday life,[23] but which is a reality that may
become actualized in the historical future by reversing the present order of the
world.

One other aspect of the political expressions of modern counterculture to be
noted is that of Marxism. Its crucial leverage against bourgeois mentality is its
formulation of dialectical materialism, which provided Marx and Engels the
key with which to unlock the hidden laws of the historic process. The intellectual progenitor of modern dialectics is commonly taken to be Hegel, but
the recent study of Benz (1968) has demonstrated the extent to which esoteric
and mystical sources figure in the German intellectual background of Hegelian
and Marxist thought. Notable sources are theosophy, philosophical alchemy,
and the Kabbalah, drawing much inspiration from the writings of earlier
mystics such as Meister Eckhart and particularly Jacob Boehme, and rein-
terpreted in early 19th-century German theosophic and evangelical circles, as
well as philosophical circles which also partook of the Romantic movement.[24]

A last consideration involving the outputs of esoteric culture to the
development of modern Western civilization is its relation to scientific thought.
The latter in its empiricist and positivistic image of an objective reality,
measurable by empirical means and existing independently of the human subject, is perhaps the key mode of thought in the modernization process which

has illegitimated and devalued the practices of occult science. Yet, paradoxically, esoteric influences in the form of symbolisms, imagery, practices,
and cosmologies, have been in much of the background of the rise of scientific
disciplines.

In the case of modern depth psychology, Bakan (1958) has brought out
various elements of the Jewish mystical tradition which frame much of Freud's
psychoanalysis; the latter's theory of the libido and the significance of symbols
in the psychic process (including the analogic linkage of symbols) may be seen
as a scientific formulation of elements of the Kabbalah and the Zohar. His
one-time heir apparent, Jung, made intensive studies of medieval and
Renaissance alchemy (Jung 1968a, 1968b) which he linked to personality
development. Freud was early influenced by Charcot's experiments in hypnotism, but the foundations of hypnotism had been laid nearly a century before
by the occultist Mesmer's demonstrations of magnetism (Mesmer 1971).

Even in the natural sciences esoteric influences have played a not insignificant role, which can only be mentioned in passing. If today the alchemical
symbols of chemical elements remain a glossed-over vestige, the development of
chemistry from its matrix in late medieval alchemy deserves mention (e.g.,
Stillman 1960). Alchemy and astrology may also have been of importance in
the rise of modern medicine, with Paracelsus being another key figure mediating between esoteric culture and modern scientific thought—the innovation
of operating on human bodies may have been guided by an attempt to establish
the correctness of astrological views that different parts of the body, and consequent pathologies, are under the influence of different signs of the Zodiac.
Astrology and theosophy were also part of the cultural baggage which was
utilized rather than rejected by modernizing scientists, such as Kepler and
even Newton (Hutin 1960). The very social organization of modern science, in
the form of academics of science, owes much inspiration to Francis Bacon's
New Atlantis with its "scientists' Paradise," a work said to come out of the
"Hermetic-Cabalist" stream (Yates 1964, p. 450).[25]

So much for some indications, necessarily brief and incomplete, of the range
of esoteric influences in the historical process of modernization.

Conclusion. Marginal as the occult revival may initially appear to sociological preoccupations, the study of the esoteric in fact touches on many facets
of our discipline, such as the sociology of knowledge, the sociology of art, the
sociology of religion, and the sociology of deviance.[26] For heuristic purpose,
this essay has mainly placed the emphasis on esoteric culture as an important

promulgator of a counterculture of long standing in the West. Essentially, we have viewed the function of esoteric culture to be that of a seed-bed cultural source of change and wide-ranging innovations in art, politics, and even science, analogous to the functions of "seed-bed societies" discussed by Parsons (1966) in the case of Israel and Greece.[27]

In discussions of social change elsewhere (Tiryakian 1967, 1970), I have proposed that important ideational components of change (i.e., changes in the social consciousness of reality) may often originate in noninstitutionalized groups or sectors of society whose paradigms of reality may, in certain historical moments, become those which replace institutionalized paradigms and become in turn new social blueprints. Relating this to the present essay, I would propose that esoteric culture, and groups of actors mediating esoteric to exoteric culture, are major inspirational sources of cultural and social innovations.

To document and validate this model is obviously no easy matter. It involves demonstrating the meaningful sociohistorical affinity between seemingly heterogenous social spheres of action, a methodological problem of exactly the same nature as the one involved in Max Weber's study of the affinity of ascetic Protestantism and the ethical basis of modern capitalism. The magnitude of the problem involved in relating esoteric culture to social innovations in exoteric culture is even greater than the Protestant case. It involves developing tools of analysis which will enable us, as sociologists, to make sense out of esoteric texts and documents, many of which depend on being able to decipher the meanings of expressive symbols which are by their nature qualitative expressions of reality, and not subject to quantitative measurement in their presentation. A promising avenue here may be the techniques of linguistic and structural anthropology, for example those used in deciphering mythologies, which have similarities to esoteric conceptions of reality. The increasing applications of phenomenology (which is, after all, oriented to the inner grasping of structures of consciousness) in the social sciences (Natanson 1973), such as those being developed by ethnomethodology, may be particularly fruitful in this vein.[28]

The problem of indicating linkages between esoteric symbolisms, imageries, and conceptions of reality to purposive social behavior, that is, the question of how conceptions of the structure of reality translate into paradigms of social action and social imagery (e.g., how the esoteric notion of the androgyne, Adam Kadmon, is linked today to fashion designers of unisex clothes) is also laden with serious methodological difficulties. And this is rendered even more serious by the fact that major mediating groups between the two cultures tend to operate in socially invisible or secret social organizations, which means a paucity of readily available informative documents, or in some cases, an undue reliance on records of governmental and other institutional agencies which have sought to repress these esoteric groups.

Nonetheless, these methodological vexations should be seen as more of a challenge to the sociological imagination than in principle insoluble. The very framing of theoretical questions concerning the relation of esoteric to exoteric culture, particularly in the area of conceptualizing the dynamics of social change, may suggest new methodological developments to the sociological enterprise.

A final note on the occult revival may be apposite in reconsidering the crucial notion of the modernization process. It may be fruitful to view modernization in a broader historical context than just that of the past 200 years or so, to view it instead as stretching back to antiquity, in the course of which modern ideas have dislodged previously institutionalized paradigms during "crucial periods"[29] of social change—a recurrent feature in the development of Western society. The net effect has been, to venture an analogy, a stochastic process of change rather than one of continuous development, one punctuated by adaptive mutations in the cultural code of Western civilization, to propose yet another analogy.

In the historical unfolding of Western civilization, occult revivals have attended such crucial periods of transition from one cultural matrix to another. The waning period of the Roman Empire is a case at hand, with a great flourish of esoteric culture and symbols (much of which was absorbed in primitive Christianity prior to its institutionalization under Constantine). The Renaissance/Reformation period is another major one of shifting cultural paradigms, representing a rejection of the rationalism of medieval scholasticism and of established ecclesiastical authority, having consequences in a variety of social domains. It is during this period, and not the antecedent medieval period, that there was a major occult revival, with esoteric culture becoming a major vehicle of new expressive symbols and belief systems, a source of new value orientations.[30]

In both of these instances the particular thrust of efficacy of esoteric culture lay, I would suggest, in the exoteric culture having what may be characterized as a loss of confidence in established symbols and cognitive models of reality, in the exhaustion of institutionalized collective symbols of identity, so to speak. There was what may be called a "retreat from reason into the occult" (Yates

1964, p. 449), a retreat not in the sense of a total "leaving of the field," to borrow from Kurt Lewin, but rather in the sense of a religious retreat, a temporary withdrawal for inspirational meditation which provides a restoring of psychic energy to be used in re-entering the everyday life with greater vigor.

The occult revival of today is, in this perspective, comparable with previous such phenomena, even including the contemporary attacks against institutionalized rationality, attacks which take irrational forms in the now generation. To make sense of the irrational, the modes and conditions in which it occurs, as well as possible societal consequences deriving from it, is a basic concern of the sociology of the occult. If we come to perceive the occult revival of today not as an ephemeral fad of mass society but as an integral component in the formation of a new cultural matrix, more likely international than national in scope, if we see it, in brief, as an important vehicle in the restructuring of collective representations of social reality, we will see (with or without the third eye) the Age of Aquarius as a major sociological happening.

REFERENCES

Arnold, Paul
    1965   *Esotéricisme de Shakespeare*. Paris: Mercure de France.

Bakan, David
    1958   *Sigmund Freud and the Jewish Mystical Tradition*. Princeton, N.J.: Van Nostrand.

Balandier, Georges, ed.
    1970   *Sociologie des mutations*. Paris: Anthropos.
    1971a *Sens et puissance*. Paris: Presses Universitaires de France.
    1971b "Réflexions sur une anthropologie de la modernité." *Cahiers internationaux de sociologie* 51 (July–December): 197–211.

Bays, Gwendolyn
    1964   *The Orphic Vision: Seer Poets from Novalis to Rimbaud*. Lincoln: University of Nebraska Press.

Becker, Howard
    1960   "Normative Reactions to Normlessness." *American Sociological Review* 25 (December): 803–10.

Bell, Daniel
    1970   "The Cultural Contradictions of Capitalism." *Public Interest* 21 (Fall): 16–43.

Benz, Ernst
    1968   *Les Sources mystiques de la philosophie romantique allemande*. Paris: Vrin.

Currie, Elliott P.
    1968   "Crimes without Criminals: Witchcraft and Its Control in Renaissance Europe." *Law & Society Review* 3 (August): 7–28.

Defrance, Phillippe, Claude Fischler, Edgar Morin, and Lena Petrossian
    1971   *Le retour des astrologues*. Paris: Les Cahiers du Club du Nouvel Observateur.

Eisenstadt, S. N.
    1971   "Some Reflections on the Significance of Max Weber's *Sociology of Religions* for the
            Analysis of Non-European Modernity." *Archives de sociologie des religions* 32
            (July–December): 29–52.

Erikson, Kai
    1966   *Wayward Puritans*. New York: Wiley.

Gould, Julius, and William L. Kolb, eds.
    1964   *A Dictionary of the Social Sciences*. London: Tavistock.

Greeley, Andrew M.
    1968   *Religion in the Year 2000*. New York: Sheed & Ward.
    1970a   "Implications for the Sociology of Religion of Occult Behavior in the Youth Cul-
            ture." Paper presented at the 1970 meeting of the American Sociological Association.
    1970b   "Superstition, Ecstacy and Tribal Consciousness," *Social Research 37* (Summer):
            203–11.

Howe, Irving, ed.
    1967   *Literary Modernism*. Greenwich, Conn: Fawcett.

Hutin, Serge
    1960   *Les disciples anglais de Jacob Boehme*. Paris: Denöel.

Jonas, Hans
    1963   *The Gnostic Religion*. Boston: Beacon.

Jung, Carl G.
    1968a   *Psychology and Alchemy. Collected Works*. 2d ed. Vol. 12. Princeton, N.J.:
            Princeton University Press.
    1968b   *Alchemical Studies. Collected Works*. Vol. 13. Princeton, N.J.: Princeton University
            Press.

Kavolis, Vytautas
    1970   "The Social Psychology of Avant-Garde Cultures." *Studies in the Twentieth
            Century* 6 (Fall): 13–34.

Keane, Jerryl L.
    1967   *Practical Astrology*. West Nyack, N.J.: Parker.

Kluckhohn, Florence
    1950   "Dominant and Substitute Profiles of Cultural Orientations." *Social Forces* 28
            (May): 276–96.

Kluckhohn, Florence, and Fred L. Strodtbeck
    1961   *Variations in Value Orientations*. Evanston, Ill.: Row, Peterson.

Lepinte, Christian
    1957   *Goethe et l'occultisme*. Paris: Société d'Edition les Belles Lettres.

Marty, Martin
    1970   "The Occult Establishment." *Social Research* 37:212–30.

Masters, G. Mallary
    1969   *Rabelaisian Dialectics and the Platonic-Hermetic Tradition*. Albany: State University
            of New York Press.

Mesmer, F. A.
    1971   *Le magnétisme animal*. Paris: Payot.

Natanson, Maurice, ed.
    1973   *Phenomenology and the Social Sciences*. Evanston, Ill.: Northwestern University
            Press.

Parsons, Talcott
    1961   "Introduction." In *Theories of Society*, edited by Talcott Parsons et al. Vol. 2. New York: Free Press.
    1966   *Societies: Evolutionary and Comparative Perspectives.* Englewood Cliffs, N.J.: Prentice-Hall.
    1969   *Politics and Social Structure.* New York: Free Press.

Pauwels, Louis, and Jacques Bergier
    1968   *The Morning of the Magicians.* New York: Avon.

Reed, Robert R.
    1965   *The Occult on the Tudor and Stuart Stage.* Boston: Christopher.

Robertson, Roland
    1971   "Sociologists and Secularization." *Sociology* 5 (September): 297–312.

Roszak, Theodore
    1969   *The Making of a Counter Culture.* Garden City, N.Y.: Doubleday Anchor.

Senior, John
    1959   *The Way Down and Out: The Occult in Symbolist Literature.* Ithaca, N.Y.: Cornell University Press.

Shepherd, William C.
    1972   "Religion and the Counter Culture—a New Religiosity." *Sociological Inquiry* 42 (1):3–9.

Shih, Vincent
    1967   *The Taiping Ideology.* Seattle: University of Washington Press.

Sills, David L., ed.
    1968   *The International Encyclopedia of the Social Sciences.* 17 vols. New York: Macmillan and Free Press.

Simmel, Georg
    1906   "The Sociology of Secrecy and of Secret Societies." *American Journal of Sociology* 11 (January): 441–98. Retranslated by Kurt Wolff in *The Sociology of Georg Simmel*, edited by K. Wolff. New York: Free Press, 1950.

Singer, Milton
    1968   "Culture." In *The International Encyclopedia of the Social Sciences*, edited by David L. Sills, Vol. 3. New York: Macmillan and Free Press.

Staude, John R.
    1970   "Alienated Youth and the Cult of the Occult." Mimeographed. Reprinted in *Sociology for the Seventies*, edited by Morris L. Medley and James E. Conyers. New York: Wiley.

Stillman, John M.
    1960   *The Story of Alchemy and Early Chemistry.* New York: Dover.

Tiryakian, Edward A.
    1967   "A Model of Societal Change and Its Lead Indicators." In *The Study of Total Societies*, edited by Samuel Z. Klausner. Garden City, N.Y.: Doubleday Anchor.
    1970   "Structural Sociology." In *Theoretical Sociology: Perspectives and Developments*, edited by John C. McKinney and Edward A. Tiryakian. New York: Appleton-Century-Crofts.

Truzzi, Marcello
    1970   "The Occult Revival as Popular Culture: Some Random Observations on the Old and Nouveau Witch." Mimeographed. Reprinted in *Sociological Quarterly* 13 (Winter 1972): 16–36.

Van Lennep, J.
    1966   *Art & Alchimie*. Brussels: Meddens.
Voegelin, Eric
    1952   *The New Science of Politics*. Chicago: University of Chicago Press.
Weber, Eugen, ed.
    1964   *Satan franc maçon*. Paris: Julliard.
Willener, Alfred
    1970   *The Action-Image of Society*. London: Tavistock.
Wilson, Bryan R.
    1966   *Religion in Secular Society*. London: Watts.
Yates, Frances A.
    1964   *Giordano Bruno and the Hermetic Tradition*. Chicago: University of Chicago Press.

NOTES

1. For a recent treatment of the secularization thesis, see Robertson (1971).

2. A justification for Greeley's terms "tribal Gods" and "tribal consciousness" is the self-designation of some communes as "tribes."

3. The late Howard Becker had developed, in an unfortunately neglected communication to the American Sociological Association (1960), a theoretical critique of the secularization model. Becker would have no difficulty in perceiving today's occult revival and the neoevangelical movement as instances of "normative reactions to normlessness."

4. Like Greeley, I see this hypothesis as having been derived from a short-sighted reading of Durkheim and Weber on the modernization process—or else as a correct reading of the mistaken notions of Spencer.

5. It is tempting to think that both artisan labor and occult work among today's college-trained youth may indicate a new nonindustrial form of inner-directed achievement orientation.

6. In the sociological literature on the occult revival, I have found commonly known instances of the occult (astrology, witchcraft, etc.) but no analytical definitions or conceptual classificatory scheme subsumed under this rubric. The *International Encyclopedia of the Social Sciences* has no entry for "esoteric" or "occult" and only passing mentions of "secret societies" in a few substantive articles. The UNESCO-sponsored *A Dictionary of the Social Sciences* does not have the following comment (by Kenneth Little, an anthropologist) under "Secret Society": "It is difficult [in this context] to discuss the nature of modern institutions, such as Freemasonry, but in primitive cultures secret societies generally constitute an integral part of the social system concerned" (in Gould and Kolb 1964, p. 624). Why the difficulty is not made clear.

7. The conceptualization and research of Florence Kluckhohn (1950, 1961) on dominant and substitute value orientations is highly relevant here.

8. It is worth noting that occultism has both a scientific and an aesthetic aspect, which relates back to our earlier remarks on the meaning of the occult revival for youth. We need not dwell on how much of scientific creativity has a pronounced aesthetic dimension, and conversely.

9. Parlor tricks or stage magic is not meant here, but rather such practices as sorcery, witchcraft, ritual or ceremonial magic, and the like.

10. For a succinct anthropological statement on divination, see Victor Turner (Sills 1968, 13: 440).

11. The academic world may be seen, through one perspective, as routinizing and secularizing the esoteric acquisition of gnosis. At lower levels, students progress through neophyte levels known as grades. At higher levels we have *rites de passage* (qualifiers, Ph.D. orals, and the like) as we initiate students into higher stages of the academic fraternity. The Phi Beta Kappa ceremony is a symbolic accolade of those who have shown particular aptitude for academic mysteries, albeit few of its recipients may be aware of its esoteric background.

12. This is institutionalized in Sweden and Great Britain where the monarch or a member of the ruling family, respectively, is the titular head of Masonry in his country; though not institutionalized in the United States, most presidents have been 33° Masons or of high rank.

13. The cultural traditions of all the major complexes of civilization and high religions have an esoteric side. Thus, Islam, Christianity, Hinduism, and Judaism have their esoteric components in Sufism, theosophy (in various forms: Illuminism, Rose Croix, and more modern versions such as those of Blavatsky, Gurdjieff, R. Steiner), Tantric Yoga, the Kabbalah, etc.

14. For a fuller discussion of the rise and characteristics of avant-garde literary culture, see Irving Howe's essay. "The Idea of the Modern" (Howe 1967, pp. 11–40).

15. In a similar vein, Edgar Morin has spoken of the revival of astrology today as a manifestation of a new gnosis (Defrance et al. 1971, p. 123). See also the remarks of Hans Jonas (1963) on gnostic features of some modern political tendencies, including the theme of alienation.

16. Students of astrological traits might note with amusement the congruence of the Promethean and the satanic with the two sides of the Aquarian-born (today's *enfants du siècle*): "A negative Aquarian is one who . . . demands licence under the guise of of liberty, and shouts for public service while serving none but himself. The positive Aquarian is . . . the humanitarian, seeking liberty not for self, but for others, dealing in the larger affairs of the country or planet, every urging humanity upward and onward, and running ahead to show the way" (Keane 1967, p. 34).

17. For a fuller statement on the social significance of Satan in the last century, see the cogent remarks of Eugen Weber (1964).

18. Note here the observation of Howe (1967) in commenting upon a passage of Baudelaire: "[This seems] the report of a desire to create . . . the very ground of being, through a permanent revolution of sensibility and style, by means of which art could raise itself to the level of white or (more likely) black magic." (p. 17.).

19. To do full justice to the role of esoteric culture as an inspirational source for avant-garde culture, one should also examine esoteric influences on earlier literary and artistic innovators, such as Shakespeare (Arnold 1965; Reed 1965) and Rabelais (Masters 1969), to say nothing about esoteric currents in painting and architecture (Van Lennep 1966).

20. In commenting on "Surrealism and Revolution," Camus stated: "The essential enemy of Surrealism is rationalism. Breton's method . . . presents the peculiar spectacle of a form of Occidental thought in which the principle of analogy is continually favored to the detriment of the principles of identity and contradiction. . . . Magic rites, . . . alchemy . . . are so many miraculous stages on the way to unity and the philosopher's stone" (Howe 1967, p. 218).

21. The hexing of the Pentagon and the Stock Exchange (to say nothing of an Establishment department of sociology) and the adoption of the acronym WITCH attest in their own modest way to the appeal of occult symbolism in some sectors of radical students. To my knowledge there was no manifest influence of surrealism in these instances.

22. Thus, the very symbols of the Great Seal of the United States (the luminous delta, the pyramid) are esoteric symbols of Freemasonry, to which belonged most of the founding fathers; similarly for the symbols of the French Republic (especially that of 1848), whose motto "Liberty, Equality, Fraternity" represents cherished ideals of Masonry formulated in lodges before the French Revolution. Simón Bolívar, the liberator of South America from Spanish rule, was also imbued with Masonic ideals, as was Garibaldi in Italy, etc.

23. S. N. Eisenstadt's evaluation of the ability of Chinese Communists to draw upon various threads of protest in Chinese society and wield them into a common cause is highly germane here. He signals in particular that such a linkage "enabled some gentry groups . . . some secret societies, some warlords and some peasant rebels to go beyond their own restricted social orientation and to find a wider basis and forge out new, broader orientations" (1971, pp. 49 f.). It is our contention that these orientations are likely to have originated, at least in part, in esoteric doctrines formulated in secret societies. In the case of China, of noteworthy mention in the rise of national consciousness is the case of the Taiping (Shih 1967).

24. Among other things contained in the esoteric conceptions of the theologian Oetinger, a generation before Marx, are such themes as an eschatological view of history and the coming freedom of man in a "Golden Age" in which the state, private property, and a money economy will disappear in communal equality and love (Benz 1968, pp. 32–53).

25. Once organized, the scientific community broke formally with esoteric culture. This was symbolized in 1666 upon the establishment of the French Academy of Sciences, membership in which excluded the practice of astrology. A few years before France had still had an official state astrologer, Morin de Villefranche, professor of mathematics at the prestigious College de France, who had sought to modernize and rationalize astrology with mathematical precision.

26. In the context of the latter, see the study of differential reactions to witchcraft in England and on the Continent by Currie (1968). For other materials on witchcraft, deviance, and social structure, see the New England study of Erikson (1966).

27. We might note in passing that Western esoteric culture has deep historical roots in cultural aspects of both Israel and Greece, notably the prophetic and Kabbalistic traditions of the former and the rituals of the mystery cults of the latter.

28. A student of Harold Garfinkel, Trent Eglin, is presently preparing an ethnomethodological study of alchemy.

29. I have taken this suggestive term from Balandier (1971a, p. 202) in preference to the overworked "periods of crisis." In this and other writings (1970, 1971b), Balandier has been developing a theory of modernity which seems particularly fruitful for reformulating the dynamics of change.

30. For an outstanding historical study of this cultural context, see Yates (1964).

Claude Fischler

Astrology and French Society: The Dialectic of Archaism and Modernity

In 1971, during a press conference, Georges Pompidou, President of the French Republic, declared, "I am not Madame Soleil." The political content of this sentence (rich though it may be) will not detain us here. Let us simply note that the President, by using this new expression to mean "I can't predict the future," certified the entry into the French language—in other words, the overwhelming reputation—of Madame Soleil, astrologer of the airwaves.

It was in September 1970 that the astrologer Soleil was first heard over a private radio station,[1] broadcasting her answers to listeners' questions. Success came very rapidly. Madame Soleil was soon receiving 25,000 letters and telephone calls a day; she was approached by several newspapers; advertis-

Materials for this essay are drawn from *Le Retour des Astrologues*, issue No. 3 of *l'obs*, Club du Nouvel Observateur, Paris, 1971. Copyright © 1971 by Le Nouvel Observateur. Mr. Fischler was one of the contributors of the issue. The present article was written with the permission of the Club du Nouvel Observateur.—Editor's note.

ments exploited her name and astrology in general. Her success also elicited a
fair number of protests and sarcastic responses, especially in Marxist or para-
Marxist circles and among the militant rationalists of the intransigent Union
Rationaliste (or what is left of it). We can distinguish two types of criticisms of
Madame Soleil, and through her of astrology: (a) the rationalist criticism,
which reproaches capitalism for exploiting astrological superstition, and (b)
"sociocultural demystification," which accuses astrology of lending support to
capitalism.

The investigation undertaken by the Sociological Diagnostic Group[2]
resulted from the astonishment in the face of the quantitative and qualitative
importance of the Madame Soleil phenomenon, which both the rationalist
criticism and the sociocultural demystification, appeared powerless to grasp.
Indeed, some ten years ago, astrology in France still appeared to be an archaic
holdover of rural beliefs, a rustic folklore of witches and conjurers. Yet here
rises Madame Soleil to the zenith of the mass media and sets herself up as a
maternal Pythoness, reassuring and comforting, with a competence extending
to all aspects of an extremely up-to-date complex of problems. The questions
asked of Madame Soleil bear the imprint of modernity: small shopkeepers
confronted with socioeconomic change; problems of men and women, parent
and child, and women's changing roles. The very observation that Madame
Soleil, rather than predicting the future, applies herself to supplying comfort,
to dressing the wounds inflicted by the modern-urban-technological civilization, led us to look more closely at the new course of astrology. Many aspects
proved worthy of attention.

A few months before the "rise " of Madame Soleil, a Parisian astrologer,
André Barbault, made a splash which was equally revealing though more localized by programming a computer installed on the Champs Elysées to give
astrological consultations based essentially on psychological considerations.
Today, half the French daily papers publish horoscopes; periodicals which
devote no space to astrology are the exception . According to a public-opinion
poll, 68% of men and 85% of women know the sign under which they were
born, and 60% of Frenchmen aged eighteen and over read, at least occasionally, their horoscope in various newspapers and magazines.

Yet is would be a mistake to reduce contemporary astrology to "mass astrology," the popular astrology of the mass media. There exists a learned astrology, speculative and philosophical, which is inherited from, or is a renewal
of, doctrinal occultism. One finds a so-called scientific astrology, compromising
with rationalism and seeking confirmation in statistics. Various astrological

currents incorporate psychoanalysis, especially Jungian, in order better to approach subjectivity. We have also detected a specifically bourgeois, or at least elitist, astrology; a medical astrology coming to the aid of diagnosis; a business astrology to which some managers resort to support decisions made in the perpetual battle with chance and risks; a show-business astrology (a milieu which is particularly sensitive to the combined whims of chance and the public—in other words, of glory). At the same time, a part of the counterculture—a militant wing of today's youth—heralds as prophecy and promise the age of Aquarius, and sees in astrology a path to existential revolution.

Given these observations, one hypothesis suggested itself at the outset: far from being a remnant of the age of witches which somehow or other found its way into the age of computers, astrology is closely linked to the advance of modernity, on the one hand, and to the crisis of modernity, on the other. But it rests upon a mode of thought and a conception of the world in the deepest and most primitive recesses of the *anthropos*: magic-analogical thought, micro-macrocosmic conception.

Any astrology rests on this postulate, at least implicitly: the universe is a living cosmic reality with man at the heart of it. The human sphere is a microcosm of the stellar macrocosm. It is analogically linked to it and corresponds to it jot for jot. The astrological symbols—signs of the zodiac, planets, houses, etc.—effect the analogical link between the human microcosm and the macrocosm. Each of these symbols bears within it the anthropomorphic or zoomorphic attribute or truth which it expresses. This micro/macrocosmic cosmology is the first unitary and coherent conception which emerges in man, and it is embedded more or less deeply in every human mind. But at the same time astrology has a scientific base: the knowledge of a celestial order. In this sense we can say that astrology is the most magical of sciences and the most scientific of magics.

From Magical Science to Mass Astrology.   A rapid historical survey reveals the interplay which takes place between these anthropological roots and the facts of culture and civilization.

The original astrology—that of Chaldea[3]—was associated with religion, and this remained true up to the time of the Macedonian conquest. From that period on, it spread throughout the Hellenistic and then the Greco-Roman syncretism,[4] it lost its religious core, and this enucleated astrology became occidental astrology. Magical science and no longer religion, it would occasionally be able to coexist with other religions, if they had a minimum tolerance for outside forms of magical belief, or with other sciences as long as they did not dissociate themselves from magic.

The next modification in France occurred in the second half of the seventeenth century: astrology was relegated to the ghetto of occultism through the combined offensive of the Catholic Church (against heresies and the remains of paganism) and the newborn "Enlightenment" (scientific-rationalist offensive against magic). Until then astrology had enjoyed the status of magical religion. It was as inseparable from astronomy as alchemy was from chemistry. Now astrology was denounced as superstition. In 1666, Colbert, minister of Louis XIV, founded the Académie des Sciences and forbade astronomers to practice astrology.[5]

Stripped of legitimacy, astrology in the eighteenth and nineteenth centuries (along with alchemy, palmistry, clairvoyance, and telepathy) encountered both legal and sociocultural repression. Consequently, during this period astrology took two forms. On the one hand, it became diffused over civilization as superstitious folk beliefs. On the other hand, it took on a clandestine aspect as occultist astrology in the doctrinal teachings of secret societies and esoteric sects. Spiritism grew out of occultism during the second half of the nineteenth century.

Occultism might appear to have been doomed, but instead it acted like a biological culture medium. From the mid-nineteenth century, especially in England, then in France, we see the old belief in ghosts reappear—not in the backward countryside, but in the cities, and even among the intelligentsia of the Romantic movement. Spiritism, far from retreating together with religion in the face of conquering science, stepped into the suddenly widened breach: death. The civilization of science is also the civilization of individualism and of the ebb of Christian immortality, and all the progress of individualism can only deepen the sorrow caused by the death of loved ones, the anguish of one's own death, and the search for an afterlife. The breach through which archaism returns to modernity is effected by the very advance of civilization.

As Edgar Morin writes, "in a world which is more and more conceived objectively by science, *there is no science of subjects*."[6] Occultism, because of enormous cultural resistance, could not be conceived as science, except in the eyes of a few people on the fringes of society. Not until hope in the omnipotence of science, in its power to find fundamental solutions for human problems, had weakened; not until religion had also weakened; not until individualism, which was still limited to the well-to-do classes, had spread and deepened, especially through the ideology of the mass media, not until then was mass astrology to emerge.

The mass media, around 1930, brought astrology once more out of occultist obscurity and at the same time condensed the haze of superstitions. Mass astrology was born with newspaper horoscopes, and from there progressed very rapidly, even though it has been in contradiction with the philosophy of the modern world, with religion, and with political ideologies.

Horoscopes appeared in the women's journals in France around 1930 in the form of a kind of psycho-astro-weather report. They made no attempt to forecast for the individual, but only collectively ("tomorrow will be unlucky"). The essential improvement in the technique of horoscopes occurred a few years later with the use of the signs of the zodiac, which divided humanity into twelve basic groups, or thirty-six if "decans" are taken into account. The appearance of the zodiac in the media ushers in a period of zodiacal literacy, of astrological vulgarization: today the zodiac is enough to symbolize astrology and to "name" the other—that is, to rid someone somewhat of his strangeness, or to bring him into the realm of the familiar. This evolution is characteristic of modern astrology, insofar as it inclines to psychologism and individualization. And at the end of this chain of increasing personalization of the astrology of the mass media, we have Madame Soleil, who restores through the radio marketplace—publicly but anonymously—the private astrologer-consultant relationship of the occultist chamber.

Astrology and Social Classes. The psychologism of mass astrology is extremely poor compared to that of learned or cultivated astrology. Along with mass astrology persists and flourishes a sophisticated, speculative, and perfected astrology, which is to newspaper horoscopes what Freudian thought is to news-column psychoanalysis. The astrologers of the elite make use of extensive information for thorough introspection. Where zodiacal astrology provides a kind of anthropometrical index of the psyche, a digest of the ego, it endeavors, by making use of the limitless range of astrological language, to denote the psyche *in extenso*: the astrology of the rich is a rich astrology.

This calls for two observations. Astrology is not strictly a fringe phenomenon; it affects the mainstream of society. Thus, the development of the most advanced feeds on astrology and is fed by it, since astrology percolates into the world of the computer and probability theory, and into the world of movie stars and celebrities. Astrology is not strictly a popular phenomenon, for we see the development of an astrology of the elite, a bourgeois astrology.

Astrology ignores the notion of social class and reaches into all strata. Its polyvalent, polymorphous character is the very mark of this: vulgar or noble, prosaic or detached, practical or speculative, it can help bring about success in love or in the lottery, it can favor cosmic speculations as well as racetrack calculations. At the same time, in the form of the horoscope, it stands for concerns shared by everyone. Although astrology does not belong to any specific class or classes, it changes somewhat from one class to another. The polarization of social forces is expressed by internal variations: here and elsewhere a hierarchy is set up in terms of wealth and culture. More refined, more personalized, more psychological, the astrology of the elite is also more marked by the cultural values acquired through education. It attempts to win over the sciences or make a pact with them. In order to differentiate itself from magic, in order to explain or rationalize the relationship between men and stars which it posits, astrology calls on astronomy and psychoanalysis. But if astrology accredits itself with the elite by relating itself to modern science, it can also imbue itself with elite culture by a different kind of affiliation. Astrology can lean on existentialist and mystical doctrines, leading to an antirationalist, antipositivistic sort of theorizing. From this emerges openly a "new Gnosis,"[7] attacking the old cultural values and taking advantage of their incipient decline.

The astrology of the poor is a "welfare" or providential astrology. As one approaches the poorest segments of society, the demand is openly magic. From occultism, from the astrologer, people in the lower strata expect happiness *hic et nunc*.

On a slightly higher level, what is asked for is help and support, succor rather than a miracle. That this "SOS" astrology is characteristic of the middle and lower classes is indicated by the broadcasts of Madame Soleil and confirmed by the statistical data which have been collected regarding these broadcasts.[8] This astrology is clearly linked to a crisis situation, be it material or affective, which favors recourse to magic and therefore to astrology. The crisis may be individual (a neglected wife, a worried mother), but it may also be social: a considerable part of Madame Soleil's clientele is composed of small shopkeepers drawn to the maternal warmth of the radio astrologer out of distress resulting from a socioeconomic change which is too rapid and inexorable.

Thus there are clear differences between the astrology of the upper classes and the astrology of the lower. But as we have seen, there is no precise border line: the widest zone is the intermediate area, the no-man's-land where the attraction exerted by one pole never excludes the influence of the other.

The middle and lower strata, then, are not free from the psychological worry which characterizes the economically favored classes—although in the case of the former it can express itself only in an extremely skeletal form of astrological language—the *abc*'s of the zodiac. Symetrically, if psychological astrology exists in a vulgarized form in the lower strata of society, SOS astrology has its counterpart in the upper strata, with the astrology of decision-making. Whereas the less economically favored groups call on astrology to remove or assume the anguish of distress which is born of a dramatic alternative, the upper classes will appeal to astrology to confirm their choices, to banish chance from uncertain decisions. In the less favored classes the need for decision arises at key moments in private life (love, affection, marriage, or a simple purchase), in the upper spheres it occurs at every instant of professional life and is linked to the daily problems of management, of technostructure, and even of power.

Conductor Milieux. It is not enough to describe the relationships between astrology and the various social classes in order to obtain a true image of the relationship between astrology and French society. For if, as we have seen, astrology in various ways affects all strata, the fact remains that there are favored terrains; we must therefore examine the milieux or social categories which prove themselves good astrological conductors. Besides the results of our own research, two public opinion polls are available for this purpose.[9]

The empirical data set forth in Tables 1 and 2 lead directly to two observations. First, the urban milieu is the most favorable to astrology, while the countryside, contrary to what is usually believed, resists its spread. Second, the groups most susceptible to astrology are women and youth.

In order to explain the preeminence of the astrology of the city over that of the country, we can put forward two hypotheses. Let us first submit, without elaborating, that the media which give the most attention to astrology are, in France, those which are least widespread in rural areas. This is the case of the important national daily newspapers and of the weekly pulp magazines.

Secondly, a characteristic of French rural life is the traditional polarization between the "red" and "white", clericals and laymen. In the French countryside, both religion and secular rationalism have remained much more powerful than in the city, and together they form a resistance to astrology. There is a shade of difference between the two: laicism combats without distinction astrology and ancient belief in magic and witchcraft, while the Church, which sees witchcraft as a work of Satan, tends to authenticate it by its very opposition.

The primacy of urban astrology is the result of the rapid progress in the city of the new standards, of the new individualism, of modernity.

In urban civilization, mass culture spreads the passwords of prestige and

Table 1. Social Attributes of Believers* in Astrology in France (I.F.O.P. Survey 1963)

Category	Percentage in Total Sample
Total believing in astrology	30
By sex	
Men	21
Women	39
By occupational group	
Professionals, managers, executives	34
Small business owners and artisans ("Commerçants")	36
Clerical and sales ("Employés")	46
Manuel workers ("ouvriers")	29
Farmers and farm workers ("agriculteurs")	15
Not in the labor force or retired	30
By locality	
Under 2,000 inhabitants	21
2,000–5,000	27
5,000–20,000	37
20,000–100,000	34
Over 100,000	40
By age (years)	
20–34	38
35–49	33
50–64	24
65 and over	20

SOURCE. P. Defrance et al., *Le Retour des Astrologues,* 1971, p. 74, from survey data gathered in 1963 by the Institut Français d'Opinion Publique, at the request of *France-Soir.*

* Persons having the three following characteristics: (a) knowing their astrological birth sign, (b) reading their horoscope at least occasionally, (c) believing "that there is something true in the character traits attributed by astrology."

Table 2. Social Characteristics of Clients of the Occult in France (I.R.E.S.—Marketing Survey 1967)

Category	Persons having consulted at least once a fortune-teller (card-reader), a seer, or another who predicts the future	Persons having consulted at least once an astrologer
Total percentage of clients	12.5%	3%
By sex		
Men	6	1.5
Women	19.5	4.5
By occupational group:		
Professionals, managers, executives ("cadres supérieurs, patrons")	11.5	4
Semi-professionals, junior executives, technical ("Cadres moyens")	14.5	4
Clerical and sales ("Employés")	15.5	4
Manual workers ("Ouvriers")	14.5	2.5
Farmers and farm workers	5.5	1.5
By locality		
Under 2,000 inhabitants	7.5	1.5
2,000–10,000	13	2
10,000–50,000	14.5	3.5
50,000–150,000	17	2.5
Over 150,000	16	5
By age (in years)		
18–25	9	1.5
26–35	12.5	3.5
36–45	13	3
46–55	13	4
56–65	13	3

SOURCE. P. Defrance, et al., *Le Retour des Astrologues,* 1971, p. 75, from survey data gathered in 1967 and published in 1968 by I.R.E.S.—Marketing.

consumerism, of private happiness and pleasure. As the motivational significance of the work situation has waned, the importance of leisure has
expanded. In private life the individual tries to find the pleasure and interest
which he does not find in his work; it is in the private sphere of love and happiness that he seeks fulfilment. Modern astrology corresponds exactly to this
individual and private demand, which increases in proportion to the growth of
problems linked to modernity. As the new standards spread, the norms which
regulated interpersonal relationships in earlier societies disappear (weakening
the old ties of neighborhood, family, proximity, and solidarity). Hence the
need to clarify private or professional relationships, to confirm the choice of
friends, sweethearts and social partners, and at the same time to face numerous decisions.

Modern man also asks more and more questions about his identity. Family
and birth, work and social status are no longer sufficient to situate and define
the individual; in this area astrology appears as the tool of tools for insight and
discovery.

But there is more than simply the advance of modernity: there is the *crisis* of
this modernity. In the urban milieu, the individual is atomized. In the French
villages of the past, the individual could depend on advisers of universal
competence—doctor, teacher, parish priest. He can no longer do so. The mass
media network of the McLuhan neovillage is now extended over the city, sub-
stituting new advisers for the fading parish priest, doctor and teacher. The
modern city exudes private suffering and calls for collective relief—Madame
Soleil, the advice to the lovelorn of the women's weeklies, Radio Luxemburg's
marriage bureau of the air. Some branches of modern astrology address
themselves to these same anxieties.

Astrology, then, makes progress in the city, in the midst of modernity which
is still developing and already undergoing crisis. But, as we have said, women
and youth are also good conductors of astrology. Examining them, we discover
vast areas of archaism ensconced in the very heart of—and developing along
with—modernity. Modern culture has as a byproduct "unculture." It bears
within itself a neo-archaism; the neovillage is also a neoghetto, peopled by
women and youth.[10]

We know, in fact, that in recent times important changes have taken place
regarding the status of women and youth. While they previously were kept
totally apart from the City,[11] now they have begun to desert their ghettos (the
housework ghetto for women, the tutelary ghetto for youth) and to enter into
modernity, making themselves into what might be termed biosocial classes.

Thus, the 1960's in France were a decisive turning point for youth, with the appearance of the "yé-yé" phenomenon,[12] that is to say, the accession of youth to consumerism and the irruption of its own culture. The affirmation of this biosocial identity showed itself in a growing pressure on the adult world, pressure which was to result in the explosion of May 1968.

As for women, they have begun to pull out of the domestic ghetto and to make an appearance in the working world, little by little gaining access to the City. More grounded in archaism than are men, they too make themselves the agents of the new modernity (the search for emotional fulfilment, for communication, for intensity). More than men, they adopt mass culture, which in turn adopts them. But, in the same shift, they bring with them their ignorance of social mechanisms, their lack of understanding of how the City functions, both of which contribute to the rise of anguish. This lack of familiarity with the workings of economy and politics, of the legal and judicial systems, induces some of them to put their hope in the omniscience-omnipotence attributed to Madame Soleil.

If women, little by little emerging from the isolation of the home, simultaneously enter into a neoghetto, young people too, to a large degree, are pioneers of modernity and the new barbarians. Less imbued than adults with the old rationalism and religious values, their antibodies for resisting astrology are fewer and less powerful—unless, flinging themselves into the cultural revolution, they deliberately refuse the old ideological, religious, humanist or rationalist values. Half-cultured, half-politicized, women and youth are, as they arrive in the City, bodies which are half-foreign. And the spread of astrology is facilitated in every zone of "unculture" of these contemporary Middle Ages.

We have seen that astrology reaches indiscriminately into all social classes, skirting ideological or cultural obstacles (Marxism, rationalism, the Catholic church), as unable to overcome them as they are to arrest it. We have seen that astrology seeps in everywhere that the old values have not been replaced, everywhere that the city and the new individualism, as well as the new "unculture" and the "modern Middle Ages" spread. The progress of astrology reveals the existence of a *process of relative ideological destructuration*. This weakening of ideological and cultural antibodies leaves defenseless vast areas which astrological germs contaminate. They take advantage of a medium which is anthropologically favorable and, to pursue the metaphor, become virulent on contact with man's deepest and most hidden tissues: those which secrete magical thought. From then on, astrological belief may take shape.

NOTES

1. "Europe 1." In France, three stations share almost exclusively the entire radio audience; there are almost no local or regional stations.

2. The Sociological Diagnostic Group (Groupe de Diagnostic Sociologique), headed by Edgar Morin, is based in Paris as part of the Center of Studies of Mass Communication (Centre d'Etudes des Communications de Masse, or CECMAS), a research laboratory of the Ecole Pratiques des Hautes Etudes. It is primarily interested in the study of the new social phenomena, often fortuitous *happenings* which being to the surface currents normally not manifest in everyday social life. Basing itself on a conception of *clinical sociology*, the diagnostic group seeks to diagnose those disturbances in the social structure which surface in the course of these happenings. The disturbance in question is traced back to more underlying structures which, in turn, place the happening in a new light.

   In the past few years, the research team has studied several such happenings. Thus, in Orléans in 1969 a rumor spread with unexpected currency concerning a white slave trade, involving the alleged disappearance of women in clothing stores owned by Jews. An on-the-spot investigation by the diagnostic group led to the publication of *Rumor in Orleans* (American translation published by Pantheon Books, New York, 1971). In 1971 the research team simultaneously carried out two studies. The first dealt with the onset in France of a Women's Liberation movement (*La Femme-Sujet: neo-féminisme et nouvelle féminité,* to be published in 1973). The second study, dealing with the spread of astrology in French society, provides the background for the present article; it was undertaken by Philippe Defrance, Claude Fischler, Edgar Morin, and Lena Petrossian (*Le Retour des Astrologues,* Paris: Nouvel Observateur, 1971). Other studies of the team, such as reactions to the setting up of a huge harbor-industrial complex near Marseille, are in various stages of publication.

3. Marguerite Rutten, *La Science des Chaldéens.* Paris: Presses Universitaires de France, 1961.

4. Bouche-Leclercq, *L'Astrologie Grecque.* Paris: Leroux, 1899.

5. Serge Hutin, *Histoire de l'Astrologie.* Verviers: Marabout, 1970.

6. *Le Retour des Astrologues,* p. 118.

7. In reference to the philosophical eclecticism of the second century A.D., we use the expression "new Gnosticism" to designate a movement suddenly surfacing in France a few years ago with the publication of the review *Planète* and the publication of the best seller by Jacques Bergier and Louis Pauwels, *The Morning of the Magicians* (1960). Positing what may be termed "realism of the fantastic" ("réalisme fantastique"), this syncretism combines hypothetical-speculative data on the immemorial past and future of the earth and the cosmos. Here are found ideas previously rejected as superstitions, esoteric doctrines of the Far East, information and hypotheses gleaned at "the confines of science," fantastic historical theses, and the sort (e.g., the prehistorical colonization of our planet by extraterrestial beings). The syncretism of magic and science into a new magico-scientific apparatus provides a new identification of man with the cosmos.

8. Michel Gauquelin and Elian de Massard, "Analyse logique et psychosociologique de Madame Soleil," *Science et Vie*, **644** (May, 1971), 77–83.

9. The first poll was conducted in 1963 by the Institut Francais d'Opinion Publique (IFOP) for the daily newspaper *France-Soir*; it is cited by Jacques Maître, "La Consommation d'Astrologie dans la France contemporaine," in *La Divination*, Vol. II, Paris: Presses Universitaires de France. The second was undertaken by I.R.E.S.—Marketing of Paris in 1967 and reported in *Bulletin I.R.E.S.—Marketing,* **22** (May, 1968). The latter is based on a representative national sample of 6,000 men and women 18–65 years old.

    We have used data from these polls as an index of the phenomenon of astrology in modern society. In addition to methodological criticisms of the research design of public opinion polls, including the formulation of questions having a bearing on respondents' answers, an additional important objection is the rationale for lumping together occupations in the same category (e.g., priests and the military). Hence the poll data have been used to complement our own observations. We acknowledge the serious problems associated with our own investigation. Not only is it difficult to quantify astrology as a social phenomenon but we have also had to carry out our own study on the basis of personal encounters and meetings with individuals having some sympathetic understanding for this kind of research. Moreover, discretion, often asked by interviewees in the reporting of data, obliges us at points to be less precise or specific than otherwise desirable.

    Our "multidimensional" method utilizes concurrently a variety of research techniques, from quasi-ethnographic participant-observation to documents obtained from questionnaire surveys. Moreover, the research team has adopted a skeptical stance concerning "scientific objectivity." Rather than deny it, we make the most of the *subjectivity* of each researcher. Thus, each team member keeps a "research diary," extracts from which are published in the appendices of our publications so that the reader is aware of the divergent areas of interest, disagreements, and even conflicts between members of the research team.

    The principles of this method are explicated at length in the concluding appendix of Edgar Morin, *et al., Rumor in Orleans* (New York: Pantheon, 1971).

10. These questions have been treated at greater length in Edgar Morin, *et al., Rumor in Orleans* (New York: Pantheon, 1971).

11. City in this context refers to citizens who participated in the political community. Formerly, women and youth did not have this full participation of citizenship, whereas they do now.

12. Starting in the 1960's, "yéyé" was the name given in France to the commercial musical and clothing fringe of the rising youth culture. It is a sarcastic rendering in French of "yeah", widely used by French rock singers desirous of indicating that their inspiration was authentically American.

Andrew M. Greeley

Implications for the Sociology of Religion of Occult Behavior in the Youth Culture

There are a number of different but interrelated strains to be observed in the deviant wing of the upper-middle-class youth culture:

1. The Woodstock syndrome: a passive, unaggressive withdrawal from the larger society—either temporary or permanent—into a subculture shaped by hallucinogenic drugs and rock music.

2. The political protest phenomenon: ranging from the Weathermen of the far left to various liberal and moderate groups concerned with active participation in the existing political processes.

3. The "communitarian" movement: ranging from the communes of Taos or the Big Sur to various kinds of encounter and sensitivity groups.

4. The "neosacral" or occult, religious or quasireligious activities of individuals and groups.

Original contribution, first presented as a paper at the 1970 annual meeting of the American Sociological Association.

All four of these strains of upper-class youth culture interact with one another. Astrology, for example, is popular with the communitarians, the protesters, and the psychedelics. Marihuana permeates all four strains. A young person can move from one emphasis to another with relative ease; someone "doing his thing" can now be engaged in protest, now drugs, now astrology, and now a Meher Baba commune.

The first three elements of the upper-middle-class youth culture are taken very seriously by social analysts. The fourth has thus far not been subject to much in the way of serious investigation. But if psychedelia and political protests and communes are thought to be important social developments, there is no logical reason for excluding interest in the occult from careful social science analysis.

One is tempted to say that many sociologists would rather like to exclude it; drugs, political protests, even the communes are somehow or other "legitimate" forms of deviance. Astrology, witchcraft, or diabolism—that is indeed another matter. The characteristic reaction of many social scientists when the subject of occultism among their students is brought up is to suggest that it is a passing fad. Psychedelia is not a fad, left-wing political movements are not fads, communes are generally not dismissed as being a fad, but occult behavior can only be explained as a fad.

One need not delve too deeply to find the reasons why the neosacral is embarrassing: it simply shouldn't have happened. In the classical model according to which most social scientists approach religion we are now in the late phases of the "secularization" process. The race is presumed to have evolved away from mythological society to a scientific society. Man no longer needs to postulate gods to explain storms or the progression of the stars across the heavens. Therefore, it is argued that he no longer needs the sacred or the religious. The more enlightened of progressive modern men, if they are not atheists, are at least agnostics, requiring neither an ultimate explanation nor any contact with "the sacred." Those who still profess a faith or engage in religious ritual are considered to represent a somewhat earlier stage of the evolutionary process, and a stage which is rapidly becoming vestigial.

Such a model is rarely stated quite so boldly or explicitly, yet it is, one suspects, a model which exists just below the surface of most social-science consciousness. Such a model obviously cannot cope with the new manifestations of the sacred on the college campus and in the communes where the collegians go when they flee the campus. It is bad enough if the superstitious—particularly the bizarrely superstitious—remains anywhere in advanced industrial society, but for it to break out in the supposed bastion of secularity—the great university—is clearly an affront to all decent, pious, agnostic men.

But despite its scandalous nature the neosacral is still very much with us. There are, it seems to me, three principal forms in which it takes.

1. Divination; that is to say, attempts either to foretell the future or to obtain divine guidance in decision-making through such traditional methods as astrology, or the I Ching, or Tarot cards.

2. Mysticism; frequently of the oriental variety and on occasion demanding long hours of silent contemplation and reflection. The Meher Baba groups seem to be particularly popular. (Indeed, I have heard of a Baba commune in Idaho called Babashire.)

3. Bizarre cultic groups such as witchcraft covens, diabolic communities, spiritualism groups, and the White Legion.

There also exist some rather strange relationships, which I must confess to not understanding completely, between science fiction and the various neosacral movements.

In the emerging literature on the communitarian movement one sees that this movement is acquiring religious dimensions. Some of the communes are explicitly religious, others use religious or quasireligious concepts to explain their purpose and behavior. Thus, the "open land" ideology frequently argues that land "belongs to God"; and the emphasis on "organic food" stresses that such food is "natural" or "the way God intends man to eat."

It is easy enough to dismiss such comments and indeed the whole resurgence of the occult as being "not serious," or "a put-on" of the scientific, rational society. The young people who say, for example, that organic food is "God's way" don't really mean God in the sense of some transcendent being. Whether they do or not is, however, precisely a question for research and not a valid a priori assumption. Much of what is going on in deviant youth culture today claims to be religious and looks and sounds as though it were religious. The serious social scientist, therefore, must deploy his tools of research in the sociology of religion and determine to what extent he can build useful models for understanding the current craze for the occult. Whether it will last or not is to some extent a research question and to some extent a question that must be left to future analysis. The relevant issue at the present time is to what extent the perspectives of the sociology of religion enable us to understand the phenomenon.

I should like to suggest that at the present state of the discipline the sociology of religion sees four principal functions that religion plays in human life:

1. It provides meaning.
2. It is a basis for community.
3. It is an attempt to establish contact with the "sacred."
4. It provides or reinforces norms according to which a man may live.

Clifford Geertz has argued that religion is a "culture system" providing a "template" by which man can "interpret" those phenomena which "baffle" him. When science, common sense, ideology, and art are not sufficient to cope with crises of interpretation and man finds himself in a situation where interpretability itself is at stake, he turns to his "ultimate" cultural system to find an explanation. Religion, in other words, is man's world view. "What sacred symbols do for those to whom they are sacred is to formulate the image of the world's construction and to program for human conduct.". . . . "A people's world-view is their picture of the way things in sheer actuality are—a concept of nature, of self, and of society. It contains their most comprehensive idea of order. Religious belief and ritual confront and mutually confirm one another. An ethos is made intellectually reasonable by being shown to represent a way of life. The world view is made emotionally acceptable by being presented as an image of an actual state of affairs of which such a way of life is an authentic expression."[1]

Geertz's frame of reference is essentially Weberian. In the Durkheimian tradition, religion is seen both as the source and the result of community ties. It is the feeling of the bonds of community which gives rise to the religious experience, and it is religion through which the society interprets and defines itself. Writers after Durkheim saw religion reintegrating the community in time of crisis (for example, Malinowski's analysis of piacular rites as reintegrating a society in time of death) and as providing social location and self-definition in the midst of a complex industrial society. (Will Herberg's development of this theme has become almost classic.) More recently, Thomas Luckman has pointed out that one feels the need of an "interpretive scheme" precisely in the act of discovering oneself as different "over against" others; but the interpretive scheme is both learned from others—as part of the early socialization experience—and makes possible social behavior with others.

Authors writing from such diverse perspectives as Mircea Eliade and Edward Shils have pointed out that religious rituals are a means of establishing contact with the "really real"; that is to say, the basic order of things which underpins the universe. Shils is quite explicit about the place of the sacred in the human condition.

> This I regard as given in the constitution of man in the same way that cognitive powers or locomotive powers are given. Like those, they are unevenly given and unevenly cultivated, so that the sense of the *"serieuse,"* the need for contact with the charismatic or sacred values, differs markedly among human beings within any society. Some persons, a minority, tend to have it to a pronounced degree and even relatively continuously; others, far more numerous, will experience it only intermittently and, except rarely, without great intensity. Finally, there is a minority which is utterly opaque to the *"serieuse."*[2]

Although relatively little has been written about the relationship of religion and ethics, it is implicit in the notion that religion is a "cultural system" or an "interpretive scheme" that religion also provides ethical meaning for life. Geertz has made the link explicit. Religion, according to him, is the "struggle for the real." It is rooted in the "insufficiency of common sense as a total orientation towards life . . . the events through which we live are forever outrunning the power of our every day moral, emotional and intellectual concepts to construe them, leaving us as a Javanese image has put it, 'like water buffalo listening to an orchestra.'"[3] And he adds: "The force of religion in supporting social values rests on the ability of its symbols to formulate a world-view in which those values as well as the forces opposing the realization are fundamental ingredients."[4] The "ethos," then, and the "world-view" are different sides of the same coin. The world-view tells us the way things really are and the ethos, how we must live to be in harmony with the way things really are.

One cannot in the present state of research on the new occult phenomenon describe with any absolute certainty the functions that the new interest in the sacred plays in the life of the devout and the initiate. One can observe that the young people who are involved strongly assert that their sacred, mystical, or occult interests do indeed provide them with meaning, with community, with a contact with the transcendent, and with norms by which to live. Indeed, they are quite explicit in contending that they have turned to or returned to the sacred precisely because the scientific, technological society has failed to provide them with faith, community, transcendence, and morality. If what they are engaging in is not a more or less authentic form of religious behavior, one wonders what kind of behavior would be acknowledged as authentically religious.

Those members of the political new left who are not yet "into" the neo-sacral seem to share the viewpoint of the neosacralists. Thus, Roszak's "counterculture" and Schaar's "new leadership" both assume that the hyperrationalism of positive and empiricist science has dehumanized the human being and human societies and that only a return to knowledge which embraces human skills in addition to abstract rationalization will save the race from destruction. Schaar's description of how a political leader ought to behave if the "rational" and "objective" mode of cognition is abandoned is strikingly religious.

> Humanly significant leadership bases its claim to authority on a kind of knowledge which includes intuition, insight, and vision as indispensable elements. The leader strives to grasp and to communicate the essence of a situation in one organic and comprehensive conception. He conjoins elements which the analytic mind keeps tidily separate. He unites the normative with the empirical, and promiscuously mixes both with the moral and esthetic. The radical distinction between subjective and objective is unknown in this kind of knowledge, for everything is personal and comes from within the prepared consciousness of the knower, who is simultaneously believer and actor. When it is about men, this kind of knowledge is again personal. It strives to see within the self and along with other selves. It is knowledge of character and destiny. . . .
>
> The language in which the knowledge appropriate to humanly significant leadership is expressed is also very different from the language profuse in illustration and anecdote, and rich in metaphor whose sources are the human body and the dramas of action and responsibility. This language is suggestive and alluring, pregnant, evocative—in all ways the opposite of the linear, constricted, jargonized discourse which is the ideal of objective communication. Decisions and recommendations are often expressed in parables and visions whose meanings are hidden to outsiders but translucent to those who have eyes to see. Teaching in this language is done mainly by story, example, and metaphor—modes of discourse which can probe depths of personal being inaccessible to objective and managerial discourse. Compare the Sermon on the Mount with the latest communique from the Office of Economic Opportunity in the War on Poverty, or Lincoln's Second Inaugural with Nixon's first.[5]

The argument of Schaar—and many of his fellow critics from the new left—seems to be that "not by reason alone doth man live." If man must have something beyond reason, then he comes dangerously close to needing something that traditionally would be called "faith"; and this is precisely what the colleagues of the new left in the new sacred movement would have us believe.

Will, the new cult of the occult survive? Perhaps in the final analysis it will depend upon how deep, how pervasive, and how permanent is the alienation of a substantial segment of the population from what they take to be the scientific and technological society. If a sufficient number do continue to be convinced that the nonrational or the transrational, or even the irrational, are an essential part of human living, then the sacred in one form or another is going to be with us for a long time to come.

The sociologist of religion ought not to be surprised; for while on the one hand he may be inclined to accept a long-range strain toward secularization, he knows his Weber and Durkheim well enough to be skeptical about man's capacity to do without faith and the sacred. While he may be somewhat startled by the vigor and variety of the new sacred manifestations, he realizes on reflection that Max Weber probably would not be at all surprised, and Emile Durkheim would even clap his hands and say, "I told you so." There will always be religion.

Or, to put the matter somewhat more abstractly, a simple, unidirectional model of religious evolution from the sacred to the secular is not able to cope with the new sacred among upper middle-class young people. Furthermore, a more sophisticated model based in part on the Weberian notion of man as a meaning-seeking animal and the Durkheimian notion of man as a community-creating animal has no difficulty in coping with the new sacred—not, at least, after the first shock on hearing of the existence of a witchcraft coven in the apartment next door.[6]

But while the sociologist of religion will not be completely taken aback by the resurgence of the sacred among the younger generation, he is, nonetheless, presented with something of a problem, a problem which neither Durkheim nor Weber were able to resolve. If the sociologist of religion is an agnostic—as the two masters were—he is caught in the somewhat ambiguous position of arguing that society needs religion—or that man needs ultimate meaning—while simultaneously asserting that he himself and most of his academic colleagues need neither religion nor meaning. Religion and the sacred are part of the human condition, but they are also a part of the human condition from which the academic considers himself exempt. He is more than somewhat dismayed that some of his students do not wish to avail themselves of such exemptions and, indeed, are on occasion wont to imply that he is somehow or other less than human himself because he has taken the exemption.

NOTES

1. Clifford Geertz, "Ethos, World View, and the Analysis of Sacred Symbols," *Antioch Review* (December, 1957) p. 426.

2. Edward Shils, "Ritual in Crisis," in Donald R. Cutler, ed., *The Religious Situation*, Boston: Beacon Press, 1968, p. 747.

3. Clifford Geertz, *Islam Observed*, New Haven, Conn.: Yale University Press, 1969, p. 101.

4. *Ibid.*, p. 426.

5. John H. Schaar, "Reflections on Authority," *New American Review*, **8** (1970), 75–77, 78.

6. A student of mine descended upon my office last fall to announce that he had been in contact with the devil. A normally sober, responsible, industrious, Methodist-turned-agnostic, the young man was visibly shaken by his experience with the diabolic. He and some of his friends had engaged in an emotionally supercharged bout with a ouija board on Halloween night and became persuaded that the devil had taken charge of the board. As my young friend pointed out, the board knew answers to questions that nobody in the room could possibly have known. For example, the board was able to tell the assembled group the year of Plato's birth and, as my friend pointed out, he was only three years off. (What kind of a devil it is who would make a mistake was an issue I did not raise with him.) I asked him what he had done with the board and he said that he and his friends had been so terrified by the experience that they brought the board to a local Roman Catholic rectory where the priest had sprinkled it with holy water and told them to break it into many different pieces and put each piece in a separate garbage can. Having some familiarity with the staff at that rectory, I can imagine that the story provided much suppertime amusement for several days afterward. The young man promised to bring me tape recordings of the Halloween interlude with the devil (and what kind of a devil would it be that would permit himself to be tape-recorded?), but returned the next day to say that his friend who had been keeping the tapes became terrified of the possibility that the devil might "adhere" in them, and had burned them. All of this at the University of Chicago!

Andrew M. Greeley and
William C. McCready

Some Notes on the Sociological Study of Mysticism

The capitol building of American social science may indeed be named after William James, although it is dubious that any of the departments housed in that flittering white skyscraper would provide Professor James with a tenure appointment should be reappear on Kirkland Street seeking admission. For when the faculty committee heard that Professor James was interested in "religious experience" and especially "mystical ecstasy" they would have shaken their heads sadly and suggested that he might better seek out some psychology department at a lesser university that was concerned with ESP and "that sort of thing." It may be all right for historians of religion like Mircea Eliade or certain anthropologists like I. M. Lewis to be interested in mystical ecstasy if they specialize in archaic or primitive cultures.[1] It is all right for an anthropologist like Lewis to say, "Belief, ritual, and spiritual experience: these are the cornerstones of religion, and the greatest of them is the last."[2] But American sociologists and psychologists can scarcely be expected to take

303

mysticism seriously. Such things don't happen anymore in enlightened urban industrial society. Abraham Maslow[3] may have written about "peak experiences," but in his final years he wandered "far to the fringes anyhow." And while the drug-induced ecstasies of the counterculture may have some interest as a form of social deviance, American social researchers simply dismiss as unthinkable the possibility that ecstatic experiences take place in "square" society. What's the point of studying something that doesn't exist?

Some psychiatrists have been concerned with the phenomenon. Prince and Savage[4] suggest that mystical experience is "like" regression. Kenneth Wapnick[5] observes that mysticism is "like" schizophrenia; and R. D. Laing[6] seems to say that transcendental experience is a form of schizophrenic behavior. Such exercises in labeling are scarcely satisfying as explanations. To say that mysticism is "like" regression or "like" schizophrenia is not to say that it is the same thing, and the various psychiatrists who have made these comparisons cheerfully admit that the mystic is not a schizophrenic or a regressed neurotic.

The conditioned reflex of many social scientists when someone raises the subject of mystical ecstasy or confronts them with a person who has had such an experience is to fall back on psychoanalytic interpretations. The ecstatic is some sort of disturbed person who is working out a personality problem acquired in childhood. That settles the issue in most instances. They "know" that the ecstatic episode is in fact some sort of psychotic interlude. With that as a basic premise, it is easy to prove that a given interlude was indeed psychotic because all mystical experiences are. Why then investigate such behavior phenomena as anything more or less than psychotic?

Two types of research evidence call into question this facile circular reasoning. First of all, it would seem that ecstatic experiences are far more common than has been supposed. Maslow suggests that large numbers of people have such experiences and that, perhaps, indeed everyone does. Mortimer Lieberman, in his as yet unpublished research, reports that 50 percent of a sample of college students he studied reported some sort of ecstatic experience, half of them without the assistance of drugs. In a pretest of items for a national sample, the authors discovered that about half of the respondents had some kind of ecstatic experience in the course of their lives.[7] Finally, Bourque and Back have used national sample data collected by the Gallup organization to document the prevalence and increase in mystical experiences within the American population.[8] The following question was asked in three Gallup polls, in 1962, 1966, and 1967: "Would you say that you have ever had a religious or mystical experience—that is, a moment of sudden religious insight or awakening?" In 1962, 21 percent of the sample answered Yes. In 1966, it was 32 percent. By 1967, 41 percent of the population could answer Yes. Bourque and Back conclude that these feelings cannot be measured by surveys alone, but it is clear that the incidence is increasing over time.

Secondly, the research done by Maslow and Lieberman offers no evidence that those who had ecstatic experiences were any more "mentally disturbed" than anyone else in society. Indeed, Maslow's subjects who had "peak experiences" reported them to be extraordinary, positive, and constructive—which is what most of the mystics of the past have said. Mystical experiences may indeed be deviant behavior in the statistical sense, and from certain philosophical perspectives they may even be considered aberrant behavior; but there is nothing available in the research literature that justifies equating the mystic with the neurotic or the psychotic.

We are speaking here of mysticism in the strict sense of the word. We are excluding from consideration such phenomena as astrology, witchcraft, divination, satanism, and the other recently rediscovered forms of religious superstition that occupy so much space on the paperback bookracks. We also exclude such forms of expanded consciousness as visceral control and trance-induced learning. The question of whether there is any difference between the so-called "natural" ecstasy and drug-induced ecstasy is likewise excluded from our discussion. We will simply assume for our present purposes that drugs may on some occasions trigger an ecstatic experience. We will suspend judgment on how this happens and whether it will happen, and whether every drug trip can be expected to result in an ecstatic experience. Two quotations from very different sources will illustrate the kind of mystical experience that primarily concerns us here. The first is cited in William James', *The Varieties of Religious Experience.* James quotes a clergyman:

> "I remember the night, and almost the very spot on the hilltop, where my soul opened out, as it were, into the Infinite, and there was a rushing together of the two worlds, the inner and outer. It was deep calling unto deep,—the deep that my own struggle had opened up within being answered by the unfathomable deep without, reaching beyond the stars. I stood alone with Him who had made me, and all the beauty of the world, and Love, and sorrow, and even temptation. I did not seek Him, but felt the perfect unison of my spirit with His. The ordinary sense of things around me faded. For the moment nothing but an ineffable joy and exaltation remained. It is impossible fully to describe the experience. It was like the effect of some great orchestra when all the separate notes have melted into one swelling harmony that

leaves the listener conscious of nothing save that his soul is being wafted
upwards, and almost bursting with its own emotion. The perfect stillness of
the night was thrilled by a more solemn silence. The darkness held a presence
that was all the more felt because it was not seen. I could not any more have
doubted that *He* was there than that I was. Indeed, I felt myself to be, if
possible, the less real of the two."[9]

The second is the opening paragraph of *The Fire of Love* by Richard Rolle,
a fourteenth-century English ecstatic and poet:

I cannot tell you how surprised I was the first time I felt my heart begin to
warm. It was real warmth too, not imaginary, and it felt as if it were actually
on fire. I was astonished at the way the heat surged up, and how this new
sensation brought great and unexpected comfort. I had to keep feeling my
breast to make sure there was no physical reason for it! But once I realized
that it came entirely from within, that this fire of love had no cause, material
or sinful, but was the gift of my Maker, I was absolutely delighted, and
wanted my love to be even greater. And this longing was all the more urgent
because of the delightful effect and the interior sweetness which this spiritual
flame fed into my soul. Before the infusion of this comfort I had never
thought that we exiles could possibly have known such warmth, so sweet was
the devotion it kindled. It set my soul aglow as if a real fire was burning
there.[10]

James describes four characteristics of such interludes:

1. *Ineffability.* . . . The subject of it immediately says that it defies
expression, that no adequate report of its contents can be given in words. It
follows from this that its quality must be directly experienced; it cannot be
imparted or transferred to others. . . .

2. *Noetic quality.* . . . mystical states seem to those who experience them
to be also states of knowledge. They are states of insight into depths of truth
unplumbed by discursive intellect. They are illuminations, revelations, full of
significance and importance, all inarticulate though they remain; and as a
rule they carry with them a curious sense of authority for after-time. . . .

3. *Transiency.*—Mystical states cannot be sustained for long. Except in
rare instances, half an hour, or at most an hour or two, seems to be the limit
beyond which they fade into the light of common day. Often, when faded,
their quality can but imperfectly be reproduced in memory; but when they
recur it is recognized; and from one recurrence to another it is susceptible of
continuous development in what is felt as inner richness and importance.[11]

4. *Passivity.*—Although the oncoming of mystical states may be facilitated
by preliminary voluntary operations, as by fixing the attention, or going
through certain bodily performances, or in other ways which manuals of

mysticism prescribe; yet when the characteristic sort of consciousness once has set in, the mystic feels as if his own will were in abeyance, and indeed sometimes as if he were grasped and held by a superior power.[12]

Richard Bucke tells us that the "person, suddenly, without warning, has a sense of being immersed in a flame, or rose-colored cloud,[13] or perhaps rather a sense that the mind is itself filled with such a cloud of haze."[14] Bucke, who was describing the kind of experience he had, adds that the mystic is "bathed in an emotion of joy, assurance, triumph, 'salvation.' "[15] He experiences "an intellectual illumination quite impossible to describe";[16] a sense of immortality possesses him; and the fear of death simply vanishes, as does the sense of sin. Bucke stresses "the instantaneousness of the illumination. . . . It can be compared to a dazzling flash of lightning in a dark night, bringing the landscape which had been hidden into clear view."[17] Also it adds "charm to the personality." Finally, the experience illuminates for the ecstatic "(1) that the universe is not a dead machine but a living presence; (2) that in its essence and tendency it is infinitely good; (3) that individual existence is continuous beyond what is called death."[18]

Abraham Maslow was scarcely less lyrical in his description of "core-religious" experiences: ". . . it is quite characteristic in peak-experiences that the whole universe is perceived as an integrated and unified whole."[19] He reports, ". . . two subjects who, because of such an experience, were totally, immediately, and permanently cured of [in one case] chronic anxiety neurosis and, in the other case, of strong obsessional thoughts of suicide."[20] "The peak-experience is felt as a self-validating, self-justifying moment which carries its own intrinsic value with it."[21] The world is seen in the peak-experience "only as beautiful, good, desirable, worthwhile, etc. and is never experienced as evil or undesirable."[22] There scarcely seems to be a positive human emotion that does not break through in the peak-experience:

> In the peak-experience, such emotions as wonder, awe, reverence, humility, surrender, and even worship before the greatness of the experience are often reported. This may go so far as to involve thoughts of death in a peculiar way. Peak-experiences can be so wonderful that they can parallel the experience of dying, that is of an eager and happy dying. It is a kind of reconciliation and acceptance of death. . . .
>
> In peak-experiences, the dichotomies, polarities, and conflicts of life tend to be transcended or resolved. That is to say, there tends to be a moving toward the perception of unity and integration in the world. The person himself tends to move toward fusion, integration, and unity and away from splitting, conflicts, and oppositions.

> In the peak-experiences, there tends to be a loss, even though transient, of fear, anxiety, inhibition, of defense and control, of perplexity, confusion, conflict, of delay and restraint. The profound fear of disintegration, of insanity, of death, all tend to disappear for the moment. Perhaps this amounts to saying that fear disappears.[23]

Maslow tells us that "The peak-experiencer becomes more loving and more accepting, and so he becomes more spontaneous and honest and innocent."[24] He is also "closer to non-striving, non-needing, non-wishing . . . "[25] Finally, the ecstatic has a "feeling of gratitude or all-embracing love for everybody and for everything, leading to an impulse to do something good for the world, an eagerness to repay, even a sense of obligation and dedication."[26]

Maslow's position ought not to be dismissed as the product of an aging psychologist who had grown ecstatic over ecstasy in his final years. One must give some consideration to the thought that his observations were valid and perceptive, a position reinforced by the fact that the mystics themselves and serious students of mysticism like William James say practically the same things that Maslow does. His writings ought to be the source of testable hypotheses to be taken seriously by social researchers who are not part of the psychedelic revolution or the counterculture. To be blunt about it, there is no good reason why Maslow's insights should be left in the hands of those who mainline sociologists would write off as "freaks."

Marghanita Laski is one of the few authors who has tried to do empirical research with those who have had mystical experiences. While her sample is not representative (it consisted of friends and acquaintances), and while her questions were simple,[27] her research is one of the earliest efforts we have presently available. It provides raw materials with which more sophisticated, systematic researchers must begin. It might be remarked, incidentally, that Laski's respondents described their experiences in much the same terms as have mystics of the past—including Richard Rolle and those cited by William James: "a new life," "joy," "knowledge," "unity," feelings of being drawn up, "fire," "light," "peace." Her Table 4b indicates that midtwentieth-century ecstasy seems to have much in common with Richard Rolle, Teresa of Avila, and John of the Cross.[28]

Laski also investigated the "triggers" of mystical experience.[29]

Art, religion, nature, childbirth, and sexual love seem to be the most frequent triggers, with sexual love being more frequent for nonbelievers than for Christians. (Laski suggests that traditional Christian suspicion of sexuality may be responsible for the difference, though surely the great mystics of the

Christian tradition did not hestitate to use sexual imagery to describe the nature of what had happened to them.) However, those respondents who said that sexual love had triggered the ecstatic experience insisted that the mystical interlude was something decisively and categorically different from the pleasure of intercourse.

Laski's respondents, like Maslow's, Lieberman's, Bourque and Back's, and the ones in our own pretest sample, seem to be ordinary human beings, leading reasonably commonplace lives. Many are not believing Christians. They report experiences similar to those that happened in the so-called "age of faith," those that happened in primitive tribes, and those that even today in many oriental religions would be considered simply the primary goal of all religious activity. Surely these people deserve more from social scientists than a casual dismissal as quasi-schizophrenics.

Mircea Eliade, attempting to draw together evidence from such disparate sources as yoga, psychoanalysis, tribal shamanism, and Christian mysticism, suggests that the ecstatic is engaged in a quest to reestablish a paradisal unity of all things:

> The imitation of the cries of animals by the shamans, which has not failed to impress observers, and which ethnologists have often supposed to be the manifestation of a pathological *possession,* actually betokens the desire to recover friendship with the animals and thus enter into the primordial Paradise. The ecstatic trance, whatever its phenomenology may be, only appears as an aberration if we lose sight of its spiritual significance. In reality, as we saw, the shaman tries to re-establish the communications between Earth and Heaven that were interrupted by "the Fall." The mastery of fire, too, is no mere superstition of savages; on the contrary, it is a demonstration that the shaman partakes of the nature of *spirits.*[30]

In the ecstatic experience, then, the boundaries between the individual self and the rest of the world are temporarily lowered or even eliminated, and reality (both upper and lower case) is experienced as rushing in and taking possession. Prince and Savage see this as a form of regression to a childhood period of development in which distinctions between self and world are vague or nonexistent.[31] They even suggest that the ecstasy is a reexperiencing of the unity with the mother that takes place while nursing at the breast. As evidence they cite—an association that only psychiatrists could be capable of—the fact that the mandala, which is frequently used in the Orient to induce meditative states as a prelude to ecstasy, can be considered to represent the female breast.

But why does one need to postulate a regression into childhood or infancy?

If we distinguish between our own "self" and the rest of the cosmos after we have acquired our own sense of individuation, it does not follow that the boundaries between self and the rest of reality are impermeable. We humans are inextricably caught up in the physical, chemical, and biological processes of the universe. We swim in an ocean of air, held by gravity to the planet earth and sustained in life by oxygen, carbon, and nitrogen cycles. We are indeed distinct from everything else, but only up to a point; and those psychiatrists who seem to think that an experience of profound awareness of how much one is involved in the natural processes is a regression to childhood have apparently come to think of themselves as archangels who live quite independently of the life processes of the universe.

Instead of describing the ecstatic as someone still suckling at his mother's breast, we might be better advised to take him at his own word. As Eliade says:

> Yet if one takes the trouble to understand the ideology that underlies all these manifestations, if we study the myths and symbols that condition them, we can free ourselves from the subjectivity of impressions and obtain a more objective view. Sometimes an understanding of the ideology is enough to re-establish the "normality" of a kind of behavior. To recall just one example: the imitation of the animals' cries. For more than a century it was thought that the strange cries of the shaman were a proof of his mental disequilibrium. But they were signs of something very different: of the nostalgia for Paradise which had haunted Isaiah and Virgil, which had nourished the saintliness of the Fathers of the Church, and that blossomed anew, victorious, in the life of St. Francis of Assisi.[32]

The ecstatic claims that he has experienced a special kind of illumination, a passive knowing in which the union between the object known and the knowing subject is immediate in the sense that there are no propositions or even mythopoetic symbols that stand between the subject and the object. The mystic experiences himself as part of the universe, which, incidentally, he is. He experiences the underlying forces of the universe as flowing through him, which, incidentally, they do. Would it not be sensible to take him at his word and try to discover both what the mechanisms of that knowledge are and what are its cultural and structural implications and consequences? A nondogmatic and expansive social science would surely proceed in this direction, rather than standing on the position that such knowledge is impossible as some have done.

The sociologist is not a specialist in the modes of human perception. He must choose between those specialists in human perception who say that mystical knowledge is possible and those who say it is not. If he chooses to take the mystics seriously, then he can proceed to investigate the structural and cultural correlates of ecstatic experience—or, so as not to offend those who say that such experiences are impossible—at least the social, structural, and cultural correlates of *reports* of ecstatic experiences. The sociologist can assume that it is possible for humans to have a capacity for intuitive, co-natural contact with the world in which they are immersed without needing the inter-mediaries of symbols or prosaic propositions. The sociologist can further assume that thus far perceptual psychology has been either unwilling or unable to discover very much about how this particular kind of co-natural knowing takes place. He can assume that like all other human capabilities, this particular one is unevenly distributed in the population. Many humans have virtually no capacity for mystical knowledge. In others the capacity is so strong that it seems to dominate their lives, and in yet others the capacity is actualized occasionally, frequently, or only once or twice. Finally, the sociologist can assume until the contrary is proven, that the mystics are sensible, rational people who are not mentally ill and who are describing as best they can something they have really experienced. Taking them at their word, the sociologist can wonder what are the correlates and consequences of such experiences.[33] We would suggest, then, that social scientists ought to become seriously concerned with the prevalence, the correlates, and the consequence of ecstatic experience in contemporary Western urban society, with particular emphasis on that very substantial number of ecstatics who have had mystical interludes without the assistance of drugs or without any kind of deliberate preparation at all.

A number of basic questions must be asked.[34] First, one must continue the inquiry into the prevalence and frequency of mystical experiences which has been started by researchers like Bourque and Back. In our own immediate network of relationships we have uncovered three mystics. One of them has had frequent experiences, though apparently at a fairly low level of intensity; another has had only one experience, but that was extraordinarily intense and has profoundly affected the course of her life; the third has apparently had "frequent and intense experiences." We hasten to add that all three are healthy, normally functioning individuals, living "ordinary" middle-class lives. They may be a little bit happier and more creative than others of their age and social class, but one would have to know the three of them quite well to perceive anything "different" or "unusual" about them. Finally, when one does discover that they are different, they are not perceived as less attractive but rather more so. In each of the three cases the person did not raise the question of his or her mystical experience but was ready enough to talk about it when we did. In two of the three cases the respondents had read none of the literature on ecstasy and were not even sure that the experiences they had could be described as ecstatic much less mystical, but mystical they surely were, even to the extent of the rose-colored or blue-colored hazy light.

Building on the work of previous researchers, we will document how widespread and how frequent ecstatic experiences are and what different varieties there are of them. The data reported by Bourque and Back would indicate that mysticism is becoming more prevalent, perhaps as a concomitant of greater social acceptance. Perhaps we will be measuring the willingness or the facility of the respondent to report ecstasy. Bourque and Back report an interesting finding relating to the ability of some people to tell others about what they have experienced.[35]

They hypothesize that there are at least two varieties of ecstatic experiences, the religious and the aesthetic. In one report they document that 47 percent of their sample answered the aesthetic question affirmatively, 32 percent answered the religious question affirmatively, and 22 percent answered both affirmatively.[36] They further hypothesize that the difference between these respondents is the language they have available to them for describing the experience. Most people referred to the aesthetic language. Those who had both the aesthetic and religious available to them, however, chose religious. This led the researchers to conclude that the experiences were the same, the respondents and their abilities to describe what happened differed.

To facilitate the use of these baselines and the replication of such measurements on different populations and at different times in the future, we are attaching, as an appendix to this chapter, the questions being used in our own national sample survey. Hopefully, some will be used by future researchers.

In particular, we wish to explore the so-called "dark nights" aspects of repeated ecstatic experiences. The habitual ecstatic has higher peaks and lower depths of experience than seem to be "normal" in the human condition. John of the Cross did ascend Mt. Carmel, but he also went down into the dark night. There is some evidence in Laski's research of experiences of "loneliness" or "deprivation." The mystical writers of the Christian tradition frequently describe their desires to escape from the "romance" in which they are caught, and there are, apparently, times with the habitual ecstatic when the alternation between peaks and valleys becomes a heavy burden. The "dark night" phenomenon is almost universally ignored in the counterculture and in the literature on mysticism. Yet one contemporary mystic poet resonates with the mystic tradition of the past when he describes in a poem the ambivalence and the reluctance of the mystic: "God damn it, Lord, is it you again?"

The most obvious questions to ask are about the "background variables" of mystical experience.[37] What correlations, if any, exist between mysticism or various varieties of mystical experience on the one hand and religion, social class, education, age, occupation, ethnic background, region of the country on the other hand? Are there certain fundamental world views (or "interpretive schemes" to use Luckmann's words or "cultural systems" to use Geertz's) that are more likely to predispose some people to mystical episodes? Are there experiences in childhood, adolescence or young adulthood that facilitate or impede the development of mystical capabilities? In a study of Catholic priets in the United States conducted by the National Opinion Research Center it was discovered that there was −.20 correlation between family tension during childhood and "religious" experience in adult life.[38] One might hypothesize that a relatively benign family environment encourages a kind of primordial and fundamental hopefulness or trust which in turn are both reinforced and represented in the almost incredible hopefulness which marks most if not all mystical interludes described in the literature.

One would want to know not only what triggers each interlude but also its social and cultural context. What are the situations which facilitate the operation of a mystical capacity and what are those that impede it? What are its special "functions" and what dysfunctions does it have? How does society "use" the mystic, and how does he "use" society?

I. M. Lewis addresses himself to these quintessentially sociological questions in his book, *Ecstatic Religion*.[39] His literary style, like many other British anthropologists, is charming and urbane but elusive and elliptical and very hard to understand if you haven't been trained in the same kind of schools in which he was trained. After a careful reading of his book, one may conclude with its author that mysticism does indeed have certain functions and that these functions vary from society to society, but such a conclusion is limited in its ability to further the sociological understanding of mysticism.

Of particular interest is the immediate personal context in which an ecstatic finds himself. Will his own interpersonal environment provide support, sympathy, reinforcement, and understanding or will it be hostile and suspicious? It seems to us possible that the power of the ecstatic experience as it has been described in the literature is such that a person who has had a particularly intense ecstatic experience in an unsupportive and suspicious interpersonal context can have a severe and depressing reaction. If a person is told he's a "nut" or "crazy" for having such an interlude, could he not in fact become mentally disturbed within that context of conflict and denigration?

In one case which came to our attention, a young woman who had an extraordinarily intense mystical episode was saved from the severe depression an extremely hostile reaction to her enthusiasm would have caused had her husband, a sensible, stolid man whose religious upbringing and Jesuit secondary school training prepared him to take for granted the possibility of ecstatic phenomena, not intervened. In a quite calm and matter-of-fact voice he observed, "Oh, sure, my wife is a mystic. I don't mind; it's a good thing. I just wish there was somebody to cook my supper until she calms down." This combination of acceptance on the one hand and firm grip on the reality of daily life on the other prevented his wife's experience from becoming a psychic disaster. Indeed, it enabled her to convert it into a positive growth-producing event in her life.

We must also examine the possibility that in the proper context and under the proper circumstances, ecstatic experiences can be extraordinarily functional for human personality development and mental health. In other words, we must take Maslow's hypotheses seriously and subject them to empirical test. With all pertinent background variables standardized, is the ecstatic less authoritarian, less racist, more trusting, more open, more "self-actualizing," more likely to report high psychological wellbeing, more tolerant of diversity, and perhaps even more inclined to loose rather than rigid sexual role definitions? Far from being "some kind of nut," it may be possible that the ecstatic is among the healthiest and most "normal" of humans. It may even be—as the religions of the East have insisted—that under some circumstances, ecstasy can be induced with the precise purpose of facilitating personality development.

We are not asserting that mystical ecstasy is necessarily a means of mental health, as do those who are so enthusiastic about drug-induced mysticism. We merely say that it is a question that lends itself to research, and it is time to begin that research soberly and seriously with all the appropriate methodological skills and restrictions. The subject should not be left in the hands of counterculture enthusiasts.[40] The methodology by which such research can be carried out will differ according to the skills and the tastes of the researchers. Our own strategy involves three phases.

(1) At the present time we are collecting data in a national study of basic belief systems in the United States from a sample size of 1,500.[41] The questions appended to this essay will be asked of all respondents. We expect that at

least 200 persons will fall into the "mystic" category. A detailed analysis of the background variables and of the present attitude and behavior of this subsample will be undertaken.

(2) If we can persuade an appropriate funding agency that there is a correlation between ecstatic experience and positive psychological health—as Maslow argues—we will then undertake a massive national "screening" project to collect a sample of 1,000 respondents who have had mystical experiences. On the basis of the analysis to be undertaken in phase 1 (which will be in effect secondary analysis of data collected for another purpose), we will compile a detailed questionnaire to measure the background, personality, attitudes, and behavior of those being interviewed.

(3) Finally, a team of clinical psychologists will interview the subsample of 1,000 mystics (perhaps 200–250) who have been chosen either because of the frequency or the intensity of their ecstatic experiences or because the relationship between their mysticism and the development of their personalities seems to offer promise of extraordinarily valuable insights into the positive potential of the mystical experience.

There are obviously a number of serious objections to such a strategy. How dare we reduce the experiences of Meister Eckhardt, Francis of Assisi or Teilhard de Chardin to questions of positive mental health? Or to questions of personality growth? Or success of human functioning? Is not the enterprise that we describe almost a caricature of social scientific behaviorism? Is it not ludicrous to think that questionnaires, IBM cards, and computer outputs can deal adequately with human experience of direct and immediate contact with the Really Real?

By definition the mystical experience is ineffable. Words are inadequate to describe it. Even the most dazzling poetry is apparently incapable of conveying what it is like. Electronic impulses on computer tape are not meant to be adequate descriptions of an ecstatic interlude. All they are is a useful tool for trying to understand a little bit better some of the aspects of the ecstatic experience. A particular advantage of using a rather rigid behaviorist approach to the study of mysticism is that it meets the behaviorist skeptics on their own ground with their own techniques. It is with their own tools and their own skills that the behaviorist's dogmatism can be exposed.

We concede that there is a certain element of folly in pursuing this kind of enterprise. However, we believe that it is only through such speculative and carefully delimited follies that new and important areas can be opened to social research. If no one engages in unusual or bizarre research enterprises, then nothing new or exciting will ever be done. The risk of failure is high; one would be much safer to develop a neat multiple regression model that explains social mobility. Many a successful academic career has been built on such research. A study of mysticism that ends up with no correlation over .1 bodes professional disaster.

But, if one can derive a multiple regression, path model to explain ecstasy, one will really rock the profession on its heels. It seems to us that that would be a useful and even gracious service to perform.

Sociology has prided itself on its courage in studying social deviancy. Homosexuals, lesbians, transvestites, prostitutes, drug addicts, prison and asylum inmates—all have been carefully, respectfully, and sympathetically studied. Heaven knows (one should excuse the expression) that the ecstatic is a deviant in contemporary society—though if one is to take him at his self-description or to consider seriously Abraham Maslow's description of him, a deviant whose only offense is to shake the faith of devout agnostics and behaviorists. The rubric which allows us to view the psychopath or sociopath sympathetically and objectively ought to allow us to take the ecstatic seriously and investigate the social, cultural, and structural contexts in which he finds himself. To do so might be to open a Pandora's box, but presumably that's what serious social research is supposed to do.

Richard Rolle described what he found in that Pandora's box:

O honeyed flame, sweeter than all sweet, delightful beyond all creation!
My God, my Love, surge over me, pierce me by your love, wound me with your beauty.
Surge over me, I say, who am longing for your comfort.
Reveal your healing medicine to your poor lover.
See, my one desire is for you; it is you my heart is seeking.
My soul pants for you; my whole being is athirst for you.
Yet you will not show yourself to me; you will look away; you bar the door, shun me, pass me over;
You even laugh at my innocent sufferings.
And yet you snatch your lovers away from all earthly things.
You life them above every desire for wordly matters.
You make them capable of loving you—and love you they do indeed.
So they offer you their praise in spiritual song which bursts out from that inner fire; they know in truth the sweetness of the dart of love.
Ah, eternal and most lovable of all joys.
   you raise us from every depth,
   and entrance us with the sight of divine majesty
   so often!

Come into me, Beloved!
All ever I had I have given up for you;
  I have spurned all that was to be mine,
  that you might make your home in my heart,
  and I your comfort.
Do not forsake me now, smitten with such great longing,
  whose consuming desire is to be amongst those who
  love you.
Grant me to love you,
  to rest in you,
  that in your kingdom I may be worthy
  to appear before you world without end.[42]

Obviously, Richard Rolle was "some kind of nut," working out his sexual frustrations.

"But what," as Tom Wolfe said of Marshall McLuhan, "if he was right?"

APPENDIX A

29. Now to something very different. With what frequency have you had any of the following experiences? READ AND CODE FOR EACH.

Hand respondent Card K

	Never in my life	Once or Twice	Several Times	Often	I cannot answer this Question
A. Thought you were somewhere you had been before, but knowing that it was impossible.	1	2	3	4	5
B. Felt as though you were in touch with someone when they were far away from you.	1	2	3	4	5
C. Seen events that happened at a great distance as they were happening.	1	2	3	4	5
D. Felt as though you were really in touch with someone who had died.	1	2	3	4	5
E. Felt as though you were very close to a powerful, spiritual force that seemed to lift you out of yourself?	1	2	3	4	5

ASK ONLY THOSE WHO ANSWER "E"; "once or twice; "several times;" often."

Many people who have had such experiences say that there are "triggers" or specific events that set them off. Have any of the following events ever started such an experience for you?

Hand the Respondent Card L.

The beauties of nature such as a sunset.
Watching little children.
Childbirth
Prayer
Reading the bible
Listening to a sermon
Sexual lovemaking
Your own creative work
Looking at a painting
Being alone in church
Listening to music
Reading a poem or a novel
Moments of quiet reflection
Attending a church service
Something else (describe)

30.B

Those who have had religious experiences have given various descriptions of what they were like. Here is a list [hand the respondent card M] of some of the things they say happen. Have any of them happened to you during any of your experiences? CODE AS MANY AS APPLY.

1. A feeling of a new life or of living in a new world.
2. A sense of the unity of everything and my own part in it.
3. An experience of great emotional intensity.
4. A great increase in my understanding or knowledge.
5. A feeling of deep and profound peace.
6. A sensation of warmth or fire.
7. A sense that I was being bathed in light.
8. A loss of concern about worldly problems.
9. A feeling that I couldn't possibly describe what is happening to me.
10. The sensation that my personality has been taken over by something much more powerful that I am.
11. A certainty that all things would work out for the good.
12. A confidence in my own personal survival.

13. A sense or tremendous personal expansion.
14. A conviction that love is at the center of everything.
15. A feeling of desolation.
16. A sense of being alone.
17. Something else (describe).

30. C

Approximately how long did your experience (s) [average time if more than one] last?

1. A few minutes or less.
2. Ten or fifteen minutes.
3. Half an hour.
4. An hour.
5. Several hours.
6. A day or more.

NOTES

1. See Mircea Eliade, *Myths, Dreams, and Mysteries,* New York: Harper and Row, 1960, and I. M. Lewis, *Ecstatic Religion,* Middlesex, England: Penguin Books, 1971. For an anthropological approach that abounds in undocumented judgments (one might even say Dogmatism), see Anthony F. C. Wallace, *Religion: An Anthropological View,* New York: Random House, 1966. Wallace tells us that the mystic has a "profound sense of dissatisfaction with [his] own secular identity, a feeling of anxiety or fear, a desperate sense of the need to be saved before being damned by some final disaster" (p. 152). He also says that religion "is doomed to die out as a result of the increasing adequacy and diffusions of scientific knowledge" (p. 265). Even in 1966, such confident, "scientific" faith must have seemed presumptuous to anyone who had read Emile Durkheim, Clifford Geertz, or Edward Shils.

2. I. M. Lewis, *op. cit.,* p. 11.

3. Abraham Maslow, *Religion, Values, and Peak Experience,* Columbus: University of Ohio Press, 1964.

4. Raymond Prince and Charles Savage, "Mystical States and the Concept of Regression," *Psychedelic Review,* **VIII** (1966).

5. Kenneth Wapnick, "Mysticism and Schizophrenia," *Journal of Trends in Personal Psychology,* **I, II** (Fall, 1969).

6. R. D. Laing, *The Politics of Experience,* Middlesex, England: Penguin Books, 1967.

7. M. Lieberman, yet to be published work from the Committee on Human Development at the University of Chicago.

8. L. B. Bourque and K. W. Back, "Can Feelings Be Enumerated?" *Behavioral Science,* **XV,** No. 6 (November, 1970).

9. William James, *The Varieties of Religious Experience* (New York: A Mentor Book, 1958), p. 67.

10. Richard Rolle, *The Fire of Love,* trans. into modern English by Clifton Wolters, Middlesex, England: Penguin Books, 1972, p. 45.

11. More recent research indicates that the ecstatic period itself may last for only a few moments—five minutes at the most. See Marghanita Laski, *Ecstasy,* Bloomington: University of Indiana Press, 1961.

12. William James, *op cit.,* pp. 292–293.

13. Mircea Eliade and some other writers describe the hazy cloud as blue.

14. Richard M. Bucke, "From Self to Cosmic Consciousness," in John White, ed., *The Highest State of Consciousness,* Garden City, N. Y.: Doubleday, 1972, p. 86.

15. *Ibid.,* p. 87.

16. *Ibid.*

17. *Ibid.,* p. 88–89.

18. *Ibid.,* p. 90.

19. Abraham Maslow, "The 'Core-Religious' or 'Transcendent' Experience" in White, *op. cit.,* p. 357.

20. *Ibid.*

21. *Ibid.,* p. 359.

22. *Ibid.,* p. 360.

23. *Ibid.,* p. 362.

24. *Ibid.,* p. 363.

25. *Ibid.*

26. *Ibid.,* p. 364.

27. The questions asked were: 1. Do you know a sensation of transcendent ecstasy? 2. How would you describe it? 3. What had induced it in you? 4. How many times have you felt it— in units, in tens, in hundreds? 5. What is your religion or faith? 6. Do you know a feeling of creative inspiration? 7. How would you describe it? 8. Does it seem to you to have anything in common with the ecstasy described above? 9. What is your profession?

28. *Table 4b.   Percentages of the Total Number of People (112) Reporting Certain Feelings*

Feelings	Number of people	Per Cent
New world/life, satisfaction, joy, salvation, glory	82	73
Knowledge by identification	76	68
New and/or mystical knowledge	61	54
Intensity	59	53
Loss of words/images, sense	57	51
Unity, eternity, heaven	56	50
Up-feelings	56	50
Contact	48	43
Loss of worldliness, desire, sorrow, sin	42	38
Enlargement, improvement	41	37
Loss of self	40	36
Inside-feelings	38	34
Loss of difference, time, place	29	26
Light/fire	28	25

Table 4b.   Continued

Feelings	Number of people	Per Cent
Peace, calm	27	24
Liquidity	26	23
Ineffability	24	21
Release	18	16
Pain	18	16
Withdrawal	10	9
Dark-feelings	4	4
Loss of limitation	3	3

SOURCE. Laski, *op. cit.,* Appendix D, pp. 488–489.

29. *Table 9.   Trigger Mentions of Christians and of Non-Believers*

The Christian group consists of all people in the questionnaire group who described themselves as Christian, no matter of what denomination; it does not include people who merely said that they believed in God. The non-believer group consists of all people in the questionnaire group who described themselves as atheists or agnostics or as having no faith or belief.

In the Christian group there are 16 people, five men and eleven women. In the non-believer group there are 32 people, eleven men and twenty-one women.

The entries for each heading are expressed as a percentage of all trigger mentions by that group.

Triggers	Non-believers		Christians	
	No.	Per cent	No.	Per cent
1. Nature	16	20.2	6	15.0
2. Sexual love	17	21.5	3	7.5
3. Childbirth	4	5.1	—	—
4. Exercise, movement	6	7.6	1	2.5
5. Religion	4	5.1	7	17.5
6. Art	14	17.7	12	30.0
7. a. Scientific knowledge	5	6.3	—	—
b. Poetic knowledge	1	1.3	1	2.5
8. Creative work	4	5.1	3	7.5
9. Recollection, introspection	2	2.5	—	—
10. 'Beauty'	2	2.5	3	7.5
11. Miscellaneous	4	5.1	4	10.0
Totals	79	100.0	40	100.0

SOURCE. Laski, *op. cit.,* Appendix D, p. 494.

30. Mircea Eliade, *Myths, Dreams, and Mysteries,* trans. by Philip Mairet (New York and Evanston: Harper & Row, Harper Torchbooks, 1967), pp. 71–72.

31. R. Prince and C. Savage, *op. cit.*

32. Eliade, *op. cit.,* p. 72.

33. It will be noted that our assumptions do not postulate the special intervention of some

external or transcendent deity. (In our own religious perspective, we would say that what
has happened is not the descent of a transcendent deity so much as the "breaking out" of an
imminent deity. For us the deity is both transcendent and imminent, and one falls back on
transcendence only when imminence is no longer adequate as a theological explanation.)

34. There is a poor fit between the time requirements of preparing this article for the volume in
which it will appear and the progress of our research. By the end of 1973, however, we hope
to be able to provide initial answers to at least some of the questions.

35. L. B. Bourque and K. W. Back, "Language, Society, and Subjective Experience,"
Sociometry, **XXXIV,** No. 1 (1971), 1–21.

36. L. B. Bourque and K. W. Back, "Social Correlates of Transcendental Experiences," *Sociological Analysis,* **XXX** (Fall, 1969), 151–163.

37. The authors of this essay are trained in the skills of survey research. Humanists,
psychologists, psychiatrists, drug freaks, and yoga and Zen enthusiasts (to say nothing of ecstatics themselves) will no doubt be extremely skeptical of the possibility of studying ecstasy
through the techniques of this primitive but stubborn discipline. We will, however, persist in
both our primitiveness and stubborness and contend that if one wants to know how many
mystics there are in the American population and what the background correlates of
mysticism are, the best way to begin is to conduct a national survey and ask people whether
they have had mystical experiences or not.

38. The questions which constituted a "religious experience" were: "An overwhelming feeling
of being at one with God or Christ; a sense of being in the presence of God; a deep feeling of
being personally loved by Christ here and now." *American Priests,* NORC Report, National
Opinion Research Center at the University of Chicago (March, 1971).

39. I. M. Lewis, *op. cit.*

40. Our guess at the present is that for personalities with a certain amount of stability, self-
possession, and integrity, the ecstatic experience with a proper context and with sympathetic
and understanding support is likely to be extraordinarily growth-producing. However, we
suspect that for weak and troubled personalities ecstasy, particularly if it is artificially induced, could be dangerous.

41. This study is being carried out at NORC under a grant from the Henry Luce Foundation.
William McCready is the study director.

42. Rolle, *op. cit.,* untitled poem, pp. 52–53.

Trent Eglin

Introduction to a Hermeneutics of the Occult: Alchemy

This paper is an introduction to an on-going study in the hermeneutics of Occult Philosophy and Science. It is restricted to predominantly methodological issues and to the study of Alchemy as one among many Occult Sciences by which considerations of those issues might best be explored. The study is an attempt to approach the Occult Sciences in a new fashion. The approach framing it relies chiefly on the work and methods developed by Harold Garfinkel.[1] As such, the approach may be termed Ethnomethodological.

Introduction. Heretofore, the Occult Sciences (the origins of which are irreparably obscure and the present extent of the activities of which is practically unassessable) have come within the province of students of history, sociology, philosophy, religion, philology, the classics and—with both moderate and deceptive success—psychology.[2] That these representatives of the analytic sciences have obscured the salient and, indeed, remarkable features of the Occult Sciences becomes clear on a careful reading of their own research "confessions." While all of these disciplines have claimed much for their findings with regard to the Occult Sciences, for our purposes, the outstanding results of their labors have been, on every hand, what they have felt constrained to omit, to gloss and to dismiss as unassimilable within the frame of their legitimate researches.

The Occult Sciences present a problem for scientific analysis precisely because recognizably sanctionable methods of observation—be they lay or scientific—of reportage, of description or of organizing evidence and formulating accounts—that is, of saying-in-so-many-words exactly and only in the ways one can be *seen* and can *make oneself seen* to be saying-in-so-many-words—rely upon an essential *ignor*ance of the reflexive or embodied character of natural language formulation for their cogency and their sense. The reflexivity of natural language formulation *as* an inexorable and at the same time *essentially uninteresting* presence on every occasion of rendering an account gives rise to apparent evidence of paradox, contradiction, absurdity, inconsistency and the rest of the list of incompetences reported with respect to the Occult Sciences, often as research findings. It is, in strong contrast, a reflexivity which, *in practice*, is prominently and characteristically "taken into account"—i.e., is *essentially interesting*—in Occult, as opposed to analytic, science, and not only demarcates the Occult Sciences' chief divergence from the analytic sciences, but guarantees their successes one and all.

The admittedly least sophisticated and yet perhaps most telling indictment against analytic forays into the realm of the Occult is simply researchers' persistent unwillingness and (with reference to the sanctionable legitimacy of their researches) inability to take the practitioners of the Occult Sciences seriously; to attend to these practitioners' claims and representations as anything other than epiphenomena, if not instances of fraud and chicanery; to resist the ever-present temptation toward reduction. All studies of the Occult or Arcane Sciences which fail to take into account the claims of its practitioners can in no way assess those practitioners' methods or achievements, and are consequently capable of bringing into view little more of ultimate interest than the invidiousness of their own investigations.

In contrast, our studies take most seriously the universal insistence of the Occult scientists that no matter the guise, no matter the variety of allegorical accoutrement, no matter the seeming diversity stretching across time and cultures, we are, when attending to the legitimate documents of the Occult Sciences, in the presence of a unitary body of thought in no wise deficient in empirical referent, in consistency, cogency, reproductibility and, specifically, in no wise lacking in sheer efficacy. In other words, it is proposed that we are in the presence of a true and, as we shall attempt to demonstrate, radical science. Although we shall see further on what is to be gained by this methodological posture, one potential benefit comes immediately to mind, viz., the Occult scientist remains no longer the mute *object* of our researches, but is transformed into their inexhaustible *resource*; indeed, their guarantor. We are subsequently in a position to free ourselves from the inevitable historicization with which studies of the Occult are generally burdened, i.e., free to confront the data unencumbered by the restrictive sense of the historically and episte-mologically situated character of Occult Science as insisted upon and reaf-firmed in previous research. This would involve, for example, the suspension of the relevance of and reliance upon dubious chronologies, arguments pitting theories of diffusion against theories of simultaneous discovery and, ultimately, of any causal reduction which invariably undercuts or trivializes practitioners' claims.

The prescriptive suspension of the relevance of historical and cultural diversity as concerns Occult Science in general, requires inevitably, a dis-tinction between *exoteric* or popular versions of Occult teachings wherein his-torical and cultural diversity is in full and rich evidence, and an *esoteric* or ex-clusive version wherein the sense of the universal profession of unity of method and content is to be sought. And, indeed, among practitioners, the distinction between the exoteric and the esoteric is explicit, virtually universal and, where referred to, its overarching importance is insisted upon. It is this insistence which renders our hermeneutical enterprise a conceivable one.

For most academic inquiries into the Occult, the exoteric, (i.e., myth, legend, religious history and, indeed, all lay-oriented representations and understandings of cosmogenesis, anthropogenesis, the nature of man and the visible order as well as of the gods and the invisible order) is inevitably seen as and understood to be a collection of accounts, standing, for all practical pur-poses, for the things and events for which the accounts are seen as names and (some kind of) descriptions. So, for example, religious histories are commonly taken as (in some sense) descriptive accounts—however attenuated—dis-playing, minimally, the features of similar and all too familiar activities of, simply, producing an account, as Garfinkel says, for-all-practical-purposes. From the point of view of this methodological presupposition, such histories reveal their patent defects as "factual accounts" when juxtaposed with the order of facticity which we, as contemporaries of science and partakers of its methodological ideals, are said to know so much better. This, it need be added, remains the case even though such accounts would not be regarded as in any sense deficient as *mythic* accounts which are characteristically treated *sui generis*. Where these accounts are treated as mythic, the emphasis of resultant studies is inevitably reductionistic and the student is in the dubious position of knowing *a priori* more of related events—psychic or physical—than those who formulated them "for the telling." We will confront this problem again later on. In any case, approaches to the documents of the Occult Sciences, and to the documents of religions, treat of them as formulations unfortunately (whatever else they may be) deficient in observation, logic, sense, completeness, cogency, etc.; that is, as the products of methodologically untrained minds, products for which the victories of science and analysis stand as correctives.

The objects and events intended, and the "meaning" underlying the documents and representations in question are, to be sure, taken to be initially opaque and thus given as "the problem." It is, however, presumably an opacity and a problem for which the analytic reductions, be they psychological, sociological, anthropological, historical or whatever, might, on every occasion, be brought to bare as method and remedy. Where Occult formulations, on the exoteric side, overlap with areas of observation organized by modern scientific disciplines, the deficiency of the former is frequently merely noted and the features of the apparent discrepancy are rarely thematicized as objects of investigation. Thus, for the modern astronomer, Astrology is simply primitive—not to say, "poor"—astronomy; for the modern chemist, Alchemy is simply primitive—not to say "poor"—chemistry, to cite two obvious examples. It is indeed the order of these misrepresentations that is expected to shed much light on our notion of progress as applied to the diverse fields of modern learning with which the notion is contemporary, and to show it to be largely misconstrued if only in point of emphasis.

All this, then, is simply another means of pointing to the essentially reflexive or self-referential character of methods of analysis, be they lay or scientific, and of indicating, in principle, that resultant accounts are themselves, so to speak, an inextricable part of the events whose very observable/accountable character is witness to their artful accomplishment and whose ways remain largely unexamined with the exception of the researches of Harold Garfinkel. We will find opportunity to deepen this formulation.

The assertion that the esoteric is everywhere contained "within" the exoteric—and, more accurately, appears *as* the exoteric—directly indicates that the former is in some sense—in radical contrast to the latter—secret. Secret, if only insofar as, first, its presence is indicated and insisted upon by practitioners but its contents are nowhere specifically revealed (i.e., in so many words). Second, it is secret insofar as even its uninterpretable presence is in no way obvious, so that, for the majority of researchers, its presence "in" their data is merely recorded as the insistence of practitioners and thereafter largely ignored. We will later go on to show (*a*) that the issue of secrecy or esotericism is indeed crucial and (*b*) that, as practitioners bear often confusing witness, it is a secrecy in two radically different meanings of the term. It is perhaps useful to anticipate our argument with the following proposal: the esoteric or true hermeneutics of the Occult is that corpus of instructions and informed teachings which are secret (fundamentally obscure as opposed to simply entirely withheld) both by design (in the fashion of the oft-repeated injunction, "cast ye not pearls before swine") *and* inexorably, irremediably. It is in light of this distinction that we must reexamine notions concerning the adjectives "occult" and "arcane."

It was held by the practitioners of the Sacred Sciences that, " . . . under the sacred histories, allegories, symbols, emblems, figures, and parables, were concealed the elements of a sublime science" (as Manly P. Hall puts it in describing the Old Testament).[3] And, in our own terms, for this science to be imparted via the structures of recognizably objective, descriptive, i.e., analytic speech or writing was itself alluded to as a special sort of impossibility, perhaps best denoted by the term "ineffable" as applied to the nondualistic experiences of the mystics. That is, inherent to and immanent in the structures of natural language formulae is the totality of the dualistic world for and within which they can be seen as adequate formulations. Ultimately, the essentially embodied, reflexive or self-referential character of those formulations conceal their own "work" whose accomplishment, first and foremost, is, in this instance, the constituting of the Occult Sciences and their objects precisely as possible subjects of investigation such and only such as they are thus "given" for those doing the investigating. Thus for those structures— again, be they lay or scientific—formulations of the Occult are holocryptic not only by conscious design, but by necessity. The elaborate symbolism dealing with and pointing to the inexorably veiled character of the Occult Doctrine attests to the contention that "it can simply be no other way." So, when Grillot de Givry says,

> Whether through fear of persecution or from that love of secret and hidden things innate in the heart of some men, these thinkers surrounded their doctrine with an illusive mystery, declared it forbidden to the profane, and insisted that knowledge of it was reserved to a very limited number of the elect . . .
>
> (From *Witchcraft Magic and Alchemy*).

or when William Leary writes, "Due to the inadequacies of ancient language [the biblical occultists] were compelled to explain their higher teachings in parable and allegory" (from *The Hidden Bible*), they are echoing at best a half-truth, and at worst, a common, persistent and fundamental misunderstanding.

In contrast to what have herein been characterized as the workings of analytic science and its formulations, the Occult Sciences *may be said* to have as their object *not* the improvement of understanding via improvements in the tools and methods of observation and formulation in and of a world pretheoretically given, but, instead, the transformation of the very structures of awareness. Their descriptions are preeminently directed not to a world presupposed and, in the words of Merleau-Ponty, "always already there," but to the very presuppositional structures of consciousness themselves from and within which such a world can arise. Further, the Occult Sciences are directed to a *transcendence* of the fundamental structures of awareness within which specific methods of making the world observable and accountable for-all-practical-purposes are employed, relied and insisted upon. The point to be demonstrated is that this "transcendence" involves, at least, a practice, a method—understood as a mode of being-in-the-world—within which the essential reflexivity of natural language formulae is of omnipresent relevance. The insistence on the part of Occult practitioners that their appropriate modes of discourse are everywhere and on every occasion those which we recognize as symbol, myth, allegory and parable, that their doctrine is fundamentally and essentially occult, assures us that, with respect to members of society's methods of making the world observable and reportable for-all-practical-purposes, we are in the presence of something interesting. The task of the present paper, then, is to locate a phenomenon which would lend these introductory remarks their sense, and do so where previous efforts have seemingly failed to find anything which would justify our interest.

Accounts of Alchemy.   Available records of Alchemy in the West can be traced to Alexandrian Egypt and date from approximately the third century A.D., although certain evidence as well as warranted inference place its beginnings considerably earlier. On the other hand, there is evidence to suggest that the Art was practiced in China at least two to four centuries before the birth of Christ. As in the West, records of Alchemy in the East fade into remote history and it is no exaggeration to say that the beginnings of the Sacred Art cannot with any certainty be located or dated. In the West, the Art's emergence into the light of history was intimately connected with the profound spiritual/philosophical climate of Hellenistic Egypt as manifested in the movements and schools which arose there in profusion out of a synthesis of Greek secular culture and Eastern mystery religion. The dominant elements of this synthesis were, according to Jonas,[4] Alexandrian Jewish philosophy, Babylonian Astrology and Magic, Eastern mystery cults become "spiritual mystery religions," Neoplatonism, Neopythagorianism and "that group of spiritual movements" known collectively as Gnosticism in which these elements were variously incorporated. Alchemy, at least at that time and place, was closely interwoven with Gnostic and related doctrines: thus, the prominent Greek alchemist, Zosimos (whose records along with those of the other Greek alchemists come to us from Alexandria by way of Byzantium) is designated both alchemist and Gnostic.

While the history of Alchemy per se is not our direct concern, some points of interest relevant to our purposes are raised with its discussion. The first of these is the inspiration for the alchemical doctrine of the transmutability of matter, specifically, of lesser metals to gold. Most historians of Alchemy have stayed well clear of a close look at the question, preferring to mention, almost in passing, an evolution of primitive metallurgy under the dominant influence of an equally primitive animism. Perhaps the most causally connected argument to this effect is that forwarded by Berthelot,[5] that the doctrine of the transmutation of metals arose, after the fashion of an understandable confusion, from the early Egyptian goldsmith's art of sophisticating or adulterating metals. He argues that it is but a short step from the sophistication of metals to the attempt at their transmutation. A. E. Waite, however, rejects this thesis, in part on the basis of Berthelot's contention that, " . . . the alchemical papyrus of Leyden connects in every respect with two in the same series which are solely Magical and Gnostic . . .", and concludes that, "It is to be understood that the Greek alchemists are by no means in the same category as the compiler of the Theban Papyrus, and that their memorials are not comparable to the note-books of artisans."[6]

It should be noted that we are not ultimately concerned with denying a thesis which combines animism and metallurgy. The point at issue is the origin of Alchemy as such and in the form in which it has survived in the West from at least the third century A.D. References to "mystico-religious symbolism" in relation to metallurgy give us no better indication concerning the origins of Alchemy per se. If such reasoning is to be allowed, it must be extended backwards in time to "in the beginning," that is, to mythic time, where or when it ceases to be an historical event or of historical interest.

Berthelot's attempt to derive Alchemy from Egyptian metallurgy takes us to the heart of the issue. He recognizes the presence of what he terms "mystical fancies" in the earliest of known alchemists; moreover, it appears from Berthelot's history that not only was the "mystical element" present from the beginning but it in fact gave rise to Alchemy per se and eventually so-called. This fact notwithstanding, the conception of Alchemy as a superimposition of a version of animism on the body of an emergent science was so difficult to lay aside—perhaps so "self-evident"—that Berthelot committed himself to a thesis which leaves Waite so justifiably incredulous on its own evidence.

The belief that Alchemy is or was merely protochemistry and that the omnipresent "mystical element" could have been and eventually was exorcized after the fashion of a superfluous addendum (to the profound benefit of, if not human knowledge in general, then certainly scientific knowledge in particular) has characterized or has been presupposed in the vast majority of accepted research.[7]

If we further examine the status of Alchemy *qua* primitive chemistry, we find that a historian of chemical science, J. M. Stillman, dismisses the contributions of the alchemists, from the earliest Greeks, through the centuries during which the Art was in Arab keeping and up to and including fourteenth- and fifteenth-century European efforts, as exhibiting no noteworthy advance " . . . over the chemistry known to Pliny or as shown in the Theban Papyri . . .", and as being of no particular importance save to those who, " . . . cultivated the philosophy of Alchemy as such."[8]

Thus in the light of the notion of the development or evolution of science, we find Alchemy—when conceived of as the beginnings of a science—seemingly stagnant precisely where and when, according to expectation, it should by all rights be developing, i.e., in Alexandria, among the Moslem Arabs and in medieval and Renaissance Europe, where otherwise the natural sciences did indeed flourish and evolve. Throughout the possibly two thousand years of its history, Alchemy undergoes no appreciable change and has contributed surprisingly little of worth to the corpus of modern chemical theory or fact, especially considering the length of its history and the diverse scientifically rich cultures through which it has passed so largely unaffected. The historians of science are apparently nonplused where they take cognizance of this fact. Stillman, for example, goes so far as to suggest—rather tautologically given his assessment of the chemistry of the particular period—that, Alchemy, when assumed to be a primitive chemistry, presents us with an inexplicably contrary nature: it simply emerges into the light of history full-grown.

> When we consider how important were the contributions of Arabian scholars in other domains of science as astronomy and mathematics it seems strange that their contributions to chemical science and practice were so unimportant. The inference seems clear that the domain of chemical science of the time, founded on the mystical alchemistry of the Alexandrian schools did not attract the ablest scholars, so that except for the work of artisans in the various trades the field of chemistry occupied the attention of students of inferior acumen and initiative.[9]

If Alchemy is a precursor of modern chemistry, we might again reasonably expect that any culture with a long-standing familiarity with its practice would eventually evolve a recognizable form of modern chemical science. That is, we might expect that its appearance would indicate the presence of at least prescientific thought presaging an evolution into more modern forms. Contrary to our common-sense expectations and to the reasonable extension of the historical view of Alchemy, both China and India, for example, "practiced" Alchemy and yet neither culture ever evolved a noteworthy natural science on its basis or any other. Experimental Alchemy was practiced in China for at least eleven to twelve hundred years and yet never evolved into a chemistry proper.

While there can be many *post hoc* explanations for these negative findings, and while the observations themselves are hardly conclusive to any effect, they are nonetheless counterintuitive and render the historical conception of Alchemy as protoscience, and the grounds upon which it rests, highly suspect. When experimental Alchemy disappears (both in China and in the West), it is not because it has in any demonstrable sense "become" experimental chemistry, but rather that its practitioners have retreated further and further from the laboratory and into purely speculative or mystical Hermetism. When chemical phenomena ceased to be regarded alchemically, it was because a new intellectual/scientific ethos had appeared and banished its predecessor, not that, for example, Newton and Boyle had succeeded in their attempts to transform Alchemy into chemistry.

Alchemy, then, from the point of view of its accredited historians is a primitive form of chemistry retarded in its development and in the rationalization of its methods by a stubborn animization of laboratory fact and a reputed disdain for experiment conformable with the pervasive reverence for and reliance upon ancient authorities. In terms of this view, the alchemist's strange persistence in the ways of his magisterium can be no better than a puzzling aberration or a willful fraud. It should be kept in mind in this connection that some of the more illustrious names in Alchemy belong to the same age as

Tycho Brahe, Galileo and Copernicus, and that Alchemy was never more widespread in Europe than in the seventeenth century which was otherwise " . . . marked by an increase in chemical experimentation and by a still greater independence of thought."[10] These men come down to us then, as reactionary vestiges of a dying age and the entire field has subsequently been abandoned to those for whom the so-called irrational aspects of Alchemy have their own fascination.

The objections to the claims of Alchemy spanning the last two or three centuries have rested, for the most part, on the fact that artificially (artfully) produced gold is not readily forthcoming, that the process, if veridical, is not "colorably" described, and that the claims are contrary to the theories and findings of modern chemistry, not to say—given the technology of the alchemists—simply preposterous.

It is *not* that we disbelieve the possiblity of transmuting metals; quite likely many men of science would allow it as one of numerous as yet unactualized possibilities. Moreover, were the fact of successful transmutation of base metals to gold to be announced from a modern university laboratory, the proverbial average citizen would likely wonder at the economic consequences, but it is unlikely that the feat would strike him as any more miraculous than countless other scientific marvels which have long since distended the boundaries of credibility and expectation to encompass the heretofore fantastic, supernatural, other-worldly, and impossible. It is rather that we disallow the specific structure of rationality underlying the methods of Alchemy as manifest in the language whereby that rationality is, on claim, demonstrated and its victories made observable.

Men are not credulous because they believe anything, but because they believe anything *within reason*: a man, that is, will be credulous according to his time. The language of Alchemy is, to the modern observer, a transparent nonsense, and, indeed, our word "gibberish" comes from the name of the Arabian alchemist, Jabir, and the European alchemist who, according to practice, assumed his name (Geber). This, however, is not equivalent to merely noting that the language of Alchemy is unintelligible, for although the language of science is largely unintelligible to the nonscientist, it is not ipso facto nonsense. The practice of Alchemy was rooted in a deeply sedimented sense of the terms and methods via which a thing's or an event's existence—no less than its rational accountability—was demonstrated and made observable.

The point here is that the naturalistic objections to Alchemy stem not so much from a rejection of its claims to transmutation, but from a rejection of the methods and terms by which its claims were advertised, communicated and, for some, adequately demonstrated. The question as to whether or not the alchemists were, in fact, able to transmute matter is far from our foremost concern, and is, in any case, not answered one way or the other by the "historical evidence." There is abundant testimony by "reliable witnesses" to the effect that such transmutations have taken place "before their eyes" and without possibility or opportunity for conjuration or fraud. There are likely an equal number of revealed attempts at conjury. We leave such testimony to those who are willing to debate the "facts" on the merits of such evidence. Aside from all of which, the list of eyewitnesses, howsoever long and howsoever dignified its members, would, in the context of the modern view of Alchemy, seem more curious than edifying.

Occular demonstration was, for the vast majority of the students of Alchemy, the end and not the beginning of their studies, studies which not infrequently demanded the better part of a lifetime, which explicitly promised to be immeasurably difficult, and which offered absolutely no guarantees of ultimate success. An alchemist has written, "To one who is acquainted with the scope and meaning of this Art, it is not so strange that only few attain to our knowledge; to him the wonder is rather that any man has ever succeeded in discovering its methods."[11] The view of Alchemy, then, as a misguided chemistry or a vain striving after riches can in no way bring to account the methods by which the quest for the Philosopher's Stone was accounted a rationally defensible, i.e., reasonable enterprise. The alternative, though presenting us with a more curious phenomenon than the one it explains, is to posit a two-thousand-year endemic irrationality, suddenly and mysteriously swept away with the advent of the Enlightenment.

The rejection of alchemical rationality stems from an explicit rejection of Occult ontology: the casual contempt and disregard shown it by modern science and philosophy is but the shadow of a former conflict to which the antagonists were then very much alive. At stake in this conflict was no less than the entire ontological orientation of Western civilization the outcome of which was finally and symbolically sealed by the acceptance of the Copernican universe. When we regard Alchemy from the point of view of the history of science, we are in rather the same position as those who, by needs, study Gnosticism from the records of the church; our being alive to the issues is prejudiced by historicization. History is, of course, written in large measure by the victors, and for that reason alone is it synonymous with progress. Our notion of progress is the ghost that haunts the hermeneutic enterprise.

SOCIOLOGICAL PERSPECTIVES

At about the middle of the nineteenth century a popular occultism flour-ished in Europe and America, and is active, indeed thriving, to this day. This
movement—assuming it may be so regarded—is interesting in many respects
and deserving of study in its own right. In terms of our inquiry it reflected
the ontological schism which emerged with the Renaissance, broadly viewed,
and from the vista of one of its poles it attempted to bring Alchemy to view in
a "new light." In 1850 M. A. Atwood's *Hermetic Philosophy and Alchemy*
was published anonymously in England. It was followed in 1857 by A. E.
Hitchcock's *Remarks on Alchemy and the Alchemists* published in America.
At the same time, the often brilliant and often doubtable French occultist,
Eliphas Lévi (Alphonse Louis Constant) was forming his own views of many
matters, including among them Alchemy. There is, as Waite observes and as
far as we know, no reason to believe that these authors were known to each
other, nor, for that matter and at that time, much outside their own countries.
Yet the views were strangely consistent: Alchemy emerges from these studies
as a mystical science of the soul veiled in the terminology and symbolism of
chemistry. Waite, who took it upon himself in *The Secret Tradition in Alchemy* to disabuse others of what he regarded as so much folly, characterized
(caricatured) this new light on Alchemy as follows:

> Man is for all adepts the one subject that contains all, and he only need be
> investigated for the discovery of all. Man is the true laboratory of Hermetic
> Art, his life is the subject, the grand distillery, the thing distilling and the
> thing distilled, and self-knowledge is at the root of all alchemical tradition.[12]

Writing from within the modern occult movement and to its students, Waite
turned his prodigious energy to the refutation of the view of Alchemy as a
mystical philosophy "talking about one thing [mysticism] in terms of another
[chemistry]." Although he readily acknowledged the fact of literatures "written from within and without," Alchemy, he claimed, was not one of them, that
is, until about the beginning of the seventeenth century and the tradition which
began with Heinrich Khunrath and Jacob Boehme. Prior to the divorce of Alchemy from the laboratory (paralleling the rise of modern science) says Waite,
the alchemists' concern was for chemical transmutation, conducted in a laboratory familiar to us from medieval renderings as crowded with well-used
crucibles, furnaces, athanors, stills, alembics, and other such standard requisite
implements. Waite's method consists, first, in quoting from alchemical texts,
recipes, and instructions which, if they were in fact a veiled symbolism would
defy recognition as such (not to mention attempts at interpretation) and which,

otherwise, are plainly what they appear to be, i.e., recipes and formulae, and second, in unmasking the curious hagiology that had grown up around and had always been an integral and interesting part of the "Lives of Alchymistical Philosophers." Waite's point is hardly to be doubted, but by proving his thesis he proves too much. There cannot be any doubt as to the alchemists' laboratory activities and goals; even the most superficial attention to the literature can rarely fail to convince the reader that he is confronted with (at least) records of the practices and results of practical chemistry.[13] Nonetheless, the whole is transfixed by a spiritual vision—in the sense of a "seeing"—which scans no less than the development and evolution of spirit in matter, Nature and God, and definitely not least, the soul of man. Hence, an explication of the whole of his activities calls for more than the no-news assurance that the alchemist was an alchemist by virtue of his being manifestly engaged in what we would unhesitatingly recognize as practical chemistry. As René Alleau writes,

> The basis of alchemy is its study of the mineral kingdom, a purely material matter, but its concept of the Philosopher's Stone starts from four fundamental abstract concepts: the desire for release, the idea of a new genesis of metal and a second birth for man, the demiurgic rite of death and resurrection, and the mystic exaltation of matter. The concrete metamorphosis of the Stone would confer analogical illumination on the spirit of the "artist" who transformed it and gazed upon it.[14]

The nineteenth-century occultists attempted to rescue the alchemists from a reductive science which, in the spirit of its century, had, if not banished the mystery from the universe, then laid siege to it in the church and was not about to credit its survival in Alchemy. The threat to those who continued to feel the presence of the mystery and to value its memorials was real enough; in 1857, for instance, the distinguished French chemist, Marcellin Berthelot, had flatly decreed, "From now on there is no mystery about the universe."[15] But the occultists were subject as well to the inherited ontological schism and resultant "negative mythology" which characterized that peculiar age; if a perfection of sorts had been obtained in science by omitting the mystery, then a perfection in mystery could be as easily obtained by omitting the science. In order to save Alchemy, they turned it "inside out" so that, with its back now everywhere to its object, it could only reflect upon itself and the quest for spiritual regeneration. The inquiry into the structure and nature of the visible was given over by default to those in terms of whose expertise all that remained was to fill in the missing pieces. Intimidated, not to mention likely repulsed, by the science of their time, nineteenth-century occultists res- cued Alchemy by removing it from the laboratories which were at that time crowded with practitioners implacably hostile to its spirit, and by proclaiming its integrity as a spiritual discipline against a science which they often hadn't the training nor perhaps the inclination to rebut. The transmutation of base metals to gold became, *mutatis mutandis*, the transformation of the lower self to spiritual or Christic gold. Alchemy became a metaphor, and the secrecy sur- rounding its teachings was often portrayed as a simple attempt to dissemble, a clever device by which to conceal its message from a jealous and spiritually bankrupt church. Those who had tried to preserve the presence of the mystery had rendered it impotent: the chemical symbolism of Alchemy was, in the case of Hitchcock, decoded with a key which, though it provided an access, revealed underneath a core of spiritual platitude, and in the case of Atwood and Levi presented a far from convincing and easily caricatured recourse to magnetism and the like.

The ultimate variation on this theme is perhaps that contained in the monu- mental works on Alchemy to which the psychologist C. G. Jung devoted decades. It suffices to quote Jung to demonstrate the ways in which the alchemist was deprived of his very phenomenon in the presence of a science whose victories are complete and unquestioned.

> [T]he alchemists were fascinated by the soul of matter, which, unknown to them, it had received from the human psyche by way of projection. For all their intensive pre-occupation with matter as a concrete fact they followed this psychic trail, which was to lead them into a region that, to our way of thinking, had not the remotest connection with chemistry. Their mental la- bors consisted in a predominantly intuitive apprehension of psychic facts, the intellect playing only the modest role of famulus. . . . The misfortune of the alchemists was that they themselves did not know what they were talking about.[16]

Reformulated by Von Franz, who adopts the Jungian perspective, it reads as an emphatic call for the remedies of plain talk and clear thinking.

> We need assume that the author [of *Aurora Consurgens*] did not express himself in clearly understandable concepts *for the simple reason that he did not possess them*, and that he was giving a stammering description of an *un- conscious content which had irrupted into his consciousness*.[17] [Emphasis in the original]

We find contained in these curious statements yet another explanation for the "secrecy" of alchemical formulations and for the particular language with which that secret was articulated. Earlier accounts had dealt with the crucial esotericism of alchemical formulations as either the strange and fraudulent claims of primitive chemists, or as the clever dodge of deviant religionists (with or without extraordinary powers). Here we encounter the alchemical secret as the more or less delusional record of premodern identity crises . . . the alchemist as patient. An adequate explanation with respect to our subject is, however, not likely such a "simple" one, and requires more than the Jungian analytic which is, by all standards, an explanation *obscurum per obscurius*, a substitution of one hidden for another by its removal from the world and its relocation in the psyche.

That Alchemy is an esoteric or secret science is precisely that which, in effect, must be ignored by the historian's (no less than by the psychologist's) view of the Art as either primitive chemistry or primitive "psychology". Their acknowledgement of the *full* seriousness of the claim would require further the acknowledgement that its purport is lost upon them and that, consequently, that which upon the testimony of practitioners is the whole of the teaching, is to them an unrelieved obscurity. Secrecy, then—the universal insistence of practitioners—is to the modern student, either a willful obfuscation and withholding of information or an ignorance of the "facts" whose remedy is, on every occasion, "plain talk" or, simply, saying-in-so-many-words. This being the case, the psychologist's condescension and the historian's impatience with the literature of Alchemy are at once perfectly understandable, and the historian's suspicion that the secret is without content fully justified.

A. E. Waite gives voice to the summary view:

> If I . . . had such a predisposition and so pursued it that I learned how to transmute metals, I should either make known my process or reserve the fact of its discovery. I should not write mystery theses to announce that I possessed the secret and place it under impassable veils, while affirming that I revealed the whole Art.[18]

Ethnomethodological Approach.   The secret of the alchemist is the secret of the production of the Philosopher's Stone by which base metals are transmuted into purest gold. Possession of the Stone consists first, in its *apprehension,* and subsequently, in its *production,* its apprehension being the beginning and most difficult stage of the work. The alchemists speak both of a "hidden" Stone and a Stone manifest. Of the former, Bonus writes,

> [It] is not sensuously apprehended, but only known intellectually, or by in-

spiration. Alexander says: There are two stages in this Art, that which you
see with the eye, and that which you apprehend with the mind.[19]

The possession of the Stone in the inexorable dual-sense of revelation or *dis*-
covery and of bringing forth or *manu*-facture—of, seemingly, ideal and real—
rewards the student with all benefits, correlatively physical/material and in-
tellectual/spiritual. The rewards may be provisionally specified thus as health,
(a sufficiency of) wealth, gnosis and transcendence.[20]

Though the method is secret, it is (of course—on claim and in some yet to
be examined sense), *nonetheless*, "revealed" in the literature, though under
the cover of various veils. The secret, that is, is not one which is entirely withheld. An obvious question arises: if the Art and the method are secret, why
then does the alchemist attempt to reveal them publicly at all, the various
guises and obfuscations notwithstanding? First, he seeks to guide the worthy
and serious student who, without aid, would be exposed to specific dangers
(both psychic and physical being variously alluded to); that is, to guide the
student who, in any case, would not otherwise attain to success in an enterprise fraught with fraudulent exponents and nearly insurmountable difficulties. And second, he is motivated at the same time or exclusively by (divine) inspiration to communicate and (thereby) perpetuate sacred and fundamental
truths. The various circumlocutions are thus designed to accomplish these
aims while simultaneously withholding these invaluable and potentially dangerous teachings from the foolish, the ignorant, the avaricious, the wicked, the
profane. There are, moreover, intimations going all the way back to the
earliest of Greek alchemists, of an oath—whether to God or men—and a
proscription, in general, with reference to revealing the method.

Those then capable of receiving initiation into the secrets of Nature and the
Soul are precisely those who, having undergone an antecedent conversion[21]
rendering them "worthy," are thus enabled to proceed on the road to initiation, i.e., precisely those whom God permits. It is not merely the clever man
who might attain to the sanctuary, but the sanctified; defects of moral or of
character are absolute hindrances to the full attainment of the work. Strictly
speaking, success in the Art is thus not attained but received: thus, the Stone is
invariably described as a "gift of God" to those deserving His mercy.[22]

The nature of this kind of secret, then, is decidedly not that of common
meaning, i.e., the matter being simply withheld or irreparably obscured: for if
the veils are such to be exclusively penetrable by the worthy and, conversely,
as to be in no way penetrable by their opposite, then a *specific* language is in-

dicated, i.e., one which speaks to and is understood by the sanctified and the wise. Geber writes:

> I therefore teach this Art in such a way that nothing will remain hidden to the wise man, even though it may strike mediocre minds as quite obscure; the foolish and the ignorant, for their part, will understand none of it at all . . .[23]

As such, a maieutic language is indicated which is directly dictated in its features by the nature of its task (that is, of keeping the profane from the gates of the sanctuary while safely bringing forth the worthy) no less than by the nature of its objects. As its task and its objects are respectively spiritual and transcendent, it is more than merely *honoris causa* that the language and the inspiration to speak are attributed, by the alchemist, to God. There is, in other words, the sense in which it is to God and to God alone that the veils, such and only as they are specifically construed, may, phenomenologically speaking, be referred. The alchemist who resorts to a language designed merely to obscure or mislead and not to enlighten, i.e., who resorts to a language which in its features does *not* lead the worthy nearer the desired goal, is chastised for his "envy" (a specific term in the context of alchemical literature). "[T]hough the phraseology of the Sages be obscure," says Bonus, "it must not therefore be supposed that their books contain a single deliberate falsehood . . . "[24]

The alchemist, himself sanctified and thus inspired to speak, is the "voice" of the language of God as well as the instrument of his will, and thus the obscurities of formulation *devolve* upon the alchemist first, as the inherited and assumed form of his *responsibility* for keeping, "knowledge of the mystery from the world," and, in their expression, as the sign and witness of his *ability* to do so while in those same formulations informing the worthy. The formulations originate with "the Providence of the Most High" who may ultimately be relied upon to, " . . . effectively guard this Arcanum from falling into the hands of covetus gold seekers and knavish pretenders to the Art of Transmutation . . ."[25] much as He could but does not reveal His secrets with the revelation of the world. The language via which the Arcanum is paradoxically both "revealed" and "withheld" is thus, *in its features*, a *specific* language. One of its features, for example, has been described as being a sort of "self-cancellation." "That is, an inquirer who does not possess the first secret must be infallibly prevented from discovering the second."[26] It is, in any case, a language with respect to which the denomination "secret"—as exoterically understood—lends no clarity whatsoever.

It follows directly upon these assertions that the language of Alchemy is secret in a correlative sense: that is, the sense in which it alone, from the pens of the alchemists and as their testimony would have it, is inadequate or insufficient to its task. For if the language is—for its understanding—dependent upon the prior or simultaneous revelation of the objects and the relations to which it applies, then, "The words of the Sages may mean anything or nothing to one who is not acquainted with the facts which they describe,"[27] such that a continual reference to Nature as the locus of these yet to be discovered "facts" is itself described as literally indispensable.[28] Presaged in these remarks is a radical contrast to the ways of natural language formulae, or of procedures for the accomplished rational accountability of witnessed things and events within which tacit reference to a world presupposed and already known in common (to an imperative, not lightly to be dispensed with, what-it-can-have-come-to-when-all-is-said-and-done) is both a characteristic feature of those formulae and the artfully managed guarantee of their cogency, their sense, their very practical accomplishments, i.e., their victories one and all.[29]

This first sense, then, in which the teachings of the alchemists are secret is one which is only nominally attributable to the willful practice of the alchemist himself. But, insofar as the instructions refer *nonetheless* or *as well* to "things" seen and touched, in the "real" world and recognizable as its objects, i.e., insofar as the instructions result in the chemical operations which have provided the historians of Alchemy-*qua*-primitive-science with indubitable material for their speculations, then—with reference to those operations and their objects—we can surely imagine that the alchemist might speak otherwise, that is, might speak "plainly."[30] Aside from the sense which follows logically from all that has been said above, that one who can perform the operations of Alchemy is not necessarily an alchemist, it remains nonetheless indicated that, on the exoteric side, there is a secret capable of being otherwise revealed which must be kept from the hands of the unworthy, not lest they become alchemists, but, "lest the world should be devastated."[31]

We are primarily interested in the second and vastly more evocative sense in which the teachings of Alchemy per se are secret; the sense, that is, in which the teachings as provided in the literature are the *best possible* description of their objects and their methods, and in which the seeming obfuscation is an inexorable one. The objects of Alchemy, the objects which make up its special gnosis, and the relations appertaining to them, are *in and of themselves* hidden to the profane and the uninitiated. All formulations referring to them are, perforce and by definition, irreparably obscure, i.e., occult. "[E]very substantial truth [is] a secret" according to Thomas Vaughn.[32] The essential obscurity results in the paradox of alchemical formulation as nowhere better related than in Geber's *Summa*:

> Whenever I have seemed to speak most clearly and openly about our science, I have in reality expressed myself most obscurely and have hidden the object of my discourse most fully. And yet in spite of all that, I have never clothed the alchemical work in allegories or riddles, but have dealt with it in clear and intelligible words and have described it honestly, just as I know it to be and have myself learnt it by divine inspiration . . .[33]

In terms then of the truth-value of formulations concerning these secrets, the traditional notion of truth as the correspondence of mind and its object appears very problematic indeed. The "objects" with which the art of Alchemy *ultimately* deals are decidedly not the "things," present-at-hand, with which we are familiar and by which we are surrounded in all directions to a distance coincident with the limits of imagination. In fact, properly speaking, they are not objects at all: they are not given with the world and, as opposed to finding them already "there" upon every awakening, we may search for them throughout a lifetime—or not—the issue having no necessary effect on our ability to conduct our everyday practical affairs in a world of normal and given objects. They are, in a word, hidden, and the first goal of the alchemical pursuit is the discovery of the very "matter" with which the science deals.

If, as we can read in Eirenaeus Philalethes and as, otherwise, all alchemists insist, " . . . the Philosophical Work is no fiction, but grounded in the possibility of Nature . . . ,"[35] then it is assuredly not the nature of *our* science, but more nearly of the science of the Greeks; i.e., nature not as the plurality of lifeless objects with which we are ontologically coincident, but as *physis*, " . . . the process," says Heidegger, "of arising, of emerging from the hidden, whereby the hidden is first made to stand."[36] Further, as one alchemist (Paracelsus) expresses it, "When the goal of the seeking is hidden, the manner of seeking is also occult."[37]

The two senses of the word "secret" now reveal themselves as two stages in the same process or Art. The first is the making visible of that which was formerly hidden and whose proper method is itself "occult", and the second is the artful manipulation of the outward sign or symbol—the "thing"—whereby its occult properties and potentialities might be *realized*. The process signified having been revealed in the properties of its sign, then the operations to be performed are themselves the recognizable recipes of chemical operations

which are described as ". . . a true woman's or cook's work."[38] Of the process
it is further said that, "Were it stripped of all figures and parables, it would be
possible to compress it into the space of eight or twelve lines."[39]

The two senses in which the word "secret" or "occult" may be applied to
the Art correspond, then, to two realms of being with which it deals inexorably (and whose estrangement—the one from the other—is the modern
legacy and the premise of modern research on Alchemy): (a) that realm in and
of the world and visible, and (b) that realm hidden from the world, though
nonetheless hidden in the world, and, as we have intimated, appearing as the
world. This is, insofar as the two realms correspond respectively to the exoteric and the esoteric in language, the emphatic sense in which the literary
method of the alchemists imitates their view of Nature (physis), that is, an
elaboration of the sense in which the resultant secrecy of formulation is attributable more so to God than to the alchemist himself. "[T]he Artist in this
profession," says Paracelsus, "ought in all things exactly to imitate Nature."[40]
To the first realm of being belongs the secret that the alchemist could but
refuses to reveal, i.e., the secret of the informed manipulation of, largely
speaking, objects with which we are either familiar or can readily make
ourselves familiar. To this familiar realm of objects belongs the just-this-right-
here and the just-that-over-there—the present-at-hand, as it were—and the
traditional motion of truth as relates to these objects is, as Heidegger concerns
himself with, the gradually accomplished correspondence of mind and thing, of
intellect and its object. The notion of truth-as-correspondence makes the world
itself out in terms of the sum of its constituent objects, of which, we might say,
man is but one, with, however, an intimation if not a promise of ultimate
mastery over the others.

The pretheoretic, ever-prior "discovery" of the World as the
phenomenological unity within which—and with perpetual tacit reference to
which—we locate not only objects but ourselves as well, needs be ignored in
order that the "problem"to which the questions of our science are ultimately
addressed appear as an essential plurality whose resolution resides in a
seemingly unending search for similarities in a universe characterized in its
very being by differences and diversity. Knowledge of such objects aspires—at
some ideal future and by way of some ideal conclusion—to specify the nature
of the world as an accomplished apprehension of the sum of and relation
between its parts. In this sense, it is an infinite program which is incapable of
having brought the world to its full accountability as yet and as such, but is
rather always on its trail, always and necessarily, at every successive moment,

more closely than ever. It is a truth with a marked history, characterized as "the human enterprise" and summarily captioned "the myth of the total explication of the world" by Merleau-Ponty.[41] What remains hidden to this view and in this world awaits the advent of better instruments, of improvements in the methods, angles, and technology of observation. Beyond all such conceivable improvements, the rest is presumably silence and darkness. It was perhaps this view the legendary churchmen opposed with their apocryphal refusal to gaze through Galileo's telescope.

We see, then, that the notion of truth-as-correspondence, from the point of view of the epistemological considerations raised here, brings us up against a rarely thematized ontology concerning the being of the objects it brings under examination ontically and which it always already has, and as a consequence, the being of the world as such (in its "worldhood") about which it is necessarily (i.e., essentially) unreflective.

In strong contrast to truth as relates to the things given with the essential and ever-prior discovery of the world, is truth as relates to things hidden. Its methods are properly phenomenological:

> Now what must be taken into account [asks Heidegger] if the formal conception of phenomenon is to be deformalized into the phenomenological one, and how is this latter to be distinguished from the ordinary conception? What is it that phenomenology is to 'let us see'? What is it that must be called a 'phenomenon' in a distinctive sense? What is it that by its very essence is *necessarily* the theme whenever we exhibit something *explicitly*? Manifestly, it is something that proximally and for the most part does *not* show itself at all: it is something that lies *hidden*, in contrast to that which proximally and for the most part does show itself; but at the same time it is something that belongs to what thus shows itself, and it belongs to it so essentially as to constitute its meaning and its ground.[42] [Emphasis in the original]

Heidegger elsewhere characterizes *truth* as related to the hidden as an "event," ". . . which occurs, so to speak, from without,"[43] as, indeed, the alchemists have always emphasized by attributing illumination with respect to such "objects" to an agency such as God or the Holy Ghost. Truth as concerns the hidden is thus precisely the moment of its (the hidden's) revelation, *dis*covery or becoming visible. "Whatever is hidden from common observation is the province of Art; but as soon as the hidden has become manifest and visible, the task of our Art is accomplished, and all that remains to be done is purely mechanical . . .," says Basilius Valentinus.[44] And from Bonus, "Find our Art . . . and you will have proved its reality . . ."[45]

We find an Art, thus, whose truth *is* the event characterized by the revelation of its object "in the first place" and as *thereby* rendered accountable in precisely the invariable fashion of its coming to be at all. The observability of its object is perforce *recognizably* coessential with nothing more and nothing less than the events produced in an order of "situated practices of looking-and-telling"[46] with which it is primordially coextensive, which observability, as an event, constitutes, as well, its truth. The reflexivity of those practices is not only irrecusable, it is *essentially interesting* as often borne witness by the sanctification or morally sanctioned inviolability of *accounts* as related to the objects of the Sacred Sciences in no lesser degree than the sanctification of the *objects* themselves with which, in this view, they are in some sense coextensive.

The language used to describe such objects and their relations, in their hiddeness—keeping in mind that they "belong" nonetheless and in some sense to what does show itself, are its ground—will inevitably exhibit certain features which lend the attribute of secrecy its distinctive character. The language, in *naming* its objects, at the same time anticipates *and* participates in their *dis*covery, and in naming what does show itself, refers—as the sign to the thing signified—to that which is still to be exhibited and made visible, where literally no alternative is conceivable. It is a language which, in order to be learned, must be known. In the *Theatrum Chemicum Britannicum*, by Elias Ashmole, we read,

> The first Paine is to remember in minde,
> How many seeken, and how few doe finde,
> And yet noe Man may this Science wynn,
> But it be tought him before that he beginn . . .[47]

In naming a thing which is familiar or can be readily made familiar, the thing named is not the more for having been named, the thing sought (in contradistinction to the "true" name of the Philosopher's Stone, known, of course, only to the alchemist). And we are assured, on every hand, that, ultimately, it is *one* thing we are seeking though, ". . . our Stone has as many names as there are things, or names of things."[48] Thus a reference to things—names—is not a reference to objects, but a reference to phenomenological attributes, both of the "thing" sought in itself, and as arise in the process—and herein the role of the alchemist—of its coming to be, that is, in the dual sense of its apprehension and its manufacture wherein the phenomenal and the phenomenological are resolved and the work complete.

> Our Stone, from its all-comprehensive nature, may be compared to all things in the world. . . . [T]here are analogies to things heavenly, earthly, and infernal, to the corporeal and the incorporeal, to things corruptible and incorruptible, visible and invisible, to spirit, soul, and body, and their union and separation, to the creation of the world, its elements, and their qualities, to all animals, vegetables, and minerals, to generation and corruption, to life and death, to virtues and vices, to unity and multitude, to actuality and potentiality, to conception and birth, to male and female. . . . [W]e have an infinite variety of names used to describe our precious Stone, every one of which may be said . . . to represent a certain aspect of the truth of our Art.[49]

In the process, then, of its coming to be, which being made observable is its truth, the names and references given the Stone exhibit prominently the following features taken up by Garfinkel under the heading of "indexical expressions": their sense is undecidable without knowledge of the purpose of the user and the circumstances of their use; ". . . descriptions involving them apply on each occasion of use to only one thing, but to different things on different occasions"; they can be used ". . . to make unequivocal statements that nevertheless seem to change in truth value"; their use refers to something not necessarily named by some replica of the work; "[t]heir denotation is relative to the speaker"; and "[t]heir use depends upon the relation of the user to the object with which the word is concerned."[50]

In strong contrast to the ways of science (for which, as Garfinkel observes, the substitution of indexical expressions by objective or context free expression is, ". . . both an actual task and an actual achievement . . ."[51] without which its victories are unimaginable), the language of Alchemy is through and through indexical and the preferred use of indexical expressions is insisted upon. That is, the reflexivity of resultant formulations is an essential feature of Alchemy as method, requiring, in the words of one of its practioners, ". . . a profound natural faculty for interpreting the significance of those symbols and analogies of the philosophers, which in one place have one meaning and in another a different."[52] "How then," Bonus might well ask, "shall we, by considering their works only superficially, and according to their literal interpretation, fathom the profound knowledge required for the practical operations of this Magistery?"[53] Perhaps an important clue is provided in the outright prescription contained in the works on Alchemy: the Art needs be rediscovered *not* as literature, but as speech directed to those phenomena on whose behalf it claims to speak, ". . . for reading is a dead speech, but that which is uttered with the lips the same is living speech."[54]

Conclusion. The modern views of Alchemy treat of it either as an art directed exclusively to a description of the properties and behavior of matter, or, conversely, exclusively to the properties and behavior of psyche; the alchemists, themselves, are respectively either poor chemists or poor psychologists. It hardly need be reiterated that the two schools reflect the two poles of the Great Schism which signalled both their emergence as autonomous modes of description, indeed, as seemingly autonomous modes of being-in-the-world, and, the death of Alchemy. In Alchemy, as we have indicated, the two poles represent, structurally, two aspects or stages of one nondualistic enterprise in which they are indissoluably linked and the nature of that indissolu-ability is specified. The thesis of the historian of science fails singularly to convince, and that, on the basis of its own evidence; the alchemists' preoccupation with the "transmutation" of self, of the structures of awareness, of "seeing," finds no place in the history of his endeavors. The Jungian thesis, as representing the opposite pole of a radical subject-object dualism and its most sophisticated and widely adopted expression as concerns Alchemy, fails, inevitably, for the opposite reason; the alchemists' insistence that theirs was a science of Nature and of matter, is dismissed as little better than a consensually validated hallucination. The two pictures, structurally enantiomorphic, are, in and of themselves, totally unable to regard the practitioners of the art they attempt to bring to accountability as other than epiphenomena in their own drama. Their resolution resides, ironically enough, in the doctrine acknowledged as the very foundation of the Spagyric Art by all the practitioners to whom it was, per se, familiar, and which otherwise is given ample testimony in all the alchemists wrote; that is, the doctrine of the Macrocosmos and the Microcosmos, attributed to the putative patron of Alchemy, the Thrice Great Hermes, Trismegistus. It stipulates, in brief, that the Great World, Nature (*physis*), is recapitulated in the Lesser World, that is, Man, although their being at a distance from each other is a fundamental feature (Alchemy is not to be mistaken for either a modern phenomenology or a true mysticism). Any description of the former, the Macrocosmos—in its essence—is, perforce, a description of the latter, the Microcosmos. "Thus the outward world represents and explains the inner one. The former is the sign, the latter the thing indicated."[55] And Paracelsus writes, "The method and most certain rule for finding out the matter of the Philosopher's Stone, as well as other subjects . . . is a careful examination of the root and seed by which they come to our knowledge."[56] The "discovery" is hardly as modern as we might believe. Alchemy thus reveals itself as a unique phenomenology which can be encountered in the methods via which it brings its world to observability, no less than to accountability, and with which, after its own lights, it presents itself as a rationally defensible enterprise. The methods developed by Harold Garfinkel, I would suggest, are singularly suited to provide access to the ways of that accountability in general, and indeed, wherever they are found and on every occasion of their use.

It is proposed that, in terms of the experiential radical dualism of subject and object, and its history and fate as the history and fate of consciousness itself, two essential languages, both as in their features conceivable, and as evidenced in history, corresponding to two ontologies, mark the trail of our being-in-the-world. It is with respect to the methods of Ethnomethodology and the " 'reflexive,' or 'incarnate' character of accounting practices and accounts"[57] as their central recommendation, that the practices of the Occult Sciences and the language of their expression may be, at least in some sense, recovered on behalf of their practitioners, that is, through an examination of the radical contrast between their methods, and the methods of "recognizably ordinary talk" in terms of which they are recognized specifically. That Alchemy defines the human enterprise and man's function in the world as that of "making visible," assures us that, with respect to the findings of Ethnomethodology, we are indeed in the presence of something interesting. "For the 'firmament,' " says Paracelsus, "needs an agent through which to work, and this agent is man and man alone. Man has been so created that through him the miracles of nature are made visible and given form."[58]

NOTES

1. Cf. Harold Garfinkel, *Studies in Ethnomethodology*, Englewood Cliffs, N.J.: Prentice-Hall, 1967.

2. Reference is made here to the works of C. G. Jung as well as to those who have adopted his thesis, for example, C. A. Burland, Marie-Louise Von Franz and the translators of *Aurora Consurgens* and John Joseph Stoudt.

3. Cf. Manly P. Hall, *Old Testament Wisdom*, Los Angeles: The Philosophical Research Society, Inc., 1957.

4. Cf. Hans Jonas, *The Gnostic Religion*, Boston: Beacon Press, 1967.

5. Cf. Marcellin Berthelot, *La Chimie au moyen âge*, Paris, 1893. Our reference is, however, to the discussion in A. E. Waite's, *The Secret Tradition in Alchemy*, New York: Alfred A. Knopf, 1926.

6. A. E. Waite, *Ibid.*, p. 68.

7. See Titus Burckhardt, *Alchemy*, London: Stuart & Watkins, 1967, p. 7.

8. John Maxson Stillman, *The Story of Alchemy and Early Chemistry,* New York, Dover: 1960, pp. 217 and 297. Cf. pp. 169, 182, and 183. In a similar vein, see A. E. Waite, *op. cit.,* p. xix.

9. John Maxson Stillman, *op. cit.,* pp. 218–219. See also his remarks on p. 273 when in another time and place he again finds Alchemy not behaving according to reasonable expectations.

10. *Ibid.,* p. 379.

11. Bonus of Ferrara, *The New Pearl of Great Price,* London: Vincent Stuart Ltd., 1963, p. 109.

12. A. E. Waite, *op. cit.,* p. 20.

13. E. J. Holmyard, *Alchemy,* Baltimore: Pengiun Books, 1957, p. 43.

14. René Alleau, *History of Occult Sciences,* London: Leisure Arts Limited, 1966, p. 73.

15. Louis Pauwels and Jacques Bergier, *The Morning of the Magicians,* New York: Stein & Day, 1964, p. 10.

16. C. G. Jung, *Mysterium Coniunctionis,* New York: Bollingen Foundation, 1963, pp. 124–125.

17. Trans. R. F. C. Hull and A. S. B. Glover, *Aurora Consurgens,* London: Routledge & Kegan Paul, 1966, p. 153.

18. A. E. Waite, *op. cit.,* p. 286.

19. Bonus of Ferrara, *op. cit.,* p. 124.

20. "Our Art frees not only the body, but also the soul from the snares of servitude and bondage . . . Indeed, it may be said to supply every human want, and to provide a remedy for every form of suffering." *Ibid.,* p. 139.

21. Conversion is a logical, if not always a temporal, antecedent: "[T]he art is sacred, and all its adepts are sanctified and pure. For 'men either discover it because they are holy, or it makes them holy.' " Bonus of Ferrara, *op. cit.,* p. 11.

22. "For this art," says Paracelsus, "is truly a gift of God. Wherefore not everyone can understand it. For this reason God bestows it upon whom He pleases, and it cannot be wrested from Him by force . . ." Paracelsus, *Selected Writings,* 2nd ed. Edited by J. Jacobi and trans. by Norbert Guterman, Princeton, N.J.: Princeton University Press for the Bollingen Foundation, 1958, p. 149.

23. Titus Burckhardt, *op. cit.,* p. 29.

24. Bonus of Ferrara, *op. cit.,* pp. 129–130.

25. Eirenaeus Philalethes & Others, *Collectanea Chemica,* London: Vincent Stuart Ltd, 1963, p. 79.

26. Fulcanelli, *Fulcanelli: Master Alchemist.* London: Neville Spearman, 1971, p. 28.

27. Bonus of Ferrara, *op. cit.,* p. 134.

28. *Ibid.,* pp. 132–133.

29. "The practice of this great work," says Benedictus Figulus, "remains our Grand Secret or Arcanum, and unless it be revealed Divinely, or by artificers, or in experiments, it also can never be learnt from books." Benedictus Figulus, *op. cit.,* p. 278.

30. Indeed, as the alchemist says, "The thing . . . is accessible and known to all men, of much superfluity, to be found everywhere, and by all." *Ibid.,* p. 84.

31. Trans. A. E. Waite, *The Turba Philosophorum,* London: Stuart & Watkins, 1970, p. 188. Note also the statement of Geber: "I hereby declare that in this *Summa* I have not taught

our science systematically, but have spread it out here and there in various chapters; for it I had presented it coherently and in logical order, the evil-minded, who might have misused it, would be able to learn it just as easily as people of good will . . ." Titus Burckhardt, *op. cit.,* p. 31.

32. Trans. A. E. Waite, *The Works of Thomas Vaughn Mystic and Alchemist,* New Hyde Park, N.Y.: University Books Inc., 1968, p. 96.

33. Titus Burckhardt, *op. cit.,* p. 30.

34. Trans. A. E. Waite, *The Works of Thomas Vaughn Mystic and Alchemist, op. cit.,* p. 103.

35. Eirenaeus Philalethes, *op. cit.,* p. 63.

36. Martin Heidegger, *An Introduction to Metaphysics,* Garden City, N.Y.: Doubleday, 1961, p. 12.

37. Trans. Norbert Guterman, *op. cit.,* p. 111. See also, trans. R. F. C. Hull and A. S. B. Glover, *op. cit.,* p. 111.

38. Benedictus Figulus, *op. cit.,* p. 242.

39. Bonus of Ferrara, *op. cit.,* p. 140. Note also the following: "Behold the base thing with which our Sanctuary has been opened! For it is a thing well known by everyone; yet, he who understands it not finds it seldom or never. The wise man keeps it, the fool throws it away, and its reduction is easy to the initiated." Benedictus Figulus, *op. cit.,* p. 316.

40. Trans. A. E. Waite, *The Hermetic and Alchemical Writings of Paracelsus,* Vol. I, New Hyde Park, N.Y.: University Books Inc., 1967, p. 113.

41. Cf. Maurice Merleau-Ponty, *The Visible and the Invisible,* Evanston, Ill.: Northwestern University Press, 1968.

42. Martin Heidegger, *Being and Time,* New York: Harper & Row, 1962, p. 59.

43. W. B. Macomber, *The Anatomy of Disillusion,* Evanston, Ill.: Northwestern University Press, 1968, pp. 61–62.

44. Basilius Valentinus, *The Triumphal Chariot of Antimony,* London: Vincent Stuart Ltd., 1962, p. 66.

45. Bonus of Ferrara, *op. cit.,* p. 88.

46. Harold Garfinkel, *op. cit.,* p. 1.

47. Elias Ashmole, Esq., *Theatrum Chemicum Britannicum,* New York: Johnson Reprint Corporation, 1967, p. 29. See also John Frederick Helvetius' tale of his encounter with an alchemist and his own quest after the key to alchemy, in A. E. Waite, note 5, p. 312.

48. Bonus of Ferrara, *op. cit.,* p. 149.

49. *Ibid.,* pp. 146–147. It might be added that, in the West, this irremediable feature of Occult formulations is at least as old as Gnosticism itself. G. R. S. Mead writes, "The Gnostics were ever changing their nomenclature. . . . He who makes a concordance of names merely, in Gnosticism, may think himself lucky to escape a lunatic asylum. . . . If they contradict one another, in the view of the word-hunter, they do not contradict themselves for the follower of ideas. G. R. S. Mead, *Fragments of a Faith Forgotten,* London: Theosophical Publishing Society, 1900, pp. 309–310.

50. Harold Garfinkel, *op. cit.,* pp. 4–5.

51. *Ibid.,* p. 5.

52. Bonus of Ferrara, *op. cit.,* pp. 134–135.

53. Bonus of Ferrara, *op. cit.,* p. 112.

54. Trans. A. E. Waite, *The Turba Philosophorum, op. cit.,* p. 131.

55.   Benedictus Figulus, *op. cit.*, p. 185.

56.   Trans. A. E. Waite, *The Hermetic and Alchemical Writings of Paracelsus,* Vol. I, *op. cit.,* p. 65.

57.   Harold Garfinkel, *op. cit.*, p. 1.

58.   Trans. Norbert Guterman, *op. cit.*, p. 112.

Selected Bibliography

This bibliography supplements the selections found in the preceding pages. The emphasis is given to scholarly materials pertaining to Western civilization. Most of the materials are still in print or generally available in most libraries.

BACKGROUND

Benoist, Luc, *L'Esotérisme.* Paris: Presses Universitaires de France, 1965.

Cassirer, Ernst, *The Philosophy of Symbolic Forms,* translated by Ralph Mannheim, 3 vols. New Haven, Conn.: Yale University Press, 1953–1957.

Eliade, Mircea, *Myths, Dreams, and Mysteries.* New York: Harper & Row, 1967.

Judah, J. Stillson, *The History and Philosophy of the Metaphysical Movements in America.* Philadelphia: Westminster Press, 1967.

Lévi-Strauss, Claude, *The Savage Mind.* Chicago: University of Chicago Press, 1966.

———, *The Raw and the Cooked.* New York: Harper & Row, 1970.

Lévy-Bruhl, Lucien, *Primitive Mentality.* New York: Macmillan, 1923.

Marquès-Rivière, Jean, *Histoire des Doctrines Esotériques.* Paris: Payot, 1971.

Ten Houten, Warren D., and Charles D. Kaplan, *Science and Its Mirror Image: A Theory of Inquiry.* New York: Harper & Row, 1973.

Zaretsky, Irving I., and Mark P. Leone, eds., *Religious Movements in Contemporary America.* Princeton, N.J.: Princeton University Press, 1974.

THE ESOTERIC AND THE OCCULT

Alchemy

De Jong, H. M. E., *Michael Maier's Atalanta Fugiens. Sources of an Alchemical Book of Emblems.* Leiden, Holland: E. J. Brill, 1969.

Demaitre, Ann, "The Theater of Cruelty and Alchemy: Artaud and *Le Grand Oeuvre,*" *Journal of the History of Ideas,* **33** (April-June, 1972), 237–250.

Eliade, Mircea, *The Forge and the Crucible.* New York: Harper & Row, 1971.

Geoghegan, D., "Some Indications of Newton's Attitude Towards Alchemy," *Ambix,* **6** (1957–1958), 102–106.

Heym, Gerard, "An Introduction to the Bibliography of Alchemy," *Ambix,* **1** (May, 1937), 48–60.

Jung, C. G., *Alchemical Studies.* Princeton, N.J.: Princeton University Press, Bollingen Series XX, 1967.

————, *Psychology and Alchemy,* 2nd ed. Princeton, N.J.: Princeton University Press, Bollingen Series XX, 1968.

Koyré, Alexandre, *Mystiques, Spirituels, Alchimistes du XVIe Siècle Allemand.* Paris: Gallimard, 1971.

Lindsay, Jack, *The Origins of Alchemy in Graeco-Roman Egypt.* New York: Barnes and Noble, 1970.

MacPhail, Ian, *Alchemy and the Occult,* 2 vols. New Haven, Conn.: Yale University Library, 1968.

Reed, John, *Through Alchemy to Chemistry.* New York: Harper & Row, 1963.

Reidy, John, "Alchemy as Counter-Culture," *Indiana Social Studies Quarterly,* **24,** No. 3 (1971–1972), 41–51.

Sadoul, Jacques, *Le Trésor des Alchimistes.* Paris: Editions Publications Premières, 1970.

Sheppard, H. J., "Alchemy: Origin or Origins?" *Ambix,* **17** (July, 1970), 69–84.

Sivin, Nathan, *Chinese Alchemy: Preliminary Studies.* Cambridge, Mass.: Harvard University Press, 1968.

Stillman, John M., *The Story of Alchemy and Early Chemistry.* New York: Dover, 1960.

Van Lennep, J., *Art & Alchimie.* Paris: Editions Meddens, 1966.

Waite, Arthur Edward, *The Secret Tradition in Alchemy.* New York: Knopf, 1926.

————, *Alchemists Through the Ages* (1888). Blauvelt, N.Y.: Rudolf Steiner Publications, 1970.

Astrology

Gleadow, Rupert, *The Origin of the Zodiac.* New York: Atheneum, 1969.

Lindsay, Jack, *Origins of Astrology.* London: F. Müller, 1971.

MacNiece, Louis, *Astrology.* Garden City, N.Y.: Doubleday, 1964.

McCaffery, Ellen, *Astrology. Its History and Influence in the Western World.* New York: Scribner's, 1942.

McIntosh, Christopher, *The Astrologers and Their Creed.* New York: Praeger, 1969.

Thorndike, Lynn, "The True Place of Astrology in the History of Science," *Isis,* **46** (September, 1955), 273–278.

Gnosticism

Doresse, Jean, *Les Livres Secrets des Gnostiques d'Egypte.* Paris: Plon, 1958.

Grant, Robert M., *Gnosticism, An Anthology.* London: Collins, 1961.

Hutin, Serge, *Les Gnostiques,* 2nd ed. Paris: Presses Universitaires de France, 1963.

Jonas, Hans, *The Gnostic Religion,* 2nd ed. Boston: Beacon, 1963.

Tanner, André, *Gnostiques de la Révolution,* 2 vols. Paris: Egloff, 1946.

Van Groningen, G., *First Century Gnosticism. Its Origin and Motifs.* Leiden, Holland: E. J. Brill, 1967.

Voegelin, Eric, *The New Science of Politics.* Chicago: University of Chicago Press, 1952.

Kabbalism

Blau, Joseph L., *The Christian Interpretation of the Cabala in the Renaissance.* New York: Columbia University Press, 1944.

Regardie, Israel, *A Garden of Pomegranates: An Outline of the Qabalah,* 2nd ed. St. Paul, Minn.: Llewellyn Publications, 1970.

Scholem, Gershom G., *Major Trends in Jewish Mysticism.* New York: Schocken, 1961.

———, *On the Kabbalah and Its Symbolism.* New York: Schocken, 1965.

Sérouya, Henri, *La Kabbale,* rev. ed. Paris: Grasset, 1957.

———, *La Kabbale,* Paris: Presses Universitaires de France, 1972.

Waite, Arthur Edward, *The Holy Kabbalah.* New Hyde Park, N.Y.: University Books, 1960.

Magic, Witchcraft, Satanism

Baroja, Julio Caro, *The World of Witches.* Chicago: University of Chicago Press, 1964.

———, *Vidas Mágicas e Inquisición,* 2 vols. Madrid: Taurus, 1967.

Bessy, Maurice, *A Pictorial History of Magic and the Supernatural.* London: Spring Books, 1964.

Cavendish, Richard, *The Black Arts.* New York: Putnam, 1967.

Cristiani, Léon, *Evidences of Satan in the Modern World.* New York: Macmillan, 1962.

Daraul, Arkon, *Witches and Sorcerers.* New York: Citadel, 1966.

Demos, John, "Underlying Themes in the Witchcraft of Seventeenth-Century New England," *American Historical Review,* **75** (June, 1970), 1311–1326.

Douglas, Mary, ed., *Witchcraft Confessions and Accusations.* London: Tavistock, 1970.

Ebon, Martin, *Witchcraft Today.* New York: New American Library, 1971.

Evans-Pritchard, E. E., *Witchcraft, Oracles and Magic Among the Azande.* Oxford: Clarendon Press, 1937.

Grillot de Givry, Emile, *Witchcraft, Magic and Alchemy.* New York: Dover, 1971.

Hole, Christina, *Witchcraft in England.* New York: Collier Books, 1966.

Hughes, Pennethorne, *Witchcraft.* Baltimore: Penguin, 1969.

Huxley, Aldous L., *The Devils of Loudun.* New York: Harper, 1971.

Jarvie, C., and Joseph Agassi, "The Problem of the Rationality of Magic," *British Journal of Sociology,* **18** (March, 1967), 55–74.

King, Francis, *The Rites of Modern Occult Magic.* New York: Macmillan, 1971.

Kluckhohn, Clyde, *Navaho Witchcraft* (1944). Boston: Beacon Press, 1967.

Kramer, Heinrich, and James Sprenger, *The Malleus Maleficarum* (1486, 1928), translated with an introduction by Montague Summers. New York: Dover, 1971.

Langton, Edward, *Essentials of Demonology.* London: Epworth Press, 1949.

LaVey, Anton S., *The Satanic Bible.* New York: Avon, 1969.

———, *The Satanic Rituals.* New York: Avon, 1972.

Lea, Henry Charles, *Materials Toward A History of Witchcraft.* Philadelphia: University of Pennsylvania Press, 1939.

Lévi, Eliphas (Alphonse Louis Constant), *The History of Magic.* London: Rider, 1969.

———, *Transcendental Magic.* New York: Samuel Weiser, 1970.

Lieban, Richard Warren, *Cebuano Sorcery.* Berkeley: University of California Press, 1967.

MacFarlane, A. D. J., *Witchcraft in Tudor and Stuart England.* New York: Harper & Row, 1970.

Mair, Lucy P., *Witchcraft.* New York: McGraw-Hill, 1970.

Malinowski, Bronislaw, *Magic, Science and Religion* (1925). New York: Free Press, 1948.

Mandrou, Robert, *Magistrats et sorciers en France au dix-septième siècle: Une analyse de psychologie historique*. Paris: Plon, 1968.

Marwick, Max, *Sorcery in Its Social Setting*. Manchester: Manchester University Press, 1965.

————, ed., *Witchcraft and Sorcery*, Baltimore: Penguin, 1970.

Michelet, Jules, *Satanism and Witchcraft* (1863). New York: Citadel Press, 1938.

Middleton, John, ed., *Magic, Witchcraft, and Curing*. Garden City, N.Y.: Doubleday, 1967.

————, and E. H. Winter, eds., *Witchcraft and Sorcery in East Africa*. London: Routledge & Kegan Paul, 1963.

Monter, E. William, ed., *European Witchcraft*. New York: Wiley, 1969.

Murray, Margaret A., *The Witch-Cult in Western Europe* (1921). Oxford: Clarendon Press, 1963.

————, *The God of the Witches*. New York: Oxford University Press, 1970.

Notestein, Wallace, *A History of Witchcraft in England from 1558 to 1718* (1911). New York: Russell & Russell, 1965.

Nugent, Donald, "Witchcraft Studies, 1959–1971: A Bibliographical Survey," *Journal of Popular Culture*, 5 (Winter, 1971): 710/82–725/97.

Robbins, Rossell Hope, *The Encyclopedia of Witchcraft and Demonology*. New York: Crown Publishers, 1959.

Russell, Jeffrey B., *Witchcraft in the Middle Ages*. Ithaca, N.Y.: Cornell University Press, 1972.

Starkey, Marion L., *The Devil in Massachusetts*. Garden City, N.Y.: Doubleday, 1961.

Summers, Montague, *The History of Witchcraft and Demonology*, 2nd ed. New York: University Books, 1956.

————, *The Geography of Witchcraft*. Evanston: University Books, 1958.

Thomas, Keith V., *Religion and the Decline of Magic*. New York: Scribner's, 1971.

Tondriau, Julien, and R. Villeneuve, *Dictionnaire du Diable et de la Démonologie*. Paris: Marabout Université, 1968.

Trevor-Roper, H. R., "The European Witch-Craze of the Sixteenth and Seventeenth Centuries," in H. R. Trevor-Roper, *Religion, the Reformation and Social Change*. London: Macmillan, 1967.

Walker, Daniel P., *Spiritual and Demonic Magic from Ficino to Campanella*. Studies of the Warburg Institute, Vol. 22. London: Warburg Institute, 1958.

Wheatley, Dennis, *The Devil and All His Works*. New York: American Heritage Press, 1971.

Williams, Charles, *Witchcraft* (1941). Cleveland and New York: World Publishing Company, 1959.

Yalman, Nur, "Magic," *International Encyclopedia of the Social Sciences*, Vol. 9. New York: Macmillan, 1968, pp. 521–528.

SECRECY AND SECRET SOCIETIES

Arnold, Paul, *Histoire des Rose-Croix et les Origines de la Franc-Maçonnerie*. Paris: Mercure de France, 1955.

Boucher, Jules, *La Symbolique Maçonnique*. Paris: Dervy, 1953.

Bourgin, Georges, "Carbonari," *Encyclopedia of the Social Sciences*, Vol. 3. New York: Macmillan, 1942, pp. 220–223.

Boutang, Pierre, *L'Ontologie du Secret*. Paris: Presses Universitaires de France, 1973.

Chesneaux, Jean, *Secret Societies in China in the Nineteenth and Twentieth Centuries*. Ann Arbor,: University of Michigan Press, 1971.

Cohen, Abner, "The Politics of Ritual Secrecy," *Man*, **6** (September, 1971), 427–448.

Daraul, Arkon, *A History of Secret Societies*. New York: Pocket Books, 1969.

Faucher, Jean-André, and Achille Ricker, *Histoire de la Franc-Maçonnerie en France*. Paris: Nouvelles Editions Latines, 1967.

Fay, Bernard, *Revolution and Freemasonry, 1680–1800*. Boston: Little, Brown, 1935.

Frost, Thomas, *The Secret Societies of the European Revolution 1776–1876*, 2 vols. London: Tinsley Brothers, 1876.

Gist, Noel P., "Culture Patterning in Secret Society Ceremonials," *Social Forces*, **14** (May, 1936), 497–505.

———, "Structure and Process in Secret Societies," *Social Forces*, **16** (March, 1938), 349–357.

———, "Dogma and Doctrine in Secret Societies," *Sociology and Social Research*, **23** (November, 1938), 121–130.

Gould, Robert Freke, *The History of Freemasonry*, 3 vols. Edinburgh: T. C. & E. C. Jack, Grange Publishing Works, n.d. (ca. 1895).

Hankins, Frank H., "Masonry," *Encyclopedia of the Social Sciences*, Vol. 10. New York: Macmillan, 1942, pp. 177–184.

Headings, M. J., *French Freemasonry Under the Third Republic*. Baltimore: Johns Hopkins Press, 1949.

Heckethorn, Charles W., *The Secret Societies of All Ages and Countries*, 2 vols. (1875, 1897). New Hyde Park, N.Y.: University Books, 1966.

Hobsbawm, E. J., *Primitive Rebels*, New York: W. W. Norton, 1965 (esp. pp. 150–174).

Howe, Ellic, *The Magicians of the Golden Dawn. A Documentary History of a Magical Order, 1887–1923*. London: Routledge & Kegan Paul, 1972.

Hutin, Serge, *Les sociétés secrètes*, 7th ed. Paris: Presses Universitaires de France, 1970.

Jennings, Hargrave, *The Rosicrucians, Their Rites and Mysteries*, 6th ed. New York: E. P. Dutton, 1921.

Katz, Jacob, *Jews and Freemasons in Europe, 1723–1939*. Cambridge, Mass.: Harvard University Press, 1970.

Lantoine, Albert, *La Franc-Maçonnerie Ecossaise en France*. Paris: Emile Nourry, 1930.

Le Forestier, René, *La Franc-Maçonnerie Templière et Occultiste*, rev. ed., published by Antoine Faivre. Paris: Aubier-Montaigne, 1970.

Mackey, Albert Gallatin, *Encyclopedia of Freemasonry and Kindred Sciences*, rev. ed., 2 vols., edited by Robert Clegg. Chicago: Masonic History Company, 1929.

MacKenzie, Norman, ed., *Secret Societies*. London: Aldus, 1967.

Magre, Maurice, *The Return of the Magi*. London: P. Allan, 1931.

Mariel, Pierre, *Rituel des Sociétés Secrètes*. Paris: La Colombe, 1961.

Mosca, Gaetano, "Mafia," *Encyclopedia of the Social Sciences*, Vol. 10. New York: Macmillan, 1942, pp. 36–38.

Naudon, Paul, *La Franc-Maçonnerie*, 4th ed. Paris: Presses Universitaires de France, 1971.

Pike, Albert, *Morals and Dogma of the Ancient and Accepted Scottish Rite of Freemasonry*. Charleston, S.C.: Supreme Council of the Thirty-Third Degree for the Southern Jurisdiction of the United States, Ancient and Accepted Scottish Rite, 1871, 1909.

Pollard, H. B. C., *The Secret Societies of Ireland*. London: P. Allan, 1922.

Preuss, Arthur, *A Dictionary of Secret and Other Societies* (1924). Detroit: Gale Research Company, 1966.

Robison, John, *Proofs of a Conspiracy Against All the Religions and Governments of Europe*. London and Edinburgh, 1797.

Simmel, Georg, "The Sociology of Secrecy and of Secret Societies," *American Journal of Sociology*, **11** (January, 1906), 441–498. Translated anew and published as Part Four in Kurt H. Wolff, ed., *The Sociology of Georg Simmel*. New York: Free Press, 1950.

Stauffer, V., *New England and the Bavarian Illuminati*. New York: Columbia University Press, 1918.

Voorhis, H. V. B., *Negro Masonry in the United States*. New York: H. Emmerson, 1940.

Waite, Arthur Edward, *The Brotherhood of the Rosy Cross*. London: Rider, 1924.

———, *Emblematic Freemasonry*. London: Rider, 1925.

Webster, Hutton, *Primitive Secret Societies,* 2nd ed. New York: Macmillan, 1932.

MISCELLANEOUS

Blavatsky, H. P., *An Abridgement of* The Secret Doctrine (1888), edited by E. Preston and C. Humphreys. London: Theosophical Publishing House, 1966.

Cohen, Daniel, *Masters of the Occult*. New York: Dodd, Mead, 1971.

Crowley, Aleister, *The Confessions of Aleister Crowley,* edited by J. Symonds and K. Grant. New York: Bantam, 1971.

Debus, Allen G., *The English Paracelsians*. New York: Franklin Watts, 1965.

Devereux, George, ed., *Psychoanalysis and the Occult* (1953). New York: International Universities Press, 1970.

Freeland, Nat, *The Occult Explosion*. New York: Putnam, 1972.

Galbreath, Robert, ed., "The Occult: Studies and Evaluation," *Journal of Popular Culture,* **5** (Winter, 1971), entire issue.

Hutin, Serge, *Les Disciples Anglais de Jacob Boehme*. Paris: Denoel, 1960.

Ouspensky, P. D., *In Search of the Miraculous* (1949). New York: Harcourt, Brace & World, 1969.

———, *Tertium Organum* (1920). New York: Random House, 1970.

———, *A New Model of the Universe,* 2nd ed. (1934). New York: Random House, 1971.

Shepherd, Arthur P., *A Scientist of the Invisible. An Introduction to the Life and Work of Rudolf Steiner*. New York: British Book Centre, 1959.

Spence, Lewis, *An Encyclopedia of Occultism* (1920). New York: Strathmore Press, 1959.

Steiner, Rudolf, *The Story of My Life*. New York: Anthroposophic Press, 1928.

———. *Karmic Relationships: Esoteric Studies,* 4 vols. London: Anthroposophic Publishing Company, 1957.

———, *The Evolution of Consciousness,* 2nd ed. London: Rudolf Steiner Press, 1966.

———, *Theosophy of the Rosicrucians,* 2nd ed. London: Rudolf Steiner Press, 1966.

———, *The Stages of Higher Knowledge*. New York: Anthroposophic Press, 1967.

———, *Macrocosm and Microcosm*. London: Rudolf Steiner Press, 1968.

Tondriau, Julien, *L'Occultisme*. Paris: Marabout Université, 1964.

Waite, Arthur Edward, *The Occult Sciences*. London: Routledge & Kegan Paul, 1891.

————, *Studies in Mysticism and Certain Aspects of the Secret Tradition.* London: Hodder and Stoughton, 1906.

————, *The Holy Grail.* New Hyde Park, N.Y.: University Books, 1961.

————, *The Pictorial Key to the Tarot.* New Hyde Park, N.Y.: University Books, 1959.

————, *The Unknown Philosopher (Louis Claude de St. Martin).* Blauvelt, N.Y.: Rudolf Steiner Publications, 1970.

Wilson, Colin, *The Occult.* New York: Random House, 1971.

Yates, Frances, *Giordano Bruno and the Hermetic Tradition.* Chicago: University of Chicago Press, 1964.

————, *The Art of Memory.* London: Routledge & Kegan Paul, 1966.

————, *The Rosicrucian Enlightenment.* London: Routledge & Kegan Paul, 1972.

Author Index

Subject Index

Abracadabra, 30
Adam Kadmon, 33n, 273
Alchemy, 41-47, 51-58, 74, 272, 326
  accounts of, 328-337
  and avant-garde science, 57
  and chemistry, 41, 46, 330-331, 334-335
  methods of explanation, 41
  and secrecy, 337-344
  symbolism in, 42-45, 334, 336, 345
Antinomianism, 185-188, 327
Arcana, 53, 66-68, 244, 339
Astral body, 77, 162
Astrology, 74, 226, 249, 272, 296, 326
  and modernity, 290-291
  sociology of, 260-263, 281-292

Carbonari, 93-100, 270
Catharism, 182, 183-184, 186-187

Charisma, 7, 8, 13n
  charismatic leader, 8, 9, 249
Clairvoyance, 163, 284
Culture, conceptualizations of, 263-264
  avant-garde, 235, 269-270
  cultura paradigm, 3, 263-264, 268, 298
  esoteric culture, 263-267

Deviance, 191-192, 200, 296, 304
  deviant knowledge, 245, 251
  and magic, 6, 227
  and systems of social control, 191-192, 200-205, 207n
Divination, 297

Ecstasy, 154, 304-316
Esotericism, 1-3, 17-25
  altruistic spirit in, 75, 146, 150
  and cultural paradigms, 3, 268

361